Computational Mechanics P~~...~~ ns

Third World Conference on Engineering Education

Edited by: **T.V. DUGGAN**, *University of Portsmouth, UK*

These volumes present the edited versions of papers presented at the Third World Conference on Engineering Education, held in 1992. The theme of the Conference was 'Engineering Education for the 21st Century'.

SET ISBN: 1853121894; 1562521179 (US, Canada, Mexico) Sept 1992 1786pp £196.00/$295.00

International, Quality and Environmental Issues

Volume 1

Partial Contents: The Changing Nature of Engineering Education and the Shape of Things to Come; Strategy for Engineering Education between USA and Japan; International Issues: CADCAM in Developing Countries; Towards Internationally Recognised Engineering First Degrees; Engineering Degrees and Foreign Languages; Quality Aspects: How Effective is Teaching of Engineering?; The Chemical Engineer in Society; Future Engineers: Are we Trying to Attract the Right People?; Environmental Engineering: Environmental Engineering in Engineering Courses.

ISBN: 1853121908; 1562521187 (US, Canada, Mexico) September 1992 590pp £72.00/$108.00

Innovation, Teaching and Management

Volume 2

Partial Contents: Courses and Teaching Issues: The Design and Introduction of Integrated, Modularised and Credit Rated Programmes of Courses from Postgraduate to Higher National Level; Widening Access: A Practice Oriented Engineering Doctorate; An Integrated Approach to Encourage Women into Engineering; Developing Desirable Approaches to Learning Among Engineering Students from Educationally Disadvantaged Backgrounds; Management: European Product Engineering and Management; A Structure and Application for Curriculum in the Management of Engineering Development; Education for Effective Project Management.

ISBN:1853121916;1562521195 (US, Canada, Mexico) September 1992 586pp £72.00/$108.00

Industrial Links, Computers and Design

Volume 3

ing:
~~...ess;~~
ing
~~S-~~
~~...nods~~
~~... ..ed~~ Learning in
M~~...~~ ~~..gn~~ and Manufacture: En~~...~~ ~~..ducation;~~ Academic-Industrial Lin~~...~~ ~~..ssional~~ Development in the Mechanical and Manufacturing Engineering Cooperative Degrees; Partnership in Education? The Management of Academic Research.

ISBN:1853121924;1562521209 (US, Canada, Mexico) September 1992 610pp £74.00/$112.00

Software Engineering in Higher Education

Edited by: **G. KING, M. ROSS**, *Southampton Institute, UK,* **C.A. BREBBIA**, *Wessex Institute of Technology, Southampton, UK and* **G. STAPLES**, *Southampton, Institute, UK*

The rapid advance in computer technology and the proliferation of new software has presented educators with a shifting scene on how best to instruct software engineers. Often the experience of others can be most valuable where the territory is uncertain, and the purpose of this volume is to disseminate knowledge gained in addressing such questions as: What are the pitfalls of teaching specfication languages such as "Z"?; How can I improve or create a first course in Formal Method?; Is it possible to judge the software quality by computer based evaluation; What are the key issues in teaching Testing and Validation?. It contains the edited proceedings of papers presented at the First International Conference on Software Engineering in Higher Education, being held in November 1994.

Topics to be covered include: Formal Methods; Object Orientation; Software Engineering of Knowledge-based Systems; Issues of Software Quality; Unifying Themes for Methodologies; CASE Tools; Testing and Validation; Teaching Techniques and Development; Environments.

ISBN: 1853122890; 1562522132 (US, Canada, Mexico) Nov 1994 apx 500pp apx £130.00/$195.00

All prices correct at time of going to press. All books are available from your bookseller or in case of difficulty direct from the Publisher.

Computational Mechanics Publications
Ashurst Lodge, Ashurst, Southampton, SO40 7AA, UK.
Tel: 44 (0)1703 293223 Fax: 44 (0) 1703 292853

Group and Interactive Learning

INTERNATIONAL CONFERENCE ON
GROUP AND INTERACTIVE LEARNING

ORGANISING COMMITTEE

H.C. Foot
C.J. Howe
A. Anderson
A.K. Tolmie
D.A. Warden
I. Robertson
University of Strathclyde, UK

EXTERNAL CONSULTANTS

H. Cowie
College of the University of Leeds, UK

E. Forman
Pittsburgh University, USA

K. Topping
Dundee University, UK

Organised by:
*The Centre for Research into Interactive Learning
The Department of Psychology
The University of Strathclyde, UK
under the auspices of the
Scottish Branch of the British Psychological Society*

Group and Interactive Learning

Editors:

H.C. Foot
C.J. Howe
A. Anderson
A.K. Tolmie
& D.A. Warden
University of Strathclyde, UK

Computational Mechanics Publications
Southampton Boston

H.C. Foot
C.J. Howe
A. Anderson
A.K. Tolmie
D.A. Warden

Department of Psychology
University of Strathclyde
155 George Street
Glasgow G1 1RD
UK

Published by

Computational Mechanics Publications
Ashurst Lodge, Ashurst, Southampton SO40 7AA, UK
Tel: 44 1703 293223   Fax: 44 1703 292853
Email: CMl@uk.ac.rl.ib   Intl Email: CMl@ib.rl.ac.uk

For USA, Canada and Mexico

Computational Mechanics Inc.
25 Bridge Street, Billerica, MA 01821, USA
Tel: 508 667 5841   Fax: 508 667 7582
Email: CMINA@com.netcom.

British Library Cataloguing-in-Publication Data
A Catalogue record for this book is available
from the British Library

ISBN 1-85312-341-2 Computational Mechanics Publications, Southampton
ISBN 1-56252-265-5 Computational Mechanics Publications, Boston

Library of Congress Catalog Card Number 94-72456

*The texts of the various papers in this volume were set
individually by the authors or under their supervision.*

Printed and bound in Great Britain by Hobbs The Printers Ltd, Southampton

PREFACE

This volume contains the Proceedings of the International Conference on Group and Interactive Learning which took place at the University of Strathclyde in Glasgow, Scotland, from 12th-16th September 1994. The Conference was held under the auspices of the Scottish Branch of the British Psychological Society and was the First International Conference of a primarily psychological nature ever held on this theme.

The impetus for the Conference came from two main sources. Firstly, early 1994 saw the setting up of the Centre for Research into Interactive Learning (CRIL) at the University of Strathclyde which developed out of a small research group of psychologists with related interests in the field of group and interactive learning at the university. Secondly, the growing network of psychologists and other academic researchers and professionals with interests in interactive work made it abundantly clear that there is a burgeoning international interest both in understanding the nature of interactive processes which promote learning and performance and in the applications of the techniques which support these processes.

The aim of the Conference was to provide a forum for the presentation and exchange of ideas in fields of group work and interactive learning. Represented at the Conference were a variety of themes which, taken together, cover virtually all the main strands of research which are actively being pursued in the mid-1990s:

- computer-supported collaborated learning
- the analysis of collaborative computer-based learning
- group work and literacy
- peer tutoring and student tutoring
- collaboration between young children
- classroom studies of interactive learning
- collaboration amongst those with special needs
- interactive learning at a distance
- effects of task, ability and interpersonal factors in group work

The settings for interactive learning are mainly educational, operating from pre-school, through primary and secondary education to further, higher and adult educational contexts. Applications of interactive technology are also beginning to be used in non–educational settings such as for team training in the armed services and within work organisations. Evidence of these applications is also offered in the Conference. The book represents the edited versions of most of the papers presented at the Conference. They have been divided into several broad sections by theme and, within sections, they are listed in alphabetical order by author rather than by their position in the Conference Programme.

We would like to extend our thanks to those who have assisted in the preparation of the Conference, especially those who helped us review the paper abstracts (Dr Helen Cowie and Professor Ellice Forman), to our Administrative Officer, Mrs Irene Robertson, who handled much of the administration so effectively, to the band of students who worked so hard as stewards and to the secretarial staff and Computing Officer of the Department of Psychology who prepared so much of the pre-conference materials. Finally, we would also like to thank the Committee of the Scottish Branch of the British Psychological Society, who guided our initial thoughts and monitored our progress in organising the Conference, and the Scientific Affairs Board of the Society which sponsored the bursaries offered to students attending the Conference.

H.C. Foot
Head of the Department of Psychology
University of Strathclyde, UK

CONTENTS

SECTION C: GROUPWORK IN ADULT AND HIGHER EDUCATION

SECTION D: COLLABORATION AMONGST CHILDREN

SECTION F: PROCESS VARIABLES IN INTERACTIVE LEARNING

SECTION A:

Keynote Addresses

Peer collaboration as situated activity: Examples from research on scientific problem solving

E. Forman

School of Education, Department of Psychology in Education, University of Pittsburgh, 5C01 Forbes Quadrangle, Pittsburgh, Pennsylvania 15260, USA

Abstract

Psychological research on peer collaboration in children has been conducted from at least two different perspectives: the individualistic and the sociocultural. The individualistic perspective views the social context as an environmental variable influencing cognitive performance. The sociocultural perspective considers individual and context processes to be mutually constitutive. This paper will outline the theoretical and methodological implications of the two perspectives and describe how these perspectives have been applied to research on peer collaboration. Implications for future research will be delineated.

1 Introduction

Psychological research on peer collaboration in children has been conducted from the individualistic and the sociocultural theoretical perspectives. The individualistic perspective views the social context as an environmental variable influencing cognitive performance. In other words, social interaction may assist or prevent learning from occurring but the learning itself is regarded as an individual process and knowledge is something one may or may not acquire. The sociocultural perspective, in contrast, does not distinguish between social and nonsocial knowledge or social practices and cognitive performance. The individual does not acquire or internalize knowledge. Instead, individual and sociocultural processes are mutually constitutive. Learning is considered not only as a constructive process, but also as a situated social practice in which the participants' interpretations are being continually negotiated.

This paper will outline the theoretical and methodological implications of the two perspectives and describe how these perspectives have been applied to research on peer collaboration. The majority of research on children's thinking in peer contexts has used the individualistic model and relied upon experimental methodology. Contrasts between this approach and an approach which takes peer collaboration as an instance of situated activity among participants within a community of practice will be made in order to illustrate the value of a sociocultural approach. First, I will contrast the individualistic and sociocultural perspectives by focusing on the theoretical and methodological differences in how actors, tasks, and context are defined. Second, I will focus on how each perspective evaluates learning. These contrasts will be used to review past reearch. Finally, I will discuss the implications of a sociocultural approach for future research on children's peer collaboration.

2 The individualistic model of peer collaboration

In the individualistic approach to studying cognition in social context, it is hypothesized that actors can acquire knowledge or skills as a result of collaborating with peers. This perspective on thinking employs what Rogoff, Baker-Sennett, and Matusov [10] call the cranial storage metaphor. By using the cranial storage metaphor one assumes that learning is a process of acquiring new information from the outside world and storing it internally. The metaphor forces one to treat cognitive processes as static mental contents or representations. Since the storage and retrieval of these mental contents are not visible, actors must be viewed as black boxes. In addition, actors are typically reduced to nothing more than disembodied minds: cognitive agents without emotions, familial or friendship affiliations, or cultural identities [9].

The individualistic approach defines tasks from the perspective of the researcher. That is, the researcher decides, apriori, what a particular task requires, in terms of scientific reasoning or problem solving skills, and then evaluates actors' expertise before and after peer collaboration from this task definition [3]. It is assumed that the children will view the task in a similar fashion and that task goals will not be renegotiated during peer collaboration. Tasks are often selected for their ties to a body of research literature rather than for their connections to the everyday lives of the actors in the experiment. Thus, actors' perceptions and evaluations of the tasks employed are rarely taken into consideration.

The social context of thinking in this approach is viewed in two ways: as a configuration of static background variables or as a set of discrete interactional variables. In the typical research study, independent variables such as gender, expertise, achievement or social status are experimentally controlled or interactional variables such as amount of talk and type of talk (e.g., number of disagreements or explanations) are treated as dependent variables [3,4].

If agents are seen as black boxes, then analyses of learning depend upon specifying the input and output conditions that result in different cognitive outcomes. Much of the early research on peer collaboration used this model. For example, children working alone on a problem were contrasted with children working with a partner in terms of gains in individual posttest scores; e.g., Doise, Mugny, & Perret-Clermont [5]. More recent research has elaborated on this procedure by including assessments of students' social interactions and then correlating these dependent variables with the cognitive gain scores; e.g., Bearison, Magzamen, & Filardo [4]. Learning is viewed as the acquisition or internalization of particular cognitive outcomes by individuals. Thus, the assessment of learning involves decisions about the content of the cranial storage device. Since the device is viewed as a container for mental contents, then learning outcomes are evaluated by making comparisons between the contents of cranial storage before and after peer collaboration. Learning processes can only be inferred, based on this comparison, they cannot be directly observed.

3 The sociocultural model of peer collaboration

Sociocultural theorists such as Vygotsky and Leont'ev argued that the appropriate unit of analysis in psychological research should not be restricted to the decontextualized, disembodied individual but, instead, must be a unit that integrates the thoughts and actions of actors with their goal-directed, culturally specific activities. By focusing on actors engaged in situated activity, one is forced to recognize the connections between what an actor does, feels, thinks, and believes; the constraints and supports provided by other actors and artifacts in that particular setting; and cultural rules, norms, and values.

Learning, from the sociocultural perspective, no longer requires the cranial storage metaphor but, instead, involves notions such as access to and participation in particular cultural practices. Lave and Wenger describe learning as a process by which a newcomer is integrated into a community of practice [2]. They call this process legitimate peripheral participation. Thus, actors derive their identity from their roles as newcomers or oldtimers in a specific community. Actors in any community are not disembodied minds; they are viewed in terms of economic status, occupational role, and kinship, friendship, ethnic and religious affiliations.

Likewise, tasks are situated in particular communities and derive their meaning from the community. Tasks embody the values of the community such that some are seen as difficult, some easy, some significant, some trivial, some for men, some for women [7].   In addition, task goals may be multiple and emergent.   That is, learning involves a constant renegotiation of task interpretations and problem solving roles [1,6].   Since task goals may change and actors' interpretations may vary from researchers', actors' view of each other's expertise may differ from that of the researcher.   Thus, children with unequal task-specific expertise (as viewed from the researcher's point of view) may or may not act the roles of "expert" or "novice" [6].

Most of the literature on peer collaboration has been conducted in an experimental setting.   From the individualistic perspective on cognition, an experimental setting allows one to control all extraneous variables so as to better observe the variables of interest in the study.   From the sociocultural perspective, an experimental setting is yet another particular cultural setting for activity.   "Extraneous" variables are no more controlled in an experiment than they are anywhere else.   In addition, the experimenter must be included as an actor in this activity setting.   Thus, "peer" collaboration research typically involves the direct or indirect involvement of one or more nonpeers.

In the sociocultural approach, the social context cannot be reduced to a set of static background variables or of discrete interactional variables.   Instead, the social context is viewed as an integral part of actors' identities, feelings and beliefs, task definitions, and learning processes and outcomes.   It also extends far beyond any particular research setting to the institutional and cultural context of that setting [9].

The sociocultural perspective argues that learning should not be depicted as a process of internalization, transmission, or assimilation of information from the external world to an internal storage device. Instead, learning should be viewed as increasing participation in communities of practice [2].   All participants in a community of practice are legitimate, but some are peripheral participants and others are full participants.   Full participants differ from partial participants in having more power in the community as well as more knowledge of its valued practices.   Peripheral participants can achieve full participation, at least in principle, by increasing their range of practice in the community over time.   As their range of practice increases, their knowledge increases. Thus, assessments of learning processes are direct: they involve observations of actors' participation patterns over time.   While both the individualistic and sociocultural approaches observe social interaction, the observations of sociocultural researchers are focused on functional not formal analyses.   In addition, because no distinction is made between social and nonsocial knowledge or practice, the social and cognitive must be integrated in the variables examined.   Finally, the unit of analysis must include both the individual and his or her sociocultural context.

4 Conclusion

The individualistic and the sociocultural perspectives offer distinctly different views of children's peer collaboration and different research methodologies. The literature on peer collaboration has been dominated by the individualistic tradition for the past twenty years and has given us a new appreciation for the role of social interaction in children's thinking. However, this literature has been limited by its reliance upon the cranial storage metaphor, its insistence upon separating social and cognitive variables, and its assumption that experimental conditions are uniquely endowed with the power to draw conclusions about causality. Recently, researchers in the field have expressed their dissatisfactions with the assumptions and methodologies of the individualistic approach [6,8]. Unfortunately, sociocultural psychology is in its infancy so that methodologies consistent with its assumptions are still being developed. Illustrations from several research programs currently under way, including the author's, will be presented so that future directions of research on children's peer collaboration can be delineated.

5 References

1.   Bruner, J. *Actual Minds, Possible Worlds*, Harvard University Press, Cambridge, 1986.
2.   Lave, J. & Wenger, E. *Situated Learning: Legitimate Peripheral Participation*, Cambridge University Press, New York.
3.   Azmitia, M. Peer interaction and problem solving: When are two heads better than one? *Child Development*, 1988, **59**, 87-96.
4.   Bearison, D.J., Magzamen, S. & Filardo, E.K. Socio-cognitive conflict and cognitive growth in young children, *Merrill-Palmer Quarterly*, 1986, **32**, 51-72.
5.   Doise, W., Mugny, G. & Perret-Clermont, A.-N. Social interaction and the development of cognitive operations, *European Journal of Social Psychology*, 1975, **5**, 367-383.
6.   Forman, E. & Larreamendy-Joerns, J. Learning in the context of peer collaboration: Individualistic and sociocultural perspectives, *Cognition and Instruction*, in press.
7.   Goodnow, J. The socialization of cognition: What's involved?, Chapter 6, *Cultural Psychology: Essays on Comparative Human Development*, ed J.W. Stigler, R.A. Shweder & G. Herdt, pp 259-286, Cambridge University Press, New York, 1990.
8.   Light, P. & Perret-Clermont, A.-N. Social context effects in learning and testing, Chapter 8, *Child Development in Social Context 2: Learning to Think*, ed P. Light, S. Sheldon & M. Woodhead, pp 136-150, Routledge, London, 1991.

9.   Minick, N., Stone, C.A. & Forman, E.A. Integration of individual, social, and institutional processes in accounts of children's learning and development, Introduction, *Contexts for Learning: Sociocultural Dynamics in Children's Development*, ed E.A. Forman, N. Minick & C.A. Stone, pp 3-16, Oxford University Press, New York, 1993.

10.   Rogoff, B., Baker-Sennett, J. & Matusov, E. Considering the concept of planning, *Future-oriented Processes*, ed M. Haith, J. Benson, B. Pennington & R. Roberts, University of Chicago Press, Chicago, in press.

Incorporating peer-tutoring procedures into literacy programs for low-progress readers

K. Wheldall

Macquarie University Special Education Centre, Macquarie University, Sydney, New South Wales 2109, Australia

Abstract

A series of experimental studies, completed in the West Midlands, UK, effectively demonstrated the power of peer-tutoring programs, using the Pause, Prompt and Praise procedures, for low-progress readers. Major gains were made by such students when following eight week programs of daily (or near-daily) peer-tutoring of about 15-20 minutes per day. In this paper, it is shown how these experimental findings were used to justify the inclusion of this form of peer-tutoring within broader, classroom-based literacy programs for children with learning difficulties in New South Wales, Australia. Several studies are reported. The first was carried out in a residential withdrawal class for children experiencing marked learning difficulties living in remote rural areas. The second study was completed as part of the Acceleration and Integration into Mainstream (AIM) program for students with learning difficulties attending the special school which forms part of Macquarie University Special Education Centre (MUSEC). The third study involved Koori (Aboriginal) students tutoring Koori peers who were low-progress readers, in an inner city primary school in Sydney. The fourth study describes the Spring Term Educational Program for Under-achieving Pupils (STEP UP) program under which low-progress students in their final term at primary school attended a special class held in their local high school. Finally, preliminary findings will be presented of the effects of peer-tutoring on the classroom behaviour of behaviourally troublesome low-progress readers in a high school context.

Introduction

The remedial tutoring procedures for low-progress readers now known as 'Pause, Prompt and Praise' (PPP) were originally developed in New Zealand by Glynn and his associates (Glynn, McNaughton, Robinson & Quinn [1]; McNaughton, Glynn & Robinson [2]). Their research showed that effective tutoring for children two or more years behind in their development of reading skills requires that tutors should: *pause* (for up to five seconds) when the reader hesitates or makes a mistake; *prompt* after the pause, if the child has not correctly identified the word, with a graphophonic or contextual cue; and *praise* the child for accurate reading, self-corrections, corrections following a prompt and for other positive reading behaviours. Major gains were made by low-progress students when following eight week PPP programs of daily (or near-daily) peer-tutoring of about 15-20 minutes per day. Glynn & McNaughton [3] review numerous studies supporting the effectiveness of these tutoring procedures, in most cases employing parents or siblings as tutors for low progress readers. Wheldall and his colleagues, originally working in the UK, focussed their attention on the use of peer tutors using the PPP procedures. In a series of studies, they repeatedly demonstrated that this form of peer tutoring led to appreciable gains in reading skill for low progress readers and, moreover, that the peer tutors themselves also gained (Wheldall & Mettem [4]; Wheldall & Colmar [5]).

The research supporting the Pause, Prompt and Praise tutoring procedures includes empirical process and product studies. These demonstrate that this form of tutoring yields superior gains for low-progress readers when compared with other listening procedures and that these gains are clearly attributable to specific tutoring behaviours. Moreover, the reading tutoring methodology is securely anchored within both a cognitive/developmental theory of reading (Clay [6]) and a contemporary 'behavioural interactionist' theory of tutoring (Wheldall & Glynn [7, 8]). PPP may be said to combine the best of both 'top-down' and 'bottom-up' approaches to the teaching of reading and, as such, may be seen to be congruent with contemporary perspectives in reading which emphasise the importance of both aspects of the reading process. This 'middle ground' position in the reading debate, sometimes known as the interactive perspective, appears to be strongly supported by contemporary research and theory.

Recent research in New South Wales

Since the original, experimental research studies on peer-tutoring using PPP were completed in the West Midlands (summarised in Wheldall & Colmar [5]), the author has moved to Sydney, Australia to take up the directorship of Macquarie University Special Education Centre (MUSEC). Beginning in 1991, a series of implementation studies have been completed in which PPP tutoring by peers and volunteers has formed the central plank of classroom-based literacy programs for children with learning difficulties. The main aim of this current paper is to review these studies, in an attempt to demonstrate how the original experimental research has helped in the development of effective literacy programs for students with learning difficulties.

1. A residential withdrawal class

A study by Wheldall, Colmar & Freeman [9] demonstrated the effectiveness of employing community volunteers as tutors in a short stay residential school for students with manifest learning difficulties living in country districts . Low-progress readers made significantly greater gains when tutored by volunteers trained to employ PPP than when tutored by untrained volunteers. Moreover, these gains were made in spite of different volunteers being employed from day to day, i.e. the gains were not dependent upon regular tutoring from the same tutor. The particularly interesting aspect of this study was that all low-progress readers in the school were also receiving intensive phonics-based reading instruction, based on procedures developed at MUSEC. The results of the study showed that PPP added another six months of reading age (on average) to the eight months gain made by the control students, leading to an average gain of nearly 14 months for seven weeks of daily tutoring. Thus, it can be shown that PPP can be effectively employed alongside other intensive reading instruction procedures.

2. Acceleration and Integration into the Mainstream Program

These encouraging findings led to the inclusion of PPP in a new literacy program called the Acceleration and Integration into the Mainstream (or AIM) Program which operates within the Special School which is at the heart of MUSEC. This program takes in from local primary schools students aged eight to eleven years who are at least two years behind in reading and related skills. The idea is to boost their literacy skills within two terms before beginning to re-integrate them back into their original schools, over the final two terms of the school year. Preliminary results are encouraging with average gains of about twenty months being recorded for the seven months of instruction completed in the first two terms. Again, this demonstrates how PPP peer and volunteer tutoring can be employed alongside more traditional phonics instruction to accelerate the academic progress of students with learning difficulties.

3. Koori peer-tutoring

In Australia, a continuing cause for concern is the poor academic progress made by children from Aboriginal backgrounds. We have carried out a series of small-scale studies exploring whether PPP peer-tutoring might prove more acceptable to local Aboriginal (Koori) students than traditional schooling methods. It can be argued that peer tutoring is more culturally appropriate for this group of students. Preliminary results indicate that Koori low progress readers make good progress when tutored by Koori peer tutors. Average gains in reading accuracy of seven months were in evidence after eight weeks of tutoring, the rate of progress being around seven times faster than they had previously achieved. Working with Koori students, however, led the research group to query whether changes to the PPP procedures might be necessary to accommodate differing cultural expectations.

4. Spring Term Educational Program for Underachieving Pupils

The idea for a Spring Term Educational Program for Under-achieving Pupils (or STEP-UP) was originally formulated in Birmingham by Wheldall and Riding but it was not operationalised until 1992 in Sydney. The aim of the program was to offer students with learning difficulties in their last term of primary school one last chance to, at least in part, catch up before commencing high school. To this end, twelve low-progress students were taught for eight weeks in a STEP-UP class held in their local high school. As part of an intensive literacy booster program, they received daily peer-tutoring using PPP by older students in the high school, following Wheldall & Mettem [4]. The mean gain in reading accuracy for the group over the eight weeks was equivalent to one year's progress, again testifying to the importance of including such tutoring as part of any literacy program.

5. Peer-tutoring and classroom behaviour

Pause, Prompt and Praise has also been (tentatively) linked to increased on-task behaviour. Pilot work carried out previously at Birmingham University, tentatively suggested that peer tutoring using PPP may be associated with gains in on-task behaviour. This is currently being followed up at MUSEC. Preliminary data is available on five low-progress readers aged 12 to 16 years (who were also behaviourally troublesome) tutored by students who were at least one year older and who were very proficient readers. They were tutored for a minimum of four times per week for six weeks. Gains in reading accuracy of 5 to 17 months were recorded (mean 12 months). These gains in reading were associated with major gains in on-task behaviour in English and History lessons. In week one of the tutoring program, on-task behaviour ranged from 5-15% (mean 10%) but increased steadily over the weeks to 21-60% (mean 47%) in week six. These are only preliminary findings and clearly considerable replication work would need to be carried out before strong claims could be made. Nonetheless, these results are encouraging and may be seen as supporting the view that inappropriate classroom behaviour may result from poor academic skills. Improving academic skills may thus improve on-task behaviour.

Future directions

In spite of the undoubted success of these procedures in the programs described above, there remains a clear need to further refine PPP. It has not yet been possible to determine the differential individual contributions of each of the various components comprising the PPP package intervention. We know that trained PPP tutoring is clearly superior to untrained tutoring but we do not yet know the relative functionality of the component parts. Current research at MUSEC is attempting to provide an empirical answer to this question. This has become more possible as the result of a more appropriate measure of successful reading behaviour having been developed which facilitates the continual repeated measurement of behaviour which is essential for determining the effectiveness of alternative interventions by means of single subject and small 'n' research design methodology. The Passage Reading Test (PRT) is a form of curriculum-based measurement, developed by Deno and his colleagues in the United States (Deno, Mirkin & Chiang [10]), requiring students to read for one minute only from an appropriate text (usually at grade level). Number of words read correctly per minute has been shown by the developers of PRT (and by our own preliminary studies) to correlate at a high level (0.8+) with standardised reading tests. This measure provides a simpler means of gathering repeated measures data than the book level measures employed previously. An example of its use in the context of PPP is provided in Wheldall, Colmar & Freeman [9]. PRT will almost certainly provide the means for the future refinement of the PPP procedures.

References

1. Glynn, T., McNaughton, S. S., Robinson, V. & Quinn, M. *Remedial Reading at Home: Helping you to help your child.* NZCER, Wellington, 1979.

2. McNaughton, S. S., Glynn, T. & Robinson, V. *Parents as Remedial Tutors: Issues for home and school.* NZCER, Wellington. Reprinted as *Pause, Prompt and Praise: Effective tutoring for remedial reading,* Positive Products, Birmingham, 1981, 1987.

3. Glynn, T. & McNaughton, S. S. The Mangere home and school remedial reading procedures: continuing research on their effectiveness. *New Zealand Journal of Psychology, 14,* 66-77, 1985.

4. Wheldall, K. & Mettem, P. Behavioural peer tutoring: training 16-year-old tutors to employ the 'pause, prompt and praise' method with 12-year-old remedial readers. *Educational Psychology, 5,* 27-44, 1985.

5. Wheldall, K. & Colmar, S. Peer tutoring for low-progress readers using 'Pause, Prompt and Praise'. In Foot, H. C., Morgan, M. J. & Shute, R. H. (eds.), *Children Helping Children.* Wiley, London, 1990.

6. Clay, M. *Reading: the patterning of complex behaviour* (second edition), Heinemann Educational Books, Auckland, 1979.

7. Wheldall, K. & Glynn, T. Contingencies in contexts: a behavioural interactionist perspective in education. *Educational Psychology, 8,* 5-19, 1988.

8. Wheldall, K. & Glynn, T. *Effective Classroom Learning: a behavioural interactionist approach to teaching.* Basil Blackwell, London, 1989.

9. Wheldall, K., Colmar, S. & Freeman, L. Employing community volunteers to tutor low-progress readers using the 'Pause, Prompt and Praise' tutoring procedures. *NSW Journal of Special Education, 14,* 23-26, 1991.

10. Deno, S. L., Mirkin, P. K. & Chiang, B. Identifying valid measures of reading. *Exceptional Children, 49,* 36-45, 1982.

SECTION B:

Computer-Based Approaches to Interactive Learning

Interactive computer-assisted reflective learning: A framework for categorising interactions in reflective learning-teaching situations

J. Cook

School of Technology and Information Studies, Thames Valley University, Ealing, London W5 5RF, UK

Abstract

In this paper we claim that reflection about problem seeking should be emphasised in creative domains, and also that reflection about learning is also a desirable goal. These claims form the basis of our proposal for a multi-level framework for describing and categorising learning and teaching interactions. The experience gained from a small formative study is used to present some practical guidelines for creating and analysing interactions in reflective learning-teaching situations. The multi-level framework appears to have general applicability to other domains and provides the level of detail required to assist in the specification of computer-assisted reflective learning systems.

1 Introduction

In this paper we define Computer-Assisted Reflective Learning Systems (CARLS) as computer-based systems whose educational objectives include the aim of promoting reflection [1] in a learner. CARLS can be divided into two broad categories depending on the amount of learner control provided to the student. The first category, Learning Environments, makes the assumption that students possess the appropriate motivation, strategies, and self-monitoring skills to control their own learning by exploration effectively. However, there are reasons to question some of these assumptions. First, research [2, 3] has shown that students may not be motivated to reflect in the manner intended by the system designers (see Table 1 for a summary). Second, Chi et al. [4] have found significant individual differences in the kind of strategies and self-monitoring that students use to explain instructional text and examples to themselves. Thus it appears that students are not equally able to study instruction effectively, and may differ in their reflective and monitoring abilities. The second category of CARLS is Intelligent Learning Environments. These aim to manage the education process interactively by engaging individual learners in some goal-directed, problem solving activity. Intelligent Learning Environments have tended to implement aspects of prominent theories that embed 'metacognition' (see Reflective Support in Table 1 for a summary). Table 1 shows a selective summary of CARLS and identifies key issues that they raise. The systems in Table 1 are still at the experimental stage. It is difficult to extract principles for designing CARLS from the systems identified in Table 1 since they vary so widely in terms of their methodology and theoretical approach. Unresolved issues that are emerging from research into CARLS can be summarised by the following questions. What teaching interventions foster reflective learning? And, what constitutes an adequate methodology for designing and building CARLS? In this paper we address these questions as follows. First, by proposing a multi-level framework for describing and categorising interactions in reflective learning-teaching situations. Second, by proposing some experiment design and analysis guidelines that make use of this framework to investigate reflective learning-teaching interactions. The framework provides the level of detail required to assist in the specification of CARLS.

Table 1. Selective summary of CARLS.

System	Domain	Reflective support	Issue
AlgebraLand [2] (LE)	Basic algebra	Trace of student's solution path	Reflective support was rarely used
Explanation Environment [3] (LE)	LISP programming	'Metacognitive' hypertext option, e.g. define your own conception of a 'New Word'	Reflective support largely ignored by experimental subjects
MEMOLAB [5] (ILE)	Experimental psychology skills	Mainly Piagetian orientation	Attempts to merge discovery learning with different levels of teaching
SCILAB [6] (ILE)	Concept learning in science	Vygotskian approach	Learner reflection requires dialogue with a teacher

(Key: LE = Learning Environment, ILE = Intelligent Learning Environment.)

2 Reflection about content and learning

The systems shown in Table 1 emphasise technical or science-like problem solving. A question that therefore arises is: what kind of reflection is appropriate for creative problem solving? Some research into the subject areas of fine art [7], maths [8] and music composition [9] suggests that *problem seeking,* or finding a problem to solve, may be a stronger indicator of true creative behaviour than the actual problem solving process. For example, in a longitudinal study of artists and the creative process Getzels and Csikszentmihalyi [7] showed that young artists whose cognitive approach emphasises problem seeking (they called it problem finding) over problem solving were more successful in their creative careers. The claim we are making here is that problem seeking is relevant to many creative problem solving activities, e.g. in the sciences and the humanities, and should be emphasised when designing CARLS. Furthermore, a small body of research [10, 11] is starting to address one of the questions posed in the introduction, i.e. what teaching interventions foster reflective learning? Bielaczyc and Recker [10] have built on the self-explanation work described above [4] to explore some of the issues surrounding learning to learn. Individual learners in the domain of LISP programming were subjected to a set of 'instructional interventions' (based on 'modelling' and 'scaffolding' techniques) that aimed to communicate good self-explanation and monitoring strategies. Learners who received strategy training (through computer-based instructional texts containing examples) not only showed improvements in the self-explanation and monitoring strategies they used, they also showed significantly greater performance gains on associated programming problems than subjects in an instructional control group. Below we incorporate these findings into an examination of (part of) the second question posed in the introduction, i.e. what constitutes an adequate methodology for designing and building CARLS? In particular we will focus on how to analyse reflective learner-teacher interactions in a way that will inform the design of an Intelligent Learning Environment.

3 Framework for the early design of an Intelligent Learning Environment

In the past the general approach to building tutoring systems has been to compress all the processing into a single level [12]. In an attempt to make use of the research into learning outlined above this situation is now changing. John Self [13] has proposed a formal, multi-level theoretical framework for describing Intelligent Learning Environments (ILEs). Current debate about Self's framework centres on the function of each level and the degree of access one level should be allowed to the other levels. Our proposed extension to Self's framework is called the Framework for Promoting Reflection in Intelligent Learning Environments or F-PRILE (see also [1], where it is called ILEA, and [12]). In the following discussion the term 'Agent' will be used to mean a human learner, a human teacher, or a computer-based teacher; 'it' will be used to refer to an Agent. The literature examined above allows us to propose that there should be two overall teaching objectives for the Teaching Agent in F-PRILE. First, to foster reflective, problem seeking in a student (i.e., the Learning Agent). Second, to encourage the student (or Learning Agent) to reflect about their own learning. In essence, F-PRILE is a taxonomy of the knowledge and processes involved in reflective learning and teaching. F-PRILE uses an **Agent-component-level** classification hierarchy, which is shown in Figure 1 and discussed below using the example domain of music composition.

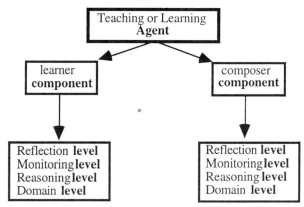

Figure 1. **Agent-component-level** classification system in
F-PRILE using example domain of music composition

Unlike Self's framework, F-PRILE makes the distinction between two different components of an Agent. A Learning Agent (or LA) has a learner component and a composer component. In F-PRILE the Teaching Agent (or TA) also has two components: a learner and a composer. The Teaching Agent has a learner component because it is itself learning (from its interactions) about the Learning Agent. Additionally, each component has four levels. The Domain level (D) contains knowledge relevant to the component. The Reasoning level (R) will represent knowledge about different methods for making use of Domain level knowledge. Goals are set and evaluated at the Monitoring level (M) for all Agent-components. The Reflection level (Ref) decides when to change a Reasoning level method and attempts to make generalisations about lower level activities. Table 2 gives a 'feel' for the structure of F-PRILE by illustrating what each **Agent-component-level** (a box in Table 2) could be doing. The examples used in Table 2 are taken from the small formative study described in section four. The examples for the composer component are for the Learning Agent.

Table 2. Examples of Agent-component-level activities in F-PRILE.

Teaching Agent or Learning Agent	Learning Agent (LA)	Teaching Agent (TA)
composer component	learner component	learner component
Ref E.g instruments can generate different moods. The flute is light. The cello is dark and meloncholic	E.g. It's good to have TAs and other LAs question why you plan to write a composition in a particular way; else I tend not to think about it	E.g. Asking the student to describe their compositional plan over the phone to a concert promoter is a more realistic scenario
M E.g. I want to move away from the sparse sound that I usually get when I compose	E.g. explaining my compositional plans to other LA's may be a good idea	E.g. Have I communicated the nature of task 3 part 2 effectively?
R E.g. Plan out the shape of a composition before looking at which notes to use	E.g. go talk to a flute player to find out ways of using the instrument in my planned composition	E.g. describe your compositional plan as if you were talking to another student
D E.g. harmony, rhythm melody	Teaching interaction (e.g. you've just described a strong musical idea)	A 'model' of the student (e.g the LA's ability to recall the structure of a piece is underdeveloped)

(Levels key: Ref =Reflection, M = Monitoring, R = Reasoning, D = Domain)

4 Guidelines for studying reflective learning-teaching interactions

Below we outline some practical guidelines for creating and analysing reflective learning-teaching situations based on a formative experimental investigation and analysis the author has carried out. The study [12] aimed to gain insight into the issues involved in examining reflective learner and teacher interaction. The outcomes of the study were intended to provide guidelines for analysing reflective learner-teacher interaction and to inform the design of a prototype ILE. Furthermore, we suggest that the approach could prove a useful categorisation framework for other studies of reflective learning-teaching interactions.

4.1 Experiment design
In our formative study three tasks were designed by the author and a music composer-teacher to encourage learners in Higher Education (BA Music, year 1

and 3) to think reflectively about problem seeking; that is, a situation where a learner could find and formulate a compositional problem of their own choosing and work towards its solution. The overall objective of the three tasks was clearly defined in advance. This was to encourage in the learner the ability to 'image' a composition accurately through reflection. Teaching interventions were prepared that we predicted would encourage learners to generate certain types of self-explanations (e.g. listen to this musical example and then describe it using the vocabulary we have developed). The self-explanations were intended to aid reflective understanding [4] and enabled us to gather verbal protocol data. Teaching interventions were particularly concerned with promoting learner activity at F-PRILE's Monitoring level (e.g. did dialogue help?) and Reflection level (e.g. can I use that approach elsewhere?). The subjects' activities (three 70 minute learner-teacher sessions) were captured by video and tape recordings.

4.2 Experiment analysis and steps for verification
Below we outline the steps involved in the use and verification of F-PRILE that were developed to analyse transcripts of the data captured by our formative experiment. F-PRILE appears to be general enough to be used to analyse experimental protocols in other subject areas; the composer components would be exchanged for a historian, mathematician, or whatever component. F-PRILE also has the level of detail required to assist in the design of ILEs. An example taken from the formative study described above will be used to illustrate the approach. (See [12] for a detailed account of these steps.)

Step 1 Separate the utterances for an Agent's 'turn' in the experiment protocol. An utterance is a unit of protocol expressing a single 'idea'. Give each utterance a unique number. The following is an utterance, U34, from one of the teacher's turns in our study: *"I'd like you to imagine that you, you are trying to describe to another student, possibly, not necessarily to me, umm, how you go, how generally you go about composing a piece."*

Step 2 For each utterance identified in step 1 define the Agent-component-level source and *intended* target. Assume that each utterance comes from the R level of F-PRILE. Using the step 1 example of U34, the source is TA-learner-R34; and the intended target is LA-learner-M.

Step 3 Examine each R level utterance(s) identified in step 2 and decide which Agent-component-level(s) collaborated internally to produced them. For example, the following Agent-component-levels in F-PRILE could lead to utterance R34:
TA-learner-M: Have I communicated task 3 part 2 effectively?
TA-learner-R: ask LA to describe how they compose (composing objective)
TA-learner-R: set scenario as describing to another student (learning objective)
Here one utterance intends to give more than one objective.

Step 4 Take the analysis to the teacher and see if they agree with it. A strategy will need to be in place so that any unresolved disagreement about interpretation can be dealt with. Get the teacher to keep a diary of their reflections on the whole exercise. Parts of the diary can be made available to the researcher at the teacher's discretion. The diary approach in our own study suggested that the teaching method used in the experiments subsequently 'transferred' to the related area of musical performance.

Step 5 Take the analysis to the learner and see if they agree with it. This may be difficult to achieve, particularly with younger learners. Students find it difficult to talk in the abstract about their own learning. Use Table 2 with empty boxes as a graphic aid to understanding for steps 4 and 5.

Step 6 Repeat the process from the experiment design stage (i.e., design some new tasks) with the same subjects to try and pin down which teaching interventions work and how they effect reflection over time.

The above six steps provide a practical link between the multi-level framework (F-PRILE) and its use in categorising reflective learning-teaching interactions.

5 Conclusions

In this paper we have proposed a multi-level framework for supporting the early design of ILEs. The experience gained from a small formative study was used to present some practical guidelines for creating and analysing interactions in reflective learning-teaching situations. The multi-level framework developed for the analysis appears to be general enough to be used to analyse experimental protocols in other subject areas. The framework also has the level of detail required to assist in the design of CARLS, and in particular ILEs.

References

1. Cook, J. Agent Reflection in an Intelligent Learning Environment Architecture for Musical Composition, *Music Education: An Artificial Intelligence Approach, Edinburgh 1993,* ed M. Smith, A. Smaill and G. Wiggins, pp. 3-23, Springer-Verlag, London, 1994.
2. Foss, C. Productive thrashing in a computerized tutoring system: the acquisition of error management skills, *Proceedings of AI-ED 87,* Pittsburgh, 1987.
3. Recker, M. and Pirolli, P. Student Strategies for Learning Programming from a Computational Environment, in ITS '92 (ed C. Frasson, G. Gauthier and G. McCalla), pp. 382-394, *Intelligent Tutoring Systems, Second International Conference,* Montréal, Canada, Springer-Verlag, 1992.
4. Chi, M., Bassok, M., Lewis, M., Reimann, P., and Glaser, R. Self-Explanation: How Students Study and Use Examples in Learning to Solve Problems, *Cognitive Science,* 1989, **13**, 145-182.
5. Borcic, B., Dillenbourg, P., Hilario, M., Mendelsohn, P., and Schneider, D. *Intelligent Learning Environments.* TECFA, Faculté de Psychologie et des Sciences de l'Education, University of Geneva, 1992.
6. Hartley, R. and Ravenscroft, A. Computer Aided Reflection: An Overview of SCILAB, *Paper presented at the SMILE Workshop, September 29th - October 1st,* Ambleside, UK, Unpublished, 1993.
7. Getzels, J. and Csikszentmihalyi, M. *The Creative Vision: A Longitudinal Study of Problem Finding in Art,* Wiley-Interscience, New York, 1976.
8. Smilansky, J. Problem solving and the quality of invention: An empirical investigation, *Journal of Educational Psychology,* 1984, **76**, 377-386.
9. DeLorenzo, L.C. A Field Study of Sixth-Grade Students' Creative Music Problem-Solving Processes, *Journal of Research in Music Education,* 1989, **37**(3), 188-200.
10. Bielaczyc, K. and Recker, M. Learning to Learn: The Implications of Strategy Instruction in Computer Programming, (ed L. Birnbaum), pp. 39-44, *Proceedings of The International Conference on the Learning Sciences,* Illinois, USA, AACE, 1991.

11. Jones, B., Palincsar, A., Ogle, D., and Carr, E. (ed). *Strategic teaching and learning: Cognitive instruction in the content areas,* Association for Supervision and Curriculum Development, 1987.
12. Cook, J. *A small study of the three reflective R's: a framework for categorising reflective composer-learner-teacher interactions.* Computing Department Technical Report, The Open University, UK, in preparation.
13. Self, J. *Dormorbile: a vehicle for metacognition.* Department of Computing, Lancaster University, 1993.

Acknowledgements
Thanks to Terri and Nancy Kinnison, Lyn Greaves, Simon Holland, Darryl Godsmark and Mark Elsom-Cook for making useful comments on a draft of this paper. Thanks again to Mark Elsom-Cook for helping me sort out the analysis.

Computer networking and collaborative learning within a departmentally focused undergraduate course

C. Crook

Department of Psychology, University of Durham, South Road, Durham DH1 3LE, UK

This paper concerns the deployment of new technology within higher education. I am particularly interested in how computer-based activities can resource the participation of undergraduates in *collaborative* learning. First, I shall discuss the context that university departments typically provide for collaborative learning. Then I shall refer to my own experience with one familiar tool of computer-supported collaboration: electronic mail. Finally, I shall summarise some impressions of how another computer resource - one less often associated with collaboration - might also support socially-organised learning: that is, I shall mention experience with hypertext, as presented on a local area network.

Educational communities

The broader context for this discussion concerns the "community" structure of educational practice. Traditionally, universities have been places that require students to *come together*: to meet with others in order deliberately to learn. Yet, it is no longer taken for granted that effective higher education must entail such a literal assembly of students. Distance learning institutions illustrate the possibility of breaking with this tradition - although often they have strived to offer summer schools, tutor meetings, telephone tutorials, and self help groups. Intriguingly, the close interpersonal dimension of even these familiar tutorial arenas is now in question. There is some feeling that such meetings might be refashioned within the technology of computer-mediated communication. Hence the masthead of the On-line Journal of Distance Education: 'In the industrial age, we go to school, in the information age, school can come to us'.

The emancipatory promise of such developments is welcome. However, although my interest is in communications technology, I am not concerned here with its possible relevance to circumstances where "school must come to us". We are *not* yet in this situation: most undergraduates still learn within a residential, full time setting. That traditional setting is the one I am concerned with: considering how its opportunities for socially-organised learning might be increased by new technology (rather than *decreased* by it - which is a common concern). In particular, I am concerned to protect (and elaborate) what I take to be a powerful feature justifying the community structure of much higher education: namely, its potential for rich varieties of student collaboration.

My enthusiasm for collaboration rests not entirely on the empirical claim typically made: the claim that discursively-organised learning leads students to perform better on some later test of understanding. That may often be the case. Nevertheless, some educationalists remain suspicious of the modern enthusiasm for forums that cultivate learning through discussion. Such an idea has recently been identified as 'one of the great untested assumptions of current educational practice' [1, p.171]. Certainly, many students survive examinations without having enjoyed rich experiences of collaboration. Yet doubts raised by such observations depend upon the credibility of empirical procedures we use to evaluate what students have learned under some regime. Exam-type tests are a controversial basis for building arguments about the effectiveness of some educational intervention [2]. However, my own case for deploying new technology to support collaborative structures does not rest upon this species of debate. For I am uneasy about the whole idea that such collaborative structures merely represent some sort of learning *method*. At least, if what this implies is that they are only a means to another end - an end to be evaluated through performance in some different arena (eg., a solitary and unsupported test).

What students should expect to gain from collaborating is exposure to the discursive practices of their academic discipline. For to claim understanding within some discipline is, in some measure, to claim the ability to participate in those discursive arenas. Even the most private acts of analyses depend upon having participated in and appropriated such practices. Indeed, beyond formal education, many graduates may find that more private, reflective states of problem solving are subservient to situations in which thinking has to be publically coordinated with others. They may find that their working communities are characterised by settings in which this is frequently what must be achieved. An occasion such as the present conference vividly exemplifies this - as we witness participants spill, animated into meeting rooms and corridors. Doing Psychology (for example) demands this social engagement and we expect any such participation to nurture new collaborative insights. Perhaps we might hope that comparable opportunities could be reproduced for our own students - and that those students would be ready to exploit them.

Traditional teaching departments as communities?

Prevailing models of computer-based learning in higher education do not obviously reflect the perspective sketched above. For example, the tradition of intelligent tutoring systems realises a more didactic style of education: typically, it offers the learner a private tutorial interaction. While simulations, microworlds and hypermedia often encourage a narrowly constructivist view of the learner - an individual exploring and experimenting, but outside of any particular social context. More in tune with the present thesis is the approach of situated or anchored instruction [3,4]. There we find an interest in mobilising technology to create for the student a more authentic contact with the concerns of some academic discipline. This approach sees new technology as able to represent, in an accessible way, those domains of practice that constitute the discipline. Thus, the technology is made to conjure up challenging but legitimate problems for learners to solve.

Situated or anchored perspectives on learning aim to draw students into genuine communities of practice. Yet, within such educational interventions, the existence of that community is easily taken for granted - or presumed to arise as an emergent consequence of richly equipping the learning environment with powerful technology-based "anchors". My own interest here is not with the design of problem spaces themselves. It is more with how the technology can supply students with better resources for communication: resources supporting the discursive activity that access to concrete problem solving anchors should stimulate. Indeed, within some disciplines, this form of interpersonal support might be the most urgent to provide. For, often, good anchors for the learner's creative activity will already be available: technology may not always be needed in this role. What is needed instead is new inspiration for supporting communication around and about these anchored experiences.

My own department's approach has been to involve students with opportunities afforded by local area computer networking [5,6]. However, first, what are the grounds for accepting that there is some real need to be met here (by networking or any other solution)? In short: how far does the residential character of traditional undergraduate education currently succeed or fail in sustaining an informal culture of communication - one that supports learning? This question suggests sampling the scope of such communication as it occurs among students themselves and between students and tutors.

Elsewhere [6], I have described some observations relevant to this interest, as gathered from within my own department - in fact, gathered prior to our investment in computer networking, This research involved (i) instituting detailed staff diaries for a two-week period, and (ii) seeking from students (unannounced and anonymous) reconstructions of how a targeted piece of coursework was prepared. Both of these exercises revealed limited practices of collaborating - either informally between staff and students or in the shape of peer-based discussion. Thus, although staff were generously available for consultation outside of timetabled teaching forums, only 12% of this time was used by undergraduates. Moreover, use was concentrated among a small group of students who staff members would be supervising for advanced project work. Similarly, in reconstructing the preparation of a significant piece of coursework (although not one contributing to final assessment), 72% of students reported pursuing no supplementary out-of-class discussion with the tutor. 62% had no discussion on the project with their peers, and of those that did, three quarters commented that these conversations were 'very brief'' or 'cursory'.

Of course, this department may not be typical; it may support an unusaul social climate. However, in standard course evaluation surveys, students reliably describe it as agreeably informal, and its' staff as very accessible. So the attitude of staff may not be exceptional. Neither are the students likely to be so: Hounsell describes a similar picture of undergraduate study elsewhere - one suggesting 'no substantive discussion of essay writing amongst peers' [7, p.113]. In citing these various observations, I mean to question whether students fully exploit social resources that are inherent within a residential and full time context for learning. We can not be sure how far my sketch above is *typical* of current practice, but my impression is that this pattern is a recognisable characteristic of many undergraduate teaching communities.

Some years ago, addressed the issue of extending the social context of learning by drawing upon the shared resources of a (campus-wide) computer network. Even in 1986, the use of network communications in higher education was not a novel idea [8]. However, existing reports refer largely to North American experience: they tend to describe activity within a more modular system in which the *course* is the principle unit of organisation. The UK system is more *department*-centred and (at least for the moment) it is more characterised by cohorts of students pursuing together a common academic path. However, apart from the fact of these differences, there remains a need for further documentation of how computer-mediated communications function in educational settings. The available research literature can not yet furnish real generalisations regarding the impact of local networks on students. What may be most valuable at the present stage of educational networking is a good corpus of case-study material: one that creates some impression of the possible trajectories associated with this kind of initiative.

Electronic mail and the department community

Surveys of how new technology has been incorporated into higher education rarely mention (or commend) network-based communication structures [9]. Yet, they seemed to us to offer a straightforward and powerful way of enriching teaching and learning within a department-centred educational framework. There are two obvious ways in which a computer network can develop existing practices. (i) It provides a powerful information server. The business of getting course materials to students can be centralised in a shared filespace: students can readily access material they need, when they need it. (ii) The network provides a person-to-person and person-to-group means of communication: email.

Care must be taken not to bolt on this infrastructure too casually. The whole constituency must have access and be well prepared. They must also have good motives for starting to use it, and conspicuous encouragement to persevere. Regarding electronic mail (my concern here), all individuals and groupings within a department need to be covered by local addresses or aliases. As described elsewhere [7], these considerations have been carefully attended to in our case. Reflecting now on eight years of our using electronic mail, prompts the following observations. First, system logging reveals that the network is very heavily used. For example, studying email directed to groups, we can calculate how quickly a message is read by half of a given constituency. During the second year of the project, this message half-life was 2 (working day) hours for staff and 10 hours for students. Second, surveys of staff and students indicate that email is very popular. Staff do not understand how they managed before, students take it for granted as an obvious part of department life.

However, my third observation is that access to this resource has not made a real impact on the problem identified above: modest levels of collaborative interaction.   Early on, staff wrote brief predictions of how networking might alter department life. It was feared that email would create an unmanageable flood of student contact. This has not happened. This conclusion is based upon accounts furnished by staff and of more detailed logging of my own email experience. Interestingly, the relevant statistics echo findings from observations of pre-network student contact mentioned above. Most student email contact arises in the context of advanced project supervision. Any other incoming mail has generally taken the form of two-turn exchanges. These arise within the context of some particular academic contract (usually a recently required piece of work): in my own case, I can only trace six items that are context-free academic inquiries - as might arise in reaction to some lecture or reading.

Of course it might be claimed that the problems here reside merely in the lack of a strong *context* for communication. However, in a recent study, Gordon Dooley and I have embedded a simple email-launching window into the graphical interface of hypertext course revision material. Being immersed in documents preparatory to an exam might seem a potent context for wanting a direct (email) link to their author (and the examiner). Even though this material was used by over 100 different students in a 3-week period, only one such enquiry was ever composed. Thus, even where the context is optimal for an electronic support of interpersonal exchange, the existence of this medium may not subvert the prevailing pattern of staff-student communication (as sketched above). Email has had an impact on much routine departmental activity and that may be reflected in more responsive and sensitive teaching. However, its effects have not been at the interpersonal/tutorial level that is often anticipated. Even though email is the most widely recognised vehicle of electronically-mediated collaboration, it may not have radically transforming impacts without some attention to an institution's existing traditions of communication.

Hypermedia and collaboration

It now seems to me naive to have serious expectations of email as a lever on the problem of supporting a collaborative culture of learning. The job of creating a community of practice really is not obstructed by inadequate media or limited opportunities for interpersonal exchange. Residential education handles this: it puts students into close contact with each other and with staff.   Email in a teaching context may help glue more firmly whatever system of exchange has evolved: it is unlikely to qualitatively transform it.   I will conclude by mentioning the species of (network-based) resource we are turning to instead.

What email illustrates is collaborative interaction *through* computers. Yet, the more familiar association between computers and collaboration involves interactions *at* the technology: small groups of learners working together at a single terminal. Elsewhere [7], I have argued for thinking more carefully about how best to *resource* collaborating learners - suggesting that computers sometimes can furnish particularly potent settings for the construction of shared knowledge. To pursue this, we have recently studied pairs of students using network-based hypertext documents (as mentioned above): interactive materials that systematise departmental lecture courses. Presence at a lecture is a common point of reference for most students; so, in combination with the interactivity of hypertext, we regarded these documents as a particularly rich resource for collaborators. To some extent this turned out to be so. Yet, not for all students. Many still found this a difficult, even uncomfortable experience. In some cases, this reflected an uneasiness about revealing to peers their own limited fluency with a topic. Sometimes it reflected too meagre a level of shared knowledge: mutual understandings were insufficient to act a platform for new exploration.

In a way the *revision* character of these documents may be the problem. They arrive too late in the overlapping experience of potential student collaborators. This suggests to us the possibility of using hypermedia to fashion a shared resource that is accessible from the start of some teaching course and that reflects its evolving concerns. Such a resource would be "local" - representing the distinctive set of interests defined for the constituency - yet (in our experience) not difficult for a tutor to design and implement. Moreover, it would be accessible by virtue of being networked, and dynamically interactive, by virtue of the hypermedia concept. Such a notion moves us from collaborative interactions *through* computers, past interactions *at* them, and towards interactions that are resourced *in relation to* them. Possibly this new media may help in the construction of mutual knowledge - an achievement that might better support truly sustained collaborative discourse in this departmental community.

References

1.   Laurillard, D. *Rethinking University Teaching*. Routledge, London, 1993.
2.   Kvale, S. Examinations reexamined: Certification of students or certification of knowledge. In S. Chaiklin and J. Lave (eds) *Understanding Practice,* Cambridge University Press, Cambridge, 1993.
3.   Brown, J.S., Collins, A. and Duguid, P. Situated cognition and the culture of learning. *Educational Researcher,* 1989, 18, 32-42.
4.   Cognition and technology group at Vanderbilt, Anchored instruction and situated cognition revisited, *Educational Technology*, 1993, 52-70.
5.   Crook, C.K. Electronic media for communications in an undergraduate teaching department. In D. Smith, (ed.), *New Technologies and Professional Communications in Education,* NCET, London 1988.
6.   Crook, C.K. *Computers and the Collaborative Experience of Learning*, Routledge, London, 1994.
7.   Hounsell, D. Essay writing and the quality of feedback. In J. Richardson, M. Eysenck and D. Piper (Eds.), *Student Learning,* SRHE and Open University Press, Milton Keynes, 1987.
8.   Sproull, L. and Kiesler, S. *Connections*. MIT Press, Cambridge, MA, 1991.
9.   Darby, J. Computers in teaching: the needs of the 90s. *The CTISS File,* 1991, 12, 9-18.

Bringing a constructivist approach to bear on evaluation

S. Draper,[a] E. McAteer,[a] A.K. Tolmie[b] & A. Anderson[b]

[a] *Department of Psychology, University of Glasgow, Hillhead Street, Glasgow G12, UK*

[b] *Centre for Research into Interactive Learning, Department of Psychology, University of Strathclyde, Graham Hills Building, 40 George Street, Glasgow G1 1QE, UK*

Our main aim in the workshop to which this paper relates will be to engage the participants in a debate about some of the theoretical issues that emerge in trying to develop meaningful ways of evaluating, or more accurately of observing and measuring, the educational effects of interventions (particularly computer based ones). We shall offer some activities and demonstrations to illustrate some of the points to serve as a starting ground. Here we discuss why we think there are debates to be resolved. The issues include the meaning of "constructivism" itself and what it implies for measuring and observing learning, the role of the learner in determining learning outcomes, the difference between deep and shallow learning, and what kinds of activity are important in learning.

Introduction

Like many others, we are interested in how to measure the effects of ("evaluate") various educational interventions (EIs). In order to illuminate and improve teaching practices, the obvious kind of knowledge to seek is knowledge about the effects of such teaching actions. Practicing teachers, those seeking to introduce new technology into teaching, and theorists seeking to demonstrate important factors underlying learning would all desire such knowledge. All of us have worked on aspects of observing and measuring the learning process. Two of us have recently (Draper et al. [1]) been involved in trying to evaluate computer assisted learning (CAL) software in universities. One approach attempted to do pre- and post-tests of learning gains surrounding an intervention of an hour or two. This method is both traditional and seems proportionate to the intervention: since the intervention is short and localised in time, it would seem inappropriate to mount enormous studies over long periods on the effect.

There are, however, several obvious kinds of criticism of so simple an approach:
a) Our measures (so far) only measure shallow learning, but surely the important aim of (higher) education is deep learning.
b) The teaching input is only one of a number of factors influencing learning, and in particular the learner's goals, i.e. whether and how they are motivated to learn, what they believe the task to be in a given situation, and how the learning task is embedded in the wider situation and organisational context are important.
c) Some authors, particularly constructivist ones (e.g. Papert [2]), suggest that the most important learning events take a long time to show their effects.

There are thus several related but not identical criticisms of a straightforward approach to evaluating and comparing EIs. The discussion in this paper and our workshop will concern what the issues are and how they relate to each other. This should inform our debate on appropriate methods of evaluation.

Immediate or delayed learning effects

Papert [2, preface], suggests that the most important learning events take a long time to show their effects. This means that a standard evaluation design of pre-test, intervention, immediate post-test and delayed post-test (used, for example, in work on deep and shallow learning by Marton et al. [3]) may not show the usual pattern of immediate gain, followed by decay between immediate and delayed post-tests, but instead might show a pattern of little immediate gain, and a large gain between the post-tests. However this also means that the learners will have engaged in other activities during that period, confounding our study.

Does this imply that we will never know what matters, and so have little hope of improving teaching or understanding learning? We would argue not. It may explain why teaching seldom improves; why particular students do well or poorly, or why the changes they make have the effects or lack of effects they see. But delayed effects are consistent with a nutrient or vitamin model of learning, and we should remember that Piaget took the concepts of assimilation and accommodation from a consciously biological metaphor.

Multi-factor models of teaching and learning

In a nutrient-like model for the teaching and learning process, you expect learning (growth) to occur best or at all only if multiple factors are all present, and present over a considerable time. Adding a pinch of nitrate, selenium or whatever seldom causes a plant to leap upwards overnight. So even if a piece of teaching does directly contribute to learning, the effects are likely to be slow; and it will only occur in the presence of many other co-factors. This implies both that measurements should extend over a long period, and that we cannot expect to understand results unless we track many possible factors. Perhaps we should abandon the hope of directly measuring the effects of individual pieces of teaching: just as missing one or more meals has little measurable effect on a person's health, so missing one or more lectures seldom has crucial effects on a student's progress. Only highly artificial experiments that completely control an organism's access to the separate components of nutrition over long periods can really establish these factors. When you know what they are, then you can analyse any input (food, teaching) for those factors, and so say what a particular input is contributing to the eventual outcome. Evaluation then becomes an analytic process on the inputs, not a matter of direct empirical measurement of effects. A weaker conclusion for evaluation would be that measurements must include not just learning outcomes, but the values of the various factors thought to be important. Simple comparisons of alternative EIs or teaching methods cannot be trusted unless the state of the other causal factors is controlled. We therefore need a model that tells us what these factors are.

The idea that learning seems to be governed by a number of factors other and larger than the teaching input has been argued both by ourselves (Draper et al. [1]) and others, e.g. Laurillard [4]. Laurillard proposes that 12 activities must occur for effective learning to take place e.g. the learner must re-express their conception of the material. Laurillard then uses the 12 activities as a checklist for analysing the teaching potential of various media: few if any support all 12, and the shortfall tells you what activities must be supported by other means.

Why is "bad" teaching still quite effective?

The problem with this is that learning seems sometimes to take place without some of the activities being supported. In other words, though evidence is often found that supporting some activity or other promotes more learning than its absence, at least some students seem to learn without it. Perhaps the basic model can be extended to explain this by arguing that skilled learners can generate the necessary activity autonomously, without external support. For instance, in a lecture a student might take notes not by dictation, but by re-expressing in their own words the key ideas, thus covering the activity of re-expression.

Although this saves the theory in the sense that we can say that all the activities must "really" occur, it is no longer true that they must all be visible or externally supported. It then becomes unclear what the implications for teaching practice are, as not all activities need be supported. Indeed, it could be argued that institutions have a duty to foster these autonomous learning skills. Since spoon-feeding students with external support will retard the development of these skills, recommendations directly opposite to Laurillard's might seem more appropriate.

The implications for evaluation however are perhaps still clear. If the theory is correct, then all activities need to be monitored (not just the overt EI). If some of these take place without external support, then we need to develop measures and extend observations to cover them e.g. observe whether students work on their notes away from the lecture theatre, and so on.

Constructivism

There is a comparable problem for constructivist theories (defined as the view that learning requires activity on the part of the learner). A lot of learning doesn't require any detectable activity, which seems on the face of it to mean that either constructivism only applies to a special kind of learning, or it is trivial. It can be argued, for instance, that for all learning there is hidden unconscious mental activity. But then, we can say the same of a tape recorder: there is fast unconscious automatic conversion and processing of the signal. This reduces constructivism to an empty claim that learning only occurs if the student's auditory neurons fire, which is a prediction of the crudest transmission theories of learning too. However, there is one key difference: constructivism makes the additional claim that the form of any activity, and thus any learning that occurs, is influenced by the knowledge that exists already (i.e. by the results of past learning). This remains true whatever the scale of activity involved. Learning may involve extensive reconstruction, in which case activity will be conscious; or it may involve simple accretion, in which case activity will be low-level and relatively unconscious. In either instance, past learning has its influence.

An example of apparently one shot passive reception illustrates the point, but also the residual problem. You need only hear once that there are photographs of a member of the royal family having sex with a Tory cabinet minister on sale at your local newsagent to remember it. In fact you are quite likely to remember this fictitious example anyway. However, the impact of this information is a function of the meaning already attached to the elements involved. Would your retention be the same if the principals were from a remote foreign country , or if they were a previously anonymous landowner and a local civic dignitary? The problem for constructivism is that under more prosaic circumstances it may be very much harder to specify or to predict what the relevant connections for a given learner will be. If they are unaware of them, how are we to find them out?

Motivation

A special class of the multiple factors determining learning is the learners' goals: whether and how they are motivated to learn, what they believe the task to be in a given situation, and how the learning task is embedded in the wider situation and organisational context. Learners' motivations appear in different theoretical roles in different areas of the literature: a) as a subset of the multiple factors acting on learning; b) the learner's grasp of the immediate task in deep and shallow learning, c) in the literature on incidental learning, d) task grasp, and the concept of learning skill (bringing different learning methods to bear depending on what the task seems to be). All of these deal with immediate motivation rather than wider scale issues (how interesting the learner finds the topic in general).

It may be helpful here to distinguish between affective reaction to a learning context and the salience of the material, i.e. what connection it makes to existing knowledge. The first is clearly problematic for constructivism, since it may involve influences such as physical health which have little or nothing to do with knowledge. The second is much less so, since, in principle at least, it ought to be predictable from prior experience. Note also that factors of this kind will often determine what processing actually occurs, irrespective of the affective system.

The implications for evaluation seem clear: standard experiments, including asking or paying students to try out materials for next year, are mostly flawed since their motivational structure is markedly different from other situations, and in particular the educational situation. More generally, we need instruments to measure what is active in terms of both affect and salience, and there is little in the literature to help on this. We might observe, though, that simply asking learners questions may only yield information on what they perceive *ought* to be the case; this may have little to do with what's actually going on.

Deep & shallow learning

Constructivism marks a denial of crude ideas of learning as a passive reception of information from a teacher. Furthermore, it tells us to attend to the differences between different learners and how that affects learning (e.g. prior conceptions). Another aspect of this is the work on deep and shallow learning: i.e. the often marked difference between learners exposed to the same material. Deep learning is associated with long retention of overall meaning, shallow learning with brief retention spans. However, deep learning could reflect how the material is structured, rather than learners having to do special work in constructing novel concepts. Effects of this kind were demonstrated by Katona [5] for learning 12 digit numbers, and by Marton for reading a newspaper article.

The notion of deep and shallow learning is a simplification of the more general notion that learners exert choice in the schema they apply to the learning material, with large effects on learning. Which kind of learning takes place is not a fixed characteristic of a learner. As Svensson [6; p.66] says, the quality of learning is the quality of the interaction between learner and material. Learners thus have a variety of learning modes at their disposal. This probably has implications for how we should test learning. Although if students are not expecting it, an open-ended comprehension test can show these differences well, if students expect and have practiced such tests they can pass them while still only learning in a shallow way. There is probably a whole skill to such tests, revolving around posing the unexpected so that learners have to go back to basics. However perhaps it means in the end that interviews not written tests should be used.

Schooling

A common assumption is that knowledge is what can be tested for in an exam: recall without prompts of any kind, and that the kind of learning done for tests of this kind is the one and only universal human learning mechanism. Cross-cultural work however suggests that proficiency at this is a function of years of practice in school (Scribner & Cole [7]). What are the distinctive characteristics and effects of informal, formal, and school-based learning? Scribner & Cole argue that school-based learning is decontextualised learning: general, abstract, rootless. It is about learning to attend to surface forms, the language itself, and to rules not effects. Margaret Donaldson points out that in normal conversation, people care only about what the speaker means, intends to convey; and not about how they say it or what the language could mean in other contexts. But school is about changing that orientation, and developing skills in literal meaning, and rule based interpretation. That is why it is unnatural.

In fact, schooling is training people to do shallow learning (for recall tests, ignoring context and meaning) that they couldn't naturally do. Cole & Scribner [8] argue that the recall tests that seem so natural to most psychologists are in fact testing only a skill specific to schooled cultures. In other cultures, people do badly at most recall tasks, and certainly at tasks about learning for recall; while they will do well at recognition tasks. But training on shallow learning, as divorced as possible from meaning and context, brings many benefits. For instance, it permits language which can cross contexts better, facilitating cultural and informational transmission and development. The great power of formalisms is that you can do rule based manipulations of surface forms without considering (using) their meaning, re-interpret the results, and get outcomes you wouldn't otherwise get. Thus you can develop rules for adding apples that are the same as for adding oranges, even though adding them together makes no sense.

As a further illustration, when you go to a doctor, you expect them to recall not only the most common drug treatment for your problem, but also the side effects of it and the situational factors that would make that treatment undesirable. These facts are often unexplained theoretically, and certainly the theories of the operation of each drug need not be known by each doctor. Thus the crucial content of education for the most important professions has a large rote learning component, and the education and assessment methods used reflect this.

It follows that concern about "shallow" learning, where pupils pass exams yet fail to understand the connection between the concepts and vocabulary they have learned and the real world fails to acknowledge that the chief aim of schooling is to suspend disbelief, disconnect from the normal effort after meaning, and attend to the surface forms of representations. Shallow learning is not the product of immature pupils, but on the contrary, of well schooled pupils who are applying the basic educated technique in an unfortunate way.

Is shallow learning bad?

Much everyday knowledge acquisition is shallow in the sense of learning common vocabulary without learning what it means. You clearly have learned something, yet you also cannot be said to understand much. However, you could now set about discovering more by enquiries. This is comparable to the situation that worries science educators, in which pupils often can pass exams on subjects and yet not relate them to everyday experience. Although making those connections is clearly desirable, and constitutes a fuller understanding, we can also see that those students have nevertheless learned something useful even if they only learn the names of concepts and substances. That is because knowledge is socially distributed, and to have learned a name is to have gained the ability to get more knowledge by asking if you ever need to. Putnam [9] has argued that in fact a lot of our basic knowledge is of that kind. Our knowledge is ultimately grounded in a social network. Many communications, particularly perhaps educational ones, are not understood in the sense of being translatable into personal knowledge, but instead equip us with the means to get further knowledge by asking other people for it should we ever need it. Why then should education aim at a different kind of knowledge? You are much better equipped for the future if you learn only the "shallow" public names, than if you learn only the private meaning. Thus shallow learning is actually appropriate very often. Again, it seems that learners exert choice over the appropriate learning strategy to apply, guided by the social demands apparent to them.

Afterword

Readers may have noticed certain contradictions in the above. Rather than resolving these here, we conclude by noting that the debate must be focused by methodological as opposed to merely theoretical concerns. The point is that the questions asked during any attempt to evaluate learning will inevitably be directed by a model (even if incomplete) of what the learning process involves, and of the factors which influence what learning takes place. The constructivist model argues that learning depends on what the students bring with them, how the EI engages this, and what activity takes place as a result. The implication is that the type of question we should be asking is about the characteristics of this sequence of interaction, rather than "how much" effect it has. What we need is a methodology for going about doing this, given that a head-on approach (e.g. asking direct questions of students) may very well not work.

References

1. Draper, S.W., Brown, M.I., Edgerton, E., Henderson, F.P., McAteer, E., Smith, E.D. & Watt H.D. Observing and measuring the performance of educational technology, Technical report no.1, TILT project, University of Glasgow, 1994.
2. Papert, S.A. *Mindstorms: Children, computers and powerful ideas*, Basic Books, New York, 1980.
3. Marton, F., Hounsell, D. & Entwistle, N. (eds). *The experience of learning*, Scottish Academic Press, Edinburgh, 1984.
4. Laurillard, D. *Rethinking university teaching: A framework for the effective use of educational technology*, Routledge, London, 1993.
5. Katona, G. *Organizing and memorizing: studies in the psychology of learning and teaching*, Hafner, New York, 1940.
6. Svensson, L. Skill in learning, ch.4, *The experience of learning*, eds F. Marton, D. Hounsell & N. Entwistle, Scottish Academic Press, Edinburgh, 1984.
7. Scribner, S. & Cole, M. The cognitive consequences of formal and informal education, *Science*, 1973, **182**, 553-559.
8. Cole, M. & Scribner, S. Cross-cultural studies of memory and cognition, ch.8, *Perspectives on the development of memory and cognition*, eds R.V.Kail & J.W.Hagan, Erlbaum, Hillsdale, N.J., 1977.
9. Putnam, H. The meaning of meaning, in *Mind, language and reality*, Cambridge University Press, Cambridge, U.K, 1975.

Group process vs group product in children's work at the computer

E. Fisher

Faculty of Humanities and Social Sciences, Nene College, Moulton Park, Northampton NN2 7AL, UK

Introduction:

The shortage of computers in primary schools has led to frequent group use of machines in the classroom. As has been reported elsewhere (Fisher 1993), pupils show an unusually focused and extended attention to work at computers. The computing setting therefore offers the potential for a rich, extended interactive/interpersonal experience. Although this potential is often not realized (Fisher, 1994) with much of the time at the computer spent in routine or superficial activities which fail to match the teacher's aims and expectations, appropriate planning and preparation by teachers can produce changes in pupil approaches (Fisher and Dawes 1994) which lead to more effective interpersonal exchanges and a more productive use of the software.

Groupwork, its underlying ideology and practice   The group-work ideology has a theoretical base in the socio-cognitivist view articulated by Vygotsky (1978) that learning occurs first in a social or interpsychological context and only subsequently becomes internalized within an intrapsychological category. Following this tradition, subsequent research has emphasized the context-specific nature of learning (Crook 1987; Edwards 1991). *Thus learning is initially a social event, transmitted through oral exchanges and closely related to the task in hand.*

The research reported here used an ethnomethodological approach and discourse analysis to examine the processes that occurred and the outcomes which followed. To illustrate the dichotomy between group processes and products, two very different examples of groupwork will be analysed in detail, followed by a discussion of a larger sample of video-recorded sessions of primary school children using computers in the course of their normal classroom activity. In all cases the software and the task were chosen by the teachers .

Example 1.   The king and the rocket: 3 - fourteen-year old girls, wordprocessing The whole class in the comprehensive school which these children attended had been engaged in a series of electronic mail exchanges with pupils in three local primary schools. Their aim was to construct a serial story, to which the younger children could respond with suggestions or questions. At the time of the recording, the exchange had been running for 3-4 weeks and the older pupils remained enthusiastic with a keen sense of responsibility to their young audience.

In the excerpt below, Jackie, Natalie and Kate were responding to a message received earlier that day. The text on the screen at the outset of this discourse extract concludes:

He called over one of his servants who brought a large glass case containing an object that looked like a rocket. What on earth is that doing? He's staring intently

Minimal punctuation is used to assist comprehension. Bracketed words indicate actions. Square bracketed utterances indicate simultaneous speech. [inaudible] indicates speech which could not be transcribed. Words in italics are those which are typed onto the screen and remain as part of the final text.

J.	1. Staring intently at the
N.	2. (typing) *at the* object
K.	3. At the
	4. At the weird
J.	5. At the weird-shaped rocket
K.	6. At the rocket-shaped object (laughs)
N.	7. No 'cos
	8. Well it is a rocket
	9. But the King's got to explain that it's a rocket
J.	10.Well in other messages we've put things like
	11.Weird thingy
	12.He was staring at the weird thing
N.	13.Yeh..so he's (types)
J.	14.So he's staring at the weird
K.	15.No
	16.Weird thing in a case
	17.You can't put 'weird thingy'
N.	18.OK (types)
K.	19.Don't put 'thingy'
J.	20.It's (inaudible) Kate
	21.You're too boring Kate

N.   22.(types - *weird thing in a case*)
       23.Do we want an exclamation mark here? (types *!*)

On paper not a great achievement. All they have added are the words 'at the weird thing in a case'. However, as their discussion shows, the girls' attention to detail of the description is considerable. Whilst they seem to be aware of a need to improve on 'object' (line 2) as a description, the constraints of the story lead through various suggestions before they make their final selection. In producing these few written words the girls showed a concern with the richness of their description (lines 3-6), the accuracy and continuity of their content (7-12) the appropriateness of their vocabulary (17-19) and their punctuation (23). They then continue:

K: 24.*The King explains what it is for* (types this in)
       25. What is it for?
N.   26. It's for Kathy's time machine
J.   27. Just
       28. Yeh but how does he know
       29. How does he know Kathy
K.   30. Yeh you can't
J.   31.Say 'I don't know what it is
       32. But I treat it as valuable
       33. One of my servants found it in'
N.   34. [inaudible] Yeh
       35. So you are gonna put 'the courtyard'
K.   36. Yeh
N.   37. It's got to be like say an old book
       38. It's written in an old book
K.   39. You've got to have (points to screen)
       40. No I'm talking about the speech things
       41. What do you want then? (N types in ..)
       42. Ah dots
N.   43. Yeh I know
K.   44. What do you want then
J.   45. Something like
       46.Do you know like medieval times
N.   47. Um well it can be written in a book
J.   48. Put in a book
       49. In a book we saw an object (laughs)
N.   50. *In a book it is written that* (K types)
K.   51. It is written that
J.   52. An object like this can create much power or something
N.   53. The rocket object
K.   54. Can be a key to power
N.   55. No it can be a key to time travel
       56. An then it gives a bit more of a clue
K.   57. Time travel
       58. Yeh
N.   59. (reads) in a book it is written that
J.   60. They didn't know about time travel in Medieval times (inaudible)
K.   61. Yeh

                62. They'd believe in it
N.   63. Yeh
                64. It'd be like um a prophecy thing
K.   65. Yeh yeh
N.   66. It is written that a rocket would be the key to
K.   67. No
                68. Put 'this object'
                69. In a book it is written that (N types) *this object is*
K.   70. Or it could be
N.   71. No put 'is'
                72. There's no doubt

In 3.5 minutes they have now only added: *The king explains what it is for. In a book it is written that the object is'.*

However, the progress of their discussion to which all three contribute indicates their concern with the quality and relevance of what they produce, and their aim to engage their audience. They have once more demonstrated their attention to precision (line 25), to continuity (28-33), shown a sense of historical perspective (37-38, 45-48, 60-65), and of dramatic content (52-59) and a need to punctuate correctly (39-43). The product of this activity is adequate but unexceptional, but by examining the process of production we can see how each girl is involved in the argument and where each benefits from building on each other's ideas.

Example 2.   Making Connections: three seven-year olds   In the next example, Richard, Gina and Anthony 'played' a mathematics game *Connections,* which according to the accompanying literature, was

designed to support the Maths National Curriculum at Levels 1 and 2. Built around the concepts of connections and patterns, the package can be used to help young children learn and understand early maths and number concepts in a meaningful and attractive way. (Sherston Software, 1990, page 5.)

The group successfully worked through the first display of six problems which required them to manipulate combinations of figures and shapes so that the total in each diagram added to 13 (see Table 1). From the outset one of the boys, Richard, dominated the group by articulating each problem aloud and deterring the other two from keying in any answers until he has checked out his calculations on a pocket calculator. Thus, although the children 'took turns' in key pressing, it was Richard's conceptualisation of the problem and his checking of it which was vital. Gina suggested answers which were correct, but which were not taken up. The third child, Anthony, adopted a trial and error approach which ultimately produced some correct answers.

TABLE 1

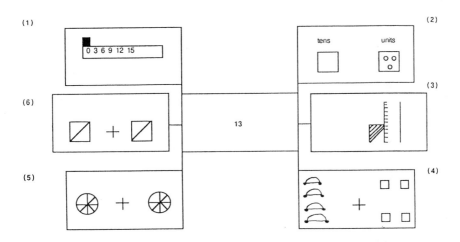

TABLE 2

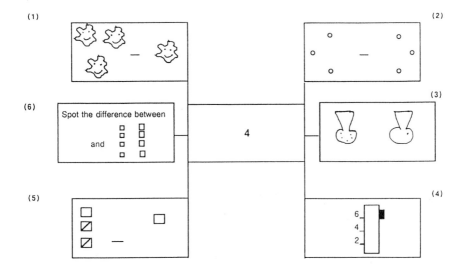

The second display (Table 2) was considerably more difficult and required the use of substraction. As before, the children were asked to alter the display so that the same (given) answer was correct for all six problems. However, the 'sums' were not always set out as straightforward 'take away' . From table 2 it can be seen that the last problem actually requires them to reverse the process and add the answer to the number of shapes in the right hand column to obtain an answer.

The children worked through the first five examples fairly quickly, though Anthony appeared to have no understanding of the activity as a computational exercise and continued to treat it as a trial and error game (at which he was intermittently rewarded with an acknowledgement from the computer of a successful choice!). Gina made only tentative suggestions and Richard's domination of the activity increased. However, problem 6 produced the first real difficulty for him and ultimately led to a shift in the balance of power in the group.

They began their attempt at the last problem on the second display as follows:

R.   1. (reads) spot the difference
G.   2. (reads) between
R.   3. nothing and whatever it asks you

Richard once again made a reasonable attempt to articulate the problem (line 3). Presumably part of the difficulty with this sum is that, if it is conceived as a 'take away' (which Anthony later suggested, and which is a perfectly reasonable approach to 'difference' sums) then the minimalist approach (i.e. making a difference sum of 4-8) would give a negative answer. It is unlikely that these seven year olds had dealt with negative numbers, but they almost certainly been told that you can't take more away from less! Thus their most straightforward approach would be to sum 8 and the answer, 4, and so place a 12 in the left-hand column. They did not propose this strategy, but continued:

R.   4. Get some more ships. Get some [more ships
A.   5.   [take
R.   6. Get some [more ships
A.   7.   [No, take away
R.   8. OK take away some ships
         (A. reaches over and presses keys, adding in a ship on the left-hand
         column)
         9. Oh that's add
G.   10.That's add. Take away (ship is deleted)

So far they seem to be confused between the notion that they have envisaged a 'take away' sum, yet by placing any ships in the left column they are adding to their total. Meanwhile, Richard continues to puzzle over what the problem actually is, using the first person singular which seems to indicate his 'ownership' of it.

R.	11. I need to... between something
	12. Press delete (points at the keyboard)
	13. Between something
	(a ship appears in the left column again)
A.	14. That adds on
R.	15. Oh
G.	16. Take way, you have to take away to get four
R.	17. Yeah I know
	18. Press that, now press that, uhh
	(Left hand column is deleted, then 2 ships reappear on the left
G.	19. No
	(R deletes the left hand column again)
R.	20. Uhh won't go
G.	21. No you have to press that (indicates the keys) all the time to make it go
	22.(points to screen) to make four, don't you?
R.	23. Yeh it won't do it
	24. Aha, I've got it, I have to make four (stands up to indicate the left hand column on the screen) on the other side
G.	25. Ah hum
R.	26. I think, I don't know, but I think you do

At line 16, Gina proposed a workable conceptualization of the problem, and Richard reworded this to come up with a more complete suggestion on lines 24-5, though he remained tentative (line 26).

The children continued on this problem for three minutes. Their difficulties were exacerbated by the fact that Anthony was 'trigger happy' and constantly pressed the keys too many times so that he overshot the correct answer.   Richard demonstrated that he understood the problem (for example, he realized that one ship in the left column and five in the right would give the correct answer), but he seemed to have lost confidence in his own solutions and they finally sought adult help.

Had this activity not been recorded, and assuming that the teacher had left the children to work until they asked for help, she would have entered at the point of them having produced 11 correct answers and having difficulty with the 12. Nothing on the screen or in any print-out would indicate:

that only one of the children (Richard) had shown an

*understanding of the aims of the activity through his articulation
of problem, though there were indications that Gina could also
solve some of the   problems. The third child showed many signs of
completely misunderstanding the whole purpose of the 'game'.*

*the strategies that had been tried when they ran into difficulty.   By
the time they sought help they were so confused that they   seemed
to have difficulty in explaining what they had tried to do.*

Thus the product of their group effort (11 out of 12 correct) is
inadequate and very misleading.

These are not isolated examples. In much of the work undertaken
by the SLANT team*, it was clear that individual contributions to
final products often came as a surprise to teachers when they
viewed the video recordings of their pupils. Perhaps more
worrying, teachers frequently assumed a level of understanding
and competence which simply did not exist. For example, all of the
10 schools in our sample possessed and sometimes used statistical
packages (Grass; Grass roots; Ourfacts). After entering raw data, the
user of these packages is able to produce on screen or paper simple
displays such as pie-charts or bar charts. Pupils seemed content to
produce these and append them to their work, but their discourse
indicated that they generally lacked explicit criteria for selecting one
display over another and, even when teachers asked for
explanations of what they had done, little justification was offered.

Further indications of the gap between process and product came
from the use of games software in which the team found that
problem solving activities might be accompanied by rich interaction
and reasoned argument or they might be carried out by one member
of the group with almost no involvement of the others and with
little consideration of the possible alternatives. What is more, these
differences occurred in the same classroom, with the same software,
but were affected by previous training in discursive skills and by the
way the teacher introduced the task. This underlines the
importance of the contextual setting and the dangers of
extrapolating findings from one setting to another. Whilst this
danger is often acknowledged in papers reporting experimental
work, many researchers nonetheless go on to draw conclusions
from their findings as if they would be little altered in more
ecologically valid settings. But these differences are not trivial.
They may represent the difference between a positive and negative
outcome. It is vital, therefore, that more research reports consider a
variety of approaches to the same problem, in which discussion of

the learning processes in a natural setting are compared with experimental data.

References:

Crook, C. 'Computers in the classroom: defining a social context' in J. Rutkowska and C. Crook (eds) *Computers, Cognition and Development,* 35-53. John Wiley, London, 1987.

Edwards, D. Categories are for talking: on the cognition and discursive bases of categorization. *Theory and Psychology,* 1991, 1, 515-542.

Fisher, E. The teacher's role, chapter 5, *Language, Classrooms and Computers,* ed P. Scrimshaw, 57-74. Routledge, London, 1993.

Fisher, E. Distinctive features of pupil-pupil classroom talk and their relationship to learning. *Language and Education,* 1994, 7:4, 239-258.

Fisher, E. and Dawes, D. Exploring through talk at the computer. *Topic.* 1994 11, 1-12. National Foundation for Educational Research, Slough.

Sherston Software. *Connections Teachers' Book.*   1990

Vygotksy, L. *Mind in Society: the development of higher psychological process.* Harvard University Press, Cambridge. 1978.

*The SLANT (Spoken Language and New Technology) Project was a joint venture between the Open University and the University of East Anglia, funded by ESRC.

Gender and the classroom computer: Do girls lose out?

H. Fitzpatrick & M. Hardman
Division of Psychology and Biology, Bolton Institute, Deane Road, Bolton BL3 5AB, UK

Abstract

This paper reports the results of two studies undertaken to compare the styles of interaction and task performance shown by seven and nine year old boys and girls (in either same or mixed gender pairs) when working on a language-based computer and non-computer task.

Introduction

Recent studies undertaken in UK schools suggest that, while both boys and girls recognise the importance of computers, boys have more positive attitudes towards computers than girls, use them more frequently at home and, within mixed sex schools, tend to dominate the classroom computer which is frequently seen as a "male preserve" (Culley, 1988[1]). Concern about girls' experience of computer work in schools has been heightened by the fact that group work with computers continues to be an economic necessity in most UK primary schools, and finding that most teachers prefer group rather than individual work, and also tend to favour mixed rather than single gender pairs and groups (Jackson, Fletcher, and Messer, 1986[2]).

The issue of whether and how girls are disadvantaged when working in mixed gender pairs is complex and has been examined in terms of task performance and styles of interaction of both same and mixed gender pairings. The majority of studies have found that the performance of mixed gender pairs is least effective when compared with same gender pairs (Underwood et. al, 1994[3]). In relation to styles of interaction, there is some support for the proposal that girls prefer a cooperative style involving the mutual sharing of ideas, and boys tend to show a competitive, individualistic style. Most research indicates that children find it difficult to cooperate in mixed gender pairs. This type of pairing has been variously described as being characterised by "task demarcation " (Underwood,

Jindal and Underwood, 1994[3]), and "constrained" and lacking in the most positive features of the interaction characteristic of both male and female same gender pairs (Tolmie and Howe, 1993[6]).

One particular aspect of collaborative work with computers which has received scant attention is the effect of the computer (or 'third partner') itself. This aspect is important for a full appreciation of the situated nature of cognition, and particularly when examining girls' apparent disadvantage in computer work in the classroom. The few studies which have addressed this (Hoyles, Healy and Sutherland, 1991[4]; Keogh, 1993[5]) suggest that the computer itself may generate different styles of social interaction which may be specific to the type of gender pairing.

The majority of previous studies on performance and styles of interaction of same and mixed gender pairs of children, and the few studies concerned with the effect of the computer itself, have examined children of at least 12 years of age. Given the importance of computer work in the primary school classroom and the influence this has on attitudes, it is important to examine younger children. The research reported in these Conference Proceedings is a brief review of the results of two studies undertaken to examine the performance and social interaction of seven and nine year old children working in either same or mixed gender pairs on a similarly structured-language based computer and non-computer task. Three specific aspects will be addressed: (i) gender pairing and styles of social interaction, (ii) gender pairing and task performance, and (iii) comparison of the computer and non-computer task. At the time of writing, the results for the second study involving the nine year old children are only available for the first of these aspects. A systematic review of the results of both studies will be presented at the conference.

Method

The two studies had a similar design, with the first study including 60 seven year old children (30 girls and 30 boys) and the second study 60 nine year old children (30 girls and 30 boys).

In both studies all children were assigned to either a same or mixed gender pairing (girl-girl, boy-boy or boy-girl) on the basis of the results of the British Ability Scale Word Definition Test (i.e. were matched in terms of verbal ability) and completed both a computer and non-computer task (the order of presentation for this was randomised). All children were subsequently given a questionnaire examining the frequency of computer use at home and school, attitudes to using computers and whether boys were better than girls at computer tasks, and asked to indicate the friendship status of the pairing. In the first study only, pre and post tests were administered to enable an assessment of learning outcome.

The computer and non-computer tasks were carefully designed to ensure their similarity in terms of the skills required and interest, their suitability for the children's ages, and lack of explicit gender stereotyping. The computer task employed a language-based computer programme (The Read Right Away series) in which children had to match the beginnings and endings of words and perform spelling tasks.   The non-computer task was designed to tap the same understanding, and was presented as a board game with a Snakes and Ladders theme, requiring the solution of similar language puzzles. The pairs of children were taken to a quiet part of the school, given a brief desciption of the task and instructed to work together to complete them. All sessions were videotaped.

The videotaped social interaction was subsequently coded into 23 verbal and non-verbal response categories, which were grouped into the following three global styles of social interaction:

assertive: this included instances where one child made a spontaneous on-task assertive statement or action (not directed to partner) followed by the other child responding with either (i) an assertive statement (assertive-reciprocal), or (ii) a passive response (assertive-dominated), which terminated the interaction.

transactive: this was cooperative, coordinated interaction where both children were actively involved in working on each others' ideas, and included instances whereby one child made a spontaneous non-assertive statement or action directed to their partner, who then responded appropriately, and the interaction continued for at least one more turn. This type of interaction was either (i) specifically directed at the set task (transactive-on task), or (ii) deviating from the task (transactive-off task).

spontaneous non-directed verbalising: this included instances whereby one child appeared to be "thinking aloud" about the task in hand, which was not directed at the other child and was not followed by an appropriate response by the other child.

A separate breakdown of the frequency of each child's individual use of "task operators" - the arrow and the return keys in the computer task and the die and the counter in the non-computer task - was also recorded.

Results

In order to examine the results, a proportional measure of each of the three global styles of social interaction was calculated for each pair. Table 1 presents a summary of these proportions for both the seven and nine year old children.

Table 1. Global proportion scores of styles of Social Interaction for each gender pair on the computer and the non-computer task

	Computer			Non-Computer		
	GG	BB	GB	GG	BB	GB
7 year olds						
Transactive	58.9	61.0	52.2	60.7	63.6	54.0
Assertive	15.5	15.1	25.8	16.0	16.3	22.9
Self-verb.	25.6	23.9	22.0	23.3	20.1	23.1
9 year olds						
Transactive	68.7	60.6	46.2	63.4	60.2	52.0
Assertive	15.8	24.2	37.5	18.1	22.2	28.3
Self-verb.	15.5	15.2	16.3	18.5	17.6	19.7

Gender Pairing and Styles of Social Interaction
Previous research suggested the problematic nature of mixed gender interaction, and it was therefore hypothesised that there would be a difference in the styles of social interaction displayed by same and mixed gender pairings. The proportions of the different styles of social interaction displayed in Table 1 indicate support for this, in that the main difference appears to relate to same gender pairs compared with mixed gender pairs on both tasks.

The significance of these differences were examined by ANOVA and t tests comparing type of pairing and task. For both age groups, there were no significant differences in the proportion of spontaneous non-directed verbalising, but there were differences in the amount of transactive and assertive interactions, with significantly more assertive and less transactive interactions for mixed gender pairs on both computer and non-computer tasks than for same gender pairs ($p < 0.05$).

Gender Pairing and Performance
On the basis of previous research it was hypothesised that same gender pairings would show better task performance than mixed gender pairings. The performance measures taken were time on task and number of errors. Analysis of the results of the first study (t tests comparing these measures according to gender pairing), suggest some support for this in that boy-boy pairs were significantly faster on the computer task than the mixed gender pairs. The same trend was apparent for the girl-girl pairs but the results did not quite reach significance. No significant differences were found between the gender pairing in relation to number of errors on the tasks.

Comparison of the Computer and Non-Computer Task
It was hypothesised that there would be a difference in styles of social interaction according to whether or not the task was computer based. However, a repeated measures t test on the data for the first study comparing styles of social interaction in the computer and non-computer task found no significant difference, and therefore did not support this.

Whilst it appeared to be the case that the style of social interaction shown by the pair was affected by the gender pairing rather than the task itself, there were significant differences between the tasks in terms of who initiated the assertive interaction. Thus, when the mixed gender pairs completed the computer task, it was the boy who initiated the assertive interaction, whereas on the non-computer task it was the girl who tended to initiate the assertive interaction. These differences were further confirmed by analysis of the frequency of use of the different "task operators", and it was found that boys used the return and arrow keys more frequently on the computer task, whereas girls used the die and counter more frequently than boys on the non-computer task.

Discussion

This brief preliminary review of the results both clarifies and extends previous proposals in relation to gender issues in collaborative work with computers. In this review we have addressed the question of whether gender pairing has an effect on the characteristics of the social interaction and task performance, as well as the significance of the computer itself in generating particular types of interaction.

In relation to gender pairing, the results regarding styles of interaction and task performance confirm previous research suggesting that mixed gender pairs are particularly problematic in the primary classroom. This style of assertive, uncoordinated responding to the task was more characteristic of mixed gender pairs than same gender, suggesting individual rather than cooperative work and the difficulties of cross-gender interaction. The finding that this had an effect on task performance - albeit in this case shorter time on task rather than improved accuracy - suggests some support for previous research on the facilitative effect of collaborative as opposed to individual work. It may well be that these results reflect motivational and attitudinal factors as well as difficulties or even hostilities in cross gender interaction, differences in friendship status or lack of experience in working together.

The finding that there were no significant differences in styles of social interaction between same gender pairs was somewhat surprising in view of previous research suggesting that boys tend to display individualistic, competitive styles of working and girls collaborative. A possible explanation is suggested by the results of a recent study which found that instructions to cooperate have least effect on mixed-gender pairs, a limited effect on pairs of girls (who tend to cooperate regardless of whether or not instructed to do so), but have the most beneficial effect on pairs of boys, causing a change in their working style (Underwood, Jindal and Underwood, 1994[3]). This suggests that the instruction to "work together" may have been effective despite concerns that this may not be sufficient to encourage collaboration.

The comparison of the two types of task raises some interesting issues in relation to gender and the disadvantages to girls of working in mixed gender pairings. The finding that there were no significant differences in styles of social interaction between the two tasks suggests it is not the computer itself which generates individualistic or competitive styles of social interaction in mixed gender pairs. Our attempt at making the non-computer task as interesting and game-like as the computer task may partly explain this for the mixed pairs, but does not explain why this style of social interaction did not also occur in the same gender pairs. The gender differences relating to who initiated the assertive interaction and took control of the "task operators" suggests that girls can be equally assertive when paired with boys, but have a particular problem in computer tasks.   Their apparent lack of confidence, and the boys' willingness to dominate in this specific situation provides additional support for current concerns about girls' experience of collaborative work with computers, and prompts caution for teachers' alleged preference for mixed gender pairs on computer tasks.

References:

Culley, L. (1988) Girls, boys and computers. *Educational Studies*, 14, 1, 3-8.

Jackson, A., Fletcher, B. and Messer D.J. (1986) A survey of microcomputer use in a provision in primary schools *Journal of Computer Assisted Learning*, 2, 45-55.

Underwood, Jindal, N, and Underwood, J. (1994) Gender differences and effects of co-operation in a computer-based language task. *Educational Research*, 36.

Hoyles, C., Healy, L. and Sutherland, R. (1991) Patterns of discussion between pupil pairs in computer and non-computer environments. *Journal of Computer Assisted Learning*, 7, 210-228.

Keogh, T. (1993) Of mice and men: an investigation of gender differences in children's engagement with an English language task presented on paper and on a computer. Unpublished M.A. dissertation, The Open University.

Tolmie, A., & Howe, C. (1993) Gender and dialogue in secondary school physics. Gender and Education, Vol. 5, No. 2, 191-209.

Is it better to work with a peer, an adult or both? A systematic comparison with children aged 5, 7 and 11 years

M. Hughes & P. Greenhough

Centre for Human Development and Learning, School of Education, University of Exeter, Heavitree Road, St Lukes, Exeter EX1 2LU, UK

Abstract

This paper reports the findings of three studies which systematically compared children learning in four conditions: (A) alone; (B) with a peer; (C) with an adult; and (D) with a peer and an adult. Children were studied at the ages of 5, 7 and 11 years using an age appropriate version of the computer language Logo. In all three studies children performed significantly better when working with an adult (i.e. in conditions C and D). However, it was only with the 11-year-olds that this effect carried over to subsequent individual performance. Possible explanations for these findings are discussed.

Introduction

Within developmental psychology, research on group and interactive learning has tended to follow one of two main traditions. One tradition, strongly influenced by theorists such as Piaget, Mugny and Doise, has focused on the potentially facilitating effects of peer-interaction on children's learning and development: researchers within this tradition have typically compared the performance of children learning in pairs with children working on their own (see [1] for a review). The second tradition, strongly influenced by the work of Vygotsky, has focused more on the potentially beneficial effects of adult-intervention in children's learning: researchers in this tradition have typically looked at children working with an adult (e.g. [2], [3]) and sometimes compared their performance with children working alone. These two traditions have tended to operate in relative isolation from one another: as a result, there are relatively few studies (e.g. [4]) which systematically compare children working alone, with a peer, and with an adult.

This paper presents findings from three studies which systematically compared children learning in four conditions: (A) alone; (B) with a peer; (C) with an adult; and (D) with a peer and an adult. Children were studied as they approached the ages of 5, 7 and 11 years: these ages were chosen as they mark the beginning and end of Key Stages within the English and Welsh National Curriculum. In each study the task involved an age appropriate version of the computer language Logo. The choice of task reflected the growing interest within Logo research in the social conditions in which learning takes place (e.g. [5], [6]). In addition, the choice enabled us to use research techniques developed in our own previous research with Logo (e.g. [7], [8]). The studies are reported in the order in which they were carried out.

Study 1: 7-year-olds

Methods:
The subjects were 144 children (72 girls and 72 boys) aged between 6 years 4 months and 7 years 6 months (mean age: 6 years 11 months). The children were drawn from nine separate classes in seven schools, with 16 children (8 boys and 8 girls) being used from each class. Nine teachers took part in the study, 8 female and 1 male. Within each class, children were assigned to one of the four conditions shown below. In the peer conditions (B and D) there were equal numbers of boy-boy, boy-girl and girl-girl pairs.

Condition A: Child alone   (18 children)
Condition B: Child plus peer   (54 children)
Condition C: Child plus teacher   (18 children)
Condition D: Child plus peer plus teacher   (54 children)

All children took part in four sessions. In Session 1, they each worked as individuals, and were introduced to the Logo Turtle and software. In this study, the children moved the Turtle by pressing one of four keys marked F, B, L or R followed by a number from 1-9. Thus F 2 moved the Turtle forward 20 cm, while R 4 rotated it clockwise through 40 degrees. The children were allowed 5 minutes free exploration, and were then given a pre-test. In Session 2 the children worked according to their social condition. Their task was to move the Turtle around an obstacle course on a large horizontal board. For conditions C and D, the teacher was asked to help the child(ren) whenever and however she/he felt appropriate. In Session 3, the children worked individually on a task similar to that used in Session 2. In Session 4 all children received an individual post-test.

Findings:
There was a significant effect due to social condition in Session 2. Children working with their teacher in Conditions C and D completed the task in significantly fewer moves than children working without a teacher ($p=0.0001$); however, children in these conditions took significantly more time to do so ($p=0.0055$). There was no effect due to social condition in any of the other sessions. In other words, the teacher had a significant effect on children's performance while he/she was present, but this effect did not persist when he/she was absent.

Study 2: 5-year-olds

Methods:
The subjects were 96 children (48 girls and 48 boys) aged between 4 years 0 months and 5 years 2 months (mean age: 4 years 10 months). The children were drawn from eight separate classes in six schools, with 12 children (6 boys and 6 girls) being used from each class. Eight teachers, all female, took part in the study. As in Study 1, children were randomly assigned to one of the four conditions shown below. In the peer conditions (B and D) there were equal numbers of boy-boy and girl-girl pairs.

Condition A: Child alone	(16 children)
Condition B: Child plus peer	(32 children)
Condition C: Child plus teacher	(16 children)
Condition D: Child plus peer plus teacher	(32 children)

All children took part in three sessions. In Session 1, they each worked as individuals, and were introduced to the Logo Turtle and software. In this study the children moved the Turtle by pressing designs on a specially prepared concept keyboard. This enabled them to move the Turtle forward through its own length, to rotate it clockwise through 90 degrees, or to make it 'hoot'. The children were also shown how sequences of commands could be entered. In Session 2 the children worked according to their social condition. Their task was to select the correct sequence of commands which would take the Turtle to particular locations on the same board used in Study 1. The task was situated within a game in which the children were asked to help the Turtle 'deliver invitations to its birthday party'. For conditions C and D, the teacher was asked to help the child(ren) whenever and however she felt appropriate. In Session 3, the children worked individually on a task similar to that used in Session 2. Unlike Study 1, there were no pre-tests or post-tests.

Findings:

The findings were very similar to those of Study 1. There was a significant effect due to social condition in Session 2: children working with their teacher in Conditions C and D required significantly fewer choices to complete the task than children working without a teacher (p=0.0001). However, this effect did not carry over to Session 3, where there was no significant difference between the different social conditions. The data from the 5-year-olds thus shows the same pattern as for the 7-year olds: the teacher had a significant effect on children's performance while she was present, but this effect did not persist when she was absent.

Study 3: 11-year-olds

Methods:

The subjects were 128 children (64 girls and 64 boys) aged between 10 years 1 month and 11 years 5 months (mean age: 10 years 9 months). The children were drawn from eight separate classes in six schools, with 16 children (8 boys and 8 girls) being used from each class. Eight teachers took part in the study, 5 female and 3 male. As in Studies 1 and 2, children were randomly assigned to one of the four conditions shown below. In the peer conditions (B and D) there were equal numbers of boy-boy, boy-girl and girl-girl pairs.

Condition A: Child alone	(16 children)
Condition B: Child plus peer	(48 children)
Condition C: Child plus teacher	(16 children)
Condition D: Child plus peer plus teacher	(48 children)

All children took part in five sessions. In Session 1, they were individually introduced to the Logo software. In this study, the children used standard Logo commands (such as Forward 100, Right 90) to move a simulated Turtle on the computer screen. The children were given time to experiment freely with the commands. Session 2 was an individual paper-and-pencil pre-test of the children's understanding of angle. In Session 3 the children worked according to their social condition on two tasks: drawing a regular 3-spoke pattern and drawing a regular 6-spoke pattern. In Session 4 the children worked individually on two tasks: drawing the same 3-spoke pattern as in Session 3, and drawing a regular 9-spoke pattern. Session 5 was an individual paper-and-pencil post-test of the child's understanding of angle.

Findings:

The findings showed a different pattern from Studies 1 and 2. As in those studies, there was a significant effect due to social condition in Session 3 (equivalent to Session 2 in Studies 1 and 2). Children working with their teacher in Conditions C and D were more likely to complete both the 3-spoke and the 6-spoke task than children working without a teacher (p=0.0001 for both tasks). Unlike Studies 1 and 2, however, this effect carried over to the subsequent individual session (Session 4). Children who had previously worked with their teacher in Session 3 were significantly more likely to complete both the 3-spoke and 9-spoke tasks than children who had not worked with their teacher (p=0.0001 and 0.01 respectively). In other words, the data from the 11-year-olds is similar to that of the 5-year-olds and the 7-year-olds in showing that the teacher had a significant effect on children's performance while he/she was present; it differs in that, for the 11-year olds, the effect persisted when the teacher was absent.

Discussion

The title of this paper asks whether it is better for children to work with a peer, an adult, or both. The data presented here suggests that it is the presence of the adult which is the critical factor. In all three studies, the teachers' presence had a significant effect on children's task performance, although in only one study did this effect carry over to their subsequent individual performance. In contrast, the presence of a peer had no significant effect on children's working. These findings are broadly in line with one of the few previous studies which have made this comparison [4].

Two questions are raised by the pattern of findings reported here. First, what is it that the teachers are doing which has a significant effect on children's performance? Inspection of the video-taped interaction suggests that, at each age level, several of the teachers are concerned to reduce the number of errors or mistakes which the children make. They use various strategies for doing this: for example, they might ask the children in advance what command they intend to enter into the computer, and then discuss with them whether this will have the desired effect. More detailed analysis of the adults' intervention strategies in conditions C and D is currently underway: this analysis makes use of a feedback model of task performance which was developed for the 7 year-olds and which is described elsewhere [9].

The second question is why the teachers' presence affects subsequent individual performance for the 11-year-olds, but not for 5- and 7-year-olds. Various possible answers need to be considered. For example, it may simply be an age effect: older children may be able to benefit more from their teacher's presence than younger ones - for example, they may have more effective strategies for requesting appropriate help. Alternatively, the explanation may lie in the different teaching approaches adopted at the different ages. In England, there is a strong tradition amongst early years teachers (3-7 years) that children should learn through self-directed discovery rather than through teacher-directed instruction. It was our impression that the teachers of the 11-year-olds were more likely to take part in 'teaching' episodes when they attempted to convey information or an understanding directly to the children: these may have contributed to the different pattern of findings for the 11-year-olds. One explanation which can be discounted, however, concerns the gender of the teachers: although it was true that the older children were more likely to work with a male teacher, there is no evidence from our data that the male teachers had a greater effect on children's learning than the female teachers.

It is clear that more detailed analysis of the interaction taking place in the social conditions (and particularly those which involve the teachers) will throw more light on both the questions raised here. Such analyses are currently underway, and the results will be reported as soon as they are available.

Acknowledgement

The research described here was supported by grant no R000232478 from the UK Economic and Social Research Council (ESRC).

References

1. Light, P. & Blaye, A. Computer-based learning: the social dimensions, Chapter 7, *Children Helping Children,* eds. H. Foote, M. Morgan & R. Shute, pp 135-147, John Wiley, Chichester, 1990.

2. Wertsch, J., McNamee, G., McLane, J. & Budwig, N. The adult-child dyad as a problem-solving system, *Child Development,* 1980, **51**, 1215-1221.

3. Wood, D., Bruner, J. & Ross, G. The role of tutoring in problem solving, *Journal of Child Psychology and Psychiatry,* 1976, **17**, 89-100.

4. Gauvain, M. & Rogoff, B. Collaborative problem-solving and children's planning skills, *Developmental Psychology,* 1989, **25**, 139-151.

5. Clements, D. & Nastasi, B. Social and cognitive interactions in educational computer environments, *American Educational Research Journal,* 1988, **25** (1), 87-106.

6. Noss, R. & Hoyles, C. Looking back and looking forward, *Learning Mathematics and Logo,* eds. C. Hoyles & R. Noss, MIT press, Cambridge, Mass., 1992.

7. Hughes, M., Macleod, H. & Potts, C. Using Logo with infant school children, *Educational Psychology,* 1985, **5**, 287-301.

8. Hughes, M., Brackenridge, A., Bibby, A., & Greenhough, P. Girls, boys and turtles: gender effects in young children learning with Logo, *Girls and Computers,* ed. C. Hoyles, pp 31-39, Bedford Way Paper 34, Institute of Education, London University, 1988.

9. Hughes, M. & Greenhough, P. (1994) Planning, feedback and adult-intervention in computer-based learning. Paper to be presented at the International Conference on Group and Interactive Learning, University of Strathclyde, September 1994.

Planning, feedback and adult-intervention in computer-based learning

M. Hughes & P. Greenhough

Centre for Human Development and Learning, School of Education, University of Exeter, Heavitree Road, St Lukes, Exeter EX1 2LU, UK

Abstract

This paper describes a particular methodological approach to studying collaborative computer-based learning. The approach gives primacy to the roles of planning and feedback in computer-based learning and in the interaction which takes place around the keyboard. The paper describes a simple feedback model developed in the course of work on young children learning Logo, and the main elements of the model are illustrated from the Logo context. It is argued that the model provides a useful basis for analysing both peer-interaction and adult-intervention during computer-based learning, and some examples are provided from our current work.

Introduction

In this paper we will describe an approach to studying collaborative computer-based learning which we have developed during work on young children learning with the computer language Logo [1],[2]. A central feature of this approach is the importance given to the processes of planning and feedback. While these processes have long been regarded as fundamental to many kinds of learning (eg [3],[4]), they are particularly relevant to understanding much computer-based learning. In particular, the computer can provide rich opportunities for learning by providing feedback to the learner (or learners) on the extent to which desired outcomes have or have not been achieved. Further, it appears that much of the social interaction which takes place around the computer keyboard is concerned with the processes of planning and feedback, and they provide a useful way of organising the analysis of such social interaction. Finally, we should mention that we consider collaborative learning to include both children working with other children (eg [5]) and children working with an adult (eg [6]).

A model of planning and feedback

The ideas expressed above can be illustrated and expanded with reference to the simple feedback model shown in Figure 1. This model, which is similar to one proposed by Norman [7], shows the main elements in a cycle which links planning and feedback.

Figure 1: A feedback model of children's task performance

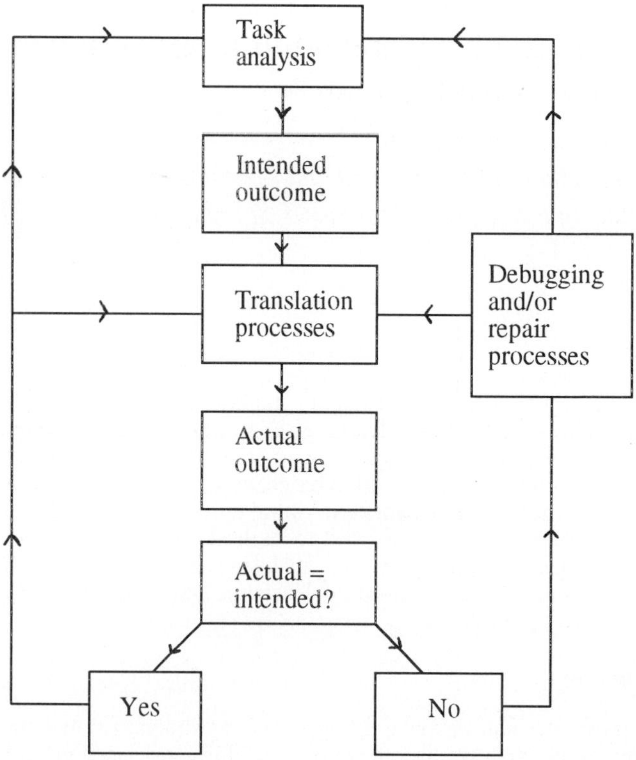

The model was developed in the course of our work with 7-year-olds learning to use a simplified version of Logo, and can be illustrated with reference to that particular application. The overall task for the 7-year-olds was to move the Logo Turtle around an obstacle track set out on a large horizontal board. The children could move the Turtle by using commands such as FORWARD 4 (which takes the Turtle forward about 40 cm) or LEFT 3 (which rotates it anti-clockwise through 30 degrees).

The model assumes that each cycle starts with some kind of task analysis. That is, the learner considers his/her overall goal (eg taking the Turtle around the track) and decides what is required next to move towards this goal. The outcome of the task analysis is thus expressed as an <u>intended outcome</u> of the cycle (eg "I want to turn the Turtle that way"). Next, this intention has to be <u>translated</u> into a specific command which the system can understand (eg RIGHT 2). The command is then entered into the computer and transmitted to the Turtle, so that an <u>actual outcome</u> is generated (a specific Turtle move). The next phase is crucial to the model; it is assumed that at some level a comparison takes place between the <u>actual and intended outcomes</u>. As a result of this comparison, the learner receives feedback which can be used to aid learning. Thus if the intended and actual outcomes coincide, then it is likely that some sort of reinforcement takes place of the original task analysis or translation processes. However, if the intended and actual outcomes do not coincide, then two further processes may be activated - <u>debugging</u> and/or <u>repair</u>. <u>Debugging</u> is a reflective process whereby the learner identifies the cause of the mismatch (eg LEFT should have been entered instead of RIGHT); this may be followed by amendment of the original task-analysis or translation processes which initially generated the error. <u>Repair</u> is a more direct response to the error, and is an attempt to correct the effect it might have had on task goals and sub-goals (eg a faulty move of RIGHT 2 might be repaired by returning the Turtle to its previous position by LEFT 2 and then adding another LEFT 2; alternatively this error might be repaired by a single move of LEFT 4).

The model is not intended to provide a mechanistic account of how learning takes place. Rather, it aims to highlight some of the key elements which might be involved in the learning process. For example, we have used the model to generate specific pre-and post-tests of children's ability to carry out task analysis, translation and repair [2]. We also argue that the model can provide a useful framework for analysing social interaction at the keyboard. This will be expanded and illustrated in the next section.

The model as a basis for analysing interaction

There are two main ways in which the model can be used for analysing interaction. First, it provides a framework for the temporal analysis of <u>when interaction takes place.</u> The main elements in the feedback model can normally be identified by specific external events (eg the entry of a command to the keyboard, or the physical movement of the Turtle) and these events provide a number of "slots" within which interaction may or may not occur. This allows us to ask various questions about the temporal location of interaction in different social conditions - eg does peer interaction occur mostly when children are discussing an intended move? How much do children discuss feedback indicating an error? Do adults intervene when children are planning a move, or do they normally wait until its outcome is known? If the latter, do they mostly intervene when an error has occurred (ie when the actual move does not equate with the intended) or do they intervene whatever the outcome?

Second, the model provides a framework for analysing the <u>content of interaction</u>. Our work on young children learning Logo in different social conditions suggests that there is usually a large amount of task-related interaction, and that most of this can be linked to particular elements within the feedback model. We can then use the model to ask various questions. At the most general level, we can simply ask how much of the interaction taking place in different social conditions is concerned with each element of the feedback model, such as task analysis, debugging or repair. We can also ask more specific questions such as: how much conflict takes place between peers when discussing intended moves, and how is this resolved? Is adult intervention after an error focussed more on repair than on debugging?

The potential value of the feedback model in providing a framework for analysing interaction can be illustrated with some examples from our current Logo work. The first example involves a conflict between two 7-year-old girls, Samantha and Hollie. Here, they agree on their intended move - to rotate the Turtle to its left - but disagree on the specific translation which will achieve this. Hollie argues that the command should be LEFT, but Samantha, possibly because the Turtle is facing towards her, thinks it should be RIGHT.

Samantha:	(gestures in anti-clockwise direction)
Hollie:	Left one
Samantha:	No!
Hollie:	Left one
Samantha:	We need...
Hollie:	Yeh, left one, or else it's going to bump in
Samantha:	(puts her finger over RIGHT key)
Hollie:	We don't want to go that way, do we? (gestures to Turtle's right). We want to go that way. (gestures to Turtle's left)
Samantha:	(presses RIGHT key)
Hollie:	Oh you. Rub out.
Samantha:	(presses 1 followed by GO) (Turtle turns in clockwise direction, towards obstacle)
Samantha:	I did it the wrong way! (laughs) (moves finger to LEFT key)
Hollie:	Left..

Here, the interaction mostly takes place during the translation stage, and is concerned primarily with the required translation. Hollie offers more than one argument to support her proposal, but these are ignored by Samantha. However, she responds directly to the negative feedback she receives from the actual Turtle move ("I did it the wrong way!"), and she immediately acts to repair the mistake. Note that there is no explicit debugging, in that no discussion takes place as to why Hollie's suggestion was correct while Samantha's was not. Nevertheless, the example shows the roles which peer interaction and negative feedback might play in children's learning.

The next example occurs when two boys, Peter and Daniel, are working with their teacher. The children enter a command which takes the Turtle too far forward (a translation error), and as a result the Turtle crashes into an obstacle. The teacher's intervention takes the form of debugging rather than repair. She goes back to the command actually entered, and asks the children to suggest a more appropriate alternative.

Daniel:	(Enters FORWARD 9. The Turtle crashes into an obstacle)
Teacher:	Oh dear. What happened there then?
Daniel:	It bumped into it
Teacher:	Do you know why?
Peter:	He pressed too much
Daniel:	It went forward too far
Teacher:	What number did you ask it to move forwards?
Peter:	Nine
Teacher:	What number do you think might have been a better number?
Daniel:	Seven
Teacher:	You could have tried seven, because you had to travel quite a fair way, didn't you?

The final example is more complex, but can still be illuminated with reference to the feedback model. Here a child, Michelle, is working with the teacher. The Turtle is at one corner of the obstacle course, and requires a substantial left turn (ideally, LEFT 9) to get it heading back in the required direction. The teacher does not wait until Michelle has made an error, but intervenes at an earlier stage to elicit her intentions:

Teacher:	Now what are you thinking of doing now?
Michelle:	Right two
Teacher:	If you go right, which way is it going to turn?
Michelle:	That way (gestures correctly)
Teacher:	Is that the way you want to go? Which way do you want to go?
Michelle:	Up there (gestures correctly)
Teacher:	So which way are you going to turn?
Michelle:	Left?
Teacher:	Does that sound right to you? Does that sound OK?
Michelle:	(Nods)
Teacher:	How far are you going to turn around do you think?
Michelle:	Two?
Teacher:	Will two be enough do you think?
Michelle:	Alright, I'll try four
Teacher:	You put in what you think.

Here, the teacher's intervention fits closely with the structure of the feedback model. Thus she first elicits an intended move from Michelle ("what are you thinking of doing now?") and then asks her to predict the actual outcome of this move ("if you go right, which way is it going to turn?"). Next, she makes a comparison of the actual and intended moves ("is that the way you want to go?") and then encourages Michelle to make a repair ("so which way are you going to turn?"). Having established the correct direction, she then repeats the process for the parameter ("how far are you going to turn?" and "will that be far enough?"). Her last comment ("you put in what you think") contains a certain amount of irony: her whole intervention has in fact been aimed at preventing the child from putting in "what she thinks", and putting in a different command instead.

This example raises a final issue which is illuminated by the feedback model - namely, when might a teacher intervene most effectively in the learning process. The model indicates that there are several possible places where intervention might take place: when the child is still formulating their intention, when they have completed the translation process but not yet entered a command on the keyboard (as in the above example), when the command has been entered but before the instruction has been transmitted to the Turtle, or when the command has been transmitted and the outcome is known. We are hoping in our current work to throw some light on whether intervention at one place in the cycle is more effective than intervention at another.

Acknowledgement

The research described here was supported by grant no R000232478 from the UK Economic and Social Research Council (ESRC).

References

1. Hughes, M. & Greenhough, P. Is it better to work with a peer, an adult or both? A systematic comparison with children aged 5, 7 and 11 years. Paper to be presented at the International Conference on Group and Interactive Learning, University of Strathclyde, September 1994.

2. Hughes, M. & Greenhough, P. The use of a feedback model in studying computer-based collaborative learning. Paper submitted for a special issue of Cognition and Instruction, Processes and products of collaborative problem solving: some interdisciplinary perspectives, eds. Hoyles, C. and Forman, E.

3. Miller, G., Galanter, E. & Pribram, K. *Plans and the structure of behaviour*, Holt, Rinehart and Winston, London 1960.

4. Karmiloff-Smith, A. & Inhelder, B. If you want to get ahead, get a theory, *Cognition*, 1975, **3**, 195-212.

5. Howe, C., Tolmie, A. & Anderson, A. Information technology and group work in physics, *Journal of Computer Assisted Learning*, 1991, **7**, 133-143.

6. Mercer, N. & Fisher, E. How do teachers help children to learn? An analysis of teachers' interventions in computer-based activities, *Learning and Instruction*, 1992, **2**, 339-355.

7. Norman, D. Cognitive Engineering, *User centred systems design*, eds D.Norman & S. Draper, LEA, Hillsdale, New Jersey.

Gender and cognitive and affective aspects of cooperative learning

K. Issroff

Institute of Educational Technology, The Open University, Walton Hall, Milton Keynes MK7 6AA, UK

Abstract

This paper discusses the gender differences found in an empirical study investigating the cognitive and motivational differences between 13 and 14 year old students working alone or in friendship pairs at the computer. Whilst there were no significant differences between girls and boys in the overall cognitive gain from working at the computer, significant differences were found in the affective measures. Differences were also found in how girls and boys value different aspects of the interaction and it is argued that these differences lead to significantly different affective outcomes for girls and boys.

Introduction

This paper discusses the gender differences found in a study of secondary school students using a chemistry data base to fill in a worksheet about the Periodic Table. The study investigated both the cognitive and affective factors pertinent to the pairs and individuals using the computer for learning.

Ames [1] claims that children evaluate their performance as a function of their perceived success or failure. Success enhances feelings of competence and failure diminishes feelings of worth. There are also other sources of information that influence students' self-evaluations and resulting motivation. What is of interest in this study, is how girls and boys evaluate their success, and what impact this has on the learning outcomes from an affective perspective. There is support for the notion that girls and boys differ in their attributions. Lyons [2] found that male and female 14 year olds have different definitions of self. She suggests that boys relate to others through their abilities, while girls relate to others through people rather than through abilities.

The aim of this study was to investigate some of the affective aspects of cooperative learning in relation to the cognitive outcomes. Affective aspects were measured by simply asking students to rate their perceptions using questionnaires both before and after collaborative computer use and cognitive outcomes involved pre, post and delayed post test scores.

Design

For the purposes of this paper, brief details of the design of the study will be presented. For further details regarding the design of this study, see Issroff [3].

The study compared pairs and individuals using a chemistry database to fill in a worksheet about the Periodic Table. The students were 13/14 year old pupils at an Inner London Secondary school. The study involved 22 teacher chosen, friendship pairs, (11 girl:girl pairs, 10 boy:boy pairs and 3 mixed gender pairs) and was carried out in the back of the science classroom. These pupils were given some training about using the software, followed by two individual pre tests, one concerning the topic area, the other focusing on the affective measures including the students' perceptions of themselves, their attitudes towards the topic and computers and their perceptions of their peers. The students then completed the worksheet using the computer. The time taken to do this ranged between 18 and 70 minutes. After they had used the computer, the students were given two post tests, one concerning the topic area, the other focusing on the affective aspects, in a similar manner to the pre test. They were also given a delayed cognitive post test, between 2 and 6 months after they had used the computer.

Results

The pupils were asked to rate on a five point scale, from very important to not important, how important it was that they got the correct answers, that they got along with their partner, that their group was successful and that they individually were successful.

There were significant differences between these ratings overall (Friedman's $\chi r^2=11.58$, p<.009). They rated getting along with each other as most important, followed by their own success, followed by group success and getting the correct answer was the least important.

However, this overall difference is accounted for by the girls. For the boys, there were no significant differences between the importance of the various factors, but for the girls, there was a significant difference (Friedman's $\chi r^2=10.735$, p=0.0488). The ordering of importance for boys and girls is shown in Figure 1 below (although there is only a significant difference for the girls):

Girls	Boys
1. get along	1. own success
2. own success	2. get along
3. group success	3. correct answer
4. correct answer	4. group success

Figure 1 The order of importance for girls and boys of various factors.

Thus for girls, getting along with each other is most important whereas for boys, their own success is most important. Also girls do not value getting the correct answer as much as boys do. The difference between the boys and girls ratings of importance of the correct answer and the importance of getting along approached significance (Get along: Kruskal-Wallis H=3.4170, p=0.0645, Correct: Kruskal-Wallis H=2.7885, p=0.0949).

The students were asked how good they thought they were at this kind of work both before they used the computer and afterwards. Overall, there is no significant change from pre to post, but there were statistically significant gender differences. Figure 2 below shows the mean pre and post ratings for girls and boys.

	Pre	Post
Girls	3.2	3.5
Boys	4.2	3.9

Figure 2 Girls and boys mean pre and post test ratings of how good they are at this kind of work.

There is a highly significant difference between the girls and boys responses to how good they think they are at this type of work, with the boys rating themselves higher than the girls (Kruskal-Wallis: H=4.0185, p<.0001) before using the computer. However, the difference between the boys and girls at the post test (Kruskal-Wallis: H=1.8218, p<.0685) is not significant. Although the majority of ratings stayed the same, there is a significant difference between the girls and boys rating change (Kruskal-Wallis: H=4.7399, p<.0295). The results found that 10 girls perceptions of themselves increased, and 3 decreased, while for the boys, 3 increased and 6 decreased. The majority of the increase in the girls were those who considered themselves average and the majority of the decrease for the boys was from those who rated themselves as very good. Thus the use of the computer increased the self perceptions of the girls who rated themselves as average and decreased the self perceptions of the boys who rated themselves as very good.

The students were asked both before and after the computer intervention to rate on a five point scale how well they got on with their partners. There was no statistically significant change overall and no significance between the girls and boys pre test ratings (Kruskal-Wallis: H=1.1424, p=0.2851). However, there was an almost statistically significant difference between the boys and girls post test ratings, with the girls having higher ratings than the boys (Kruskal-Wallis: H=3.5893, p=0.0582).

The students were asked to rate on a five point scale both before and after the computer intervention how interested and motivated they were towards chemistry. Gender differences were found in the students post test ratings of their motivation towards chemistry (Kruskal-Wallis: H=2.1417, p<0.0322). The boys had higher post test ratings than the girls and there was more change in the boys ratings than the girls. Therefore using the computer increased the boys perceived motivation towards chemistry, but had no effect on the girls.

There was a significant difference between the students' pre, and post and delayed post chemistry test scores (pre to post: t=9.48, p<0.0001, pre to delayed post: t=8.29, p<0.0001). Figure 3 below shows the mean pre, post and delayed post test scores for the boys and girls.

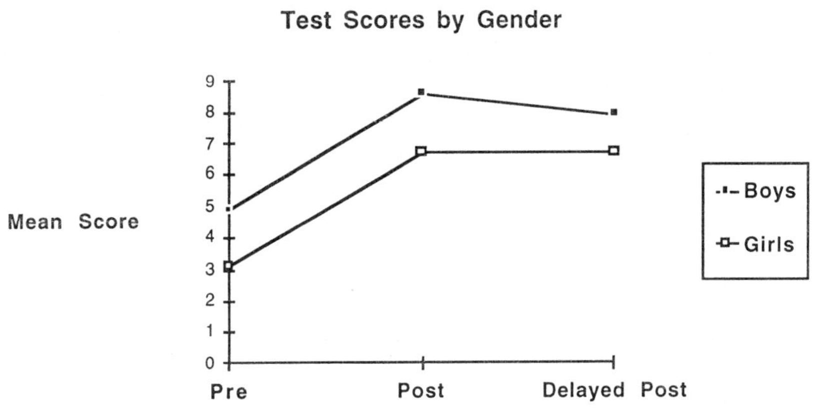

Figure 3. Mean scores on pre, post and delayed post tests for girls and boys.

The boys start at a higher level than girls and this continues through the immediate post test to the delayed post tests. The average girls' scores improve from immediate post test to delayed post test whereas the boys average score decreases but these differences are not statistically significant. This is slightly surprising because several studies have found gender differences in students use of computers in favour of boys. However, it appears that this software is not more beneficial for boys than for girls in cognitive terms.

The students were asked to rate on a five point scale how successful they thought they had been. Sixty percent of the students thought that they were more successful than average and very few students rated themselves below average. There were no significant differences between boys and girls (Kruskal-Wallis H=0.3732, p=0.5413).

Discussion

There were no significant differences in cognitive outcomes between boys and girls, and therefore this type of software does not benefit boys more than girls in these conditions. There were also no significant differences in perceived success between boys and girls. However, significant differences were found from an affective perspective.

The important factor for the girls in this study, was getting on with their partner. Thus their focus was on the social aspects of the interactions. Consequently using the computer collaboratively had an impact on their perceptions of themselves and on their ratings of how well they got on with their partners relative to the boys.

However, the use of the computer had a different effect on the boys. The boys did not think that getting on with each other was more important than other factors, and their success seems to have been judged by what they had achieved. Their success led to the boys having significantly higher motivation towards chemistry than the girls.

Conclusion

This study found that girls and boys find different factors salient in cooperative interactions. Although there were no significant differences between the boys and the girls actual success (as measured by pre, post and delayed post cognitive scores) and their perceived success, it has been argued that the fact that girls find getting on with each other significantly more important than other factors whereas there is no significant differences for boys, leads to different affective outcomes. In particular, the collaborative use of computers led to an increase in how good the girls think they are at this type of work and their ratings of how well they got on with one another, and an increase in the boys motivation towards chemistry. Thus the impact was on social factors for girls, but on task related factors for boys.

Acknowledgements
I would like to thank Ann Jones, Eileen Scanlon, Karen Littleton and Janet McCracken for commenting on drafts of this paper.

References
1.   Ames, C. (1984). Competitive, cooperative and Individualistic Goal Structure: A Cognitive-Motivational Analysis. *Research on Motivation in Education. Vol 1: Student Motivation.* Orlando, Florida., Academic Press Inc.

2.   Lyons, N. P. (1983). Two perspectives: on self, relationships, and morality. *Harvard Educational Review* 53 (2): 125-145.

3.   Issroff, K. (1993). *Motivation and CAL in different learning situations.* Artificial Intelligence in Education, 1993, The University of Edinburgh, Edinburgh, Scotland, Association for the Advancement of Computing in Education.

Case studies of children cooperating with computers: A time based analysis

K. Issroff, A. Jones & E. Scanlon
Institute of Educational Technology, The Open University, Walton Hall, Milton Keynes MK7 6AA, UK

Abstract

This paper reports the results of a Timelines[1] video analysis of pairs of students working cooperatively. Timelines is a system for video annotation, and was used to analyse students' interactions. The analysis showed differences both between and within the pairs in terms of the symmetry of their behaviours and the nature and timing of different types of talk. Additionally, there was evidence of the development of modes of interacting over time in two of the pairs. The paper discusses the students interactions and relates this to their cognitive pre and post test scores. The effectiveness of using Timelines in this context is discussed.

Introduction

This paper reports on the qualitative analysis of videotapes of pairs of students using chemistry software collaboratively. There has recently been much interest in collaborative use of computers in classrooms (see special editions of Learning and Instruction (Mevarech and Light [1]) and Social Development (Howe [2])). In this study, a video annotation tool was used to analyse the interactions and led to a comprehensive study of the nature of the

---

[1]Developed by Russell Owen, Ronald Baecker and Beverly Harrison at the University of Toronto for the Ontario Telepresence Project and the Institute for Robotics and Intelligent Systems

interaction, focusing on the students' behaviours and their dialogues.

Timelines

Timelines is a system for annotating or coding videotape data (see (Harrison and Chignell [3])). It supports three different types of qualitative data: events, intervals and comments. This analysis involved only the use of intervals. A set of finite categories were used which applied to the type of talk, the actions of either of the individuals and other external events. The videotapes were analysed using the software which then produces two types of ouputs: 1. a summary with the total number of entries, the number of categories and for each category, the total number, their total duration and their average duration and 2. a timeline display which shows the categories on the y-axis and time on the x-axis. The timelines can be edited so that they only incorporate selected entries.

Empirical Design

The empirical study was carried out in an Inner London secondary school. The students were 13 and 14 year olds and the study was conducted at the back of the classroom. The study involved teacher chosen/friendship pairs of pupils in two cooperative conditions: cooperative task structure condition where the pair of students shared training worksheets and a non-cooperative task structure condition where each student had their own training and worksheet. The task involved using a database of information about the Periodic Table to answer both factual and conceptual questions from the worksheets.

Five pairs were selected for in-depth analysis of their interactions. These pairs were chosen to cover a range of criteria. One mixed gender pair, two girl:girl pairs and two boy:boy pairs were chosen. Within this, two successful and two unsuccessful pairs were chosen.

Summary of the Five Pairs

Steve and Donna are both rated as having high abilities and motivation. Steve showed a higher pre to post gain than Donna. Nick is rated as having high ability and motivation, whereas Mike has low ability and motivation ratings. Mike was a new boy to the school and Nick was acknowledged as the cleverest boy in the class. Nick showed a pre to post test gain, whereas Mike did not. Sue and Jane both have low ability and motivation ratings. Jane showed a higher pre to post gain than Sue. David is rated as having average ability and motivation, while Andy is rated as having low ability and motivation. They both showed a very high pre to post test gain. Debbie and Kara are both rated as low in ability and motivation. They both showed a high pre to post test gain.

Results

In this section, some of the results of the video analysis are presented. The average time that these pairs spent on the worksheet was 40.46 minutes. David and Andy and Debbie and Kara spent longer completing the worksheet than the other pairs. There are large variations in the amount of time spent talking. Debbie and Kara spent 61.41% of their time talking whereas Steve and Donna only spent 26.7% of their time talking.

The pair's talk was divided into 4 categories: topic, next, control and other. This analysis of talk is relatively broad, but still enables patterns of talk to be elucidated and it brings out distinct differences between the pairs. Topic talk refers to any talk about the chemistry that the students were studying. For example:

Jane: reading "What does the atomic number of an element represent?"
Jane: "It's the ...um...."
Sue:"...nucleus..."
Both: "..neutrons...around the shells"

Next talk refers to any discussion about what to do next in terms of how to use the software. For example:

Kara: "Less than 5."
Kara: "Go to database."
Debbie: "I am. I'm trying to get it..."
Kara: "Go to atomic number."
Debbie: "Um .. what have we got to do?"
Kara: "Less than ...less than"

Control talk is talk about the use of the hardware, for example:

Steve: "You can do this one."
Donna: "OK, thanks."

Other talk refers to any off task talk. For example:

Sue: "I have to get another pair of (inaudible) I think my brothers taken it."
Jane: "What? Do you think she might be (inaudible)' .. she should be ..
(inaudible)"
Sue: "I haven't seen her have I?"
Jane: "No, I'm not going to see her either."

There was a large amount of variation in the different types of talk which occurred during the interactions. For all the pairs except Sue and Jane and Debbie and Kara, over half the talk was concerned with the topic. Sue and Jane and Debbie and Kara spent more time than the other pairs discussing the interface and what to do next. Nick and Mike spent over a quarter of their talk time discussing the interface and what to do next. David and Andy spent nearly a quarter of their time talking about non-task related aspects and this is reflected in the length of time they spent completing their worksheets. In contrast, Steve and Donna spent less than 3% of their time discussing non-task related things. David and Andy did not discuss the control of the hardware, whereas Steve and Donna spent 14% of their time discussing control.

David and Andy and Kara and Debbie did considerably more off-task activities than the rest of the pairs and they were the only pairs in which both members achieved a pre to post test gain. There was variation within the pairs. Steve did more off-task activities than Donna, and this was predominantly while Donna was using the hardware. David spent double the amount of time off-task than Andy, but this was also while Andy was using the hardware. In general, the time spent off-task was minimal.

Development of ways of interacting over time

The timelines summaries show evidence of a development in the way that the students interacted with each other over time for the two pairs that spent more then one session using the computer. For David and Andy's first session, the hardware use was evenly distributed between them, but during the second session, Andy dominated the hardware. Changes over Debbie and Kara's two sessions can be seen in their use of the mouse and the amount of writing. They physically fought over the use of the mouse. Kara dominated the first session. Debbie used the mouse for the majority of the second session, insisting that Kara write.

The timelines also show the distribution of the different types of talk over time. Steve and Donna's timeline (Figure 1) shows a decrease in talk about the interface (next talk) and an increase in the amount of topic talk over the session.

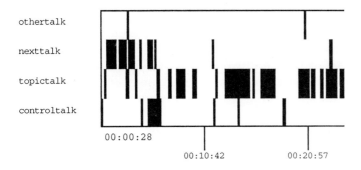

Figure 1 Steve and Donna's talk Timeline

In contrast, Sue and Jane's timeline (Figure 2) shows no decrease in next talk, with a slight increase in topic talk. This reflects the fact that they never fully mastered the software. The timeline also shows the relatively large amount of other talk that occurred.

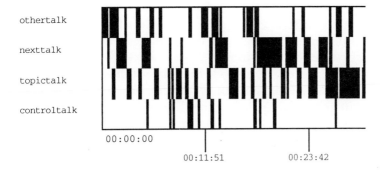

Figure 2 Sue and Jane's talk Timeline

Results of the Analysis

Pair	Own or shared worksheet	Total Time	Total Talk	Dominant Talk
Steve and Donna	own	low	low	topic and control
Nick and Mike	own	low	medium	topic and next
Sue and Jane	shared	medium	high	next and other
David and Andy *	own	high	high	topic and other
Debbie and Kara *	shared	high	high	topic and next

The two pairs with high pre to post gains (denoted by a *) spent longer than average completing the worksheet, talked more than average and spent more time off-task. Sue and Jane were the only pair in which topic talk was not dominant and they were the pair that achieved the least. Debbie and Kara, Sue and Jane and Nick and Mike spent considerable amounts of time talking about how to use the software. For Nick and Mike, this predominantly consisted of Mike telling Nick what he was doing. However, for the other two pairs, this talk shows that they never understood how to use the software. Steve and Donna are the only pair who discussed control to a significant extent. Therefore, it appears that the control of software is normally 'assumed' between the pairs. However, for Debbie and Kara, control was gained by physical fighting.

Evaluating the use of Timelines

The first important factor to consider in evaluating the use of Timelines is the period spent on the analysis. Video analysis is known to be time consuming. In this analysis, the ratio was 2:1, which represents a significant time saving. The summaries that Timelines produces allows the analysis of interindividual, inter-pair and intra-pair differences and from the timelines, patterns of behaviour and changes in behaviour over time can be seen. One of the major difficulties with using this type of tool is selecting the appropriate categories/events/intervals and the level of granularity for the analysis. For example, in this study, the behavioural categories were fine grained, while the talk categories were at a higher level. This is suitable for the present analysis but a finer level of granularity may be needed to fully explore the dialogues.

Conclusions

From this small sample of pairs, several features are apparent. The pairs that spent more time off-task have greater cognitive gains. This may be a reflection of consolidation during off-task periods. These pairs also spent longer on the task. The control of the hardware is often tacitly assumed, with only Steve and Donna discussing control and Kara and Debbie fighting over control. In the pairs that spent more than one session using the computer, there are clear developments in the ways that they interact.

This is a report of a small part of a large data set (for a fuller discussion of these pairs, see Issroff [4]). Our experience of using Timelines has led us to believe that it is a useful and effective tool for analysing cooperative interactions.

Acknowledgements
Thanks to the teachers and pupils for their time and enthusiasm. Special thanks to Blaine Price for help with setting up Timelines.

References
1. Mevarech, Z. R. and Light, P. H. (1992). Cooperative Learning with Computers. *Learning and Instruction* **2**.
2. Howe, C. (1993). Peer Interaction and Knowledge Acquisition. *Social Development.* **2** (3):
3. Harrison, B. L. and Chignell, M. H. (1994). Multimedia Tools for Social and Interactional Data Collection and Analysis. *The Social and Interactional Dimensions of Human-Computer Interfaces.*
4. Issroff, K. (1994) *Case studies of children cooperating with computers on a chemistry database task.* CALRG Report no. 141 Institute of Educational Technology, The Open University.

Talking and learning: A preliminary investigation into productive interaction

R. Joiner,[a] D. Messer,[b] P. Light[c] & K. Littleton[c]

[a] *Psychology Department, University of Leicester, University Road, Leicester LE1 7RH, UK*

[b] *Psychology Division, University of Hertfordshire, Hatfield Campus, College Lane, Hatfield AL10 9AB, UK*

[c] *Psychology Department, The University of Southampton, Highfield, Southampton SO9 5NH, UK*

Abstract

This paper reports an investigation into the linguistic structures that are thought to support productive interaction. A study was carried out concerning the benefits of peer interaction on computer based problem solving. The study had three sessions: a pre-test, an interaction session and a post-test. We analysed four pairs with very similar performance levels in the pre-test, two pairs who were successful and two pairs who were unsuccessful. The more successful pairs had more of the linguistic structures than the unsuccessful pairs, thus supporting the argument that language is important in productive interaction.

Introduction

There has been considerable interest in understanding the process of collaborative learning, in particular research concerning collaboration and computer based activity in schools. This interest in computers and collaborative learning has arisen partly because of resource limitations; partly because of technical innovations and partly because of the proposals that learning is promoted though social interaction [5,7].

Early research from a Piagetian perspective on the benefits of collaboration, both with computer and non computer based tasks, tended to focus on outcomes [1]. More recent work based on the writings of Vygotsky has begun to examine and articulate the processes mediating productive interaction [2]

A number of these researchers have started to examine the role of language in supporting collaboration. Roschelle and Behrend [6] report a microgenetic analysis. They identify a number of linguistic structures, which they argue can function to maintain a shared and mutual understanding of a task. Similarly Garton & Renshaw [3] have argued that 'communication style' is an important factor in productive interaction. They report that learning was most noticeable in children who were communicating responsively, who listened and responded to their partner's statements. Unfortunately neither investigation evaluated whether 'communication style' was related to productive interaction. This paper reports a preliminary analysis of the communicative style of successful pairs compared with the communicative style of unsuccessful pairs. The aim is to investigate whether communication style is related to productive interaction.

Method

The subjects (n = 120) were 11 to 12 year old children. The children were randomly assigned to one of two conditions; either a paired condition (45 pairs) or an individual condition (30 children). The task employed was a complex route planning problem in the form of a computer adventure game called the Honey Bears. The experiment had three sessions; a pre-test, an interaction or individual session and a post-test. The children's performance was classified into 8 levels, level 0 being the lowest and level 8 being the highest. This paper is only concerned with the performance of the pairs (see [4] for the other results).

Results

This report concerns a limited number of pairs. The full analysis will be presented at the conference. We analysed the discourse of the 4 pairs. Two pairs (1 and 2) where both participants progressed and the 2 pairs (3 and 4) where neither participant progressed (see Table 1).

Pairs	Subjects	Gender	Performance Level		
			Pre-Test	Interaction	Post-test
Pair 1	M	Boy	1	8	5
	G	Boy	1		7
Pair 2	B	Boy	1	6	7
	D	Girl	1		7
Pair 3	I	Girl	0	1	2
	H	Girl	1		0
Pair 4	H	Girl	0	1	2
	S	Girl	1		1

Table 1 : Performance of the 4 pairs.

Coding Framework

Roschelle & Behrend identify a number of conversational structures that they argue support the construction of shared understanding. The coding framework used in this study is partly based on their work.

Repairs are periods of conflict and follow a breakdown in mutual understanding. The repair of a breakdown is evidence of the participants desire to maintain mutual intelligibility.

> X   : Shall we go back to Brockly by boat with the honey
> Y   : No the honey monsters will get us
> X   : Oh yeah
>   : Right I know we'll take the plane

Collaborative Sentences   are linguistic structures that support the co-construction of problem solving knowledge. A typical example is where one participant begins a sentence or idea and the other participant completes it.

> X   : Lets take
> Y   :   Airbear in the plane.

Collaborative Plans are also collaborative completions. They are when one participant starts a plan and the other participant completes it.

> X   : Lets go on the pony
> Y   : with Ponybear
> X   : Airbear
> Y   : and Waterbear

(Note a collaborative utterance was coded as one of these types.)

Simultaneous Utterances. This is when both participants make the same utterance simultaneously.

	Successful Pairs		Unsuccessful Pairs	
	Pair 1	Pair 2	Pair 3	Pair 4
Repairs	8	3	4	2
Collaborative Sentences	0	1	0	0
Collaborative Plans	8	9	2	5
Simultaneous Utterances	5	4	0	0
Total	21	17	6	7

Number of Linguistic Structures

Table 2 : Discourse Analysis of the 4 pairs.

The discourse of all four pairs was analysed and a record kept of the number of times each of the linguistic structures was observed. As can be seen from the analysis (see Table 2). The pairs who succeeded (pairs 1 and 2) have more of these linguistic structures than the two less successful pairs (pairs 3 and 4). In particular pairs 1 and 2 appear to make more simultaneous utterances and make more collaborative plans than pairs 3 and 4. There is only a slight difference between the pairs in terms of the number of repairs observed. The unsuccessful pairs made slightly fewer repairs than the successful pairs. Finally, we only found one example of a collaborative sentence.

Conclusions

In conclusion, from our preliminary analysis of these four pairs, it appears that more successful pairs had a more productive communicative style than less productive pairs. This finding supports Roschelle & Behrend's arguments for the importance of language in productive interaction. Further analysis with a greater number and range of pairs will be used to extend this finding.

References

1. Doise, W. & Mugny, G. Individual and Collective conflicts of centrations in cognitive development, *European Journal of Social Psychology*, 1979, **9**, 105-109.

2. Forman E. A. & Cazden C. B. Exploring Vygotskian Perspectives in education: the cognitive value of peer interaction. In J. V. Werstch (ed.) *Culture Communication and Cognition*, Cambridge University Press, Cambridge, 1985.

3. Garton, A. F. & Renshaw, P. D. Linguistic processes in disagreements occurring in young children's dyadic problem solving, *British Journal of Developmental Psychology*, 1988, 6, 275 - 284.

4. Littleton, K., Light, P., Joiner R., Messer, D., & Barnes P. (1992) Pairing and gender effects in computer based learning. *European Journal of Psychology of Education*, 7, (4), 1-14.

5. Piaget J. The *Moral Judgement of the Child*, Routledge & Kegan Paul, London, 1932.

6. Roschelle, J. & Behrend. S. The construction of shared knowledge in collaborative problem solving. In C O'Malley (eds.) *Computer Supported Collaborative Learning* (in press).

7. Vygotsky, L. S. Mind *in Society: the Development of higher psychological processes*, Harvard University Press Cambridge, Mass, 1978.

The use of the computer as a therapeutic tool for children

A. Jones[a] & H. McMahon[b]

[a] *Institute of Educational Technology, The Open University, Walton Hall, Milton Keynes MK7 6AA, UK*

[b] *School of Education, University of Ulster, Coleraine, UK*

Abstract

A computer program, Bubble Dialogue, (O'Neill and McMahon [1]) may be a useful therapeutic tool for children who have suffered disruptions in parenting, for the following reasons: computers are an engaging medium for children and are part of their culture; the program operates within a comic strip type environment which is also a genre that children find fascinating, and finally, that this, coupled with a 'role play' scenario may encourage children to express their feelings in an unthreatening environment. The educational use of Bubble Dialogue suggests that it encourages children to reflect on situations and to express their feelings, and examples of this are given. The current project investigates its use with children who have suffered disruptions in parenting.

Background and literature

The literature on the effects on children of disruptions to (or loss of) their relationships with their parent(s) suggests that there are often long term emotional and scholastic consequences, which are likely to be inter-related: *"The available data are not satisfactory but consistently show that patterns of upbringing involving ..discontinuities in parenting..carry a high risk that the children will show socio-emotional or behavioural problems...".* (Rutter [2] p95). Children will often need help to express and deal with their negative feelings. For many children, the new parent will need to play the role of therapist, along with the many other roles of parenthood. This paper argues that a computer program called Bubble Dialogue may provide a useful therapeutic tool for parents or professional therapists to use with children who have suffered disruptions.

Children growing up in substitute families (i.e. without either birth parent) have suffered the loss of their relationship with their birth parent(s). In a new substitute family setting the child may need help to cope with this loss and with the consequences of an early disrupted life. The work by Tizard and Hodges [3] suggests that although the cognitive ability of children who have experienced institutional care in infancy, can, following substitute family care, match those of children who have not had this experience, differences in children's socio-emotional behaviour may be more persistent.   There is also strong evidence that children in care underachieve in education (Jackson, [4]). Rutter (op. cit.) suggests that family disruptions affect scholastic performance more by their effect on socio-emotional and behavioural functioning than by directly affecting cognition. Regarding the persistence of such effects, there is also evidence that difficulties in forming and maintaining relationships as a child often remain in adulthood (Duck, [5])

Children with socio-emotional difficulties can find it hard to focus on a task and to sustain concentration and may have poor social skills. They may also need help in dealing with their loss. Some children's problems will be viewed as severe enough for therapy to be sought for their difficulties, but this is often difficult to obtain. A few others may receive additional educational support. In the main, however, most of the work will come from their substitute parents. Foster carers are given some guidance in how they might deal with emotional problems, but the tools for them to use, to date, are limited and include "life story and tracing" work, expressive drawings and various games and exercises designed to explore the child's difficulties and feelings.

Bubble Dialogue

Bubble Dialogue captures dialogue in a role play situation. It has hitherto been used largely for educational purposes, but the evidence suggests that it may provide a bridge between a child's private and public world: that it "offers a new window into...those aspects of our thinking which we have become expert at guarding". (O'Neill and McMahon, op. cit., p25). It can therefore play an effective role by providing a medium for story telling, already established as a tool for educational therapy (Barrett, [6]), but in addition, can give the child the control, distance and interaction which dictating a story cannot achieve. It is best illustrated through an example. At the start of a session users are given a particular scenario via the "prologue", shown in figure 1. The characters are also introduced here. Clicking on the dialogue icon (the hand) takes the user to the next screen to begin the dialogue. Now the user is invited to create the characters' dialogue and thus produce a script. Each character has both speech and thought bubbles, and they take it in turn to speak, think, or speak and think. In figure 2, the opening dialogue is shown, where Bobby is speaking. Typically this will already be provided by the teacher. At this point, there are two options; Bobby can also be given a thought bubble, or Debbie can take up the dialogue. The next move is Debbie's and she can opt for a speech or thought bubble or both. From this point on, the dialogue continues until the users decide they have finished.

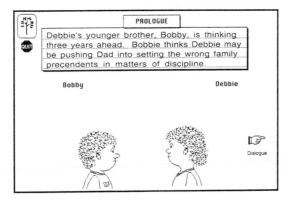

Figure 1   A first Bubble Dialogue screen showing the prologue

Figure 2   Second screen: the opening dialogue

There are two modes. Creation mode is illustrated above and here the only movement is forward to the next think or speech bubble. In review mode, however, users can move backwards or forwards and add notes, speech or thought, and this mode is intended to encourage users to be reflexive.

Bubble Dialogue has now been used in a number of diverse situations and its power and potential lie (we believe) in two features: the ability to operate in both public and private domains through the speech and thought bubbles and also in its versatility which allows it to be tailored rapidly to suit the learning (or therapeutic) needs of particular children in highly relevant contexts. Prior to this study, Bubble Dialogue has not been used for specifically therapeutic purposes, but evidence from its educational uses suggests that it may encourage children to reveal their private worlds and can help them reflect on situations with problematic outcomes, and to explore the consequences of their behaviour and how it might feel to be in another's place. This is nicely illustrated in an example given by the Language Development and Hypermedia Research Group [7]. They report how, during a group session, one of the boys became angry when the others in the group disciplined him for inappropriate behaviour, and a fight ensued between the two boys. The teacher asked the researchers to use Bubble Dialogue to investigate what had occurred. The boy who had initiated the fight chose not to play himself in the Bubble Dialogue role play but showed considerable insight into the feelings of his victim, who likewise showed compassion for his attacker, resulting in a new understanding about how to handle such situations in the future.

Episodes such as this illustrate Bubble Dialogue's role in exploring children's perceptions of particular social situations. The particular focus of this study, however, is on Bubble Dialogue's potential for helping children to express their feelings about loss.

Work so far

This project is in its early stages and the use of Bubble Dialogue is being piloted with a small number of children. Contact has been made with a therapist whom we hope to work with in future, and with families of adopted children. We are developing a range of scenarios which will have a general title: "It's not fair" . This has been chosen as the issue of "fairness" and dealing fairly with people is of interest to all children, though it may be a more sensitive area for children who have suffered disruptions and may have very low self esteem and perceive themselves to be victims of "unfairness". Such scenarios, then, can provide a continuum from "ordinary" children dealing with social and moral issues through to children with disruptions. In these scenarios, the central characters are the children Jo and Thomas, who live with their aunt, Auntie May. This family appears in several scenarios, with the issues becoming more personal and sensitive, e.g. in the last scenario, the two characters are Jo and his birth mother whom he is meeting for the first time in 2 years. An example scenario, *The birthday party*, is given below:

The birthday party
It's Jo's birthday party and Aunt May has promised to take Jo and two of his special friends to the ice rink. At the last minute Aunt May decides to bring his little brother Jo as well. Opener: "Aunt May says: "What's wrong, Jo? Why are you looking like that? Don't you want Thomas to come too?"
We have piloted two of these scenarios with Mark, a boy of 9, who is being adopted by the foster parents with whom he has lived for 3 years. Whilst it is too early to have definite results at this stage, the issues that have emerged from the pilot studies are:

What are the factors that contribute to a scenario that works?
One early scenario, *the school register*, was intended to be realistic, but not too close to home, or threatening. Unfortunately it was perceived as trivial, and the ensuing script, although interesting, was rather short. There is a need, therefore for the scene to present a real problem or issue that will engage the child for long enough. It is also important to avoid defining the scenario too closely, and in the process removing from the child the chance to explore the issue in their own terms as they create the dialogue. In this instance, for example, restricting the prologue and the opener is more likely to ensure that it is the child, not the parent or therapist who has to come up with the reasons why it's not fair.

How much control should the child be allowed?
Mark soon wanted to create his own situation, rather than working with a pre-canned script. Bubble Dialogue is designed to allow this to happen. Given practice, a new scenario can be created in a few minutes, and if this is done in negotiation with the child, the process of setting the scene, deciding who the characters are, what the problem is, and so on, allows the focus to be on the central issue (e.g., the child's concept of fairness) and ensures that it is explored in a context which is meaningful to the child.

Mark's high degree of acceptance of social conventions/behaviour
Mark constantly challenges authority and expresses a desire to be grown up so as to have more control over his life. He finds it hard to accept that any adult should have any authority over him. Yet in his

role play in Bubble Dialogue, he was at pains to be fair, to follow social conventions, and when one of the characters (played by the adult) was rude to the teacher, he was outraged! It was interesting to see this acceptance of conventional social rules being expressed in this form, where they are not always evident in his day-to-day life.

Conclusions

Our work so far supports our contention that Bubble Dialogue may have potential as a therapeutic tool for children and that children enjoy working with it. Earlier experiences from its educational use, and Mark's keen observance of social conventions whilst role playing would suggest that one useful role for Bubble Dialogue may be to help children reflect on difficult situations, such as fights, as shown in the earlier example, and to give them a way of exploring the creation of an alternative, positive outcome. This in itself may be quite illuminating for children who find it hard both to anticipate and deal with the consequences of their actions and the idea that there may be different ways of handling situations that may have different outcomes.

References

1   O'Neill, B. and McMahon, H. (1991) Opening New Windows with Bubble Dialogue, *Computers in Education,* Vol. 17. No. 1, pp 29-35,

2   Rutter, M. (1985) Family and School Influences on Cognitive Development, in Social relationships and Cognitive Development , edited by R. A Hinde, A Perret-Clermont and J. Stevenson-Hinde, Oxford University Press.

3   Tizard, B. and Hodges, J (1978) The effects of early institutional rearing on the development of eight-year-old children. *J. Child. Psychol. Psychiat,* **16**, pp 61-74.

4   Jackson, S. (1989) Education of children in care, in Kahan, B (ed); Child care research, policy and practice. Hodder and Stoughton.

5   Duck, S (1991) Friends for life, Harvester Press

6   Barrett, M. and Trevitt, J. (1992) Attachment Behaviour and the Schoolchild: An Introduction to Educational Therapy, Routledge.

7   Language and Development Hypermedia Research group (1991) Bubble Dialogue: A New Tool for Instruction and Assessment ETR&D, Vol 40, No. 2 pp59-67.

Advanced learning technology: Where's the *real* support for learning?

T. Mayes, P. McAndrew, C. Gunn, C. Smith & L. Coventry

Institute for Computer-Based Learning, Heriot-Watt University, ICBL, Riccarton, Edinburgh EH14 4AS, UK

Abstract

This paper forms the basis for a workshop where the main aim is to explore some of the fundamental issues in advanced learning technology from a learning theory perspective. The following questions are addressed:

- What aspects of the learning process are most effectively supported by ALT(Advanced Learning Technology)?
- What is the case for *multimedia*?
- Where is the real value of *interaction*?
- How can technology support *cooperative* learning?

These are deceptively simple questions, and the workshop attempts to highlight the contrast between the implicit assumptions underlying the rapid development of ALT in education (particularly in the context of the TLTP programme in UK higher education) and the evidence from research. The workshop also addresses the questions in the context of four projects in ALT, somewhat different in aims, but emphasising several of the underlying issues.

Models of learning

Every teacher, learner, instructional designer or courseware developer holds an implicit model of learning, even if it is never articulated. Shuell [1] has discussed the characterisation of these. The most common implicit theories of learning are probably the following:

- knowledge reception
- discovery
- learning by doing

Knowledge reception is by far the most deeply ingrained assumption about learning. It underlies most thinking about educational technology, and entails a belief that knowledge is something that can be passed, largely intact, from teacher to student or from author to reader. It underpins an "expository" form of teaching - teaching by telling. In its more sophisticated form it involves identifying the deficit in a learner's current understanding, and then supplying the missing knowledge. Papert [2] has called this approach "instructivist" (to contrast with "constructivist"). This view sees learning as essentially a process of knowledge acquisition rather than knowledge construction. A more subtle version of this, identifiable in the intelligent tutoring systems approach, is that learning occurs through an instructional dialogue in which the learner's misconceptions, or missing conceptions, are gradually identified and corrected through individualised instructional explanation. This leads to a view that one only has to organise knowledge in an appropriate form to match the conceptual state of the individual learner and learning will occur inevitably. An alternative view is that knowledge, in the form of information, cannot be 'delivered' in that sense at all. Knowledge is constructed, not 'acquired' (see, for example, Duffy, Lowyck & Jonassen, [3]).

Discovery learning is at the other end of a passive/active dimension. According to this, learners will understand little from didactic or expository instruction ("pre-digested knowledge") but must come to develop their own framework of understanding through exploration and active seeking of comprehension through discovery. The 'microworld' movement, inspired by LOGO's potential for allowing the discovery of principles and relationships through programming, was closely identified with this model. Similarly, exponents of hypertext and hypermedia as learning environments, embraced the notion of learning by browsing. Exploratory learning environments were designed to allow the learner complete control. In recognition of the inefficiency of waiting for the learner to discover target concepts, however, subsequent work has led to a less extreme version of this model, in which the task of the designers is to build guidance and support tools into the learner's environment (Hammond, [4]).

Learning by doing assumes that learning occurs primarily as a result of performing tasks. The kind of learning will, of course, depend on the nature of the task but the essential point is that learning is most likely to be successful if it is oriented towards the achievement of some goal. With this view, learning is a kind of by-product of the cognitive processing which accompanies the purposeful manipulation of information (Mayes [5]). Of course, it begs the question to talk in general terms about learning 'tasks': the difficult thing is to design tasks which will lead to the right kind of learning, will be meaningful to the individual learner, and will require thinking at the right conceptual level. Also it leaves open what is meant by a task. Is a "thought experiment" a task, or a conversation? None the less, it emphasises the main goal for teaching: to focus on what the learners do, rather than on what information is presented to them.

None of these implicit models can be said to be wrong, merely incomplete. In the case of the knowledge reception model it is so incomplete, and its emphasis so misleading, that it leads to a ineffective instructional approach. Much current educational technology will fail because it is based on a simple knowledge reception model of learning.

Case studies

Four projects have each had to develop a view on the possibilities for ALT. The first of these has developed an overall framework for its use in telematics. The three further case studies each emphasise that the role for ALT is the support for the reconceptualisation process, through tools for structuring and communication tasks which require the learner to think and reflect at an appropriate level for durable learning.

Learning through telematics

In this project [6] we have developed a framework for understanding the relationship between varieties of ALT, and categories of learning. Our basic description of learning is of a cycle of conceptualisation and re-conceptualisation, a process of iterative refinement of understanding. There are three fundamental components:

• Conceptualisation

- initial conceptualisations flow from the contact the learner has with other peoples' conceptualisations. This involves an interaction between the learner's pre-existing framework of understanding and a new exposition.

• Construction

- the application and testing of developing conceptualisations in the performance of meaningful tasks.

• Dialogue

- the creation and testing of new conceptualisations during conversation with both tutors and fellow learners, and the reflection on these.

Each component is then expanded into a similar cycle. The analysis of learning emphasises the need for learners to perform meaningful tasks, and for the resultant understanding to be reflected on, and discussed with others. The optimal form in which the 'primary exposition' is presented - the explanation from which the learner forms an initial conceptualisation - is dependent on what the learner already knows, rather than on intrinsic features of the presentation. This contrasts with the prevailing view, both in the choice of methods of the higher educational system, and in the assumptions of the multimedia industry, that the main contribution of technology is to present the primary exposition in an interactive and enticing form.

We also describe three kinds of learning technology, distinguishing between 'delivery' of content, tools for performing tasks from which learning is a by-product, and technology for supporting dialogue. The classification of the technology is mapped directly onto the description of learning.

The DELTA Co-Learn project

The Co-Learn project, part of the current DELTA R&D programme, is exploring the question of how cooperative teaching/learning can be best supported at a distance through a virtual teaching/learning environment. One way to investigate how new technologies might influence learning is to create a 'concrete instantiation' of the envisaged technology and position it in real teaching and learning situations. The Co-Learn project has adopted this approach and has built a prototype virtual teaching/learning environment using ISDN networks and multimedia technology. Ten teaching institutions, one of them the largest distance learning provider in Europe, are now using Co-Learn in selected parts of their teaching programmes.

The Co-learn prototype is designed to provide a virtual classroom for teachers and students using any of four teaching/learning scenarios:
- a lecture;
- interactive group-work for small groups;
- one-to-one tutor assistance for students learning independently with computer based resources or tools;
- learning through delayed-time discussions and group project work.

Co-Learn's four virtual classrooms provide information displays and interaction mechanisms appropriate to the character of each teaching/learning scenario. Each room can be further configured according to the teacher's or learner's requirements for a particular session by *adding more mechanisms for articulating interaction*, such as a virtual pen, private chatting via text messages, voting forms, and stop watches, or by *altering these mechanisms/interaction protocols* for different types of users, e.g. negotiated turn taking for students, or teacher priority for controlling a virtual pen.

The Co-Learn prototype takes into account the need to support not just highly collaborative and tightly coupled teaching/learning activities, but also those that appear less interactive. We consider whether real value in interaction is not only in the most obvious direct peer collaboration, but also in those interactions that endure over a longer time frame and in the wider pedagogical context. Often it is the less direct, more subtle interactions between tutors, students, and peers which form, maintain and distinguish different pedagogical situations. These interactions pivot on the expertise of a tutor who subtly controls the behaviour and atmosphere of a classroom session or a project according to individual, social and work demands.

Supporting both explicit and subtle classroom interactions at a distance clearly puts a heavy burden on human communication. We discuss some examples from Co-Learn trials which illustrate the distinction.

The TLTP CLASS project

The objective of the CLASS Project is to produce a widely applicable, computer based tool kit which will help undergraduate students develop the skills necessary for effective performance in all areas of study. Two main assumptions underlie this work:

a) there are an identifiable set of generic skills which are involved in effective study across all academic disciplines

b) these skills can be developed through use of software which has been specifically designed for the purpose

Two separate aspects of skills development are addressed: a) development of study techniques and skills, such as writing, reading, working in groups, information handling and managing time, and b) development of executive processing ability which means students will be aware of the range of possible alternative strategies for approaching a given task, and able to correctly judge which is most appropriate to the particular task and the context in which it will be completed.

One important aspect of software development focuses on group based and collaborative learning situations. While much attention has been given to the processes and outcomes of students' performance in groups, it has largely been assumed that individual skills necessary for effective collaboration already exist. The skills referred to include communication, self confidence, attention, listening, negotiation, leadership, understanding alternatives etc.

The Introductory Module of the CLASS Software Environment (CSE) does not accept this assumption as a starting point. It attempts to provide diagnostic and instructive material to help students recognise and reflect on their personal interactive style. Also covered is a basic understanding of the effects of personal performance on the behaviour of others, whose own styles may be radically different. Finally, an attempt is made to provide a learning environment where students can build enough confidence in their own abilities before being expected to contribute effectively 'in public', to group performance.

The Introductory Module, as the name suggests, provides for basic skills building as a lead in to other topic based CSE modules, one of which is wholly devoted to the area of group working. The Group Working Module demonstrates the implications of different interpersonal styles by providing students with the opportunity to examine alternative perspectives and outcomes in a realistic, task based environment.

The HIPERNET project

The HIPERNET (High Performance Networked Multimedia for Distributed Language Training) project is designed to make full use of broadband technology to deliver language learning. This project is funded under the EC RACE programme and involves IBM in France and Germany, Cap-Sesa Telecom (France), AND Software (Holland), Ascom Technology (Switzerland), GEC-Marconi, Cambridge University Language Centre and ICBL at Heriot-Watt as partners.

The initial system will run on the Cambridge GRANTA backbone, a high performance metropolitan area network. This existing network will be enhanced by equipment from some of the partners to provide very high speed ATM (Asynchronous Transfer Mode) connections to meet the requirements for delivery of multimedia and the additional needs of language learners.

Preliminary work within the project had concentrated on the feasibility of converting an existing course based on a series of BBC TV programmes called "French Means Business". The technology available would be harnessed to integrate these different media and deliver them over the network. It is clear that this is feasible using the intended technology of multimedia servers and high speed networking to deliver the material to relatively low cost PC based learner machines.

However, an approach based purely on conversion of an existing mixed media course to multimedia delivery raised questions about the motivations that learners would have for using the system, and what advantages would be gained from the move to multimedia presentation. This analysis identified the importance of designing the system around the learners' tasks, and the opportunities that the technology provided for the design of tasks based on cooperation.

The current design now has an emphasis on the use of technology for human-human communication. It had always been intended to incorporate a "help-desk" into the system to provide human assistance to learners over the network. The broadband technology allows screen sharing and video and audio conferencing facilities between workstations. This has now been integrated into the learning provision of the system by centring the learning tasks around communication between users. Two forms of communication task are envisaged, role-play conversations and exchanges of information. The multimedia course material now provides a resource to aid the learner in preparation for these communication tasks.

REFERENCES

1.   Shuell, T. Designing instructional computing systems for meaningful learning, In *Foundations and frontiers in instructional computing systems*, eds P. Winne & M. Jones, Springer-Verlag, Heidelberg, Germany, 1992.
2.   Papert, S. An introduction to the 5th anniversary collection, In *Constructionist Learning*, ed I. Harel, MIT Media Laboratory, Cambridge, MA, 1990
3.   Duffy, T., Jonassen, D., & Lowyck, J. (eds) Designing constructivist learning environments, Springer-Verlag, Heidelberg, Germany, 1993.
4.   Hammond N.V. Learning with hypertext: problems, principles and prospects, In *Hypertext: A Psychological Perspective*, eds A. Dillon & J. Richardson, Ellis Horwood, Chichester, 1992.
5.   Mayes, J.T. Cognitive tools: a suitable case for learning, In *Cognitive Tools for Learning*, eds P. Kommers, D. Jonassen & J.T Mayes, Springer-Verlag, Heidelberg, Germany, 1992.
6.   Mayes, J.T., Coventry, L., Mason, R., & Thomson, A. Learning through Telematics: A learning framework for telecommunicaation applications in higher education, Report for BT Labs, 1994.

Interactivity at a distance: Motivation and the distant learner

A.E. McCormack
Northern College, Gardyne Road, Dundee DD5 1NY, UK

Abstract

The bulk of research in distance learning addresses the structures and procedures required by both tutor and learner in order to achieve effective learning. What is of crucial importance in the area of tutor support are the characteristics of the tutorial/counselling processes as the interactive dialogue in maintaining the distant student.

Within this study, motivation in starting and continuing the DASET course of study is examined.

The aim of the current study is to investigate students' motivational patterns throughout a distance learning course.

The objectives are

> *to gather data on students' reasons for embarking on a course of study;
> *to gather data on reasons for continuing the course of study;
> *to identify support/interactive mechanisms for students.

The study group comprised past and current students on the now DASET course, who were asked as part of the methodology to complete a postal survey questionnaire, with selected follow up interviews. The analysis comprises basic tallies cross item analysis and computerised content analysis of open ended comments/statements.

The paper addresses interactivity at a distance and the importance of the tutor/student relationship. The role of psychosocial support is explored.

Introduction

This study on motivation and the distant student was conducted within the context of the distance learning (DL) Pathway of the Post Graduate Diploma in Applied Studies in Education & Training (DASET). DASET is a new course, evolving from the former PG Diploma in Educational Technology, a DL course which has been available for almost twenty years. DASET grew out of the recognition of the need and the desire to update the course and widen the market to embrace health and social services personnel and trainers in industry and commerce. DASET is an 8 module award, constituting around 700 hours of study including assessment. Each of the six single modules are assessed by essay while the core module Key Study is a two module project elected by the student.

Literature Review

The majority of the literature on adult learning deals with face to face, full time education. From this, it is clear that personal support is of great significance (McCombs[1]) and while more powerful, intrinsic motivation is easier to 'turn off than on' (Reeve[2]). Marton[3] proposes that the way a learner experiences a learning situation is related to his/her conception of learning. What is important also is self awareness and responsibility for the student's own learning as personal growth (Drummond & Croll[4]; Kinzie[5]).

In terms of distance learning, Schuller[6] states that :

'The individual's commitment to participate often stems initially from a development of his or her own occupational skills'.

It has been found (Knowles[7]) that most students enter the distance learning process in order to advance their career pathway.

'Adults are motivated to learn as they experience needs and interests that learning will satisfy'.

Baath[8] suggests that students receiving computer assisted tutoring started submitting more assignments than students receiving traditional tutoring by mail.

It has been observed through professional practice that students' motivation fluctuates throughout their course of study.   The motivation to embark on the course may be quite different that of continuation on it.

Study Group

The sample comprised 100 past and current students on the DASET/(DipEdTech) Pathway.

Methodology

It was proposed to use a standardised instrument to evaluate student motivation.   The Academic Motivation Scale, translated from French and validated in Canada (Vallerand et al[9], Baker & Siryk[10]) was discarded as it had been developed for full time face to face education.

A questionnaire was designed, and piloted with ten colleagues who were former students.   The questionnaire, with appropriate changes is available on request.

The random sample population were contacted by mail and asked to complete the questionnaire.   Six past/current respondents were followed up with a personal interview by a research assistant.

Results

Full results are available on request.   There was a 46% response rate to the mailed questionnaire and this was deemed adequate. The majority of respondents were male, in promoted posts, in the age range 30/39.

Analysis

Analysis was by basic tallies on individual items and cross-item tallies.   A content analysis of open ended comments is in progress.

Discussion

Distance learning courses by their very nature, place an onus on students to be responsible for their rate of progress, often in the most trying circumstances.   DASET courses encourage the students to customize the course through the tasks they undertake, and the opportunities to choose at least some elements of their course of study.

Colleague/Personal Support
Most respondents noted the support of valued colleague/friend as

a kind of self-help/support dyad, and many remarked on the support of their partner/spouse in their course of study.

Allocated study Location / Time
Students reporting success in maintaining motivation had allocated specific time and study space to their course. This 'location in space' seemed to legitimise their taking time out to pursue their own course of study. It is proposed that this allocation of space and time may alleviate feelings of guilt/selfishness but this was not in fact investigated in any kind of depth within the confines of this study.

College Support
While praising the tutorial system within College, it was clearly evident from the returns that College support is of lesser significance than local peer/personal support in distance learning. This supports the shift in DASET away from the need for in-College blocks, but clearly puts in question the role of College delivery in maintaining interactive support for distance learners. The follow up interviews further questionned the value of the termly newsletter sent to students in an attempt to maintain a spirit of cohesion and interactivity.

On Line Communication
It is proposed that in future students will have the option of access to tutorial support and inter-student communication through on-line services via First Class/COSY using a modem. Baath[8] found that students completed their studies more fully and more rapidly when received by computer assisted correspondence. This may be due to novelty, or to immediacy of response.

Conclusion

The results of this course related study clearly confirm other findings (McCombs, Drummond & Croll, Kinzie, Reeve op cit) that motivation in distance learning is based primarily on intrinsic factors inherent to the individual learner, but that personal networks of support are more important than those provided by the institution delivering the award. Tutorial support is accepted as the norm within the context of delivery.

Interactivity therefore relies on personal rather than institutionalised psychodynamics, and motivation on the personal support systems to which a learner has access.

Access to all the data from this study are available from the author.

1.   McCombs, B. L. Unraveling Motivation, *Journal of Experimental Education*, 1991, **60**, 3-88.

2.   Reeve, J. Intrinsic Motivation and the Acquisition and Maintenance of Four Experiential States, *Journal of Social Psychology*, 1989, **129**, 841-54.

3.   Marton, F. Towards a Phenomenography of Learning. III: Experience and Conceptualisation 1982:02. Goteborg University, Molndal (Sweden), Dept of Education.

4.   Drummond, R. J. & Croll J. C. Intrinsic and Extrinsic Motivation and Attitudes toward Professional Continuing Education: Implications for the Counselors, *Journal of Employment Counseling*, 1983, **20**, 88-96.

5.   Kinzie, M. B. Requirements and Benefits of Effective Interactive Instruction: Learner Control, Self-Regulation and Continuing Motivation, *Educational Technology Research and Development*, 1990, **38**, 5-21.

6.   Schuller, T. *The Democratisation of Work: Educational Implications in Schuller & Megany* (eds) Recurrent and Lifelong Learning, Kogan Page, London, 1979.

7.   Knowles, M. *The Adult Learner*, Gullf USA, 1990.

8.   Baath, J. A., *Postal Two-Way Communication in Correspondence Education. An Empirical Investigation*, EDRS, 1980.

9.   Vallerand, R. J. et al, On the Assement of Intrinsic, Extrinsic and Amovitation in Education: Evidence on the Concurrent and Construct Validity of the Academic Motivation Scale, *Educational and Psychological Measurement*, 1993, **53**, 159-172.

10.   Baker, R. W. & Siryk, B. Measuring Academic Motivation of Matriculating College Freshmen, *Journal of College Student Personnel*, 1984, **25**, 459-464.

Collaboration and discourse during computer-based problem solving

K. Pheasey & G. Underwood

Centre for Research in Development, Instruction and Training,
Psychology Department, University of Nottingham, University Park,
Nottingham NG7 2RA, UK

Abstract

Children worked in pairs on a computer-based language problem-solving task, and their keyboard activities were monitored along with their discussions of the problems. Previous investigations have indicated that suggestions and evaluations are associated with improved task performance. The gender composition of the pairs has also been found to influence performance. In the present Cloze task, however, boy-girl pairs showed only slightly lower levels of verbal interaction and task performance than did single gender pairs.

1 Introduction

When children work in groups there are benefits to be gained, but group work also carries risks. These risks are particularly high for certain combinations of children, computer role and task. It is this interaction between the social structure of the group, the computer as a possible 'other' person within the group, and the task in hand, which we will focus upon here.

The nature of the co-operation between the participants may differ within and between these learning environments. Currently terms such as group work, co-operative and collaborative learning are used very loosely in the literature. The central concept refers to learning environments in which small groups of students work together to achieve a common goal. In achieving that common goal, however, the members of the group may choose to take responsibility for sub-tasks and work co-operatively, or they may collaborate and work together on all the parts of the problem. If the learners collaborate and share in the decision making process the level of social interaction is necessarily high, but this is not necessarily so for co-operative workers.

There are essential differences in the level of interaction in co-operative versus collaborative work group, so how might these affect learning? There is a myriad of questions still to be answered in this area. What do children gain from social interaction and under what circumstances do those gains occur? What aspects of social interaction contribute to children's advances? How do variations in the nature of the group, such as whether the partners are adults or peers, the extent of their expertise, their authority or equality relative to the learner, and the extent to which partners share in decision making, affect the nature of the interaction and therefore the learning that takes place? Are there any differences in the role of the interaction depending on the age of the children? Essentially here we will be considering the circumstances under which children's thinking can gain from co-operative problem-solving with computer-based activities, and the causes of these gains.

The positive aspects of collaborative work have been well documented, and aside from any benefits for social development or communication skills, as important as these are, there are also benefits for children's powers of thinking. Ann Cale Kruger [1] has recently reviewed the evidence that suggests that when pairs of children solve a problem together, they think more effectively than when they work alone. This generalisation is good for a variety of tasks, including Piagetian conservation, logical thinking, moral reasoning, and mathematics. Different theoretical perspectives on this advantage give different explanations of course, but Kruger's explanation points to the similarities between them.

The Piagetian perspective argues that gains are made through socio-cognitive conflict, which acts against ego-centric thought. By coming up against the ideas of a co-worker children see a challenge to their own interpretation of the world. This social conflict requires a cognitive resolution, and so cognitive gains are made. On the other hand, the explanation from Vygotsky's perspective is that social co-operation results in a new cognitive product based upon joint definitions. Whereas the Piagetian perspective sees conflict as the key, Vygotskian approach is to emphasise the value of co-operation. Kruger's resolution is through an analysis of the interactions between children attempting to solve problems together, and her account provides us with an explanation of why some groups of children working on a computer task perform better than others, as well as giving some hints about how the effective classroom will be organised.

In our previous classroom experiments pairs of children have worked on a computer-based task, (e.g. Underwood, McCaffrey and Underwood [2]). Where performance varied our informal observations suggested that there was also variation in the amount of discussion between the members of the pair. On the basis of Kruger's analysis we might expect discussion of alternative hypotheses and alternative solutions to predict performance on the problem. In the present study all children were given an individual practice session and a paired practice session. The length of time allowed for each session was increased from ten to fifteen minutes, to allow a greater opportunity for problem-oriented discussion and for the children to increase their familiarity both with the task and with their partner. Although children in the Underwood, Underwood and Turner [3] study both worked together for two sessions (once on TRAY and once on ROAMER), they were not given any individual training on either task. It is hoped that increased training will lead to improved interaction and performance on task. Increased interaction will hopefully lead to the identification of the specific components of discussion that are associated with variations in task performance. In this study children were told to cooperate, but were not instructed to take individual turns as in the previous experiment. It is thought that this instruction may have affected the interaction of the pairs. More detailed measures of how pairs interact at the keyboard can then be taken. A key behaviour associated with the Cloze task is control of the keyboard, particularly the cursor. Only by moving the cursor using the arrow keys can words be attempted. Other behaviours may also be identified which may indicate a collaborative style of working.

2 Method

Subjects

The children participating in this experiment were aged between 9 years 4 months and 11 years 1 month, (mean age 10 years 5 months) and came from a single school in which testing took place. A total of 60 children took part in the study (30 boys and 30 girls). The children were divided into 10 pairs of each gender arrangement; girl/girl pairs, boy/boy pairs and girl/boy pairs. Children were drawn from three parallel classes and were in either year 5 or year 6.

Procedure

All children were initially tested using the GAP reading comprehension test. Children were allocated randomly to groups. The mean reading age of each group was found not to be significantly different (boy/boy pairs 126.6 months, girl/girl pairs 125.75 months, girl/boy pairs 124.85 months). Within each group, children were paired with a child who was of similar reading age, but from a different class. This was to minimise the chance of more friendship pairs occurring in single sex pairs than mixed gender pairs. All chidren were asked if they would work with their partner beforehand.

Subjects were given two practice sessions; one individual and one paired session, and a paired test session. Children were allowed 15 minutes working with each incomplete piece of text, or until completion. All sessions were video-taped.

The 'Infant Tray' Cloze Task
This task involves the completion of a paragraph in which letters have been replaced by hyphens. The text was prepared using the MEP programme 'Infant TRAY' using a BBC B microcomputer. All pieces of text contained no dialogue and no hidden proper names. The text used in individual training was taken from 'James and the Giant Peach' by Roald Dahl. Children were given instructions on how to use the program and any help they required to be able to use the program and the computer effectively.

The text used in paired training was from 'Tales from Allotment Lane School' by Margaret Joy. This passage had been previously used in studies by Underwood et al.[1,3]. The pairs were told to cooperate when deciding what actions to take. No intervention was provided by the experimenter if the children did not cooperate.

Children were tested again with the same partner under the same conditions as the practice session. The section of text used was taken from a collection of stories called 'The Downhill Crocodile Whizz' by Margaret Mahy, and is shown below.

```
THERE WAS ONCE A B== C==L=D ETHELRED W== W==
RE==Y F== A==T====. H= L=V=D I= A T=== RI=== N=X=
T= O== O= T==S= B== JU====S F==L O= CR==OD===S,
T=GE==, RUINED C====S A== S==N= STATUES C=V==ED
W==H V=N==.
```

Measures taken for each session were the number of letters and words, attempted and correct. For each child or pair, a letter efficiency score was obtained by finding the percentage of letters correct from letters attempted. From the video, all conversations were transcribed. Data was also collected about the frequency of key presses, the length of turn of each member of a pair, and the amount of keyboard sharing. Keyboard sharing describes whether the pairs took distinct turns at the keyboard, or if they divided the parts of the task. For example, if one child entered all the letters whilst the other child moved the cursor and pressed return, this would be coded as keyboard sharing. It is expressed as a percentage of the total number of key presses. This measure was adopted because it was thought that keyboard sharing could indicate a more collaborative style of working.

3 Results

The number of letters and words attempted and correctly entered, the letter efficiency, the time taken on task, the number of letters entered by children seated to the left or the right of the keyboard, and the amount of keyboard sharing of each pair is shown in Table 1. Separate analyses of variance were performed for each measure.

No significant differences were found between groups for any of the measures of task performance: letters attempted ($F = 1.49\ df = 2,27$), letters correct ($F = <1\ df = 2,27$), words attempted ($F = <1\ df = 2,27$), words correct ($F = <1\ df = 2,27$), and letter efficiency ($F = <1, df = 2,27$). There was a reliable difference for the % keyboard sharing ($F = 10.490\ df = 2,27\ p = 0.0004$) and for the % letter keys pressed by the left or right hand person ($F = 3.245\ df = 2,27\ p = 0.05$). An unplanned comparison revealed that in girl pairs the person occupying the chair to the left of the keyboard pressed more keys than in boy pairs ($p = 0.05$). There was also a significant difference between pairs in the level of keyboard sharing. Pairs of girls shared the keyboard more than boy pairs ($p = 0.01$) and mixed pairs ($p = 0.01$).

Table 1. Summary of performance scores for each pair type

| | PAIR TYPE | | |
	Girl Girl	Boy Boy	Girl Boy
Number of letters attempted	130.6	137.3	115.6
Number of letters correct	63.6	64	59.1
Letter efficiency %	50.92	49.47	53.02
Number of words attempted	27.89	28.7	27.2
Number of words correct	26.2	26.4	24.8
Time (seconds)	792	716.09	731.2
Letter keys pressed % left	66.43	48.31	61.68
Letter keys pressed % right	33.53	51.69	38.32
Keyboard sharing %	65.95	36.97	21.14

Bales Analysis

All conversations from the final paired session were scored using Bales Interaction Process Analysis (Bales [4]).Because trials were of different lengths the number of statements per minute was used as the unit of analysis. A separate analysis of variance was performed on the category B statements (suggestions, evaluations and analysis, information, clarification and repetition). A significant interaction occurred between pairing and category ($F = 4.716$, $df = 4,54$, $p = 0.0025$). Mixed pairs gave more B6 statements but less B4 and B5 statements. Category 4 statements were subsequently re-analysed to separate solution-related suggestions (B4a) from other suggestions (B4b), for example, which word to try next. Paired comparisons revealed the difference to be in the number of solution-related suggestions given. Single gender pairs made almost twice as many suggestions as mixed gender pairs ($p = 0.01$). Due to the low number of entries in certain categories, categories A, C and D were collapsed to give a single score. An unplanned comparison revealed that boy pairs gave a greater number of negative utterances (category D) than mixed pairs ($p = 0.05$)

Table 2. Showing Mean Number of Statements Per Pair For Each Bales Category

pair	A1	A2	A3	B4a	B4b	B5	B6	C7	C8	C9	D10	D11	D12
GG	Mean0.14	0.63	0.64	4.20	0.57	1.11	2.28	0.33	0.06	0.15	0.34	0.11	0.02
BB	Mean0.09	0.30	0.60	4.22	0.74	0.98	2.81	0.29	0.05	0.14	0.33	0.10	0.23
GB	Mean0.04	0.36	0.31	1.99	0.31	0.84	3.26	0.16	0.05	0.03	0.06	0.05	0.02

Transaction Analysis

Conversations were also scored for transactional statements. These are spontaneously produced critiques, refinements, justifications, evaluations and elaborations of a solution (Kruger, [1]). No significant differences were found between groups due to the small number of statements that were included in these categories.

Performance measures were correlated with dialogue measures. No significant correlations were found. However, significant correlations were found within each group of scores. Several of the Bales categories correlated. Correlations significant at the 0.01 level are shown with an asterisk in table 3.

Performance measures recorded from both paired sessions were correlated. Letters correct and attempted, efficiency and words correct were all significantly correlated ($p = 0.01$) between trials.

Performance on the paired test session was predicted by regression analysis with R^2 (adjusted) = 62.0% by five variables - reading age (41%), paired practice session letter efficiency score (21%), the number of transactional statements per minute (4%), the number of category D statements per minute (2%), the number of category B statements per minute (1%) - with $F = 20.2$, $df = 5, 54$ $p = 0.001$.

Table 3. Significant correlations between Bales categories.

	a1	a2	a3	b4a	b4b	b5	b6	c7	c8	c9	d10	d11	d12
a1	1.00												
a2	0.38	1.00											
a3	0.74*	0.42	1.00										
b4a	0.47*	0.54*	0.63*	1.00									
b4b	0.06	0.22	0.33	0.35	1.00								
b5	0.46*	0.78*	0.63*	0.72*	0.28	1.00							
b6	0.12	0.25	0.12	0.32	0.00	0.42	1.00						
c7	0.54*	0.30	0.76*	0.73*	0.04	0.64*	0.36	1.00					
c8	0.43	0.32	0.54*	0.35	0.10	0.40	0.40	0.50*	1.00				
c9	0.65*	0.27	0.67*	0.64*	0.18	0.53*	0.31	0.74*	0.46*	1.00			
d10	0.15	-0.07	0.18	0.29	-0.16	0.24	0.09	0.50*	0.00	0.48*	1.00		
d11	0.28	0.32	0.36	0.54*	0.12	0.33	0.33	0.46*	0.29	0.69*	0.14	1.00	
d12	0.48*	-0.12	0.52*	0.27	-0.12	0.09	0.18	0.51*	0.46*	0.74*	0.45*	0.60*	1.00

4 Discussion

The results do not replicate the significant gender differences in performance measures found previously, but differences in process measures such as verbal dialogues and keyboard behaviour are present. The results do show the same pattern as in previous experiments. Mixed pairs show lower levels of verbal interaction and slightly poorer performance than single gender pairs.

The differences between groups for keyboard sharing behaviour are of interest. It is notable that pairs of girls spontaneously adopt a collaborative style of working. A further experimental manipulation would be to force children to adopt this style of working. Interdependence may lead to greater verbal interaction and increased task performance.

Informal observations of cursor control indicate that in the majority of mixed pairs it is the boy who moves the cursor most often, and decides when the pair should move on to a new word. This is of significance because control of the cursor is the key to the Cloze task. Although access to the keyboard is necessary to enter letters, answers cannot be entered unless the cursor is in the right place. Dominance of boys in mixed pairs undertaking a computer task has been observed in other studies (Littleton et al.[5], Fitzpatrick & Hardman [6]). The input device could be manipulated so that letters can be entered using either a real keyboard, or an on-screen keyboard using a mouse, in future studies. Roles may be undertaken simply because of seating arrangements. This cannot be investigated from the current experiment, but perhaps could be in future.

The majority of the verbal interaction is positive and task oriented. Lack of suggestions from mixed pairs is compensated for by a greater level of commentary and re-reading of the text (Bales B6). However, correlations are low between all performance and process measures so it would be difficult to draw any strong conclusions about the components of dialogue that indicate successful task performance. It seems the features of conversation that are frequent and easily measured are not those which predict task performance reliably. The regression analysis shows a relationship between transactional statements and task performance (letter efficiency). These analytical statements, though infrequent do seem to be linked with task performance. More analysis is needed to unpack the significance of these statements. The regression also shows a small, but significant relationship, between lack of negative statements and task success.

One major problem we have come across is the lack of in depth discussion between pairs when they are not experiencing any difficulty with the task. It is only when the children hit upon some problem that 'real discussion' begins to take place. Although children are asked to discuss and choose together a course of action, there is no penalty for wrong guesses and no need for discussion when the right answer is reached. Therefore, in future a version of the task with a scoring system that deducted points for wrong guesses and gave points for right answers could be used. This would hopefully limit random guessing. Restructuring the task in this way would limit the problem of one person taking control of the task.

It seems that most children prefer to test their ideas on the computer rather than discuss whether a suggestion is correct with their partner. The relationship between the computer and the children is an unequal one in that the computer has all the right answers and the children may not.

This task is limited in the type of interaction it allows. A richer verbal dialogue would be gained by using a different task. The scope of the task as currently used on the BBC is restricted because of the small amount of text that can be displayed on the screen. Longer interactions can only be obtained by using a longer, more difficult piece of text. Many of the children may have been approaching ceiling for the task, or may have run out of suggestions of possible answers. Two sessions is probably not enough to develop a stable working style. This could be remedied by even longer or repeated sessions of paired work. Experimenter pairing using reading age is not the best way of pairing. In future, it would be better to use pairs in which the children had chosen their partner. Although all children agreed to work with each other, this did not guarantee they would cooperate closely.

References

1.   Kruger, A. (1993). Peer collaboration: conflict, collaboration or both? Social Development, 2(3), 165-182.

2.   Underwood, G., McCaffrey, M., & Underwood, J. (1990). Gender differences in a cooperative computer-based language task. Educational Research, 32(1), 44-49.

3.   Underwood, G., Underwood, J., & Turner, M. (1993). Children's thinking during collaborative computer-based problem solving. Educational Psychology, 13(3 & 4), 345-357.

4.   Bales, R. F. (1951) Interaction Process Analysis, Addison-Wessley Press, Cambridge, MA.

5.   Littleton, K., Light, P., Joiner, R., Messer, D., & Barnes, P.(1992). Pairing and gender effects on children's computer-based learning. European Journal of Psychology of Education, 7(4), 311-324.

6.   Fitzpatrick, H., & Hardman, M. Girls, boys and the classroom computer: an equal partnership. In B.P.S. Developmental Section Annual Conference, University of Birmingham: (1993)

Laptops down under: The construction of knowledge at an Australian college

M. Rawlings

Methodist Ladies' College, 207 Barkers Road, Kew, Victoria 3101, Australia

It has been argued that the computer is the latest addition to a range of tools, such as chalk, paper and ink, abacus and calculator, that have been technological aids in helping individuals process new information. More strongly it is argued that the computer, if used as a tool, becomes an amplifier of human capabilities and a catalyst to intellectual development. Computing can change the nature of the task, and so alter the cognitive processes of the problem solvers.

Our human activities shape the environment to which we react. The transmission of skills, knowledge and behaviours renders the world different to the receiver from the world of the transmitter, in which such knowledge was formed. Vygotsky (1978) recognised that

the signs (symbols of language) act as an instrument of psychological activity in a manner analogous to the role of a tool in labour. (p.52)

Rowe (1993) has made a distinction with respect to the use made of computers. Those machines which do our work for us, the washing machine, the car, the programmes to teach touch typing, or multiplication tables represent the technologies available in our current environment. In contrast, the machines with which we work, the synthesizer for composition, the pruning shears, the pencil and aerogramme, or the language in which we choose to programme, are instruments that we adapt to our own purposes. In the latter situation, computers are an extension of ourselves, but in the former these machines are 'significant others'. They are agents of our present environment. This appears to be the logic behind Papert's (1980) proposal of computer programming environments in which students can explore the abstract by making their thinking processes concrete in terms of Logo. They can predict translations, rotations or reflections, for example, and use the machine to verify the outcomes. They can 'create' by repeating such instructions to a degree that they cannot imagine, and can find the product pleasing.

The technologies available as fruits of other programmers, however, cannot be ignored in the educational process. Computer aided instruction (CAI) in typing and tables has already been mentioned. If Logo-writer has the instructions in French or German, then the jargon must be acquired and used for access to the programme. The whole gamut of Western business culture, can be conveyed through computer managed instruction (CMI) within pre-programmed microworlds.

Laptops were introduced into Methodist Ladies' College in years 5 and 7 in a small number of classes in 1990. The parents had to fund this addition to their daughters' learning tools. Word processing has been a compulsory part of the year 7 curriculum (using the College's existing desktops in large purpose-built classrooms) since 1988 and there was an existing business studies course for years 11 and 12 entirely supported by CAI. In 1994 there are a few students in years 11 and 12 who do not have laptops, although they have their own passwords and access to the school network in these large classrooms of computers and printers. Laptops are not compulsory until year 5, but are introduced through class sets of machines from year 1. Teachers are given a grant of $700 in the first year towards the purchase of their own laptop and attractive deals are offered on College approved models. A further $700 is provided in the following year for the purchase of supporting hardware or software.

The college principal, David Loader has encouraged a proactive philosophy in this independent (non-government) school. It has an enrolment of 2235 (day and boarding students) this year. Consequently the school is administered in four relatively autonomous sub-schools. Another 4000 adults and young people are enrolled in after (day) school programmes (evenings and weekends) in Community Education. MLC accepts that a future must be chosen and then achieved. A combination of 'bold imaginings' and real appraisals of the market situation in enrolments has seen it maintain and strengthen its position in a decade of recession and school closures. A traditional curriculum, prescribed by the Victorian Board of Studies, still dominates in years 11 and 12, and percolates into other aspects of school life. Since the late eighties there has been a concerted effort to move curricular philosophy towards a more constructionist approach. Piaget first suggested that "knowledge is built by the learner, not supplied by the teacher". This 'constructivism' has been extended by Papert to 'constructionism' which includes

the further idea that this happens especially felicitously when the learner is engaged in the construction of something external..." (Polin, 1990, p.6)

Unlike Piaget's stage theory, Papert's 'constructionism' implies that students can use their own initiative to build a curriculum suitable to their present cognitive needs. Students should become empowered in the sense that they would recognise that they have control over their own ideas and thought processes, that they can describe what they are thinking to others. Psychological literature refers to this sense of empowerment as metacognition. MLC has consciously moved to encourage curricular initiatives that will result in student metacognition.

Basic to this philosophy is the idea that the portable computer is 'personal'. The file organisation, the choice of programme, the educational activities, games, down-loads from the network and virus checks are all the responsibility of the student. For each girl, there is a personal world to which she may choose to invite or exclude others. The school insists on an IBM compatible platform, while providing ample support for rebels, who insist on keeping to 'other' ways.

For the teachers in years 5, 6 and 7, Logowriter was the chosen medium for Maths, Science, English, Geography, History and Biblical Studies. It provided

facilities for the writing of procedures, the manipulation of a micro-world, the production of graphics, animation, music, the provision for word processing and a data base (Baker, 1989. p.4)

Teachers of these core studies adopted a team approach to produce integrated experiences involving process skills from each of the studies. Inevitably the environments created as a result of integrating the laptop are reminiscent of the free school movement of the 1960s. Expectations of society and parents are no longer as certain as in that period of nearly full employment. There is a much greater acceptance of the College's move from 'an organisation for learning to a learning organisation' (Grasso and Fallshaw,ed., 1993, appendix). Few are willing to predict the skills that will be marketable in the twenty-first century. Hence a flexibility of approach across a range of disciplines seems attractive. Teachers have not abrogated their roles in providing guidance to the students to bridge the gap between the students' understandings of the tasks and the outcomes that are expected in the objectives. In fact, the teachers' explorations of the new medium have intensified their own perceptions of themselves as learners. This reflectivity has improved their understanding of the need for *scaffolding* appropriate to a particular learner's personal perspective. The 'zone of proximal development' (Vygotsky, 1978. p.68) has become all too real to teachers relying on their peer support as they explore and create in the laptop classroom.

If students are assessed in the classroom, obviously a new and radical initiative in teaching should be assessed as well. Papert has stressed that he has sort to decenter the perception of the Logo experience. He observed that children have access to programming and other computer applications in a multitude of ways and not just at school. He revealed a strong preference for anecdotes, single classroom case studies, and ethnographic research methods. He derided methods of cause and effect, as ill-suited to revealing the multiplicity of factors that affect students' performances (Rowe, 1993). At MLC the appraisal of change caused by the introduction of laptops and appropriate curriculum has been carried out by Helen McDonald, a former staff member and a Ph.D. student from the Education Faculty of Monash University. The Faculty's commitment to qualitative, descriptive methods and case studies was seen to be 'appropriate' to the cultural ethos defended by Papert. McDonald together with case study interviews with selected students and staff, administered a questionnaire to all year 7 students in 1991 and 1992. In the first year 8 of 10 classes used laptops and were following new innovations in curriculum. In the second year all 10 classes were using laptops.

There was clearly a feeling of pioneering a change and the very positive responses to student questionnaires must be interpreted in this light. In the second year, 1992, the laptops were somewhat less of a novelty to the students. The program was established, although still in an evolutionary phase.(McDonald, 1994.)

In 1991, 95% of students claimed that they liked using a laptop computer in their studies, while in 1992, 83% of students agreed. In 1991, year 7 students were entirely divided on the issue of whether a laptop made learning easier, with 50% returning a positive response. The 1992 cohort had 38 % agreeing that learning was easier on a laptop, but only 13% in 1991 and 16% in 1992 felt that the laptop made learning harder. Eighty-nine percent of students in 1991 (80% in 1992) thought that programming taught them a lot, while ninety-eight percent (92% in 1992) felt that they had acquired new skills with the computer. With the statement, 'I can do things on the computer that I can't do in other ways", 89% of students in 1991 and 88% in 1992, expressed agreement.

Use of a laptop was seen as a time-saver by approximately 70% in both years and ninety percent in 1991 (80% in 1992) were pleased with the appearance of work produced by the computer. In 1991, seventy percent of students felt that they wrote more using a computer, although only 53% of the 1992 students did. As to whether they felt empowered by using a computer, only 32% in 1991 and 33% in 1992 felt greater control, whereas twenty-nine percent in 1991 and 49% in 1992 felt more frustrated when working with the computer. This latter figure may have been a reaction to the evolving nature of the programme in 1992. More staff were being brought 'on line' and more teachers were willing to take risks with the exploration of new approaches. Thirty-three percent in both years admitted to confusion when trying to use their laptops, reflected in 17% in 1991 and 25% in 1992 reporting that they 'lost too much work' on the computer. However 81% (1991) and 67% (1992) felt more organised when using a computer and 85% and 70% respectively admitted that they preferred using a computer to pen and paper. Most noted greater ease in finding their work on computer files (86% in 1991 and 77% in 1992). Just over sixty percent in both years tired less quickly when working on a computer.

Games have been a vexed area for a Christian school. Copywright is the last thing on students' minds as they swap with each other. Pragmatically, viruses tend to be the second last thing. Nevertheless, ninety-three percent in 1991 (81% in 1992) confessed to using the computer for their 'own interests'. Eighty-six percent (1991) and 68% (1992) agreed that learning with a laptop is fun, and eight percent (1991) together with 28% (1992) considered the process to be boring. A significant proportion of students (32% in 1991 and 51% in 1992) felt that there were too many things that can go wrong with computers, and just over eighty percent in both years noted that the re-charging aspect was annoying.

Focussing upon teachers and teaching styles, approximately ninety-four percent of students in both years felt that they were trusted to work alone on projects. Eighty-two percent in 1991 and 73% in 1992 noted that they progressed at their own pace, while 86% (1991) and 74% (1992) agreed that students helped each other more. Over seventy-five percent in both years agreed that they were given more responsibility, and learnt more independently than in the previous year, when approximately two-thirds of students were at a different school. In both years only a third of the students expected their teachers to 'know all about Logowriter', although approximately 90% expected the teacher to 'know enough to appreciate' what they had done. There was a change of perception of students to teacher attitudes. In 1991, eighty percent agreed that teachers did not mind whether a task was completed with pen or paper or on the computer, but in 1992 this figure was 69%. This may reflect the effort teachers were putting into the inception of the new ethos.

The students from the 1991 cohort are now in year 10 and all have a laptop. The intention is to survey these students again about their attitudes to the use that is being made of the computer in their current learning situations.

References

Baker, R. (1989) Computers and independent learning: A year 7 project. CEGV Computers in Education Conference.

Grasso, I and Fallshaw M. (eds.) (1993) <u>Reflections of a learning community: Views on the introduction of laptops at MLC.</u> Kew, VIC: Methodist Ladies' College.

McDonald H. (1994) personal communication.

Papert, S. (1980) <u>Mindstorms: Children, computers and powerful ideas.</u> Brighton: Harvester Press.

Polin, L. (1990) What's hot and what's not. <u>The Computing Teacher,</u> August/September.

Rowe, H. A. H. (1993) <u>Learning with personal computers.</u> Hawthorn, VIC: Australian Council for Educational Research.

Vygotsky, L. S. (1978) <u>Mind in society: The development of higher psychological processes.</u> Cambridge, MA: Harvard University Press.

A gender perspective on collaborative working with science simulations

E. Scanlon

Institute of Educational Technology, The Open University, Walton Hall, Milton Keynes MK7 6AA, UK

Abstract

Groupwork has particular relevance for science learners. This paper reviews experiences of groups working with science simulations in relation to gender effects on science learning. The groups discussed range from pairs of adults working together on computer simulations at a distance, or side by side, to pairs of fifteen year olds with computer simulations and larger groups of younger children working cooperatively on combinations of computer simuations and real science experiments. Gender differences in the most productive way of forming groups to work at the computer on science simulations are considered.

1 Introduction

In recent years there is an appreciation of the benefits that can be obtained by students working with computers collaboratively. For example, Eraut and Hoyles [1] reviewing recent classroom based studies of cooperative learning such as Slavin [2] stress that short and long term benefits for both academic achievement and social goals have been demonstrated. There is some difference of opinion as to how this enhanced learning takes place. The overall experimental evidence concerning the effects of cooperative activity on individual learning and development is rather complicated. Benefits appear to be dependent on a number of task specific factors, research findings are not always replicated and researchers are divided about the underlying mechanisms responsible for conceptual change. The research on collaborative learning raises a number of questions about how such group working can best be facilitated. With particular reference for science group work, there have been well documented differences in the way that girls and women approach their science learning and suggestions are made (e.g. Morgan, [3]) that developing certain science skills is problematic for girls due to the level of confidence needed to put forward ideas and participate in group discussions.

2 Working with science simulations

Three research projects which involved OU researchers and a range of students working with computers on science topics will be discussed in relation to three areas of research on collaborative learning: conflict, nature of task, and communication in mixed groups. Conclusions from these studies should influence the best way to arrange for effective learning for students working with computers on science topics. These projects were not laboratory experiments but were carried out in the appropriate setting, real classrooms for the first two and an industrial research laboratory using communications technology in use by the scientists who worked there. Each of these projects have particular implications for the gender composition of groups.

Conflict
Much of the research about children learning science deals with what is going on in the individual pupils' heads as they grapple with the new concepts which they have to assimilate. We know that each individual will have some view of any topic under study. Much of the time children spend on classroom activity will be organised in groups. Some guidance documents for teachers suggest that children could be allocated to groups on the basis of age, ability, friendship or interest. Recently some research has examined how such groups should be structured. For example, Christine Howe and her co-workers [4] have experimented with the groups working together, varying the cognitive conflict in the group. Howe and the other researchers were not working in a classroom. They found that groups with more differences in the children's views on the topic area they are studying eventually produced more learning but stressed that these results do not provide evidence that the superiority (of the groups with more differences) was immediately apparent. Indeed there was a strong suggestion that the progress that occurred took place after the group tasks, indicating that interaction when concepts differ is something of a catalyst for development. Howe also suggests that setting primary children to work on science investigations in mixed ability groups promotes more effective learning than streaming children into groups where they possess similar ideas and levels of knowledge. She suggests that allocating children at random is good enough to provide these mixed ability groupings. However this conflicts with a need to consider gender

distribution within the groups. Other researchers have suggested that there might be a need to ensure a critical mass of girls in a mixed sex group, or girls will be left out. This will be discussed further in a later section.

There is evidence that there are gender differences in the way that conflict is percieved. For example, Galton [5] suggests that children's reluctance to work collaboratively in groups could be to do with mixed emotions involving fear of failure combined with a desire to own their own work. Smith [6] reviews this work and other work which suggests that boys and girls react differently in these group settings. However one set of experiments provides evidence for the productive behaviour of groups of girls who have similar views of a topic. Whitelock et al., [7] found that, in a situation where secondary students worked in a group with a mechanics computer simulation on the Computer Supported Cooperative Work in physics project, pairs with similar views did just as well as pairs chosen with different starting views of the physics under study. The task was to make some predictions about the behaviour of a set of pucks using the Laws of Conservation of Momentum and Energy in a computer simulation called *Puckland*. Pupils were pretested with a questionnaire before using the simulation. Then the subjects had access to the simulation where they are given time to check out their predictions and to experiment with any other situations which interested them before completing the problem solving exercises. A post test was then administered. Single gender pairs of 15 year old British schoolchildren formed by analysis of the performance on pre tests of eighty children were studied. Four types of pairs were formed: boy/boy pairs with similar views of the physics concept, and girl/girl pairs with similar views and two further groups with differing views on the physics. Overall all the groups increased their scores on the post test but it was similar pairs rather than the different pairs which improved the most. 'Girls similar' improved most of all with 'boys similar' coming next, with 'boys and girls different' being equal third. On inspection, the 'girls similar' had the worst scores on their pre-tests however. When we examined the dialogues the girls appeared to have less experiential knowledge of collisions than the boys (i.e. they did not play snooker, hockey or football and did not use analogies from their sporting experiences to make predictions.) Girls were disadvantaged by their lack of practical experience of collisions. This type of gender effect has been commented on before (see e.g. Johnson and Murphy, [8]).

Nature of Task
The Conceptual Change in Science project aimed to improve the science understanding of a mixed group of twenty-nine thirteen year olds using specially designed computer software. The concepts to be studied were those from Newtonian mechanics. Our curriculum involved a scheme of work based round four scenarios

(the Rocket Skater, the Parachutist, the Speedboat, and the Supermarket). Children worked in affinity groups chosen by the class teacher which were operated for a two week trial period before the main experiment but there were no mixed sex groups in the main experiment. Individual student performance on a pre and post test was measured and we experienced some significant improvement in pupil performance (see Hennessy et al, [9]). No gender effects were noticed in the statistical analysis of results but several observers did comment on the different behaviour of the all boy as opposed to all girl groups. It seemd that the girls' groups behaved more cooperatively. We need to review our audiotapes and videotapes of the groups as they worked at their tasks to try to characterise these differences. Many of the girls said they preferred conventional to computer practicals.

This project was not designed to investigate gender differences. Scenarios were designed to appeal to both boys and girls, and our findings on conceptual change show no particular advantage or disadvantage for boys or girls groups. However, our anecdotal evidence suggests that the groups did behave differently. This behaviour is related to the effects noted in a study of groups working on primary science investigations without a computer (see Scanlon et al., [10]).

Mixed gender working

The effect of gender distributions within groups of science learners has been studied by various researchers. For example, Kempa [11] reports that a critical mass of girls in any one group may be necessary to create an environment which will encourage active participation of girls in science tasks. Where there is only one girl in a group with two or three boys the girl is likely to get left out, and this can mean that as a non participant she benefits less from the interaction than other group members. Whether this gender effect is specific to science is unclear. Bennett and Cass [12] have looked in detail at the effect of group composition in nine groups of eleven and twelve year olds using a computer to a perform a task involving historical sites and settlement patterns. In contrast to the findings of the other researchers we have mentioned, in their groups of two boys and one girl, the girls tended to talk more frequently.

The Shared Alternate Reality Kit project involved adults working in mixed and single gender pairs at a simulation of the "running in the rain" problem (de Angelis, [13]). In these experiments two users are in seperate rooms with a workstation each and communicate through a high fidelity hands free audiolink with a camera monitor device called a videotunnel which enables eye contact. We used the problem of whether it makes more sense to run or walk in the rain without an umbrella. (On the one hand, running means spending less time in the rain, but, on the other hand, as you run into some rain, you might end up wetter than if you had walked). Video protocols were analysed and utterances related to eye contact and simulation events. Utterances were categorised in a variety of ways. One striking finding from this experiment was the important role of eye contact through the videotunnel in establishing successful collaboration (Smith et al., [14]). In the experiment, subjects could be both face to face through the video tunnel and side by side through the interface. Some subjects worked together well and some subjects were at times uncomfortable working through the videotunnel. Male/female pairings seem to find the negotiation of their problem solving more successful than male/male pairings. In the case of male/female couples, the videotunnel achieves a distancing effect but at the same time makes it possible for subjects to negotiate their gaze patterns which allowed subjects to relax with one another. The one male/male pair we observed had problems in communication which got worse. The time spent by this male/male pair on "social interaction" was much less that that spent by three male/female pairs.

An illustration of the degree of comfort felt by the mixed sex groups was their use of humour or banter. One interchange referred to the "rain runner" as Gene Kelly, another to the location of the experiment as Glasgow, Scotland (notorious for wet weather). One pair evolved an extended fantasy of how they approached their role and task division with the male as hunter-gatherer out chasing escaped features of the interface while the female collected harvests of raindrops. One of their summarising conclusions gives a flavour of the interchange:

> What we found out was that thin people got less wet than fat and that by running faster the fat person seemed to get less wet than the thin person correspondingly running faster.
> That was about it, wasn't it?
> *So would you say a thin person should run fast?*
> I wouldn't bother... Do you think a thin person should run in the rain?
> *Yes but not as much as a fat person should lose weight!..*

More protocols collected with a similar set up are needed to check out how these findings apply to other groups and to female/female groups and we are planning further studies.

Conclusions Students who use science simulations in groups make learning gains. Gender effects appear and have to be considered when decisions about the nature of the task, the composition of the group and the degree of conflict within it are made. It may be that some problems posed by mixed gender working can be eased by technology.

Acknowledgements My thanks are due to coworkers on the projects mentioned above and in particular to Sara Hennessy, Tim O'Shea, Josie Taylor and Denise Whitelock.

References

1.   Eraut, M. and Hoyles, C. Groupwork with computers, *Journal of Computer Assisted Learning,* 5, 12-24, 1988
2.   Slavin, R. *Cooperative Learning.* Longman, New York,1983
3.   Morgan, V. Primary Science - gender differences in pupils' responses, *Education 3-13,* 17, 2, 33-37, 1989
4.   Howe, C,. Learning through peer interaction, *Presentation to the British Assocation for the Advancement of Science Meeting,* Southampton, August, 1992
5.   Galton, M. Grouping and groupwork. In Rogers, C. and Kutnik, P. (ed) *The social psychology of the primary school,* London: Routledge, 1990
6.   Smith, R. *Gender and Language in Science Education.* Open University internal document, 1993
7.   Whitelock, D., Taylor, J, O'Shea, T., Scanlon, E.,.Clark, P., O'Malley, C., Collaborative working in physics using a computer simulation, *Paper presented at the ICTE conference,* Boston, March 1993.
8.   Johnson, S. and Murphy, P. Girls and Physics: reflections on APU survey findings, *APU Occasional Paper No 4., D.E.S.,* 1986
9.   Hennessy, S., Twigger, D., Byard, M., Driver, R., Draper, S., Hartley, R., Mohamed, R., O'Malley, C., O'Shea, T., and Scanlon, E. A classroom intervention using a computer-augmented curriculum for mechanics, *International Journal of Science Education,* in press.
10.   Scanlon, E., Murphy, P. , Hodgson, B. and Whitelegg, E. A case study approach to studying collaboration in primary science classrooms, *(see this conference proceedings)*
11.   Kempa, R.and Aminah, A. Learning interactions in group work in science, *International Journal of Science Education,* 13, 3, 341-354, 1991
12.   Bennett, N. and Cass, A. The effects of group composition on group interactive processes, *British Educational Research Journal,* 15 (1) 19-32, 1988
13.   De Angelis,E. Is it really worth running in the rain? *European Journal of Physics,* 8, 201 -202, 1987
14.   Smith, R., O'Shea, T., O'Malley, C., Scanlon, E., and Taylor, J. Preliminary experiments with a distributed, multimedia, problem solving environment, In: J. Bowers and S. Benford (Eds.), *Studies in Computer Supported Collaborative Work: Theory, Practice and Design.* Elsevier Science Publishers, *1991*

Gender differences in communicative style: Possible consequences for the learning process

R.B. Thompson

Department of Psychology, University of Edinburgh, 7 George Square, Edinburgh EH9 8JZ, UK

Abstract

Preschoolers' communication styles were observed in the problem-solving setting, to determine what gender differences, if any, emerged. In a second phase of the study adult subjects were presented with video clips of children matched for ability and asked to make evaluative judgments of ability based on differing communicative behaviour. Results indicate significant gender differences in communicative style; and that these differences do influence the beliefs of adult observers. Results are discussed in terms of social learning and self-fulfilling prophecy.

Introduction

Gender differences in communication, and *Observer Bias,* are two concepts with extensive research histories. Research findings available about gender differences in communication style include speech among girls that is particularly deferential (Haas[1]; Ahlgren[2]) or among boys that is domineering and competitive (Sheldon[3]). In most of these studies, though actual ability is equal, the recurring theme is one of female deficiency in the levels of overt confidence; and these behaviour differences are perceived by adults and peers in everyday interaction. Studies looking at ability *and* behaviour are able to point out the interpretive dilemma caused by communication which does not reflect ability (Jacklin[4]).

One example of children's differing styles of communication is provided by Sheldon's observational study using preschool children, which revealed striking differences in male and female discourse. In sequences of fantasy play involving disputes over a toy, girls interwove their dispute over a desirable toy into the fantasy dialogue (of a domestic nature), thus extending the intact story-line over a longer period of time than the boys. Sheldon concludes that though competition for resources (in this case a toy pickle) is equal between boys and girls, there was a more cooperative and collaborative motivation among the girls.

Close to *cooperativeness* in meaning, but far more in evaluative tone, is *compliance*. This perceived construct was studied by Gold, Crombie and Noble[5] who found that only among girls was *compliance* a factor in teachers' opinions. The more they perceived in an individual child, the lower their opinion of their problem solving ability. Research dealing with adult differences in communicative style finds parallels. Newcombe and Arnkoff[6] (1979) reviewed Lakoff's work on speech styles in connection with their own results in a language study. They concluded (along with Coates[7], Sheldon and Trudgill[8]) that females use more tag questions, (equivocations at the end of a declarative statement, e.g. "It's really cold in here, *isn't it*?") along with more qualifiers such as "*I guess*" or "*maybe*" and more requests rather than direct commands (e.g. "*won't you* close the door?") Newcombe and Arnkoff concluded that tag questions and qualifiers did lessen the perceived assertiveness of speech. Their results indicate that people do believe that females are less assertive, not necessarily because they are female but because of the systematic interpretation of typically female speech styles.

It seems important to revisit the literature concerned with gender differences in confidence levels and achievement motivation, and look at it with a critical eye. In many cases conclusions are drawn that imply the now debunked "female failure trait" or "female fear of success" concept. A review by Lenney[9] helps establish a more plausible picture. Girls, it appears, do seem to be influenced by the social nature of a problem solving situation; however achievement motivation, she claims, is only a function of perceived sex-appropriateness. Girls frequently display communicative behaviour which in a very facile way have been paired with traditional sex role stereotypes. Modesty, for example, has not precluded motivation for success (Lenney); nor has cooperativeness precluded achievement (Maccoby and Jacklin[10], Maccoby[11]) However, as the Gold, Crombie and Noble study shows, this is not how girls' behaviour is usually construed.

While studies on both *communication differences* and *gender bias* are abundant, they range across numerous contexts, and rarely appear together as a discussion about cause and effect. Nor do many examine problem-solving as an important context for a biasing dynamic to occur. Children's thinking, according to Belmont[12] is a "goal-directed strategic activity that, although ultimately internalized, must nevertheless develop and operate within an influential and responsive social context." In terms of the social-interactional nature of the learning setting there are important parallels with Vygotsky's[13] Zone of Proximal Development.

The intent of this study therefore, is to examine the use of some important communication behaviours. These include help-seeking vocalisations, deferential speech. (e.g. hedging statements) and eye-contact. These are elements which feature significantly in the literature concerned with gender differences. This study will use the problem-solving context to determine what gender differences, if any, occur whilst very young children are engaged in a challenging problem. The results will be considered in relation to actual ability. Secondly, these communicative behaviours will be used directly (via video-clips) with adult subjects to study what role any communication differences play in the evaluation of ability.

METHOD: Study I: Children's Communication Styles

Design

Girls' and boys' spontaneous communication in a problem-solving setting was compared. Frequency of behaviours relating to help-seeking was studied, in relation to performance on the problem-solving task.

Subjects

30 Children (14 girls, 16 boys) ranging in age from 2.9 years to 4.8 years, (mean age 3.9) from the University of Edinburgh Psychology Department Nursery, and the Liberton Nursery School, Edinburgh, have so far participated in this ongoing study.

Procedure

In the experimental sessions each child was asked first to do an easy jigsaw puzzle to familiarize them with the test setting (to "warm-up") and to bring them to a base-line level of achievement that would be immediately obvious to the child. Having completed the first puzzle, they began the second puzzle which they had not seen before, depicting a red double-decker bus, of considerably more detail and complexity than the first. They were timed, but without mention of any time limits, or puzzle difficulty, so as not to pre-empt their attitude in any way. Before beginning the second puzzle each child was asked about the content of the puzzle, covering every major aspect of the picture depicted, so that no child had any puzzle solving advantage due to awareness of pictorial arrangement.

These sessions were videotaped, and then analyzed for puzzle solving performance. This was determined to be cumulative on-task time elapsed from the start of the second puzzle to completion. The frequency of certain verbal and nonverbal communication behaviours were recorded. These included help-seeking vocalizations, which were defined as any verbal statement or question which clearly implied a request for help (e.g. "I can't do this"; "Will you help me?"; "Where does this piece go?", etc.); eye contact with the experimenter, and hedging statements (e.g. "This piece goes here, *I think*".) Mann-Whitney U tests were conducted to compare boys' and girls' mean help vocalizations per minute, hedges per minute and eye-contacts per minute. A two-tailed unpaired t-test was conducted on the children's elapsed times for the puzzle, comparing the performance of boys and girls.

RESULTS

In this experiment no significant difference in puzzle solving speed occurred between the girls and boys (p = .7083). The mean male time was 259 seconds, with a SD of 127 and a range from 70 - 531 seconds. The female mean was 287 seconds, with a SD of 154, and a range from 108 - 613 seconds. Nor was there any significant difference in the amount of off-task time that elapsed during the experimental sessions (p=.8619).

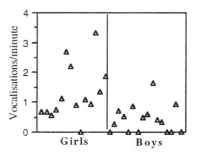

Figure 1: Help-Seeking Vocalisations

A highly significant difference (U = 36, p = .001) emerged between the boys' and girls' "help-seeking" vocalizations (Figure 1). The girls had a far higher frequency of "help-seeking" behaviours (girls' mean = 1.3/minute, SD .91, range 0 - 3.3; vs. boys' mean = .42/minute, SD .46, range 0 - 1.6/min). Girls used more hedging statements, but not to a significant degree (U = 82; p=.23), with greater variability among the girls (mean = .43/min.; SD - 2.7; range, 0 - 1.8/min. vs. male mean = .25/min.; SD - 1.8; range, 0 - .9/min.). No significant differences occurred (U = 83, p=.1981)with the measurement of eye-contact frequency (Girls: mean=.67/min. SD=.73, range 2.07/min.; Boys: mean=.28/min., SD=.42, range 0 - 1.3/min.

DISCUSSION

In terms of the frequency with which children say things which might be interpreted as "help-seeking", the results of this experiment suggest a dramatic gender difference. Girls said such things as "I can't do this", "Where does this piece go?" and "Will you do this one?" significantly more often than the boys. They also used more hedging statements, although this difference did not reach significance. However, they did not differ in their ability to solve the puzzle, both in terms of finishing (all the children did) and in elapsed time.

In the light of their equal ability, the girls' greater amount of "help-seeking" may be part of a naturally fluent and spontaneous repertoire of socially engaging behaviour; whilst for boys, "help-seeking" behaviour may have a more limited, task orientated function.

METHOD: Study II: Adult Evaluative Interpretation

Design
Study II, examined adults' evaluative judgements of ability, based on the spontaneous communicative behaviours of a girl and a boy, individually engaged in a problem-solving task.

Subjects
22 middle-class adults were selected from undergraduates and post-graduates from Edinburgh University and the Edinburgh area. Ages ranged from approximatly 18 - 50 years. The sample included 13 females and 9 males.

Stimulus Material
The materials included video clips of preschool children solving a jigsaw puzzle individually with an adult. These video clips were taken directly from the Child Communication Style study (Bus Puzzle). They were selected for equal ability (using on-task elapsed times), and markedly differing styles of communication, on the basis of frequency of help-seeking vocalisations. There were two clips, one of a highly communicative girl and one of a less communicative boy. The clips shown were full-length and unedited except for the removal of clearly off-task periods of time, therefore what the subjects saw was actual, "real-time" solving of the puzzle.

Two questionnaires were administered, one following each video clip, which asked questions pertaining directly to the performance of the child just seen. The target questions included the following: 1) "Did you think this puzzle was appropriate for the child's age?" 2) Do you feel the child could have used some extra help?" 3) How much confidence did the child seem to have in solving the puzzle?" and 4) How many correctly placed puzzle pieces do you think were through luck?" Subjects responded using a scale of 0 - 5 to indicate for each question, the strength of their belief.

Procedure

Subjects were invited to participate in an assessment of certain puzzle types and were instructed that they would be viewing video clips of children from the nursery. Subjects were told they would be filling in a brief questionnaire about the puzzle for each child. The order in which subjects viewed the boy and girl was counter-balanced.

The ratings of each subject were collated. These data were analyzed using Wilcoxon Signed-Rank tests, to compare each subject's opinion regarding the boy and girl on each question.

RESULTS

Target question 1 resulted in a significant difference (p = .02). Subjects believed that the puzzle was less appropriate for the girl, considering it harder for her to complete. Target question 2 also produced a significant result, (p = .003) indicating that subjects believed the girl would have benefitted from additional help to a greater extent than the boy. Target question 3 revealed a significant difference (p = .03) indicating that subjects believed that the girl had less confidence than the boy. Lastly, target question 4 resulted in a significant difference (p = .01) The Girl was thought to have relied more on luck (vs. skill) than the boy.

DISCUSSION

A trend seems to have emerged in the overall opinions of the subjects in this experiment. In spite of equal ability in solving the puzzle, on the dimension of elapsed time, the subjects considered the girl to have been less confident (Target Question 3), and in three different ways (Target Questions 1, 2, 4) expressed their belief that the girl's performance was not as good as the boy's. On the direct analysis level, the results seem to support the initial hypothesis. It seems likely that the level of help seeking behaviours (e.g. expectant looks to adult, overt requests for help and comments of uncertainty, all of which the girl in this study was selected for) did indeed shape the observer's belief about confidence and performance, resulting in rather disparaging opinions about the girl's ability.

When communicative style does not reflect ability, observer bias seems very likely to occur, as demonstrated in this study. This raises issues for any learning context, for both groups and adult/child dyads. One is the phenomenon of the self-fulfilling prophecy, which is well known and well researched. The meta-analysis of Harris and Rothenthal[14] provides a compelling set of premises and conclusions which speak effectively to the issue of biased teaching in the classroom. Adults' belief about the ability of girls, particularly at the early developmental ages, may not come in the form of overt disapproval, but more often will occur as a subtle shaping of the children's self-concepts.

In future research, further variables and methodological improvements will be added. In the child study, the sample size will be increased, and children's age and puzzle difficulty will be included as variables. In the adult study, experimental sessions using other combinations of gender and communicative behaviour will be conducted, in order to better understand how and when bias may occur.

REFERENCES

1 Haas, A. "Male and Female Spoken Language Differences: Stereotypes and Evidence", *Psychological Bulletin* , 1984, **20**, 83 - 88.

2 Ahlgren, A. "Sex differences in the correlates of cooperative and competetive school attitudes" *Developmental Psychology*, 1983, **19**, 319 - 322.

3 Sheldon, P. "Pickle Fights: "Gendered Talk in Preschool Children", *Discourse Processes* , 1990, **13,** 5 - 32.

4 Jacklin, C. N. "Female and Male: Issues of Gender" *American Psychologist*, 1989, **44,** 127 - 133.

5 Gold, D. Crombie, G. & Noble, S. "Relations Between Teachers' Judgments of Girls' and Boys' Compliance and Intellectual Competence" *Sex-Roles* Abstracts, 1987, **16**, 351 - 358.

6 Newcombe, N. & Arnkoff, D. "Effects of speech style and sex of speaker on person perception", *Journal of Personality and Social Psychology*, 1979, **37**, 1293 - 1303.

7 Coates, J. *Men Women and Language*, Longman, Inc. New York, 1987.

8 Trudgill, P. *Sociolinguistics: An Introduction to Language and Society*, Cambridge University Press, Cambridge, England, 1983.

9 Lenney, E. "Women's Confidence in Achievement Settings", *Psychological Bulletin* , 1977, **84**, 1 - 13.

10 Maccoby, E. & Jacklin, C. *The Psychology of Sex Differences* , Stanford University Press, 1974

11 Maccoby, E. "Gender and relationships: A developmental account", *American Psychologist.*, 1990, **45**, 513 - 520.

12 Belmont, J. "Cognitive strategies and strategic Learning", *American Psychologist* , 1989, **44**, 142 - 148.

13 Vygotsky, L.S. *Mind in Society: The Development of Higher Psychological Processes*, 1978.

14 Harris, M. and Rosenthal, R. "Mediation of interpersonal expectancy effects: 31 meta-analyses" *Psychological Bulletin*, 1985, **97**, 363 - 386.

Using a multimedia cooperative toolkit for distance learning support

S. Tian & D.G. Jenkins
Department of Computing and Information Systems, University of Paisley, High Street, Paisley PA1 2BE, UK

Abstract

The group interactions in tutorials and seminars need distributed groupware support if these are to be used in distance learning. We present the features of a multimedia toolkit as appropriate for the support of such, presenting the procedure, task, action process model of this toolkit and showing how both seminar and tutorial sessions can be supported using this model. The advantages of this toolkit and the future work to be carried out are described. Finally experience with previous applications with similar demands leads us to anticipate evaluation in a distance learning situation once the necessary communications infrastructure is in place.

1. Introduction

Seminars and tutorials encourage interactions among participants, and group work oriented computing systems [2,10] need to be developed which provide the collaborative learning environments required to support these interactions. This paper shows how the Multimedia Toolbox for Cooperative Applications (MMTCA) can be used here, drawing on experience with providing tutorial support to a distance learning course mounted in the Far East, thus going beyond the proposal of [3] in which only a virtual lecture theatre is foreseen. Further, ongoing research into CSCW support of engineering design will provide further insight drawing on the analogy between learning and design as intellectual processes. MMTCA has been developed using desktop conferencing techniques and a brief introduction to these follows:

Basically, there are two strategies for building desktop conferencing systems [4,8]: developing specialised *collaboration-aware* tools or using *existing single-user* tools. The second strategy is used in most desktop conferencing systems as it is easy to make extensions and the tools are already familiar to users. Two approaches adopted in the second strategy are introduced below.

Shared-output (figure 1a): Only one copy of each single-user tool executes; a conference agent (CA) receives input from one site (i.e. the current floor-holder site) and forwards it to the tools; at the same time, the

CA distributes output to all conference sites for display, including the local window system.

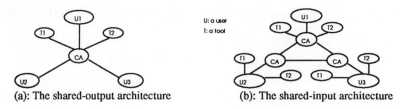

(a): The shared-output architecture   (b): The shared-input architecture

Figure 1: Architecture of the shared-input and shared-output desktop conferencing systems.

Shared-input (figure 1b): A copy of the tool runs at every site in the conference; under a floor-control policy, input is generated at one of the conference sites (i.e. the current floor-holder site) and is distributed to all copies of that tool; the output from each copy only appears locally; because all copies have the same input, their states remain synchronised, generating identical displays at each conference site. The main advantages and disadvantages of these two approaches are discussed in [4,8]. In terms of performance, the shared-input approach is the winner. But sometimes special application contexts may contribute to a decision as to which approach to adopt. Implementing a desktop conferencing system within a local area (e.g. across an Ethernet on a campus), a shared-output approach may be used, since in this case, the advantages of the shared-output approach may outweigh its disadvantages. For MMTCA, one of the design issues is that the developed toolbox is expected to be used in a distributed manner (e.g. under WAN environments); hence, the shared-input approach has been adopted, although it is a challenging selection [8].

2. Requirements for Group Work Systems

Communication, co-operation, and co-ordination are three key areas needed to be supported for group work [7]. Based on these three key areas, basic requirements for groupwork-oriented computing systems are discussed below:

• The system should provide mechanisms to facilitate communications among users. A multimedia approach is preferable.

• The system should be able to build an environment under which users are able to carry out collaborative activities, synchronously or asynchronously.

• The system should provide a mechanism to integrate existing single-user tools, ensuring the appearance and configuration of shared tools being the same on all participants' displays.

• The system should route work to individuals based on relationships between units of work. It should allow users to access and perform the work which they have to do, by providing an "intray-list" which contains work in progress as well as new work to be performed.

- When necessary, the system should allow for human intervention in determining what sequence of actions is required to perform tasks. On the other hand, automatically executing tasks should be accommodated as well, where actions can be decided in advance needing no further human intervention.
- The system should provide both programming and run-time support mechanisms for group leaders to instantiate and start a collaborative process, as well as to view the structure of a process.
- The system should support monitoring of an on-going process. The progress of work in each process generates reports on the status of all activities. This measurement enables a feedback loop whereby an organisation can improve its processes.
- The system should be open, in the sense of being based on industry standards for operating systems, networks, file systems, databases, and window system services, and in the sense that users are able to build their own customised collaborative applications. It should operate in distributed environments.

3. Approach

According to the above requirements, a *Procedure-Task-Action* (*PTA*) model has been designed and implemented for MMTCA. This *PTA* model is "action-driven", since it is through *actions* that actual work is carried out.

Actions are most elementary. Performed by individual users or groups, *actions* are equivalent to program activation (e.g. use word processor to write a letter, use a database program to find a customer's record, use a CAD program to draw a machine part, &c.). Each *action* is a single "unit of work" with clearly defined inputs and outputs.

Tasks introduce order to the *actions* of an individual user or a group of users. *Tasks* can be regarded as mini-programs which specify how a set of *actions* should be carried out by a user or a group responsible. *Procedures* are at the highest level and correspond to a "project" in management terms.

Procedures are provided to introduce order to *tasks* carried out by individual users or groups of users. *Procedures* can, as in the case of *tasks*, be regarded as programs which specify how *tasks* are to be carried out by the individuals or groups responsible. For example, in the context of a *procedure*, the time sequence of *tasks*, their inter-dependencies in terms of *documents* (e.g., *task A* produces *document A1*, which is required input for *task B*, which produces *document B1*), &c. are specified. In the context of a *procedure* we may specify loops of *tasks*, alternative paths, &c.

The *PTA* model forms a comprehensive representation of how people carry out their work in a modern organisation, providing obvious ways to cater for the three key areas of communication, co-operation and co-ordination. It can support collaborative activities in a *synchronous* or *asynchronous* manner. In the case of *asynchronous co-operation* no special provisions have to be made. The *task* is performed by a single user in a manner quite similar to that of normal PC usage. The only difference is that MMTCA will guide the user as to what programs to load and which files to use, according to the *task's* specification. For *synchronous co-operation*, rather than a single user, a group of users carry out the *task*. They all run their individual single-user tools (as specified by the *task*), view the same *documents*, and are aware in real-time of each other's actions.

4. Application Scenarios

Shipping and banking scenarios were set up and fully evaluated in MMTCA [11], showing that the requirements stated above have been satisfied by the project. As indicated above, two distance learning scenarios (the seminar and the tutorial) exist and corresponding procedures have been designed. In each, the supporting distance learning material is considered to have been prepared and distributed with the lecture series being delivered at the remote sites by independent means. However, evaluation awaits establishment of the communications infrastructure required.

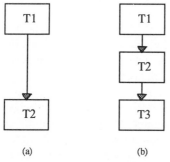

(a)   (b)

Figure 2: Distance Learning Procedures.

Distance Seminar. In this scenario two tasks, T1 and T2 (see figure 2a), occur in sequence. The first, T1, an asynchronous *task*, is used for preparation, and the second, T2, a synchronous *task*, is the seminar process itself. In T1, the speaker of the seminar informs other participants of information about the up-coming seminar. Changes (e.g. using an alternate date, etc.) to the seminar plan can be made if necessary. T2 will be run automatically when T1 is ended (marked as complete). In T2, a presentation is given by the speaker and other participants act as passive receivers (watching the shared workspace and watching the speaker's video image as well as listening). After the presentation, a discussion is held, and finally, T2 is ended by the speaker. The output of the seminar (e.g. discussion records, seminar materials, etc.) is filed at the speaker site and distributed to other sites if necessary.

Distance Tutorial. Figure 2b shows the procedure designed for a distance tutorial scenario. It aims to complement the distance lectures which have been previously held (or may still on-going). T1, an asynchronous task, starts at about the same time as the first lecture starts and is designed for preparation. The tutor informs other participants of relevant information about the tutorial. As in the case of the distance seminar, changes to the tutorial plan can be made if necessary. After T1 is ended, T2, an asynchronous task, starts. During the process of T2, the tutor and his/her students extensively exchange ideas about the on-going lectures. The aim of T2 is to identify points which have not been well understood rather than to solve problems (of course, simple questions could be answered by the tutor at the time). After a period of several lectures, when the tutor thinks the time is appropriate (the final tutorial materials should be formed by then) he/she will end T2, and T3 will be run automatically (a synchronous task). Discussions are carried out throughout the process of T3; the tutor gives explanations, and the participants listen and discuss with the tutor as well as with others about their understanding. Finally T3 is ended by the tutor, and the output (e.g. discussion records, tutorial materials, etc.) of the tutorial is filed at the tutor site, and distributed to other sites if necessary.

5. Differences between MMTCA and Related Work

• For teaching applications, our system has the functionality which can provide a collaborative environment; teaching and learning processes are facilitated by multimedia communication (voice, video and a shared workspace), and can be carried out synchronously and asynchronously. Other systems [2,10] have similar functionality, but they cannot provide our complete range of functionality.
• Many desktop conferencing systems [4,9] cannot support a workflow control mechanism, while our system can.
• Although workflow mechanisms are also supported by some systems [5], our system provides users with a collaborative environment, in which they can select standard single-user tools (theoretically, no limitation to the number of tools selected), while other systems just support one specialised single-user tool (image management or engineering product data management, &c.).
• Although some "office procedure" systems [12] available provide functionality which overlaps with our system (i.e. they can support workflow control, multiple single-user tools, &c.), our system can support synchronous collaborative applications as well as asynchronous ones, whereas those systems can only support asynchronous applications. To support synchronous collaborative applications through the shared-input approach is more difficult [8] than to just support asynchronous ones.
• While both our system and some "office procedure" systems [13,6] have similar graph-based tools to describe sequencing dependencies among tasks in a co-operative process; our system can modify the structure of a process dynamically, while other systems cannot.

6. Future Work

Distributing input events reliably: Errors can occur when data are transmitted across local or wide area networks. TCP/IP stream sockets provide reliable data transmission, and we are currently using datagram sockets with an acknowledge mechanism when sending events. In WAN environments, the probability of getting errors will increase; we will do some investigation into this.

Multicasting messages: Most messages (e.g. input events) transmitted in the MMTCA environment belong to multicast messages (i.e. the server needs to distribute one single message to multiple recipients). At the moment, a point-to-point transmission is used to simulate the multicast feature. When MMTCA is used across a wide area network, a true multicasting mechanism is necessary in order to obtain better performance. We are going to investigate multicast mechanisms in LAN and WAN environments.

Voice and video conferencing: Communication among distributed participants is important. Two point-to-point voice and video conferencing products have been used with MMTCA so far. The effectiveness of such a feature on group collaborations has been recognised. The voice and video conferencing mechanism should be able to accommodate multi-user contexts, in order to cater for a co-operative session with more than two participants. We are currently investigating this.

Multimedia document handling (MDH): The current tool-integration mechanism supports activation of a number of tools (e.g. MSWord, Paintbrush, etc.) for a co-operative activity, therefore users are able to access both text and graphics files. In order to further enhance the system's capability of facilitating collaborative activities, we will investigate advanced MDH techniques (e.g. exploring Windows OLE capability [1]).

Comprehensive management support: A mechanism has been built in MMTCA to monitor executing processes. We will upgrade this mechanism to support recording of progress of work and generating reports on status of all activities, so that with the help of this measurement, the quality of management of teaching could be improved.

Automatic task execution: The current workflow mechanism supports automatic task scheduling and automatic task ending. We are going to upgrade this mechanism to cater for automatic task execution as well.

Mixed co-operation style: MMTCA can support synchronous and asynchronous tasks, which are independent components within the workflow control framework. It is necessary to support a mixed co-operation style - allowing a synchronous task to take place within a period of an on-going asynchronous task. The idea is to allow a user who is working on an asynchronous task to hold a co-operative session with another colleague when necessary, in order to obtain comments on his/her work.

7. Conclusion

We have presented the application of a distributed, decentralised, groupware system, MMTCA, to the support of distance learning via distance seminars and tutorials, to complement the well established one-way presentation of lecture material. The features of MMTCA are seen as appropriate to the support of the management and carrying out of such sessions, and, based on experienced in the completed MMTCA project, we anticipate favourable evaluation of the application of this system to distance learning.

ACKNOWLEDGEMENTS

MMTCA is an ESPRIT-funded project. Seven organisations are involved in the research and development work, - Intrasoft SA (Greece), Novosoft SA (Spain), Paisley University (UK), Robotiker SA (Spain), Intracom SA (Greece), BDC (a Spanish bank) and ISL (a German shipping company). The authors would like to thank John G Gammack, Sandy Kydd, Stuart McColl, Paul E Oldfield, Margaret Struthers, and their research colleagues for their valuable review and support work during the writing of this paper.

REFERENCES

1. Baer, J. and Bauder, I. Windows 3.1 INTERN, Abacus, 1992, ISBN 1-55755-159-6.
2. Beckwith, R. C. LIVE-NET - From video to multi-media, IEE Colloquium, 7 Feb., 1991, Digest No.032, 151/33/08, AVS, pp 1/1-1/2.
3. Cochrane, P. Education, technology and change - a personal view, Computing & Control Engineering Journal, April 1994, 52-54.
4. Crowley, T., Milazzo, P., Baker, E., Forsdick, H. and Tomlinson, R. MMConf: An Infrastructure for Building Shared Multimedia Applications, *CSCW* 90 Proceedings, 1990, 329-342.
5. Dwight, B.D. Software That Makes Your Work Flow, DATAMATION, April 1991, 75-78.
6. Ellis, C.A. and Bernal, M. Officetalk-D: An Experimental Office Information System, Proceedings ACM-SIGOA Conference on Office Information Systems, June 1982, 131-140.
7. Ellis, C.A., Gibbs, S.J. and Rein, G.L. Groupware: some issues and experiences, Communications of The ACM, Jan. 1991, Vol. 34, No. 1, 39-58.
8. Lauwers, J.C., Joseph, T.A., Lantz, K.A., and Romanow, A.L. Replicated Architectures for Shared Window Systems: Critique, 1990, ACM 089791-358 2/90/0004/0249, 249-260.
9. Lantz, K.A. An Experiment in Integrated Multimedia Conferencing, Proc. *CSCW*, Dec.1986, 533-552.
10. McConnell, D. Case Study: The educational use of computer conferencing, Educational and Training Technology International, Vol.27, No.2, May 1990, pp 190-208.
11. MMTCA Documentation, Toolbox Evaluation, University of Paisley, Aug.1993.
12. Sarin, S.K., Abbott, K.R. and McCarthy, D.R. A Process Model and System for Supporting Collaborative Work, ACM 0-89791-456-2/91/0010/0213, 1991, 213-224.
13. Zisman, M.D. Representation, Specification, and Automation of Office Procedures, PhD dissertation, Wharton School, Univ. Pennsylvania, 1977.

Computer-directed group activity and the development of children's hypothesis testing skills

A.K. Tolmie & C.J. Howe

Centre for Research into Interactive Learning, Department of Psychology, University of Strathclyde, 40 George Street, Glasgow G1 1QE, UK

Abstract

Two studies were conducted to examine whether on-task guidance of group activity was an effective means of promoting hypothesis testing skills. Groups of pupils agreed which factors they thought affected outcome in a given domain and then carried out joint tests of their hypotheses. Progress was directed by a computer, which detailed objectives and requested information on decisions. Inappropriate or inaccurate decisions led to prompts for these to be reconsidered. Individual pre- to post-test gains in hypothesis testing skills were examined in relation to measures of on-task dialogue and other activity, and compared to values for groups who worked with a version of the software that provided no prompts. In both studies, prompting produced substantial improvements in on-task performance. However, the benefits of this for individual progress were restricted by negative influences on group dialogue, underlining the need for careful coordination of different factors affecting learning.

1 Introduction

Contemporary science education recognises conceptual grasp as a major obstacle to pupils' progress. Children's pre-existing ideas about scientific phenomena offer stiff resistance to new learning (Driver & Easley [1]), and more accurate concepts cannot simply be imparted, but have to be built onto the understanding that is there already. In practice, this means pupils testing out their ideas; success depends on them making sense of the results of this process.

Yet even informal hypothesis testing is a complex affair, and our earlier research (Howe, Tolmie & Sofroniou [2]) shows that children have considerable difficulties in generating and interpreting evidence. Pupils aged between 9 and 14 were individually interviewed to identify whether or not they thought certain factors affected outcome in each of four domains. After their beliefs had been ascertained, pupils were asked to plan, carry out, and interpret tests on selected factors to demonstrate whether or not they were correct. Irrespective of domain, virtually all pupils were capable of describing what occurred on a test. However, few thought that testing was simply about varying the factor they had been asked to explore, either when making plans or manipulating the equipment. Moreover, having manipulated other factors, pupils further betrayed their lack of understanding by explaining their predictions or conclusions as if this had not been the case. Not surprisingly, they frequently carried out many more tests than necessary to form a proper conclusion.

This suggests that planning and carrying out valid tests (i.e. manipulations of the factor under consideration with all others held constant) constitutes a major problem for pupils of all ages. The further implication, though, is that if pupils could be brought to recognise this one requirement of hypothesis testing, substantial improvements in all other aspects of performance would follow, although attaining the highest levels might require further insight.

Achieving progress would therefore seem to lie in getting pupils to carry out valid tests first, and then building up understanding around this. The point is important because whilst our previous work (e.g. Howe, Tolmie & Rodgers [3]; Tolmie, Howe, Mackenzie & Greer [4]) shows that dialogue between peers with conflicting views leads to *conceptual* change, research by Wood [5] suggests that "scaffolding" or contingent support (the provision of guidance dependent upon current performance of an activity) is more effective for promoting *procedural* skills. The implication is that intervention in the form of contingent support would be more likely to result in advances in hypothesis testing skills than the kind of conflict task used in our earlier research, although dialogue might still serve a useful back-up role in extending pupils' grasp of those skills.

However, providing contingent support using human tutors would be labour intensive and potentially less systematic than desirable. Our solution was to use a computer application, implemented in HyperCard, to direct the progress of groups of pupils on hypothesis testing tasks employing physical materials. In its "supported" version, this software provided prompts intended to correct misplaced activity and promote discussion about the conceptual bases for these corrections. The software was evaluated with 9 to 14 year olds in two domains, water pressure and shadows, by comparing its effectiveness with that of an "unsupported" version which did not provide contingent prompts.

2 The Pressure Study

Both the supported and unsupported software were used alongside equipment which allowed observation of the effects of five factors on the distance travelled by a jet of water. Each factor had three levels, one of which was designated the "standard". After seeing the equipment in operation at the standard setting on all factors, groups of pupils were directed by the computer through a sequence of hypothesis testing activity in which they: 1) agreed which factors affected outcome; 2) selected a factor for testing; 3) planned what needed to be changed during testing; 4) decided on a manipulation of the equipment; 5) predicted the outcome of that manipulation; 6) observed and recorded the outcome; 7) compared the outcome to previous tests; 8) recorded an interim conclusion about whether the factor affected outcome; 9) decided whether to carry out any more tests; and 10) drew an overall conclusion about the factor. Groups could carry out as many test cycles (i.e. stages 4 to 8) as they wanted. Once they had finished, the sequence from stage 2 was repeated for a second factor.

At each stage, the computer asked groups to register their decisions on-screen. The unsupported software simply saved this information to a seperate file. In the supported version, however, any departure from the requirements of valid testing (stages 3 & 4), inconsistency of report (stages 5 to 7), or inaccurate conclusion (stages 8 & 10) resulted in prompts for reconsideration being issued. Two levels of prompt were used. The first indicated that there was a problem, and asked the group to discuss their decision further. If the response was still inappropriate, a second prompt detailed the precise nature of the problem and again requested further discussion. If an error was repeated a third time, it was accepted and activity proceeded to the next stage.

Prior to taking part in the group sessions, pupils were individually pre-tested using the interview format of Howe et al. [2] outlined earlier. A total of 94 pupils aged between 9 and 14 were pre-tested in this way, and then assigned at random to 25 small groups (n = 3 to 5), each drawn from within a single school class. Of these groups, 13 were allocated to work on the supported software and 12 on the unsupported. Approximately three weeks after the group sessions, which were videotaped in their entirety, all pupils (bar 5 who were then unavailable) were post-tested using the same procedure as the pre-test.

Pre- and post-test responses yielded eight measures. Pupils' **plans** for the tests needed to establish whether their idea was correct, **manipulations** of equipment, **predictions** of outcome, descriptions of **observations**, **comparisons** between observations, **interim conclusions** after each test, and **overall conclusions** drawn at the end of testing, were each scored on scale from 1 to 4 according to their approximation to an ideal performance. In addition, a note was made of the number of test **cycles** carried out in examining each factor. Individual change on each measure was calculated by subtraction.

Group activity was indexed by eight variables recovered from software records: 1) the time spent on task; 2) the number of moves made (i.e. on-screen responses); 3) the number of test cycles; 4) the number of valid tests; 5) the number of accurate reports of outcome; 6) the number of appropriate conclusions drawn about factors; 7) the time spent planning tests; 8) the number of moves made whilst planning tests. For the supported groups, a record was also kept of the number of level 1 and level 2 prompts received. The videotapes of the group sessions were used to count the incidence of fourteen categories of dialogue at each stage of the hypothesis testing sequence. These included requests for a contribution from other group members; suggested manipulations, predictions, observations or conclusions; and statements relating activity to previous test cycles, or to general principles of hypothesis testing. Reliabilities for pre- and post-test scores, and for dialogue frequencies were ascertained via independent coding of 20% of the data. Overall agreement was 92% and 86% respectively.

Table 1: Mean change on eight aspects of hypothesis testing for Supported and Unsupported conditions (Pressure).

	Supported	*Unsupported*
Plans	+ 0.09	+ 0.07
Manipulations	+ 0.01	+ 0.01
Predictions	+ 0.18	+ 0.06
Observations	+ 0.06	+ 0.06
Comparisons	+ 0.55	+ 0.32
Conclusions (I)	+ 0.33	+ 0.18
Conclusions (O)	+ 0.72	+ 0.41
Test cycles	- 0.63	- 0.60

Analysis of the data showed significant pre-to post-test progress in comparisons, interim conclusions and overall conclusions, along with an encouraging decline in the number of cycles. There was, however, no significant difference between the conditions in change on any variable (see Table 1). Despite this, the conditions did differ in performance on-task: those who worked on the supported software conducted nearly ten times as many valid tests (32 in total as against 3 in the unsupported condition), and drew 50% more appropriate conclusions. They also made more moves, especially whilst planning their tests.

In a sense, then, the supported software proved successful, and yet despite our assumptions, carrying out valid tests had little impact on learning: the only identifiable benefit was a correlated reduction in test cycles at post-test, and this was unrelated to change on other variables. Closer examination of how conducting valid tests related to other group activity in the supported condition suggested why learning was not better. Whilst making more moves when planning tests might seem to be indicative of extra care, this was not the case, since these moves were *negatively* associated with the number of valid tests, and positively associated with the number of prompts issued at both levels. In addition, the total amount of dialogue in half of the categories was positively associated with level 1 or level 2 prompts (or both), and also with the number of moves. In general, then, receiving prompts led to more dialogue and to more moves being made, with less chance of a valid test emerging. Amount of dialogue was associated with an *increase* in cycles at post-test.

The picture seems to be one of prompting producing confusion, except that *something* in the supported condition must have promoted valid tests. Since there was no positive effect of dialogue, it seems it can only have been the software itself. The implication is that prompting helps, but beyond a certain point it leads to a profusion of activity that undermines learning. These negative effects related to prompting in general, though, not just that which occurred during the setting up of tests. Thus some types of prompting could perhaps be removed without reducing the relative incidence of valid tests. This might in turn assist learning.

3 The Shadows Study

Taking this message to heart, the software for the second study focused more closely on aiding the production and interpretation of valid tests, this time during investigation of the factors affecting the size of a shadow projected onto a screen. Prompts were only provided for manipulations, predictions, observations and overall conclusions. There was no initial stage of planning the factors that ought to be manipulated, nor of explicit comparison between observations. In other respects the procedure was equivalent to the pressure study. Individual pre-tests were administered to 112 pupils aged 9 to 14. These pupils were then assigned to foursomes. Of the 28 resulting groups, half worked on the supported software and half on the unsupported. Some five to six weeks later the 107 pupils then available were individually post-tested. The system used for scoring pre- and post-test responses and for coding group dialogue was as before, and yielded comparable rates for inter-rater agreement of 85% and 93% respectively.

On this occasion there was significant pre- to post-test advance in all aspects of hypothesis testing, plus a significant decrease in the number of cycles, but once again, except for comparisons, both conditions had an equal impact on change (see Table 2). However, those in the supported condition still made more valid tests on-task (39, against 20 in the unsupported condition), and drew 50% more appropriate conclusions. There was now no difference between conditions in the number of moves made by groups, and the number of valid tests was the main influence on learning in the supported condition, being positively correlated with change on all variables except observations and comparisons.

Table 2: Mean change on eight aspects of hypothesis testing for Supported and Unsupported conditions (Shadows).

	Supported	*Unsupported*
Plans	+ 0.74	+ 0.89
Manipulations	+ 0.52	+ 0.78
Predictions	+ 0.79	+ 0.63
Observations	+ 0.33	+ 0.42
Comparisons	+ 0.41	+ 0.08
Conclusions (I)	+ 0.37	+ 0.43
Conclusions (O)	+ 0.45	+ 0.38
Test cycles	- 0.98	- 0.69

There were improvements in the supported software's effectiveness, then, but it still failed to produce greater learning than the unsupported. Once more, examination of influences on the incidence of valid testing within the supported condition proved illuminating. Overall, the number of test cycles conducted whilst groups investigated their *second* factor was the major positive influence. Interestingly, amongst 9 to 10 year olds level 1 prompts were positively related to these second factor cycles, whilst level 2 prompts had a negative effect. Amongst 11 to 12 year olds prompting at both levels had a negative effect. For 13 to 14 year olds the number of *first* factor cycles was a negative influence, with these first factor cycles strongly associated with level 1 and level 2 prompts.

What seemed to be involved then was a graded negative effect of prompting. For younger pupils, learning took place if groups picked up how to conduct valid tests whilst examining the first factor, and then practised this, without much prompting, during tests for the second factor (though for 9 to 10 year olds some amount of reminding was still helpful). For the oldest pupils, the impact on learning was negative unless they avoided prompts during the first factor tests by picking up what was required more or less straight away. That they could to some extent work this out for themselves was evident from the fact that this age group produced most of the valid tests conducted in the unsupported condition. Once again, dialogue had negative effects on learning. In particular, level 2 prompts for manipulations were associated with increased requests for others to suggest the way forward (perhaps implying a kind of abdication), something that reduced the likelihood of the all-important valid tests being carried out.

What promoted change in the unsupported condition is harder to see, since there was no detectable influence, positive or negative, from either task activity or dialogue. This might suggest simple exposure as a source of progress, but there is little evidence of a relationship between change and time on-task to back this up. Interestingly, numbers of second factor cycles and valid tests were related here too, but in this condition valid tests did not result in learning. This seems a clear indication that *systematic* progress required both practice and some external confirmation that groups were on the right track.

4 Conclusions

The studies were informative in many respects, then, confirming that contingent support can promote valid tests, and that this in turn can result in wider learning. At the same time, even scaled down prompting had negative effects, indicating the need for it to be applied still more sensitively, especially with older children.

The difficulties of external direction signalled by this are consistent with the results of one of our earlier studies (Tolmie et al. [4]), where it was found that requiring children to summarise their observations by choosing between rules provided for them was entirely detrimental.

In the present circumstances, the key to these negative effects is the fact that the software was more successful in promoting activity than dialogue which aided understanding of that activity: groups did better if they said less, followed instructions on tests for the first factor, and then practised what they had picked up on the second. What would seem to be better would be to provide early prompts, perhaps solely on the preparation of valid tests, and then to withdraw these unless actively requested, in order to give groups an opportunity to reflect; or alternatively to change the form of later prompts entirely so that dialogue itself becomes the focus.

This has important implications about methods for promoting the acquisition of skills. Whilst contingent support does seem to be capable of producing improvements in pupil performance of relatively complex sequences of activity, it also (at least in the form it took here) tended to provoke dialogue which was antagonistic to both performance and learning. Since we have consistently found positive effects of dialogue on learning across seven previous studies, this came as something of a surprise. There are various possibilities as to why prompting might have had this effect, including the incidence with which it occurred and its perhaps over-directive wording. Clarification awaits further work, but for us identifying techniques of marrying contingent support to the instigation of productive dialogue is sufficiently important to render this a major research priority. We believe that the present work provides at least some clues as to how this might be achieved.

Acknowledgements
This research was supported by Economic and Social Research Council Grant No. R000233481 to Christine Howe and Andrew Tolmie. The assistance provided by the ESRC, by the schools involved in the research, and by Nick Sofroniou, Claire Stevens and Stuart Ross, is gratefully acknowledged.

References
1. Driver, R. & Easley, J. Pupils and paradigms: a review of literature related to concept development in adolescent science students, *Studies in Science Education*, 1978, **5**, 61-84.
2. Howe, C.J., Tolmie A., and Sofroniou, N. Hypothesis testing in nine- to fourteen-year-old children. BPS Developmental Section Annual Conference, Birmingham, UK, 1993.
3. Howe, C.J., Tolmie, A., and Rodgers, C. The acquisition of conceptual knowledge in science by primary school children: group interaction and the understanding of motion down an incline, *British Journal of Developmental Psychology*, 1992, **10**, 113-130.
4. Tolmie, A., Howe, C.J., Mackenzie, M. and Greer, K. Task design as an influence on dialogue and learning: primary school group work with object flotation, *Social Development*, 1993, **2**, 183-201.
5. Wood, D. Aspects of teaching and learning, *Children of social worlds: development in a social context*, eds M. Richards and P. Light, Polity, Cambridge, 1986.

The evaluation of a computer based case-study across two cultures; The UK and Holland

M.J. Wrennall[a] & R. Slotman[b]

[a] *Department of Psychology, Glasgow Caledonian University, Cowcaddens Road, Glasgow G4 0BA, UK*

[b] *CETIS, Hogeschool, Utrecht, The Netherlands*

1 Introduction

The need for new forms of course delivery in Higher Education has been highlighted by a report from the Committee of Scottish University Principals on Teaching and Learning (1992). Increasing demands on staff time, rising student numbers and the need for cost effectiveness is placing a strain on traditional course structures; this cannot be alleviated by the simple practice of increasing class sizes. In this context, a computerised case-study has been developed for teaching Industrial/Organisational (I/O) Psychology on Business degree courses, the purpose of which is to replace a labour intensive conventional small group seminar system with more student directed learning, where the individual controls the interaction and learning process and which at the same time enhances the teaching of Psychology on these degrees. Colleagues in Holland indicated that the case study, as well as being a vehicle for learning about psychological aspects of organisational problem solving, would also be of great use to students learning business English .

2 Characteristics and problems of case studies

The use of case studies and simulations is well established, but the distinction between the two may not be clear cut. Armitage (1993) sees simulations as integrating tools, bringing together theory learned over several courses and providing an opportunity for experimentation and review. Simulations can provide the student with opportunity to develop communication skills; experience team decision making; conflict resolution and group development. When computer based, they expose students to information technology. Vilsteren (1993) identifies the main features of case studies as: being based in a real life event; data are given about the real life events; there is a question, problem/assignment for the student to analyse within the data or find a solution to the problem; there are several possible solutions to the problem or several possible answers to the question; the case handles a specific domain of knowledge; the case is used in an educational setting to reach certain learning objectives.

Most case studies, because of presentational difficulties, are relatively short abstractions and give little indication of the complexities and actualities of the organisational context within which they are based. There is often little space in which to develop the characters, personalities, issues, problems, organisational structure, politics and the history of the organisation in which the case is set. In short the student does not get a 'feel' for the totality of the organisation for which diagnoses and solutions to problems are being generated. Some business simulations and games do increase the level of complexity but they often induce high levels of competitiveness and group decision making which may alter the pedagogical rationale for using cases (e.g. Anderson & Lawton, 1991; Wolfe, 1987).The need for new types of business games and simulations, which express not only the complexity but also strong interactions between elements and delays between actions and their effects, has been emphasised by Machuca (1992). Similarly, Krut and Bulgen (1990) have argued that "management behaviour is not about 'rights' and 'wrongs' [but] is about weighing complex variables, making responsible decisions and living with the consequences". Simulations and case studies need to offer more substantial and lifelike environments in which a wider range of skills are practised.

3 The computer based case study

In the light of the above discussion, our computer based case study approach represents a method of introducing and exposing students to the application of psychological theory and principles to a (simulated) real-life business situation. The use of the 'electronic delivery' provides students with the degree of complexity which is required to make case studies meaningful learning experiences and at the same time moves towards a more student centred learning approach (e.g. Jacobs, 1992; Muns and Slotman, 1992); it also requires the use of a wide range of skills and abilities (Linstead, 1990). Use of a computer format means that the case study can be updated and modified as required.

The case study requires the user to adopt the simulated role of an I/O Psychologist tasked with solving a number of organisational problems. Using Hypercard stacks, the user can move through an organisation, consulting items such as personnel records; memoranda; minutes of meetings; reports and consider job satisfaction and attitudinal data. The student can also 'observe interviews' carried out by a consultant. By this process various organisational problems can be identified relating to psychological issues in individual and group behaviour, motivation and leadership, job satisfaction, organisational change, the implementation of new technology, stress etc. As currently used, the student is required to produce a consultant's report to the management of the company, identifying the problems, highlighting the likely causes and offering recommendations, but other problems and issues can also be raised. Contact time with computer delivered case study is between 3 and 5 hours and the report forms part of the course work assessment. A major advantage of the case study is that it can be used to satisfy a variety of educational objectives.

4 Problems of evaluation

A major criticism of simulations and case studies is the general lack of evidence as to the utility of such approaches. Klein and Fleck (1990), reviewing 30 years of simulation, pointed out the crucial need for evaluation and the possible methods and problems of carrying out these evaluations. Miller and Leroux-Demers (1992), reviewing evaluation studies of management training simulation, indicated that issues of validity can be difficult to address in an educational context since a whole variety of 'validities' can be considered.

Content validity relates to the extent to which the material of the case study reflects the real world. **Internal validity** relates to the extent to which the procedure meets the aims of the training course within which it is operated (i.e.

whether the performance of students is improved by the activity in comparison with alternative activities). **External validity** relates to the extent to which the experience gained as a result of the procedure enhance the performance of students in later working situations. These validity problems can be tied into the more general question of 'does educational technology work?' Wrennall *et al* (1992) and Kearsley (1993) have indicated that there are a number of methodologies which can be used to answer this question: **Comparison studies**: Two methods of delivery of *the same material* can be compared to test the effectiveness of the delivery method; **Cost effectiveness studies**: Can the same material and learning be delivered cheaper?; **Feasibility:** Is it feasible to deliver education or training using a given method?; **Learning improvement studies**: Does the delivery method facilitate more sophisticated forms of learning such as critical thinking and problem solving? A further complication arises when educational or training material is transferred from one culture to another. Most textbooks in I/O Psychology are produced in America using American terminology and materials and certainly UK students often object to this. Mackenzie (1993) has indicated some of the difficulties in moving training across cultures and the many problems that this can generate particularly the use of technical terms and analogies.

5 The cross-national evaluation study

Some of these issues were addressed in an evaluation of the case study carried out in two countries; Scotland and Holland during 1994. 90 Scottish and 33 Dutch students on a variety of full time and part time Business Studies courses used the electronic case study as part of their studies. The Scottish students were studying I/O Psychology as part of their business courses and the Dutch students were studying Managerial problem solving in an international context. As part of this course the Dutch students were learning English.

Both groups of students completed a biographical questionnaire, an attitude to computers questionnaire (Todman & File, 1990) and rated the amount and type of experience they had with computers. They then worked on the electronic case study. The Scottish students worked individually and produced a written report on the case study for assessment by teaching staff. The Dutch students worked in small groups and produced an oral report presented in English in front of teaching staff for assessment.

After completing the work involved, all participants filled in questionnaires on what the benefits of the case study were to them and what they had got out of the case study method. (The questionnaires have been used in previous evaluation studies of case studies and management simulation e.g. Miles, Biggs & Schubert, 1986). In addition, open ended comments on the case study both positive and negative were obtained as were statements as to how participants felt the case-study could be improved. Finally they rated their overall feeling about the case-study as a learning experience on a satisfaction scale.

6 Results

Biographical characteristics.
The Scottish and Dutch students did not differ in terms of their mean age (23.4 years, and 24.7 years) or amount of work experience, but did differ in terms of gender distribution, Scottish, 73% female, Dutch, 12% female. They also differed in term of claimed computing experience. All students had some computing experience, but of Scottish students, 45% claimed they had a small

amount of experience, while 55% claimed a fair or good amount of experience. In the Dutch group, 18% claimed a small amount of experience while 82% claimed a fair or good amount of experience. This probably reflects the stage of the course being undertaken since a large number of the Scottish sample were in the first year of their courses, while the Dutch were at higher levels.

Feelings towards the case study.
The main differences between the two groups were in terms of their feelings towards the case study as a learning experience. This was measured using a Hoppock type satisfaction scale.

Table 1. Feelings towards the case study as a learning experience for Scottish and Dutch students

Feeling response	Scottish	Dutch
I hated it	2%	0%
I disliked it	12%	0%
I didn't like it	18%	0%
I was indifferent to it	14%	9%
I liked it	38%	55%
I was enthusiastic about it	10%	27%
I loved it	3%	3%
	n=90	n=33

Chi-squared, (DF7) = 23.29, p<0.002

Dutch students, on the whole, rated the learning experience more positively than the Scottish students. Administrative difficulties which affected some of the Scottish students may have influenced responses to this question although some students, as can be seen from the open ended responses, did actively dislike the case study.

Open ended responses.
Open ended responses to what the participants liked about the cases study; what they disliked; what they felt the had learned from the case study and how it could be improved for future users were obtained. Combining the responses for both groups, the following trends emerged; (Numbers given are number of item responses from total responses given in that area)
Liked: It was fun/interesting/different (47/145); shows how organisations work/reflects real life/gave experience; (34/145); problem solving/practical application, (19/145); self teaching or self paced working (13/145); applies theories/integrates lecture material (9/145); using computers (9/145); nothing (8/145); others (7/145).
    Students saw it as a different approach and that it could be related to real life experiences. It allowed a degree of self paced learning and provided some integration of lecture materials. Some students indicated their animosity to the package.
Disliked: Time consuming (35/162); too much information/too complex/too long, (31/162); no note taking/printing/WP facilities (20/162); computer unavailability, (16/162); interface problems/screen size (15/162); lack of integration with seminars and lectures (13/162); not stimulating/boring/not enjoyable/nothing (8/162); English language (2/162); other (13/162).
    Major dislikes revolve around complexity and time required to collect information. This is a potential problem since one of the major aims of the case

study is to provide complexity but it could be a functional problem for first year students with little knowledge of business. Interface problems can be alleviated as can the integration of lectures and seminars. Two students wanted the package in the Dutch language!

Learned from Case study: Problem solving in organisations/ reality of organisations/gathering information in organisations (55/123); relating lecture material and theory (31/123); how to apply psychology in work settings (14/123); use of computers (6/123); other (10/123).

The case study would appear to be fulfilling some of the educational objectives in that it gives the student experience of 'reality' and problem solving and allows them to apply lecture materials and theories learned in the abstract. Some students liked the way of presentation using computers.

Improvements suggested: Better interface/add sound/colour/note taker, allow downloading. etc.(39/132); give less information/make less complex (18/132); more preparation/help with report writing/tutor discussion (26/132); allow more time (15/132); use paper version (14/132); use the Dutch language (2/132); other (20/132).

The interface and additions are to be expected. The package was written to run on a Mac Plus since these were readily available to the Scottish students; many students now expect a higher level of sophistication in computing. Making less complex again appears, but more preparation and assistance is seen as an issue. This can obviously be dealt with as an administrative aspect of implementing the case study. Allowing downloading was mentioned by a number of students and many wanted to print out all the material. This was deliberately restricted in the design since an important pedagogical aspect and task was to develop skills in reading information and abstracting the important points from it. Students found this very difficult and is further exemplified in the 'time consuming/long/complex' responses given.

Differences between Scottish and Dutch students.

Students completed questionnaires on 'the benefits of the case study to them' (19 items) and on the 'general utility of the case study method' (8 items). There were surprisingly, few significant differences between the two groups given the different objectives in using the case study. Scottish students rated a question "has participating in the case study allowed you to gain new knowledge about how a business operates?" in a more positive way than the Dutch students, but this probably reflects the level of work experience, more of the Dutch students having worked full time.

Dutch students rated the question "has participating in the case study increased your effectiveness as a participant in group problem solving?" more positively than Scottish students. This indicates the question has face validity since the Dutch worked in groups whereas the Scots worked individually.

Case study method: The main differences between the two groups concerned how students saw the integrating effect of the case study. Scottish students thought it was of more value than the Dutch students in "...helping understand better the basic principles of the course";"....adding a lot of realism to the course". The Dutch students saw the case study as "...bringing together material learned on several other course" The Dutch students also rated the case study more positively as "... being liked by most of the students", and being "...worth the time it took to do it". The differences probably reflect the amount of experience of the students; their maturity and the stage of their educational careers.

7 Conclusion

The case study does seem to be meeting its stated objectives in both cultures of providing new forms of learning which are student centred, which allow the student to apply theoretical concepts to 'real' situations and which tap a range and variety of skills such as critical thinking and problem solving not normally encountered in traditional lectures and seminars. There are differences between how students in each culture respond to the method, but these are relatively small and probably reflect teaching and stages of learning rather than vast cultural differences. Improvements can be made to the package, but students are responding positively towards it. A further benefit of the case study is a saving in staff time. Students can work in time normally allocated to seminars, and do not need to be supervised. In one set of courses this has saved 75 staff contact hours. Further evaluation is required and this will be carried out in the near future.

References

Anderson, P. H., & Lawton, L. (1991). Case study versus a business simulation exercise: Student perceptions of acquired skills. *Simulation/Games for learning*, 21(3). 250-261.

Armitage S. (1993). Guidelines for enhancing learning opportunities in computer-based management simulations. In Percival F., Lodge S., & Saunders D. (Eds.), *Simulation and gaming yearbook, 1993* (pp. 14-26). London: Kogan Page.

Jacobs, G. (1992). Hypermedia and discovery based learning: A historical perspective. *British Journal of Educational Technology.*, 23(2), 113-121.

Kearsley, G. (1993). Educational technology: does it work? *Ed-Tech Review*, Spring/Summer, 34-36.

Klein, R. D., & Fleck, R. A. (1990). International business simulation/ gaming: an assessment and review. *Simulation and games*, 21(2), 147-165.

Krut, R., & Bulgen, M. (1990). Changing manager's behaviour through computer simulation. *Personnel Management*. (May), 61-63.

Linstead, S. (1990). Computer-based systems in management education and Development. *Management education and development*, 21(1), 61-65.

Machuca, J. A. D. (1992). The need for a new generation of business games for management education. *Simulation/Games for Learning*, 22(1), 40-47.

Mackenzie, D. (1993). Multilingual CBT. In Maurer H. (Ed.), *Proceedings of ED-MEDIA 93*, Charlottville, VA: AACE.(318-323)

Miles, W., Biggs W., & Schubert J., (1986) Student perceptions of skill acquisition through cases and a general management simulation. *Simulation/Games for Learning*, 17(1), 7-24.

Miller, R., & Leroux-Demers, T. (1992). Business simulations: Validity and effectiveness. *Simulation/Games for Learning,* 22(4), 261-285.

Muns, G., & Slotman, R. (1992). Organizing the use of CBT at home - An organizational approach to educational technology. In Fricker J. (Eds.), *Proceedings ETTE 1992 - Improving Business Performance Through Training Technology* Amsterdam: ETTE.

Todman, J., & File, P., (1990) A scale for children's attitudes to computers. *School Psychology International*. 11, 71-75.

Vilsteren, V. (1993). *Case-methodology for distance education*. Report of the Dutch Open University, Heerlen, Holland.

Wolfe, J., & Jackson, R. (1989). An investigation of the needs for algorithmic validity. *Simulation and Games*, 20, 275.

Wrennall, M. J., Britten, R. A., & Daffurn, R. (1992) Learning and Hypermedia: Hype or hope? The Scottish Communication Association Annual Conference, Stirling.

SECTION C:

Groupwork in Adult and Higher Education

The effects of peer evaluation on the behaviour of undergraduate students working in tutorless groups

D. Abson

Division of Marketing, Newcastle Business School, The University of Northumbria at Newcastle, Newcastle upon Tyne NE1 8ST, UK

Abstract

There appears to be no substantial evidence that group work is necessarily an efficacious learning strategy. Research is starting to indicate that there may be much dysfunctional behaviour in student groups. One mechanism both to avoid "free riders" in a group and to provide a basis for grading individual students is peer evaluation. This paper suggests this, in itself, can be abused by students and have undesirable effects on individuals in the group.

1 Introduction

Group work here is defined as "...two or more individuals in face to face interaction, each aware of his or her membership in the group, each aware of the others who belong to the group, and each aware of their positive interdependence as they strive to achieve mutual goals." Johnson and Johnson [1].

Much is claimed for its power in helping cognitive gain, stimulating deeper, more critical evaluation of material, changing attitudes and increasing the students tolerance of others. See Jaques [2], Bligh [3], Rau and Heyl [4], Johnson and Johnson [5], Lambiotte, Dansereau, O'Donnell, Young, Scaggs and Hall [6]. However none of these presents any substantial evidence that the use of groups is always and inevitably beneficial to the student. Topping [7] in a substantial review of literature reports a dearth of evidence.

As the evidence on group work builds, it becomes apparent that it has its critics. It is suggested there may be ethical objections, i.e. that groups are an unacceptable form of social control. Others feel certain types of students may be disadvantaged. There are concerns for disproportionate effort from some students, the ineffectiveness of peer tuition, and disproportionate learning experiences. See Quicke [8], Miall [9], Kerr and Bruun [10] and Sheingold, Hawkin and Char [11]. Perhaps the most serious fear is that the process, in itself, might socially damage some students. See Campbell and Ryder [12] and Salomon and Globerson [13].

In my teaching of Marketing Research, I use tutorless group work extensively. The self selected groups are involved in a project which involves them in applying Marketing Research methods to a problem of their own choosing. The groups work together on their own for approximately 3 months with weekly contact with myself to check progress and give advice. I am concerned to ensure equality of student effort and to provide a mechanism by which the abilities of individual students can be assessed. This has led me to use peer evaluation, the effect and effectiveness of which I now wish to describe and question.

2 Method

In order to prepare a case study of behaviour, one group of students was asked to participate in individual interviews during their Marketing Research project. Each student was interviewed after a month into the project and at its end. A semi-structured questionnaire was used with probing as and when appropriate. All interviews were tape recorded and transcribed by myself.

3 Description of events

The group is selected at random from a class of 25 students, working in five groups of five. I felt the group to be typical.

The students are in their second (final) year of the Business and Technician Education Council's (B.T.E.C.) Higher National Diploma in Business and Finance. Their pseudonyms are Carol, Tony, Jocelyn, Susan and Rose. They have worked in groups before as almost 50% of their assessed work for the course is in groups. They have not worked in this group before. All except Rose live in the same house. Carol and Rose are friends from school. Jocelyn and Tony are "going out" together although during the course of the project she starts to "go out" with one of his friends. Susan is a year older with a working boyfriend (who lives elsewhere). They intend to buy a house together next year.

The Marketing Research project contains two assessed reports, the first - a Research Proposal - has been submitted for marking with the confidential peer evaluations (see Figure 1).

After grading the report, the evaluations appear to show poor performance by Susan. The scores for all are; Carol 53, Rose 56, Susan 32, Tony 51 and Jocelyn 52. The individual scores for Susan are shown in Table 1.

When applied to the overall grade for the assignment, this produces the following individual B.T.E.C. grades. Susan is given a "Pass", Rose receives a "Distinction". All the others are awarded a "Merit".

Figure 1 : **Peer evaluation form**

PEER EVALUATION FORM FOR GROUP PROJECTS [14]

This is an opportunity for you to evaluate the contribution made by each member of your group to the project on which you have been working. Your response will be used as guidance on how credit should be distributed for the work you have done together and will be kept completely confidential.

To use this form, fill in the name of each member except yourself, then assign points for each category and total the points. You may add comments and explanation at the bottom, if you wish.

0 = No Work 1 = Not Good 2 = Average 3 = Good 4 = Excellent

NAMES   Co-operation   Ideas   Effort   Reliability   TOTAL

COMMENTS:

Table 1: The rating of Susan by the others:

	Co-operation	Ideas	Effort	Reliability	Total
Jocelyn	2	2	2	3	9
Rose	2	1	2	3	8
Carol	2	1	2	2	7
Tony	2	1	2	3	8
Total	8	5	8	11	32

Shortly after this, Tony approaches me to complain that he feels he should have had a Distinction as he did more than the others. Similarly Susan sees me to complain of being unfairly punished. These complaints, particularly the latter, seem to me from my knowledge of the group to be possibly justified. Consequently the group is called together and I facilitate a discussion where they are given an opportunity to reconsider their grading of each other. Tony withdraws his complaint, but the group, whilst admitting the imprecise nature of the gradings, is not prepared to re-do the evaluation. The grades are left as they are.

The final interview presents an opportunity to discuss the effect that peer evaluation had on individual behaviour. The salient, edited student responses are as follows [15]:

Tony

Q. Did peer group appraisal affect you?
A. ... I was determined to do better after the grades, I think two people tried harder, one definitely rested on her laurels.

Carol

Q. How did peer appraisal affect the group?
A. ... there was one who worked harder and there was one who decided only to do things that they thought were important to get good grades.

Q. How does the group behave now?
A. ... I feel we'd never work in a group together again.

Jocelyn

Q. Did peer group appraisal affect you?
A. ... I was determined to do better after the grades, I think two people tried harder, one definitely rested on her laurels after the first set ...

Q. Is the group still behaving as before?
A. After the first peer evaluation it was a bit tense in the house ... there was tension between her (*Susan*)and another girl (*Carol*) and that got even worse during that time because she felt it must have been her that marked her down.

Susan

Q. What about everyone pulling their weight?
A. ... I tried to be seen to be doing more, even though I was probably doing the same. One person was always trying to make it look as if they were doing more.

Q. What about arguments?
A. .... Tony even admitted to Jocelyn that what she was doing socially (*going out with one of his friends instead of him*) affected his grade for her.

Q. What about social relationships?
A. Well I don't really do what they do. .... Last year I used to be really sociable but this year I've got a boyfriend ... so I've not had time to be with them. I've seen a maturing in myself and I don't want a student life anymore.

Rose

Q. What was the effect on you of peer assessment?
A. ... I was less inclined to disagree 'cos I didn't want to appear too pushy. You could clearly tell other members who felt they should have done better and they were purposely trying to put others down to try to get better grades. It completely changed the group afterwards.

Q. In the wrong sort of way?

A. People were trying to make sure everyone realised what their contribution had been, there was a sort of "bitchiness" at the end of it.

4 Discussion

Whilst a single case cannot be held to be conclusive, and this case may be atypical as (retrospectively) it was found the majority of the students shared accommodation, there appear to be many issues worthy of consideration and further research.

Student responses indicate that peer evaluation might make them work harder. It does provide guidance in grading to tutors. The more serious concern is the apparent dysfunctional behaviour that appears to have been generated and the validity of the students' assessment of each other.

Consider the possible social damage to Susan: was she penalised for poor participation or because of her challenging approach and different lifestyle? What of her opinion that she, in fact, worked no harder, just made it more apparent what she was doing? Does peer evaluation merely produce the masquerading of effort?

Are students tempted into "putting down" the effort of others to try to attract better marks, as some have reported here? Do others reduce effort with a good evaluation behind them? It could be we are encouraging a cynical and instrumental attitude to study.

What of the vengeful use of peer evaluation by Tony to settle social scores with Jocelyn? Can we afford to overlook the social dynamics of the groups.?

It seems that peer evaluation may only be creating the illusion of solving some of the inherent problems of group work. One wonders exactly what behaviour is being encouraged. Does it brings with it perhaps more serious dysfunctional behaviour? Research on a larger scale may support this suggestion and uncover other issues.

My position now is closer to that of Campbell and Ryder [13] who argue:

"It is crucial that teachers avoid putting students in situations that they themselves have not experienced and which they lack experience of handling."

5 References

1. Johnson, D.W. and Johnson, F.P. (1991) *Joining Together: Group Theory and Group Skills, 4th Ed,* Prentice-Hall International.

2. Jaques, D. (1984) *Learning in Groups,* Croon Helm.

3. Bligh, D.A. (1974) *What's the Use of Lectures? 3rd. Ed.*, Penguin Educational.

4. Rau, W. and Heyl, B.S. (1990) Humanising the college classroom: Collaborative learning and social organisation among students, *Teaching Sociology*, **18**, 141-155.

5. Johnson, D.W. and Johnson, F.P. (1978) Co-operative, Competitive and Individualistic Learning, *Journal of Research and Development in Education,* **12**, 3-5.

6. Lambiotte, J.G,. Dansereau, D.F., O'Donnell, A.M., Young, M.D., Skaggs, L.P. and Hall R.H. (1988) Effects of cooperative script manipulations on initial learning and transfer, *Cognition and Instruction*, **5**, 103-121.

7. Topping, K. (1992) Cooperative learning and peer tutoring: An overview, *The Psychologist*, **5**, 151-157.

8. Quicke, J. (1985) Charting a Course for Personal and Social Education, *Pastoral Care in Education*, 3, 91-9.

9. Miall, D.S. (1987) Learning in Autonomous Student Groups, Learning Skills as a Predictor of Satisfaction, *Studies in Educational Evaluation*, **13**, 175-183.

10. Kerr, N. and Bruun, S. (1983) The dispensibility of member effort and group motivational losses: Free Rider Effects, *Journal of Personality and Social Psychology*, **44**, 78-94.

11. Sheingold, K., Hawkins. J. and Char, C. (1984) "I'm the thinkist, you're the typist": The interaction of technology and the social life of classrooms, *Journal of Social Issues*, **40**, 49-61.

12. Campbell, L. and Ryder, J. (1989) Groupsense: When Work in Groups Does Not Add Up To 'Group work', *Pastoral Care in Education*, **7**, 22-30.

13. Salomon, G. and Globerson, T. (1989) When teams do not function the way they ought to, in Webb, N.M. (Ed.) Peer Interaction, Problem-solving, and Cognition: Multidisciplinary Perspectives, *International Journal of Educational Research*, **13**, 89-99.

14. Peer evaluation form designed by Jerry Lynn, College of Journalism, Marquette University, Milwaukee, USA

15. For fuller transcripts see D.J. Abson (1992) The Efficacy and Behavioural Dimensions of Long-Term Tutorless Groups in Higher Education: A Case Study, *MEd. Dissertation*, University of Sunderland

Innovative approaches to learning in an applied psychology degree

R. Bray & L. Holyoak

Department of Psychology, Faculty of Health, University of Central Lancashire, Preston PR1 2HE, UK

Abstract

In recent years there has been increasing attention paid to the idea that undergraduate psychology courses should adopt a more skill based, experiential approach to learning. The University of Central Lancashire has, since 1990, developed a new Applied Psychology degree encompassing a variety of methods in order to achieve this aim, including: Group based learning, distance learning, work placement, informal peer tutoring, peer assessment, interpersonal skill development and deep learning techniques. The implementation of these is outlined, together with a variety of evaluation data indicating a high level of student satisfaction and employability associated with the course.

Introduction

The changing context of Higher Education

Higher Education is, as Barnett [1] puts it, a 'contested concept': increasingly, traditional assumptions concerning its methods and very aims are being challenged. In particular learning and teaching styles are being fundamentally re-examined as we move towards the so-called 'learning society' (Evans [2]).

The traditional approach to degree level teaching can be characterised as focusing on teaching rather than learning, on understanding rather than ability and on teacher-managed rather than learner managed learning (Graves [3]). Innovatory approaches to Higher Education, in contrast, often stress the importance of experiential methods (Kolb [4]) and skill based learning outcomes.

Along with this interest in activity based learning has come the realisation that learning is facilitated by social interaction. The traditional Higher Education experience has relied on numbers of individuals working in isolation (e.g. in the lecture or revising for traditional exams) while innovatory methods stress the value of learning in groups, whether in more formal contexts (such as group based problem solving using case studies in seminars) or more informal (such as peer tutoring and mentoring).

These two relatively new approaches (of activity and group based learning), together with technological developments (such as multi-media) are beginning, it can be argued, to revolutionise the way in which Higher Education is conducted. It should not be surprising, then, if Psychology, as a discipline within which the concept of learning plays such a pivotal role, is at the forefront of such developments.

New approaches to Psychology degrees

Arnold et al [5], however, suggest that the British Psychology degree has continued to overemphasise the acquisition of knowledge of facts and theories - that is, propositional knowledge (Yinger [6]) - at the expense of Transferable Personal Skills - which are a cornerstone of procedural knowledge (i.e. 'how to' knowledge). They call for "a modest but significant reorientation" of courses to make such skills "more explicit and important within the curriculum" reflecting the fact that "scholarship is not simply learning new information". Such a reorientation, they suggest, would not only increase student employability, given research findings which indicate that many employers select individuals largely on the basis of such skills, but also increase general, long-term personal effectiveness. Within such a context, therefore, the introduction of skill based learning is supported as much by educational arguments (i.e. relating to individual self-development) as by economic imperative. Nevertheless the employability of graduates remains an important criterion: while the traditional degree may prepare students well for academic or professional training it does little for the career prospects of the 75-90% who enter occupations unrelated to Psychology.

The centrality of Transferable Personal Skills to such a change is reiterated by Arnold and Newstead [7] in their telling critique of the orthodox Psychology degree. Such skills, they propose, include: Communication (oral and written), problem solving and decision making, to which Hayes [8] adds (inter alia) interpersonal awareness and information-finding skills. However, it should be noted that the concept of Transferable Personal Skills is not one free from controversy, as it can easily be perceived - together with the allied notion of competence (Caird [9]) - as an excessively mechanistic, reductionist approach to learning, which is overdependent on an obsolete behaviourism. Transferable Personal Skills are not, however, purely behavioural but often depend on higher order cognitive skills. Indeed Peterson et al [10], among others, point out the critical role of metacognitive awareness in the development of such skills.

There seems to be, therefore, a coherent and cogent case to be made for innovation within the Psychology degree which stresses experiential and group based activity through the medium of Transferable Personal Skills. But what methods are most effective? The rest of this paper presents a case study of how one degree introduced and evaluated such innovation.

Innovation on a new Applied Psychology degree

In 1990 the Department of Psychology at the University of Central Lancashire (then Lancashire Polytechnic) decided to develop a new degree of Applied Psychology which would run in parallel with an existing and well established B.Sc. Psychology course. After a common first year students in year two would have the opportunity of taking a (new) 'Introduction to Applied Psychology' unit (14% of that year's credits) which would render them eligible to opt for the Applied Psychology degree in year three. This involved a new 'Techniques in Applied Psychology' unit (17% of the year's credits), the option of a innovatory work placement (8%) and a number of existing options.

Given that the new degree would share as much as 85% course content with the established course the problem emerged of how to ensure that it had a distinctive profile which would underline its applied nature. The decision was made to use the opportunity to make the new units as skill-based as possible, using a variety of methods including group based learning, distance learning, shadowing, informal peer tutoring, peer assessment, interpersonal skill development and deep learning technique.

Group based learning, peer tutoring and interpersonal skills development
For the core level 3 course unit on the Applied Degree (Techniques in Applied Psychology) it was decided to adopt a group based learning approach. It was hoped that in this way certain things could be promoted: informal peer tutoring; learning to work in 'imposed' work teams (team composition was decided by the tutor, avoiding putting known friends together) and fostering a deep approach, by tackling applied problems. Informal feedback indicated that students did indeed learn extensively from one anothers' experiences within and outside the educational system. It was certainly the case that the groups (even though composed of seemingly unlikely combinations of individuals) learnt to work well together, devising their own methods of tackling exercises. The high standard of coursework submitted indicated that students had a good level of understanding the material with which they had been presented.

Distance learning
Certain level 2 course units were made available as distance learning packs. One of these (Introduction to Applied Psychology) is the pre-requisite for the above. The need to produce the pack was seen as an opportunity to put together materials which introduced appropriate theoretical content, but which were 'punctuated' at regular intervals by exercises, large and small, which

required the reader to reflect on the material just presented, and/or to try out very basic skills. These packs were particularly designed for part-time, mature students, and feedback again suggests that these students enjoy the pack, particularly the way it relates to their life experiences, and emphasises the 'reality' of psychology.

Work Placement and Peer Assessment
It was decided that students on the Applied Psychology degree would be offered the opportunity to undertake a short work placement, which would take the form either of shadowing a psychology graduate in their workplace, or carrying out a short 'project' in a place where psychology is practised (e.g. personnel department). The aim of the placement was firstly to increase students' awareness, and development, of personal transferable skills; secondly to show psychological techniques in practice; and thirdly to facilitate career choice decisions. To aid this the placement was assessed in three ways: a diary kept during kept during the placement; a report on some aspect of the placement; and a peer assessed talk. The three aims were met, to different degrees. Much of the 'mystery' surrounding performing a job disappeared, and the students realised that they did not have most (if not all) of the basic skills required. Whether the students saw psychological techniques in practice depended very much on the nature of the placement; however it was not easy to identify which would - and which would not - fulfil this aim. What is most evident is that students, after having sampled a possible career, increase their commitment to it, or decide against it completely, feeling fortunate for having been able to find out in advance that it was not for them.

Deep Learning
Convinced of the efficacy of deep learning it was subsequently decided to apply the principles to a Level 3 option available to students on Applied Psychology, that is, ergonomics. The approach adopted was slightly different from the 'Techniques' course, in that although students were divided into groups, they were put in the role of ergonomics consultants and given case studies to tackle with the help of large quantities of relevant journal articles etc., the reading of which was to be divided between members of the group. The hope was to encourage the making of the link between the theory and practice of ergonomics; to aid the development of an understanding of the subject, rather than a superficial learning of facts; and to encourage a group approach to learning, with its concomitant benefits. The approach was not as successful on this unit as it was on Techniques. Students felt that they did not want to rely on others for their learning, and were 'overwhelmed' by the amount of materials they were asked to read (even though it was no more than they would be directed to after the normal lectures). Their assessment marks were good, however, the mean being higher than the previous year which used a more traditional approach.

Evaluation

As has been indicated, some of these innovations have met with more success than others. All bar the Distance Learning pack have been assessed using formal, quantitative feedback methods.

The Techniques unit is always rated highly by participants, and although they may like some topics more than others, when asked how it might be improved, can only suggest such things as free coffee and biscuits at the interval!

For the work placement, feedback has been obtained from both the students and the supervisors. Supervisors see benefits for themselves; and the students see nothing but good coming from the experience, for example the gaining of insight into a job and the accruing of valuable experience.

Deep learning on Ergonomics received a more mixed response. Reported understanding of the course varied from very poor to excellent; the majority thought the learning strategy was awful or poor; and there was a fairly even split between those who were pleased they had undertaken the unit, and those who were not. Students were also asked to complete the abridged Approaches to Studying Questionnaire [11] at the beginning and the end of the option. The scores suggest that instead of fostering a deep approach to learning, the opposite effect was achieved, although it was impossible to control the influence of other learning experiences these students were having.

For the Applied psychology degree as a whole, students are generally happy with their experiences. The increasing popularity of the course (suggested by the growing numbers transferring onto it) is in part from word of mouth recommendation from previous final year students. Another attraction might be the comparative employment/unemployment rates. The data from students on which we have information indicates the following unemployment rates six months after graduation.

Table 1: Graduate unemployment rates

	1992			1993		
	Number graduating	Number responding	Unemployment rate (%)	Number graduating	Number responding	Unemployment rate (%)
Psychology	66	37	16.2%	62	41	4.9%
Applied Psychology	32	27	7.4%	24	21	0.0%

Conclusions

The innovations introduced into the Applied Psychology degree have, in general, achieved their aims: skills have been developed without sacrificing academic quality; a high level of student employability has been achieved and student satisfaction is very high. Yet unresolved issues remain. In particular there exists a clear incongruence between the skill based nature of these courses and the traditional format of assessment: coursework focuses on writing skills to the exclusion of all others just as much as examination (whether seen or unseen). The assessment of oral presentations provides one solution to this problem, but in its turn creates new ones: students need to be properly prepared in presentation techniques, but where is the space in an already crowded curriculum, while increasing student numbers makes individual assessed presentations a time consuming option. Peer assessment has provided a partial answer here, but in its turns poses new questions. Moreover, all innovations in assessment have to ensure that academic rigour is maintained, within a context of increasing anxiety that relative decreases in resources per student are endangering educational quality. For some, educational innovation is perceived as a thinly veiled ideological attack on the independence of Higher Education with the aim of driving it into the arms of industry. The perception of this particular innovation in delivering a Psychology degree is, however, that neither intellectual integrity nor academic rigour need be sacrificed in order to enhance the relevance - and enjoyment - of the learning experience.

References

[1] Barnett, R. *The Idea of Higher Education*, Society for Research into Higher Education, London, 1990.

[2] Evans, N. *The Knowledge Revolution*, Grant McIntyre, London, 1981.

[3] Graves, N. *Learner Managed Learning: Practice, Theory and Policy*, Higher Education for Capability, Leeds, 1993.

[4] Kolb, D.A. *Experiential Learning*, Prentice Hall, New Jersey, 1984.

[5] Arnold, J., Newstead, S.E., Donaldson, M.L., Reid, F.J.M. and Dennis, I. Skills development in undergraduate psychology courses, *Bulletin of the British Psychological Society*, 1987, 40, 469-472.

[6] Yinger, R. Journal writing as a learning tool, *Volta Review*, 1985, 21-34.

[7] Arnold, J. & Newstead, S. Working with Psychology, Chapter 2, *A liberal Science: Education in Psychology past present and future*, eds Radford, J. & Rose, D. pp48-60, Society for Research into Higher Education, London, 1989.

[8] Hayes, N. The skills aquired in Psychology degrees, *The Psychologist*, 1989, June, 238-239.

[9] Caird, S. Problems with the identification of Enterprise competencies and the implications for Assessment and Development, *Management Education and Development*, 1992, 23 (1) , 6-17.

[10] Peterson, G.W., Sampson, J.P., & Reardon, R.C., *Career development and services: A cognitive approach*, Brooks/Cole, Pacific Grove CA, 1991.

[11]. Entwistle, N. *Styles of Teaching and Learning*, Wiley, Chichester, 1981.

Empirical projects and small group learning

M. Callaghan, A. Knox, I. Mowatt & G. Siann
Glasgow Caledonian University, City Campus, Cowcaddens Road, Glasgow G4 0BA, UK

Abstract

The aim of the research was to evaluate the use of a non-assessed empirical project carried out by small groups of third year media studies students (total n=31: 21 females, 10 males) as a preparation for similar assessed individual empirical projects. As an aid to the group project, students received detailed handouts covering relevant aspects of research methodology and information technology (IT). Questionnaires were administered at three month intervals: at the beginning of the group project, immediately afterwards and three months later. The questionnaires investigated (i) students' knowledge of, and confidence in, the use of IT and (ii) their attitudes to the experience of working in both assessed and non-assessed groups.

Results indicated : (i) A general increase in skills and confidence in the use of IT after the group project. (ii) Significant gender differences were shown in that males reported making more use of IT than females as well as more confidence in its use. (iii) Analyses of attitudinal items indicated that following the group experience students reported that, while non-assessed group work was preferable with respect to group dynamics, assessed group work was preferable with respect to learning outcomes. Analyses of students' extended comments indicated that students were more positive to group work three months after the end of the group project than they were immediately afterwards.

This evaluation of the group project procedure has led to modifications of the procedure in the subsequent two academic years and details of these modifications are reported.

1   Introduction

The current expansion in the numbers of students entering Higher Education in the United Kingdom has not been accompanied by a commensurate increase in teaching staff. Consequently many institutions have moved towards group projects as a means of more efficiently deploying teaching resources. Simultaneously movements within education as a whole have also emphasised the pedagogic benefits of group projects. First as aiding the movement away from student passivity and towards student centred learning (Rogers[1]); second within a theoretical perspective which sees education as affecting not only cognitive but also personal growth (Bowen[2]); third as serving as a means of enhancing creativity (Hare[3]) and finally as enhancing social skills (Cassels[4]) Thus recently there has been a shift from lectures and seminars towards group-based projects.

Annette Kolmos discussed this shift (Kolmos[5]) with reference to a group-based project undertaken at a Technical University in Denmark. In her paper she emphasised both the cognitive and affective aspects of the group work experience. Cognitive aspects were defined as: the demands on the group for the analysis of the problem, the direction for their project and the methods used to solve the problem, while the affective aspects involved were defined as: identity, feelings, attitudes, values and experience.

Kolmos also noted that teachers and students need to be aware of the cognitive and affective aspects in order to be productively involved in an "active investigating learning process." (p112.) She further claimed that emphasising such metacognitive aspects (i.e. cognitive and affective) tends to accelerate the learning process.

Finally Kolmos noted that student group work can cover differing strategies. One strategy she highlighted as particularly effective involved students undertaking problem-based projects which require the group to formulate a research question and then undertake a joint endeavour to provide empirical data impinging on the question.

In the present study this particular small group methodology was incorporated as part of a third year course on mass communications. Students were required in groups of between three and six to formulate a question relating to the impact of the mass media and were then required to carry out, as a group, an empirical investigation of the relevant question. This group investigation was to be unassessed but was to provide a learning experience which would provide the basis for similar assessed individual projects.

The unassessed group project replaced a set of six lectures and seminars on research methodology which had, in previous years, preceded the individual empirical projects. As these changes were introduced students' attitudes towards such group projects were monitored as was their use of IT facilities relevant to the carrying out of such empirical projects.

2   Method

Thirty-one third year students (21 females and 10 males) were required to complete three questionnaires relating to their attitudes towards group projects and their use of IT facilities . The first questionnaire was given out before the start of the group project, the second (which was identical to the first) was given out three months later, after the completion of the group project and the third (again identical) after a further three months, at the end of the relevant academic year.

3   Results

Because there was a high level of attrition in responses to the third administration of the questionnaire, the quantitative results below are reported only for the first two questionnaire administrations.

3.1   Use of IT

To measure the increase in skills relating to information technology the students were asked about their use of, and degree of confidence in, several aspects of IT such as using the Library Dynix system; using CD ROM literature and research records and using Apple Macs for both word processing and the analysis of statistical data. Following the group project there was a general increase in the usage of Library IT facilities and, in particular, in the use of Psyclit facilities which none of the students had used before.

Gender differences were shown with t -tests indicating that male students were more likely than females students to report on the questionnaires that they felt 'very' or 'quite' confident about using IT ($p < .05$). Males also reported making significantly more use of IT ($p < .05$). However, when staff looked at the extent to which students made use of IT in their own individual projects which were carried out following the group projects, no evidence was found that females students made less use of IT than their male peers. These findings with respect to gender are in line with other research which suggests that there are minimal gender differences in ability in IT, but that females consistently rate themselves as lower in ability than do their male counterparts [7].

3.2   Attitudes to Group work

3.21   With respect to learning outcomes. A number of items on the questionnaires covered attitudes to group work with respect to learning outcomes under two conditions, assessed and non-assessed. (For example 'working in an assessed (or non-assessed) group is better than working on my own with respect to formulating ideas about a project/ analysing what is needed/writing up.) A composite scale was calculated from these items and analyses of variance were performed for the first two administrations of the questionnaire with reference to both assessed and non-assessed group work. With respect to this scale there were no significant differences between liking for assessed versus non-assessed group projects on either questionnaire administration , but after the conclusion of the group project there was a significant increase in liking for assessed group work (p <.03) and a non-significant increase in liking for unassesssed group work. This finding can probably be ascribed to the students' recent experience of completing a non assessed group project and consequently being likely to encounter problems with such projects. Whereas when responding to items about assessed group projects they had no such recent experience to call on.

3.22   With respect to social dynamics. A similar sub-scale was calculated incorporating items in the questionnaire which were concerned with social dynamics (for example 'do you think working in groups improves class cohesion/ makes you more confident/ makes students less reliant on staff). Over both administrations students indicated a more positive attitude to non-assessed groups projects than to assessed (p<.05) but following the group project there was a significant decline on the scale with reference to non-assessed group work but not with respect to assessed group projects. Once again we ascribe this to the students' recent experience with non-assessed, but not with assessed, group projects.

Scrutiny of individual questionnaire responses reinforced the impressions noted above that students regarded assessed group projects more favourably with respect to learning outcomes, but non-assessed group projects more favourably with regard to group dynamics.

3.3   Extended Comments. Students were encouraged to make extended comments about their experience of the group project. Twenty-four students responded to this in each of the first two administrations and sixteen in the third administration.

Responses before the group project centred around two issues. The first of these was the extent to which members of a group were prepared to participate in the group task (e.g. *'some people tend to* dominate in all aspects of group work which results in the breakdown of communication within the group', '...from previous experience lazy people remain lazy and get away with it'. A second aspect dealt with the 'chance' aspect of the group experience; the group experience could be either positive or negative. It depended on the luck of the draw in the how members of the group worked as a team: 'if everyone is motivated and willing to do their share of work then the group will be successful'.

Finally some comments took up general issues such as the extent to which staff were prepared to monitor the group process. Following the group experience, comments were on the whole less positive and tended to centre on the negative aspects of group participation. For example 'Sometimes organising times to meet can be difficult, people don't always turn up and others get annoyed'; '...it depends on who is in the group; their qualities, their motivation, their personality'.

Despite the fact that a number of students made negative extended comments following the group projects, other students endorsed group work quite forcibly. For example: 'Working in groups is so much more effective a means of learning, education needs more of this'.

Comments made on the third administration of the questionnaire were in general more favourable to group work than those made immediately afterwards and this resonated with discussion with students at the informal level. Further when the different group presented the results of their group projects to the class as a whole, shortly before the commencement of their individual projects, there was unanimous agreement that group learning is superior to the traditional lecture and seminar approach although there was a widespread feeling that the groups should be smaller and that there should be some mark awarded for the group project in succeeding years.

4   Conclusions

In general as the results section indicates, students regarded their experience of the group project favourably although with strong reservations about group composition. In the two subsequent years staff have taken this reservation on board in restricting groups to a maximum of four with a recommendation of three as an optimum number. Further care has been taken in monitoring students' self-selection of members of individual groups in order to minimise differentials in the degree of participation.

In the year following this study, as a result of students comments, a small proportion of course marks was awarded to the group project. Staff, however, felt that doing this did not offer any obvious benefits in practice and in the second year following the study staff reverted to non-assessed group projects.

Comparison of the individual projects over the three years since the replacement of seminars and lectures by group projects has shown a steady increase in quality as staff have gained in the experience of administering group projects. Informal monitoring of the group projects has continued and, accompanying the increase in confidence amongst staff, there has been a steady increase in favourable comments about the group experience.

In general staff administering this course concur with Hare's premise that small groups can be powerfully involved in 'creative shift' in that they provide a forum for offering individuals new perspectives in learning situations. Furthermore the staff concerned are increasingly aware that group learning contributes positively to social dynamics within classes.

References

1. Rogers, C.R. *Freedom to Learn*, Columbus, Ohio: Merrill, 1969.
2. Bowen, H.C. *Froebel and Education by self activity*, London: William Heinemann, 1907.
3. Hare, A.P. *Creativity in Small Groups*, London: Sage, 1982.
4. Cassels, J. *Britain's Real Skill Shortage*, London: Policy Studies Institute, 1990.
5. Thorpe, M. & Grudgeon, D. (eds.) Kelly, P. Tutorial Groups in Open Learning, *Open Learning Learning for Adults*, Harlow, Essex: Longman, 1987.
6. Kolmos, A. Metacognitive Aspects in a Group-Based Project work at Technical Universities, in Gender and Science and Technology, Volume **1**, pp.111-120, *Contributions to the East and West European Conference, Eindhoven*, The Netherlands 1992.
7. Siann, G., Macleod, H.A., Glissov, P. & Durndell, A.J. The Effect of Computer Use on Gender Differences in Attitudes to Computers. *Computers and Education*, **14.2**, pp.183-191, 1990b.

Supplemental instruction - A model for supporting student learning

C.E. Healy

Energy and Environmental Engineering Department, Glasgow Caledonian University, City Campus, Cowcaddens Road, Glasgow G4 0BA, UK

Abstract

The study investigates the effectiveness of the Supplemental Instruction Model. Supplemental Instruction has been employed successfully for over 20 years at universities in the USA, e.g. Martin[1]. It is suggested that Supplemental Instruction may help to overcome some of the problems facing Higher Education now and in the next century.

The model was recently introduced into the United Kingdom. It is now being tested at Glasgow Caledonian University and a number of other universities in the United Kingdom. Preliminary results indicate: a) improved performance in the students' annual examinations; b) reduction in students' drop-out rate; c) enhanced communication and other transferable skills and d) deeper understanding of engineering principles. Further details of the challenges encountered in implementing the program will be discussed.

Keywords: Supplemental Instruction, learning facilitation, learning to learn

Context

Examination of UCCA and PCAS applications and admissions statistics over the past 8 years reveals that the number of applicants per place for many engineering courses has dropped from approximately 2:1 in 1985 to just over 1:1 in 1992.[2 & 3]. Together with the trend to widen access to Higher Education, this has led to increased diversity in the student population. These students as a whole have a broader spectrum of skills and experiences; many are mature (29% over 21). Some have a range of educational qualifications which differ from students entering Higher Education directly from school.

Engineering, like medicine, is essentially a vocational subject. Rye [4] argues that relevant learning techniques adopted early in a course will not only benefit the student throughout the course - they will be invaluable throughout a professional career, where knowledge and techniques are rapidly changing. Zuber-Skerritt [5] argues for a more holistic and dialectical model of knowing and learning in which the learner is conceived as an active construer of knowledge through cycles of problem-solving. She also concludes that high quality education is linked to the development of intellectual independence which can be achieved through certain processes (...collaboration, group processes..) Earwalker [6] suggests a method of supporting students which is part of the curriculum and not as some extra-curricular activity for which time has to be found. Sheer size indicates that many courses can in no way be thought of as a community, and the complexity of timetabling means that any unscheduled 'meetings' is virtually impossible to organise.

In common with many other engineering departments we were concerned with progression rates. The growing ideas and debates about peer support for learning seemed to offer a way forward for

*   using the experience and skills of students from diverse backgrounds
*   encouraging the development of learning strategies
*   developing student confidence through teamwork and associated interpersonal skills

The research referred to earlier is representative of some of the issues which I believed would contribute to the success of the scheme we adopted.

Introduction

In the summer of 1992 I was invited to join a task force which was considering ways of improving progression rates in one of our engineering courses. Supplemental Instruction was suggested as one strategy for achieving this, having been used successfully in an engineering department at Kingston University in the previous year.

The scheme is built around the concept of a Student Leader as a facilitator for the learning of others. This Student Leader is a 'model student' in terms of organisation of their own learning. An SI co-ordinator organises the scheme.

The course being considered was the combined first year of a BSc/HND in Computer Aided Engineering (CAE) and Electronic Engineering (EE). At the end of first year students split into the two streams. Approximately 10% of the cohort, chosen by their overall academic performance, are offered transfer to the BEng(Hons). 36 students attended at least one SI session, with 19 students attending three or more sessions. 199 students were registered, but not all of these were 'current' students.

Supplemental Instruction

SI is a student centred scheme which helps students to acquire and use study skills by providing a structured, proven, non-threatening active learning environment for interaction between students of the same course. SI is not another form of teaching - it is not about content of course work, but about preparation for learning. Course content is used in the SI sessions to develop study skills. The scheme supports and complements normal teaching support.

The scheme has been used most frequently with first year students on difficult, content-laden courses. These students attend a one-hour SI session once per week. The session is led by a second (or exceptionally third) year student on the same course. Student leaders are trained for their role, both at the start of the scheme and throughout the year of operation. Group dynamics, verbal and non-verbal communication skills, theory of learning and dealing with problems outwith their expertise are among the skills developed during training. Structuring SI sessions is also dealt with. At the beginning of the academic year the student leader structures the sessions, but later students themselves take some responsibility for the content of the sessions.

SI is not a remedial scheme; it will help students with academic difficulties, but it targets high-risk courses rather than high-risk students. A member of academic staff takes responsibility for the scheme, but day to day running is the responsibility of an SI co-ordinator. Ideally this person would be a recent graduate from the same department, but if the scheme runs in several departments one co-ordinator could take organisational responsibility for all of these. Student leaders and the SI co-ordinator meet for one hour per week for feedback, reflective discussion and dealing with problems. This meeting is friendly and relaxed. Attendance at SI sessions is voluntary and confidential to encourage trust between the SI leader and students who attend. Leaders provide feedback to academic staff, either through the co-ordinator or directly.

Planning

Second and third year students from the course were invited to volunteer for a session which presented the ideas behind the scheme. Fifteen students attended and subsequently all of those students agreed to take part and to undertake the required two days of training, with a view to final selection of only those who successfully completed the training. In fact, all of these students, who had selected themselves initially, became Student Leaders. A slight problem arose, in that three of these students were direct entrants from other Institutions to second year, and had not followed precisely the same curriculum as their peers. This meant that they had not been through the same lecture programme as the students they would be required to help. Remembering that the scheme is about facilitating learning and the fact that these students had shown many skills during training they were invited to continue in the scheme. Questioning all of the leaders revealed that they

> "wanted to help others"
> "wanted to help themselves"
> "recognised the difficulty of Higher Education"
> "recognised the expertise within a self-help group"

In discussions on learning theory during the training it became clear that some students were aware of the concepts of deep learning, shallow 'rote' learning and a strategic combination of the two.

Attendance

The desired attendance was for one third of all of the first year target group. This did not mean that one-third would come every week but that over the course of a year one-third would have experienced at least three SI sessions. A number of difficulties arose in achieving that aim. One of the difficulties was timing of sessions, which required a common 'free' slot with first years and their Student Leaders. Four of those sessions occurred at lunch times after a three hour teaching block. Evaluation of the timing problems in year 1 led to SI being included at a more suitable time for the second year of the scheme. Another problem was that of physical space - this has become more difficult to find over the past two years. Some available rooms are either laboratories with fixed high benches, or lecture rooms with fixed seating. Neither of these are suitable for SI sessions, which require a 'round table' setting. Academic staff awareness of the scheme was built up slowly, but initially limited staff awareness meant that students may not have perceived strong support for the scheme, even though this did exist.

Evaluation

Table 1 early evaluation 1992-1993

	SI	non SI
Engineering Practice	69%	63%
Computer Technology	70%	63%
Communications&Industrial Studies	67%	62%
Electrical Engineering Principles	61%	46%
Mechanical Electronic Systems	64%	53%
Manufacturing Technology 1	62%	48%
Mechanical Engineering Principles	57%	43%
Technical Maths 1	66%	54%

In earlier results from USA and from Kingston University a statistically significant increase in course grades ($p \leq 0.05$) was observed in those students participating in the scheme. [1 & 4]

Evaluation was begun with student leaders during the second year of the scheme. They were asked to undergo reflective self and peer evaluation. Each leader completed a questionnaire for him/herself and for one other student leader. The following skills were considered

Verbal communications
Non-verbal communications
Learning techniques
Interpersonal skills
Attitude

A 'marking scheme' was devised for this but it is incomplete and we are treating this as a pilot scheme in devising further research. Those students who took part certainly reflected on their technique and behaviour.

Discussion

The scheme benefits SI attendees, SI leaders and academic staff. SI attendees show improved academic performance. SI leaders have been invited to take part in staff-student consultative groups because of their keen interest in the course as a whole, and because of their well-developed communication skills. Academic staff get better feedback, through communication with the student leaders and the SI co-ordinator on how students are reacting to lectures, laboratories and tutorials. Some of the SI leaders have changed their career aspirations because of their experiences. "Before I attended this University I hoped to obtain a degree and then get a job within the engineering industry. Now I feel I would possibly like to become a teacher of technical subjects within schools". One of our current leaders had originally embarked on a two year HND course, but his progress allowed him to continue to BSc level. He too wishes to proceed to a career in teaching: "I volunteered for SI with the idea that first year students walk a very fine line between passing or failing, depending on outside influences. A friendly face, someone to help identify problems or to sympathise can help someone carry on rather than give up."

Conclusion

Supplemental Instruction develops confident, active and successful learners and stimulates intellectual excitement which the students discover for themselves as they learn how to understand difficult concepts. SI has begun to break down the barriers between years, especially since second and third year students were involved. Effective administration of the scheme is essential - our experience indicates that an SI co-ordinator who is a recent engineering graduate from the same department is ideal, since they know many staff and can use their own recent experiences. SI leaders have developed their own personal transferable skills in group working, leadership, personal responsibility and self confidence and more research is required into benefits to SI leaders. Implementation of SI is evidence of the first steps in a major cultural change and support for staff implementing it is crucial. Further research is also needed on the further progress of SI attendees when they have progressed to later years of their course.

References

1.   Martin, D.C., Blanc, R.A. & De Buhr, L, *Breaking the attrition cycle: the effects of supplemental instruction on undergraduate performance and attrition,* Journal of Higher Education, 54(1)

2.   *The Universities Central Council on Admissions*

3.   *Polytechnics Central Admissions System*

4.   Rye, P.D., Wallace, J, Bidgood, P. Instructions in learning skills: an integrated approach, *Medical Education,* 1993, **27**, 470-473

5.   Zuber-Skerritt, O, *Professional Research in Higher Education: A Theoretical Framework for Action Research,* Kogan Page, London 1992

6.   Earwalker, J., *Helping and Supporting Students,* SRHE and OUP 1992

Developing a learning organization at the university level

E.-L. Kronqvist & H. Soini

Faculty of Education, Department of Behavioral Sciences, University of Oulu, PO Box 222, FIN-90571 Oulu, Finland

Abstract

The Peer Tutor Model was applied to university studies in two courses one in the course of education, the other in the course of psychology. The teachers of the course acted as lecturer and as consultants for the small groups and the peer-tutors' group. The model was evaluated by students and peer tutors. The Peer-Tutor Model was seen as very useful in higher education, but the role of the peer-tutors needed some clarification. This model has implications for developing the university organization at the departmental level.

I Introduction

University - its organization as well as teaching and research have been subjected to criticism in many countries in Europe. This criticism is directed against an unclear and conflicting mission and goals, which may be seen in close relation with problems and discrepancies in study programmes and curricula, inappropriate methods of teaching and learning, inflexible curricula and programmes which lead to a high rate of drop-outs and long duration of studies, and finally, poor organization of postgraduate studies and the research domain. In the Finnish universities the essence of criticism is similar (Educational Faculties and Teacher Education in the Finnish Universities 1994). Widespread changes have taken place in university studies between the 1970's and the 1980's or 1990's. The universities themselves have undergone a powerful process of rationalization, there have been increasing demands for efficiency, and greater emphasis has come to be placed on administration. The consequences can be viewed from the point of view of both the student and the teacher-researcher.

Research concerned with university students and the student culture in Finland has shown that students place particular emphasis on gaining their degree as quickly as possible and finding themselves a good job which correlates with their own interests. This requires self-discipline from the student, but a goal-directed planning of studies as well. There is a tendency for students to adopt a more instrumental attitude towards knowledge and study. Studying is "training" for a career, and it is not particularly closely connected with the individual's way of life as a whole.The most far-reaching changes , however, have taken place at the level of the hidden curriculum (Aittola 1988). University studies have come to be arranged more in the form of fixed courses and the burden on students has increased. This has in turn generated greater pressures in terms of performance and led students to be guided to an escalating degree by the hidden curriculum. However , according to Aittola (1988), the students did not strive very hard to influence their own situation in life or do away with the problems caused by the strict curriculum.The students regarded the university as a   very massive and bureaucratic place where they did not receive much attention (Aittola 1988).

The above- mentioned tendencies of crisis are reflected not only by the students but also by the teachers and researchers of the university. Teaching is considered a marginal activity at the university. The development of teaching and the different kinds of experiments are easily left to the level of individual courses (Gröhn et al.1993). The changes in teaching require cooperation in the whole department as well as the active participation of the students in the development of teaching.

Naturally, one may ask if it is even possible for a student in this kind of situation to take any other attitude than an instrumental one towards knowledge and studies.The same question may also be asked from the point of view of a university teacher.As the opposite of instrumental studying , the developmental attitude towards studying and studies has often been offered. The psychosocial theories (eg. Rogers 1990) describe the developmental change during the student days also from the standpoint of stress and conflict. If a person does not experience conflict, dissonance, situations and crises, which are difficult to handle, the person will not develop. So, at the same time , studying at the university means establishing a young adult's own academic and personal identity. The critical nature, the learning to think scientifically as well the deepening and widening of one's own personal philosophy of life are some of the targets in studying at the university (Rogers 1990).

All these changes which I mentioned just reflect the crisis in which our universities find themselves, and in particular the crisis of learning, a situation which has in recent times led research into university education to develop various models which place emphasis on the active handling of information and a more critical attitude towards the material taught. At the Department of Behavioral Sciences at the University of Oulu a programme has been developed,which is based on three theoretical principles: 1) systemic psychology, 2) communicative handling, and 3) the theory of social learning. The model is described elsewhere (Järvilehto1994). In this article will be handled the various models of developing research and teaching in the department and especially the tutoring models as a part of the developing model. Tutoring models can be viewed as instrumental or as developmental models. In instrumental tutoring the meaning is mainly to take care that the studies proceed according to the degree requirements and that the aim concerning the career are achieved. Tutoring can also be seen as developmental, in which the crucial point is to reflect on one's own function as a person as well as a member of the group in a wider perspective. The attention is also a way of examining the subconscious factors that prevent learning in both the individual and the group (Soini & Kronqvist 1994). Both the tutoring models have their own functions and the combining of them is problematic, but the model used in this experiment is specifically based on the developmental point of view In it the roles of both the teacher and the peer-tutor are estimated again. Tutoring is closely connected and integrated into the teaching and contents of a course.The peer tutors act as helpers in the small groups. They are trained for their tasks. In education the emphasis has been on the theoretical studies of group dynamics, but also on consultations where the peer tutors are able to run through their experiences with group work.

In this report I examine the university's organization from the point of view of learning, changing, and developing. The emphasis has been put especially on examining the readiness to change as experienced by a student.The aim is to develop forms of work where the students are allowed to participate in the development of teaching and where the students can support each other by taking responsibility for both the teaching and their own learning.

II Method

The tutoring models which are used in this project are: 1) Personal Teacher Model and 2) Peer Tutoring Model. The first of these means that each of the students is assigned a personal teacher of his own who guides and supervises his studies throughout the span of his studies. Experience with these models has been very positive, but some problems are connected with them. First ,the models are developed apart from the teaching and research of the department. Secondly , there can be problems of commitment on the teachers' as well as on the students' level.

The second one is The Peer Tutoring Model, in which an older student meets with first or second-year students to study with them or advise them in their studies. In a sense this takes after Vygotsky's idea that the learning of new skills or facts is based to a great extent on social interaction, i.e. that through interaction an individual or group can aspire to skills that could never be achieved when working alone. This implies that each indivudual in a group is able to take advantage not only of the capabilities of the leader but also of those of the other members.

Study I: A Course - Higher Education

The purpose of the first study was to evaluate the Peer Tutoring Model in higher education and the students' experience with peer-tutors and their own function in small groups. The course has been a traditional series of lectures consisting of a certain amount of literature and lectures. In the experiment the course was changed so that it consisted of the following units:
1. Introduction to Higher Education in Finland
2. Small groups
3. A lecture on the theme "Teaching and Learning in Higher Education"
4. Small groups
5. A lecture on the the theme "The Support to the Student in Higher Education"
6. Small groups
7. The results of the small groups and the summary of the lecture series

In every small group there was a peer tutor, whose task it was to 1) help the group through intervening to proceed at a parallel with the primary task , 2) act as an equal member of the group, and 3) examine the group phenomena in the students' small groups. The peer tutors formed their own group , which met regularly and was led by two teacher-consultants. In a group they examined the group phenomena that occurred in the small groups. Also the matters that were connected with one's own way of action and the examination of own behaviors were brought up in the consultant groups. All peer tutors were interviewed (N=5).The students in the course filled out a questionnaire (N=30).

Study II: A Course- Social Psychology

This course was realized in such a way that four peer tutors helped the teacher-consultants in their work. The aim of the course was 1) to familiarize the students with the theoretical questions related to social psychology, 2) to study the phenomena of group dynamics from the viewpoint of learning and teaching, and 3) to give every student the opportunity to learn and examine his own behaviour as an individual and as a group member.

The course was built on lectures and small group activities.The activity of the peer tutors concentrated on large group exercise, in which they acted as consultants for small groups together with the the teacher-consultants. The peer-tutors helped the small groups with questions to define the goals for their group work, and to see if all the resources were available. The students worked in small groups with special themes which were based on the lectures and the set literature of the course. They prepared a poster together, and it was presented at the end of the course. In this case the peer tutors were not participating in the course, but they were seen more as facilitators, as group members.

In this article the results are described from the viewpoint of the students' experiences of the model, focusing on three themes: 1) what was the influence of the peer tutor on the small groups' activity, 2) what is the meaning and function of the Peer Tutor Model in higher education, and 3) how do the students evaluate the model and how do they think it should be developed in the future?

III Results

Clearly over half of the students on the course of Higher Education estimated that in addition to the studies themselves they had learned especially to identify their own way of acting. Especially the problems concerning individual action were taken up in group situations.How to take responsibility in a group? The difficulty of changing , individual passivity and the unwillingness to commit oneself were mentioned. So the students mentioned that they had learned to make observations of all these things - and especially of themselves.

In general the approach was considered positive, but there seemed to be certain needs for the development as well. It is still necessary to think about the practical questions connected with this approach, as well as the theoretical knowledge of group dynamics. According to the students, the role and the task of the peer tutors still needed some clarifying. The tutors were expected to be the leaders of the groups.The peer tutors emphasized that acting as tutors in the groups had given much information about their own learning, but especially about how a group works and how it learns. There are many latent features and phenomena in the groups, which cannot be seen directly, but which can be detected only indirectly. The peer tutors pointed out that the work had been very important to them. In the words of one of them," It was the first time during your study you got a task where you could do it independently and which had a real meaning for you".

The adaptability of the model on the course of Social Psychology was evaluated as good. The students on the course evaluated the role of peer tutors as facilitators. He or she helped but was not very active in determining the activity of the group. The tutees were to understand that they themselves should do the work and not the tutor.The role and the personality of the tutor had an effect on the function of the group. A peer tutor who was very active and immediately shared his opinions seemed to confuse the group's activity. He or she took the leadership to him/herself although the group did not give it away.Also a very passive and quiet peer tutor had a controlling effect on the group.

Some of the students thought the working model was "unnatural" and far away from "real life",   but mostly, the students argued that the model was very realistic and a good practice for orientation to working life. In their words,"There is need for more new situations, difficulties and conflicts. Throughout these the individual learns more about himself, too. The whole university-studies can be developed in a more communicative direction.

DISCUSSION

The development of the Peer Tutoring Model was a part of the developmental programme at the Department of Behavioral Sciences. Various models for teaching and especially learning have been developed in the programme, especially where the students as resources are better taken into consideration. The results indicated that the small group activity and the Peer Tutor Model was reasonable in higher education too, where the subject aims are as important as the aim of group functioning. The role of the peer tutor was a little ambigious. What is the real effect of peer tutoring on the primary task-function of the small group is difficult to say, because the same effect could result from the activity of a group member or a teacher when he is functioning as an intervening consultant. In this model we supported the function of the groups with Peer-Tutor Model, but the same positive results could be possible in another way, too.

In another study the function of the Peer Tutor Model was evaluated very good as complementary to the lecturing practice. The communicative and interactive activity is a very important part of the university studies and should be promoted with various methods.The tutees described the feelings of envy, competition and conflicts to be a part of the groups' activity and that is how the model could give opportunity and readiness for the real working life. The results of the model imply that there are possibilities for a developmental relationship to the studying at the university level. The criticism against an unclear mission and inappropiate methods of teaching and learning has resulted in many various teaching experiments in Finnish universities, but it is important that these do not remain as experiments of some sporadic courses but that they could be one part of the developmental work at the whole department and faculty. Only then we can speak about changes at the organizational level.

REFERENCES

Aittola, T. Study Choices and Learning Styles of Students. Higher Education in Europe, 1988, XIII,4,pp 5-13.

Educational Faculties and Techer Education in the Finnish Universities: A Commentary by an International Review Team, ed. J. Vähäsaari, Helsinki, 3, 1994.

Gröhn,T., Kauppi,A., Ranta, M., Jansson, J. & Paananen, S.   Developing teching and learning in higher education,Helsinki University Press,1993.

Järvilehto,T. Yhteisöllisen oppiminen ohjelma: Käyttäytymistieteiden laitoksen koulutukssen kehittäminen, Department of Education, University of Oulu,1994.

Rogers, R. Theories, Concepts and Ethics, Part One, Student Development in Higher education, ed. D. Creamer, pp10-95, ACPA, New York.

Soini,H. & Kronqvist, E. The signifigance of group dynamics in peer-tutoring in higher education, Faculty of Education, University of Oulu,1994.

Managing-resource based learning

O. Liber

Information Technology Consultancy Unit, Notting Dale Technology Centre, 189-191 Freston Road, London W10 6TH, UK

Abstract

Teachers manage the complexity of their students' learning needs. Management cybernetics is concerned with the management of complexity, and so can help to reinterpret teaching methods in this light. The use of this approach shows that formal teaching restricts the expression of the complexity of learning needs, whereas group and resource-based teaching recognises the variety of students' needs, but at the cost of increased administration. Computer based tools can help alleviate this, and the HyperSMILE[1] system provides an example of a set of such tools for use with a large resource-based learning scheme for mathematics education.

Introduction

The argument of this paper is that teaching involves the management of complexity, and that the science of cybernetics can be used to provide a new perspective on different teaching methods as devices for the management of complexity. Debates on the effectiveness of different teaching methods have usually been around their educational merits; seeing them from this new perspective can help in their evaluation.

In cybernetics, variety is the formal term used as the measure of a system's complexity, and is defined by Ashby[2] as the 'number of possible states of a system'. His Law of Requisite Variety states that 'only variety can soak up variety'. Applied to the teaching situation, this means that the variety of learning needs must be balanced by the learning opportunities. Either the former must be somehow reduced, or the latter must be amplified, or some combination of the two; but the two sides of this equation must balance if the system is to survive.

According to Stafford Beer[3], a pioneer in management cybernetics, 'the tool for handling complexity is organization'. The way in which teaching is organized determines how students' variety is managed, whether it is ignored or respected.

The formal lesson goes back a long way. Everyone, no matter where in the world, would recognise a teacher expounding at a blackboard as the standard educational form, and to many it is the only proper way of teaching. I argue in this paper that no matter how good the teacher's exposition, it is essentially a 'low variety' device. Most educational establishments are set up to support this type of teaching, which, however, can be unhelpful for other teaching methods.

The last quarter century has seen the introduction of new teaching methods, along with new learning technologies. These make different demands on teachers and on their supporting institutions, the impact of which has not yet been fully understood. They can create a 'high variety' learning situation, but can have significant administrative requirements.

This paper sets out to use management cybernetics to help assess the effectiveness of different teaching methods, and suggests a role for computer-based systems. Finally it describes one such system that was developed for use in the teaching of mathematics.

Requisite Variety and organization of learning

The way in which Beer[4] has applied Ashby's Law to organizations can be partially described by figure 1:

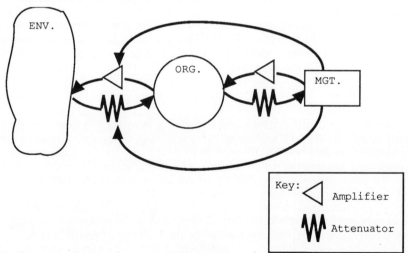

Figure 1.

Management is less complex than the organization it manages, which in turn is less complex than the environment in which it exists. Management is able to steer its organization by controlling the way in which the organization responds to its environment. Re-interpreting this for the classroom, teachers cannot hope to match the variety of their students' learning needs, and students cannot cope with the complexity of the potential learning possibilities that exist. What teachers can do is to manage the interaction between students and the "learning environment".

Teaching methods and modes of classroom organization, then, can be seen as being essentially devices for managing complexity. They can be characterised as falling into two broad categories; "low variety", seeking to reduce complexity; "high variety", seeking to permit the maximum possible expression of complexity.

Low variety

Low variety approaches attempt to make the students' expression of their complexity as difficult as possible. A number of devices can be seen to play a role in this. Grouping by ability, for example, reduces the population of students to a number of categories. Convincing students that their needs are identical controls the expression of individual complexity (although it usually emerges at some point). Detailed syllabuses limit the expression of students' learning desires. Formal teaching treats the group of students as if they were one.

Having been the principal mode for the delivery of learning for so long, formal teaching is difficult to challenge. Nevertheless, it is a low variety device *par excellence*, inhibiting the expression of the complexity of the group, and providing little scope for individual interaction between student and teacher. The learning offered to students is totally controlled by the teacher, all knowledge being filtered through him/her.

High variety

Higher variety learning can be made possible through the use of various strategies. For example, well-planned group work can get students to soak up each others' complexity without overwhelming the teacher. Using a wide range of learning resources can amplify the teacher's complexity. Resource-based learning can allow the provision of different learning programmes to suit individual students' needs.

Resource-based learning replaces the teachers' exposition with learning materials. It requires the development or collection of materials specifically designed for learning, including information and activities to support that learning. The materials can have different versions, each suited to a different learning need. The prime motivation of resource-based schemes is to enable learning that recognises and respects the variety of learning needs of any group.

In a resource-based situation, the teacher's role becomes the planning of programmes of study for learners that involve the use of these resources. They can, of course, adopt different strategies; they can have all students working on similar content but using different learning materials; they can organise the class into small groups; or they can have completely individualised learning.

The flexibility of learning programmes is to some extent constrained by how fine grained learning resources are. The shorter the unit length, the larger the resource base, and the greater the variety of learning options becomes.

However, there is a price to be paid; the greater the flexibility, the more difficult the management process becomes for the teacher.

Software Tools for Resource-Based Learning

Computer-based tools can help with managing variety, and the rest of this paper is devoted to giving a brief description of a prototype software system that was developed with that purpose in mind.

In 1989, my company was funded to design and implement a computer system to help with the management of SMILE, a resource-based learning system for mathematics education in schools. The project was funded by the Learning Technologies Unit (LTU) of the Training Enterprise and Education Directorate of the Employment Department.

SMILE had been in operation since the early 1970s, and was a response to the massive range of learning needs of schoolchildren. Over the years, the system had grown to incorporate nearly 2000 items of learning material, with corresponding answers and assessments. Whilst experienced teachers were able to cope with this proliferating variety, it was becoming increasingly difficult for newcomers to get to know the materials well enough to set them for individual students, and to make sense of student records. Various paper based devices had evolved to help with the management of the system, but it was apparent that computer management could have much to offer.

The LTU recognised the problems that could arise with resource-based and flexible learning systems, and funded the project as a prototype, to demonstrate an approach to handling these problems. The project took nearly three years, and there were several revisions in that time. However, there is not the space to describe the project here, but rather to give an outline of the resulting system.

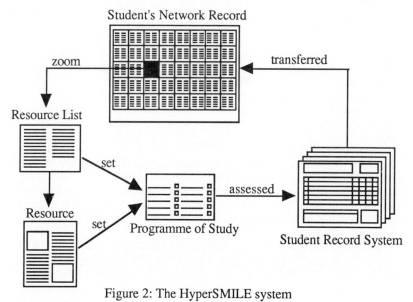

Figure 2: The HyperSMILE system

There are two main sources of complexity that HyperSMILE helps the teacher to manage: the learning resource base, and the student group (figure 2). Computer based tools need to make each of these more manageable, and make it possible to accurately match one to the other.

Resource management

Resources can come in all shapes and sizes. As well as specifically written learning materials, they can also include source books, tapes, videos, software and other equipment. One of the problems HyperSMILE set out to address was that of giving teachers the ability to get to know the materials that make up the SMILE system. HyperSMILE provides an on-screen browser that presents the materials according to their topic and level of difficulty. This two dimensional index can be scrolled around and "zoomed" in on, and any item can be displayed in an on-screen version (on-screen versions of all the materials were created as part of the project). Facilities to allow materials to be found by name have been built in. Model answers, tests and test answers can also be viewed.

Setting work for students

A copy of the resource browser (known as the student's network record) are automatically set up for each student when they are added to the system. Teachers can use the browse facility when designing a programme of study for the student, viewing and/or setting the materials with a click of the mouse.

As soon as an item is set, it is highlighted on the network record, providing a visual representation of the student's work to date. When a programme of work is set, it can be printed for the student along with any worksheets and tests

Record management

Keeping track of student progress is difficult in a resource-based individualised or group based situation, since each student may follow a unique programme of study. Good record keeping is essential, if subsequent programmes of work are to be planned on the basis of previous work.

HyperSMILE automatically records work set on a student's record card. A range of information can be recorded here on the student's work, including test scores, weighting of activities, and multi-level comments. Test answers are provided on screen when required by the teacher, but the decision was taken not to support computer marking of tests, since it was felt that teachers need to do this themselves to get a good feel for the students' understanding of the material. Various totals, averages and aggregates are automatically calculated. The records are also automatically transferred to the student's network record, thus allowing their progress on each category of the system to be monitored, and for this information to be available when the teacher is setting the next programme of work.

Class management

Students and classes can be added and removed from the system, and student records can be moved between classes. Class lists can be easily generated, and various batch facilities are provided to speed up these processes. Students' records can be exported to other packages such as spreadsheet or databases, allowing for their further analysis.

Summary
HyperSMILE provides a set of facilities that help with managing the complexity of a large resource base, and students on individualised programmes of study. By making the process easy to manage, and providing detailed information at appropriate places, it reduces the administrative overhead and removes the limitation this would have brought to the size and complexity of the resource base. As such it provides a model for the use of computers in supporting resource-based approaches to learning.

Conclusion

This paper has sought to reinterpret teaching approaches as devices for managing the complexity inherent in a class of students, using concepts from management cybernetics. Formal teaching methods have been characterised as seeking to reduce complexity, whereas resource-based and group learning strategies are identified as seeking to respond to the expression of students' individual learning needs. However, the more fine grained and varied the resource-based scheme, the greater the problem of administration becomes. Computer based learning management systems can help overcome this problem by providing tools to make a large resource base tractable, and by providing record keeping systems that allow accurate matching between students and learning resources.

Management cybernetics can be also be applied to help understand the structure of the whole educational establishment. Its organizations exist to allow lessons to take place; but their structure supports certain styles of educational delivery and discourages others. Cybernetic tools provide insights into how these structures enable the management of complexity, and can help with their redesign to support different educational approaches.

References

1. Liber, O., *HyperSMILE Project Final Report,* Department of Employment, Sheffield, awaiting publication.
2. Ashby, W.R., *An Introduction to Cybernetics*, Methuen, London and New York, 1956.
3. Beer, S., *Platform for Change*, John Wiley, Chichester, 1979.
4. Beer, S., *The Heart of Enterprise*, John Wiley, Chichester, 1979.

Learning about the learners - The impact of a peer tutoring scheme

J. Mallatratt

Department of Computing, Hanover Building, University of Central Lancashire, Preston PR1 1HE, UK

Abstract

The paper reports on a peer tutoring scheme established in the Department of Computing at the University of Central Lancashire. The scheme was used to provide support for a particular course unit. Students in successive cohorts have found the work covered in this unit difficult and have consistently performed badly in this area. In the evaluation of the scheme, three main themes have been addressed. Firstly, consideration has been given to the extent to which the peer tutor support has been taken up by students. Secondly, the perceived effects that the support has had on tutees have been analysed. Finally, consideration has been given to progression statistics both prior to and since the scheme's introduction.

1 Background

This paper gives a description of, and evaluation of, a peer tutoring scheme introduced in the Department of Computing at the University of Central Lancashire. The scheme was initially staged in the first semester of the 1993-94 academic session.

The scheme was designed to make peer tutor support available to students on the first years of the HND Computing and the HND Software Engineering courses. In the first year this meant that a total of approximately seventy students (50 on the HND Computing, 20 on the HND Software Engineering) were included. These courses were chosen because the Department was less than satisfied with their wastage rates (see section 4.3 'Progression') and was eager to discover whether peer tutoring could constitute (part of) a solution. In particular, it was decided to focus support upon a course unit appearing in both programmes (Principles of Computer Systems (PCS)) that traditionally had a higher than average failure rate. The scheme was universal, in contrast to some computing schemes developed elsewhere (eg McDonnell [1]). The absence of a control group placed a constraint upon design of the scheme's evaluation, but it was felt that it would be unethical to withhold access to a potentially beneficial supplement from a subset of the student cohort (Goodlad and Hirst [2]).

Peer tutors were recruited from second and third year degree students. In the first year of the scheme, four students took on the role of peer tutors. The basic intention of the scheme was to provide one hour per week additional (peer tutor) support to all the HND students. As there were four tutorial groups, one peer tutor was assigned to each. Before any tutoring was provided, the tutors had to attend an intensive two day training course, loosely based upon materials developed for use with peer tutors at University of Missouri - Kansas City. Thereafter, they had timetabled support of an hour per week with the member of staff responsible for the scheme.

The group of staff that established the scheme had identified two sets of objectives for peer tutoring. The first set related to the Department and the recipient students. These were:

* To reduce drop out rates on the Department's courses

* To reduce failure rates on (a) course unit(s) which traditionally caused students problems

* To provide extra support to students

The second set concerned the peer tutors. For them, two objectives were identified:

* To promote deep learning of the material being tutored

* To develop the skill of providing learning support to others

Peer tutors enrolled for a course unit (Computing Peer Tutors' Unit) which had its own set of learning outcomes and assessment strategy, part of the latter being based upon feedback gathered from tutees via a questionnaire.

It was decided that the focus of the support to be given by the peer tutors to their tutees was support to develop the skill of being independent learners. That is, rather than peer tutoring becoming another means by which answers about subject content were provided, sessions were intended to provide the time in which help could be given to tutees to discover the nature of the gaps in their knowledge and the means of how to address them. Apart from requiring that this principle guided their actions, there were no further rules imposed upon the tutors about the way in which tutoring sessions should operate.

2 Evaluation

The evaluation strategy comprised of five components:

- A questionnaire for completion by all actual, and potential, tutees
- A critical review written by each peer tutor
- Comparison of drop out rates from the course before and after the innovation
- Comparison of student grades on the PCS course unit before and after the innovation
- Evaluation by an 'external' evaluator

The comments that follow are based upon the information gleaned from this combination of sources.

3 Use made of the peer tutoring scheme

The questionnaire was administered (anonymously) at the end of the semester to all the students on year 1 of the HND Computing and HND Software Engineering courses. From the responses to the questionnaire, it would appear that approximately 64% (44) of students made some use of the sessions, with just under half of these (43% - 19 students) attending four or more sessions. (One student did not respond to this question.) These figures seem to compare favourably with a scheme developed in the computing domain elsewhere (Ball [3]). According to the tutors, the figures might be slightly inflated as they exceeded their personal 'impressions'. However, as the tutors were not required to keep registers and were, indeed, warned of the possible disadvantage of being seen to do so (i.e. running the risk of being accused of passing the information back to lecturers - students attending peer tutor sessions were given assurances that their confidentiality would be respected), this perspective cannot constitute a formal triangulation.

The reasons why students first attended a peer tutoring session are shown in Figure 1. These results indicate quite clearly that students were more motivated by their own perception of needs (i.e. they were seeking to obtain a better grade or were having difficulties with the course) than they were by being exhorted by others around them (fellow students or lecturing staff). Of those students who didn't use the scheme, 60% (15 students) indicated that it was because they were not having difficulties with the course. This, and other reasons for non-use of the scheme are shown in Figure 2.

Figure 1 Reason given for first attending a peer tutoring session

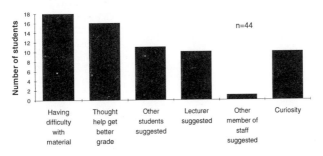

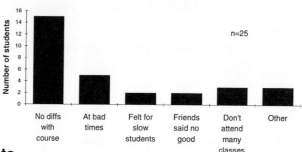

Figure 2 Reasons given for never attending a peer tutoring session

4 Effects

4.1 Understanding of PCS and study skills improvement

The extent to which tutees felt that peer tutor support had helped them with their understanding of PCS and the development of their study skills is shown in Figure 3. Inspection of the chart shows that, out of those students who attended peer tutor sessions, most felt that they had been supported to tackle their coursework and to get a better grade for PCS. Regarding this latter point, there would appear to be corroborating evidence since both the average grade and the average pass grade were better for this cohort than for any of the other cohorts for which data is available (see Figure 4). The scale of the improvement in the pass grade (approximately 31% over the previous year) is particularly pleasing as it might be indicative that those students who were motivated to do well were finding a more accessible mechanism to support that objective. However, more longitudinal data is required before too many inferences are made about causation.

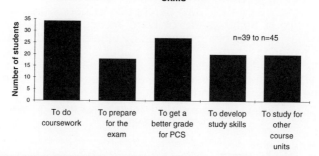

Figure 3 Ways in which peer tutoring was felt to have helped - understanding of PCS and study skills

Figure 4 Average grades obtained in PCS		
	Average grade	Average pass grade
1991-2	7.5	6.6
1992-3	8.8	7.5
1993-4	7	5.2

Returning to the findings shown in Figure 3, fewer students indicated that peer tutor support had helped them to prepare for the exam than might have been anticipated. However, as the questionnaire was administered before the exam was taken, it could be that many respondents were unwilling to commit themselves until they were clear how appropriate their exam preparation had been.

A sizeable proportion of the students indicated that they had either developed their study skills (20 out of 41 respondents) and/or improved their study of other course units (20 out of 39 respondents). Whilst this is a pleasing result, it might have been expected that the numbers would have been higher given that one of the intentions was that the peer tutors would concentrate on developing the independent learning skills of their tutees. However, tutor reviews revealed that two of the four tutors felt more confident in delivering PCS content (and did so) than in supporting study skills development and so this could account for the result.

4.2 Confidence and comfort

It could be argued that any well-founded increase in a student's confidence, their level of comfort with their course, or with their host Department, must be beneficial. Twenty nine students felt more comfortable with the course and 14 felt themselves to be more a part of the Department as a consequence of the introduction of peer tutoring. By comparison, the fact that only nine students claimed to feel more confident in their studies may initially seem disappointing. However, this number has to be set in the context of how many students staff would wish to feel more confident. The staff perception is that although there is a minority of students whose lack of confidence is woeful, there is also a large number of students who are over-confident. The students who fall into this latter category can generally be found amongst those who have previously taken Computer Studies at National Diploma level, a group which accounts for over 50% of the cohort in most years.

4.3 Progression

An extremely surprising result was that a total of seven students indicated that peer tutor support had been the critical factor in preventing them from leaving the course. When this question was drafted, it was expected that no more than one, if any, student would respond positively to it. Doubts about its reliability came to the fore when seven did. However, some supporting evidence suggests that it might be reliable. Admittedly some of this is impressionistic, such as the unsolicited praise for the scheme given by student representatives at their course committee meeting. Other evidence is as yet incomplete. For instance, drop out statistics from the previous two years show that the proportion of students who embarked upon the first year of the HND Computing who failed to proceed into the second year was 53% in 1992 and 44% in 1993. In the current year, so far eight students out of the original fifty eight that enrolled (14%) have withdrawn. Clearly this figure can only deteriorate between now and October 1994 when the second year enrolment figures will be known, but at this stage there is still reason to be hopeful that the progression statistics will represent an improvement over previous years.

Figures for the HND Software Engineering are similar although, as it is a newer course, there is only one previous cohort with which to make comparisons. In 1993 53% failed to proceed from enrolment in the first year to enrolment in the second. At this stage in the current year, withdrawals from the course account for 10% of the original first year cohort.

Even if the final figures, when they are available, show a marked improvement in progression, there can be no certainty that the improvement is attributable to either the direct or indirect effects of the introduction of peer tutoring. However, a pleasing result would at least suggest that there is merit in continuing to collect data relating to the innovation for at least another session if for no other reason than to enable some longitudinal analyses to be made.

5 Conclusion

Although the effects of this innovation have been more systematically investigated than would be normally be the case in a Department where teaching is the prime function, it is clear that there are a number of shortcomings to the design of the evaluation. Little attention has been given to the extent to which the tutors' depth of understanding of the PCS material has changed during their involvement with the scheme. Consideration has not been given to the learning styles of the tutees and the extent to which the peer tutor system has either supported or confronted these. Instead the evaluation design has been driven by the pragmatics of costs and benefits, that is how can the most benefit from an evaluation be derived without sustaining unacceptable costs. The inclusion of a specialist input from psychology would probably have been helpful. However, if inspection of the processes of learning became intrusive, beneficial effects of the scheme could be undermined. It is a valued component of the scheme that the attendance of any tutee is not a matter of report to any member of staff; close observation could jeopardise this anonymity.

References

1. McDonnell, J.T. Peer tutoring: a pilot scheme among computer science undergraduates in Proceedings of Conference on Developments in the Teaching of Computer Science, University of Kent, April 1992

2. Goodlad, S and Hirst, B Explorations in peer tutoring, Chapter 1 in *Explorations in Peer Tutoring*, ed S Goodlad and B Hirst, pp1-25, Blackwell Education, Oxford, 1990.

3. Ball, D Supplemental Instruction: a student centred approach to transferable skills development at Hatfield Polytechnic. Paper presented at Higher Education for Capability conference on peer tutoring, University of Plymouth,1993

Co-operative learning using self and peer assessment in Public International Law

J. McCrae & I. Scobbie

Department of Law, Department of Psychology, University of Dundee, Dundee DD1 4HN, UK

Abstract

Courses in Law are traditionally heavily content focused and individualistically oriented. The redesign of the Public International Law course at the University of Dundee aimed to mirror the central course aim of 'stimulating and encouraging a critical approach to law', within the student learning experiences and assessment procedures. The introduction of co-operative interactive learning coupled with a structured and developmental assessment schedule which utilised mutually generated assessment criteria and self and peer assessment activities, provided students with an opportunity to enhance skills which will benefit career development.

Background

Public International Law is an honours level class in which 11 students enrolled during the pilot study. Participants are expected to undertake approximately 8-10 hours of preparatory reading of texts and case law prior to attending the two-hour weekly seminar classes. To date the traditional method of course assessment had been a three-hour examination which accounted for 100% of course marks.

The course addresses three broad areas of International Law: the use of force in international relations; aspects of international humanitarian laws of war; and issues arising from the process of international adjudication. Consequently much of the law has immediate application within the current world political scene. One of the key aims of the course is to stimulate and encourage a critical approach in these areas of law.

Co-operative learning activities

At the heart of the course redesign was the desire to reflect the development of a 'critical approach' in aspects other than simply the course content. The development and enhancement of skills of analysis and criticism, the public presentation of investigative findings and an accurate awareness of the quality of one's own performance have been identified as factors which contribute to success in graduate employment.[1]

The course redesign also afforded an opportunity to develop a new assessment schedule. The traditional three-hour end-of-year summative examination, contributes little to the formative development of student learning and understanding. The introduction of self and peer assessment techniques which not only contributed to formative learning but also carried 15% of course marks was unique within the Faculty. The schedule was designed to involve students in the generation of criteria for assessment in relation to various activities and in the allocation of marks. Seeking formal approval for these new assessment procedures precipitated significant debate at both Departmental and Faculty Board meetings. It was a condition of Board approval that the lecturer had to seek the support and agreement of the students who had registered for the course.

Enhancing learning through co-operative written tasks

It is an almost universal feature of higher education courses that the majority of marks which count towards a degree award are allocated for written essays, be they completed in term time or during the final examination period. It is rare for any 'tuition' to be provided in the development of essay writing skills *within* specific discipline areas. It is also uncommon for the criteria on which the assessment of essays is based to be made available to students prior to the submission of essays. It may even be that the criteria for 'success' varies between departments and disciplines. Most often the feedback on the quality of one essay is not received in time to inform improvements in a subsequent essay. Examination essays are often never returned to the student. In short, the use of essays solely as a form of summative assessment contributes little to the learning cycle by way of feedback for reflection.

In order to address some of the deficiencies outlined above and to utilise written tasks to aid student learning, three increasingly complex writing exercises were undertaken prior to the completion of the final examination essays.

The first exercise required students to complete a shared reading assignment to be undertaken in pairs and to be presented in a written format as key points for a summary argument. Prior to embarking on the task students identified the criteria by which the summaries would be assessed: structure, brevity, canvassing both sides of the argument, identification of the main points, identification of contentious points which require discussion and legibility.

Summaries were then submitted for tutor marking, however initially tutor marks were withheld so that students could review each others work and comment on the degree to which they believed that their colleagues' summaries met the mutually identified criteria. No course marks were allocated for this exercise.

Peer co-operation was encouraged on three levels: researching the topic in pairs; preparing the argument summary; providing feedback on the summaries produced by other pairs. At the completion of the exercise all summaries were made available to other class members. As well as constituting the foundation exercise in the preparation of essays, this also provided a precursor for the oral presentation aspect of the course.

The second written task was a short essay (maximum 1500 words) which was undertaken individually. The topic choice however, was so designed as to allow for the cumulative short essays to provide an overview of a substantial content topic area of the course. Thus the individual's essay contributed co-operatively to the gaining of a wider topic perspective by other members of the class. Again the assessment criteria were mutually identified prior to the submission of the essays.

Following the marking of the short essays by the tutor (with tutor marks withheld), the essays were returned during class time for students to mark the essays of four peers in accordance with the agreed criteria. The tutor subsequently aggregated the peer marks and allocated 5% of the course marks for this exercise. Comparison between tutor marks and peer marking on this exercise revealed such a high degree of congruence that no tutor adjustments were required in relation to the peer allocation of marks.

The final written task was the completion of the long essay (5-10,000 words) worth 20% of course marks. For this essay students were required to include a self assessment assignment attachment - a self reviewing mechanism, the criteria of which had been refined during the course. The tutor was committed to returning this essay prior to the final examination so that feedback and comments might be incorporated during final preparations for the examination.

These three exercises were designed to provide incremental complexity in written tasks. Co-operation between students was actively encouraged during the completion of the tasks. Students co-operatively with their peers and tutor, generated the assessment criteria which they subsequently applied to each others' work - the resulting peer marks being highly congruent with those of the tutor. Not only did each individual student benefit from the range of comments received but each student also had the opportunity to compare and contrast the quality of work of their peers. Many students go through university without sighting any other student's work apart from that of friends - and even then the work may be limited in allowing the student to appreciate the range of assignment quality.

Enhancing learning through oral presentations

Good quality presentation skills are of particular importance within Law although only a limited number of opportunities exist to develop these skills within formal courses e.g. Moot Court.

As with the written tasks, the oral presentation sessions were structured such that the first presentation was considered as the preparatory 'test run'. Consequently, no marks were allocated for the first presentation. Paired co-operative work was again encouraged, with students researching the topic in pairs with both contributing to the oral presentation allotted time.

Assessment criteria to be applied to the presentations was again originally generated by class discussion and subsequently refined and enhanced for the second presentation.

Each speaker was required to complete a self assessment or reflection sheet on the basis of her/his presentation and then received copies of comments and feedback from the rest of the class. Students were encouraged not only to indicate the numerical rating but also to provide their peers with written comments.

The second presentation was a sole presentation and was awarded 5% of course marks. As with the peer assessed written exercise, peer marks were collated and combined with the tutor's allocation of marks. The same close alignment of peer marks with tutor marks was evidenced - rank order of marks was almost identical.

Enhancing learning through assessment

In the above sections, brief details have been provided about self assessment/self reflection sheets which were developed for both written exercises and oral presentations (details of these will be provided at the conference presentation).

These were augmented by the peer assessments and feedback undertaken using the mutually generated assessment criteria for the summary argument and short essay. Peer assessment criteria for the oral presentation were also developed and refined during the course.

The final component of self and peer assessment undertaken in the course was the allocation of a further 5% of the course marks in relation to the individual student's contribution to the course. This list of assessment criteria was compiled throughout the year by the tutor on the basis of other lists of criteria, comments and discussions.

Students were firstly asked to rate themselves on the list of items relating to contribution to, and participation in, the seminar programme. These individual self assessments were then transferred to a tally sheet, immediately photocopied and redistributed to class members for review. Essentially students were involved in a peer verification process of each individual class member's self assessment of her or his contribution to the seminars.

Each student was invited in turn to indicate whether there was any rating which s/he would like to alter in the self assessment. Class members were then invited to make comments as to their opinion of the accuracy and appropriateness of the ratings which individuals had allocated to themselves. By mutual agreement some scores on specific items were increased or decreased as a result of the discussion which ensued.

Discussion

Essentially this course redesign has utilised assessment as the focus to bring about change in the ways in which students interact. This focus has allowed for restructuring of seminar activities to encourage the development of co-operative learning. Much of the theoretical underpinning of the above practices is based on the reflective practitioner approach espoused by Schon[2], the suggestions for the practical application of self and peer assessment in higher education by Boud[3] and the meta-analysis of studies in self assessment by Boud and Falchikov[4].

The word 'assess' is derived form the action 'to sit down beside' (C15 <OF assesser, <L assidere). The concept of 'sitting down beside' portrays a picture of closeness, support and perhaps consultation and mutual decision making. It does not readily accord with the more modern educational interpretation in general practice of assessment being a removed, detached (sometimes anonymous), non-consultative, judgement resulting in the allocation of marks or grades.

The redesigning of the Public International Law course was modelled on the original derivation of the word 'assess'. By applying it to the notion of self and peer assessment as outlined above, there are the beginnings of an acceptable foundation on which to expand the sound educational principle of co-operative learning.

The ability to sit beside ones self or ones peers and examine the work or activity with honesty and constructive criticism - is an essential and integral key in our learning processes.

Conclusion

The Public International Law course was itself subject to evaluation by the participants. (A summary of the evaluation will be provided at the conference). When students were asked: "In what ways (if any) was this course preferable to lecture based courses?" the replies included:

- Made you think - not just listen.
- The way we have to work on our own 'stuff'.
- The discussion was good and in my opinion the only way such a course could be learned - lectures would not work.
- Smaller classes = better atmosphere = more individual contribution.
- Involvement equals interest. Not just cardboard lectures.
- It wasn't - too much time taken up in discussing assessment e.g. today;
- Lively discussions. Presentations helped me to learn in detail aspects of the course.
- More room for discussions.

When asked whether this type of learning activity should be repeated in another Law course and whether the same course format should be retained for next year's students, all but one student responded in the affirmative.

Students also offered suggestions about how the course could be improved and these will be taken into consideration when planning for next year.

Perhaps the most important finding for note by traditional academics, is that in both the written short essay exercise and the oral presentation assessments, peer assessment ratings matched those ratings given by the tutor (much to the tutor's surprise and relief). Thus when assessment criteria are co-operatively generated, overtly stated and a minimum amount of 'practice' time is allocated, not only is there high inter-rater reliability, there is also a significant contribution to the formative learning process of students.

References

1. *Enterprise in Higher Education Key Features of Enterprise in Higher Education 1990-91,* Employment Department, Sheffield.

2. Schon, D. *The Reflective Practitioner,* Basic Books, New York, 1983.

3. Boud, D. *Implementing Student Self Assessment,* HERDSA Green Guide No. 5. 1986.

4. Falchikov, N. Boud, D. Student Self-Assessment in Higher Education: A Meta Analysis, *Review of Educational Research,* 1989, 59 (4), 395-430.

Cross year peer tutoring with Law undergraduates

S. Moody & J. McCrae
Department of Law, Department of Psychology, University of Dundee, Dundee DD1 4HN, UK

Abstract

A pilot project in cross year peer tutoring was undertaken in the Department of Law at the University of Dundee. Four student tutors conducted tutorials for 157 first year students. The project was implemented on the basis of a systematic and strategic plan with significant attention being paid to the training and debriefing of student tutors. An evaluation of the tutorials by student participants and a review of the experience of the student tutors were undertaken. The project was deemed highly successful with 83% of students indicating that student-led tutorials should be offered to next year's students and 80% indicating that they personally would wish to repeat the experience.

Introduction

Peer support for learning could be described as the 'untapped resource' of higher education. Students naturally seek the support of their peers in the extra-curricular activities of their university experience and informally tap the knowledge and understanding of their fellow students in the library, tutorial or laboratory class. The concept of students helping each other to learn and in the process consolidating their own learning was proposed by scholars of ancient times, was utilised by Lancaster and Bell in the late 18th century and is again being examined as a viable approach to learning in higher education.

Goodlad and Hirst[1] indicate that they identified, between 1975 and 1989, over 1000 papers published on the topic of 'Peer Tutoring'. Whitman[2] states that a review of the American literature shows that the cognitive processing used to study material to teach is different from studying for a test, that peer learners benefit because of the ability of peers to teach at the right level and that both the student teacher and learner appear to benefit from the co-operative relationship that peer teaching generates. Whitman concludes that: "Providing opportunities for students to teach each other may be one of the most important services a teacher can render". (v)

The same report indicates that staff who are about to undertake the introduction of a peer teaching programme might benefit from adopting a systematic approach. The development of the University of Dundee's Peer Tutoring in Law project took cognisance of these suggestions and adapted and augmented the components of the strategy:

- a tactful 'public relations' campaign to promote the introduction of student tutors both in relation to staff and students
- project goals and objectives to be identified clearly in writing
- staff should be involved in the recruitment, selection and training of student tutors
- student tutors should receive adequate orientation and training
- where possible training should be augmented by 'guidance notes' or manuals
- student tutors should receive adequate debriefing and an opportunity to reflect on their experiences
- student tutors should receive acknowledgement for the responsibilities which they have undertaken
- pilot project results need to be evaluated and communicated to the wider staff group

This paper will address briefly each of these aspects in relation to the Dundee project.

Background

First Year LLB students undertaking a compulsory course on the Scots Law of Delict (civil liability arising from non-contractual obligations) are taught mainly by lectures which take place three times a week for twelve weeks. As with other First Year courses tutorial sessions are offered to students approximately every other week, a total of five. Unlike lectures, attendance at tutorials is compulsory and a register is taken.

Tutorials for courses such as this generally involve students in finding solutions to fictitious problems. While students were advised in the Course Guide about the general topic which would be addressed in the tutorial in only one case were they given the problem in advance and asked to prepare an answer. The student-led tutorial followed the usual pattern with students attending lectures the week before the tutorial on the subject matter to be covered in the problem. The problem, which focused on the delictual responsibilities of employers, was not given to students until the tutorial itself. As with the other tutorials both the problem itself and the notes to assist tutors were provided by the course organiser.

Methodology

'Public relations'

Although the original intention had been to run student-led tutorials in parallel with the standard tutorials, and thus be able to draw comparative results, it was considered by the Head of Department that this might raise concerns among the recipients about differences in teaching provision. Therefore to accommodate the pilot project an extra compulsory tutorial was added to the Delict course. This took place in Week 10 after students had already participated in three other tutorials. This approach could also be interpreted as the Department's strategy for limiting any possible negative repercussions from the pilot activities.

The existing complement of course tutors consisted of the course organiser, another experienced staff member and 2 external tutors, both graduates with legal practising certificates but no previous experience of running tutorials. These tutors, unlike the student tutors, received no formal training for the task since this is not standard practice in the Law Department. The course organiser did discuss the aims and objectives of the tutorial and different approaches to the process with them individually and was available for advice.

Departmental staff were made aware of the pilot project. Students were informed both by information in the course handbook as well as by announcements at lectures.

Project Goals

In the early stages of the project the aims of the project were outlined:

- to recruit four advanced Delict course students to undertake three tutorial groups each with 12-14 students studying Delict at a more basic level
- to ascertain the effectiveness of using students as tutors
- to evaluate student tutors as a contribution to peer support for learning in higher education.

An outline of the anticipated advantages and disadvantages for the first year students, the student tutors and the department was developed and a timetable for implementation was identified.

Recruitment and selection

Prior to the recruitment of student tutors, staff identified what they believed to be the criteria for 'good student tutors'. Nine applications (5 third years, 4 fourth years) were received for the four advertised posts. Each applicant was required to submit a short application form and to indicate reasons for applying and any previous experience which might be relevant to the role of student tutor. Two staff members, including the project leader, conducted the fifteen minute recruitment interviews.

For the most part interviewees made excellent suggestions for dealing with difficult situations. They were particularly aware of the need to encourage students to participate, to ensure that students' understanding is enhanced and to make the tutorials interesting!

Any of the nine candidates would, we believed, have performed well. In the final event the following criteria were applied:

- ability to communicate clearly
- maturity and confidence to cope with awkward situations
- willingness to look to students' needs - not their own
- a relaxed but planned approach to the tutorial.

Two students were chosen from third year and two from fourth year All demonstrated a variety of approaches to learning. Gender differences were reflected in three females and one male.

Orientation and training

Student tutors, unlike other tutors, had the opportunity to participate in two training sessions. The first two hour session was taken by a representative from the Psychology Department who was also present at the recruitment interviews. The subsequent session was delivered by the course organiser.

The first session focused on pedagogical issues and aspects of group dynamics. The student tutors' expectations and needs with respect to the training sessions were addressed. Participants identified what they considered to be the criteria for a 'good tutorial'. Student tutors were introduced to the concept of different learning styles and discussion on the implications for tutorial groups ensued. Details were outlined on the process of planning a tutorial and the session concluded by addressing 'problems and questions' which the tutors posed. Student tutors were also provided with a 'Handbook' which had previously been prepared for a more extensive training session with student tutors who had participated in the University's Summer School.

The second training session focused on the content of the tutorial i.e. the problem to be solved. Tutors had an opportunity to tackle the problem unseen, thus placing them in the same situation as their subsequent tutorial participants. The four tutors were asked to identify appropriate self assessment criteria which they might apply to their own performances following the tutorial session. The remainder of the time was used to finalise administrative details e.g. attendance sheets and room allocations.

At this meeting student tutors agreed to allow their third tutorial videoed for debriefing purposes. It is anticipated that the excerpts from these videos together with the video of the debriefing session may contribute to a training video for subsequent student tutor training sessions.

Debriefing and acknowledgement

A debriefing and feedback session was held the week after the student-led tutorials. This session was videoed.

All the student tutors indicated that they had found it beneficial to have spent time preparing for the tutorials by reviewing the training material, familiarising themselves with relevant tutorial material, identifying aims and objectives, preparing an outline of the process and, where appropriate, reviewing their strategy in the light of earlier tutorial experience

All but one student tutor found the video camera intrusive and would have preferred to have gained experience of videos in an earlier training session prior to the tutorials. However, they had no difficulties with the use of the video cameras thereafter in the debriefing session. Different views were expressed about the responses of the students themselves to the camera. One tutor felt that students became more nervous, two thought that students were more supportive of the student tutor when the video camera was present and one considered that it made no difference.

Student tutors were not aware of any progression from the first to the third tutorial group although two did feel more relaxed in later sessions. They were surprised by the difference in group dynamics and were quickly aware of established patterns within groups - a product of the interaction between individual students and the approach adopted by the usual tutor. Since students are in the same tutorial groups every week and may have the same tutor over a period of ten weeks it would be unrealistic to expect that student tutors would to be able to easily influence such established patterns. The variance in the students' preparedness, knowledge and understanding was also noted.

Student tutors believed that these problems might be overcome by allowing them to run a series of tutorials dealing with different issues.

Student tutors did not consider that different groups of students in terms of sex, age or previous experience presented particular difficulties. Tutors had anticipated experiencing problems with mature students - this did not materialise. Mature students per se were not more demanding or less easy to control - these aspects depended more on the personality of the individual students and the already developed group pattern.

All the student tutors had been required to deal with the unexpected. Students perceived some ambiguity in the problem which had not been anticipated by the course organiser. Students also inevitably suggested possible but unlikely solutions which were not included in the 'Notes for Tutors'. The students apparently dealt well with these surprises, either by tackling them head-on and in the way which the course organiser would have done or by indicating that they did not know the answer but would find out.

All student tutors encouraged participation and attempted to answer questions adequately. They kept to time and summarised the key points at the end.

The size of the groups varied from 5 to 19 - it was anticipated that groups should comprise 10 to 13 students. This required students tutors to be adaptable with one tutor dividing the first two tutorials into two, with one group representing the employer's case and the other advising the employee. This had been very successful, especially the second time this strategy was adopted. However, the third group was far too big for this and the video camera added to the difficulties.

Tutors were critical of their own performances with no one rating her/his input as excellent. There were noticeable differences between tutorials with three tutors finding the second tutorial most successful. The lowest ratings were for management of the tutorial. However all agreed that this would improve with experience and increasing confidence.

Student tutors all agreed that they had enjoyed the experiment and would recommend it as a learning experience:

> *The major benefit I found was that it helped me to tackle problems like this logically. The issues were very clear in my mind; I felt I knew what the students' problems were and how to deal with them.*

Tutors indicated that they had gained in confidence as a result of the experience and had developed their communication skills:

> • *it improved my communication skills and presentation abilities*
> • *it has made me less shy about speaking in front of groups*
> • *I learnt ways of getting a point across to people*
> • *it provided a boost to my confidence when talking to a group of people.*

It also gave them the opportunity to get to know some of the First Year students and to break down barriers between themselves and new entrants. They considered that it would have been better had they led more than one tutorial with the same tutorial group earlier in the year:

> • *the project should be initiated earlier in the academic year so student tutors do not inherit problems that have developed over the year..and are more approachable and accessible to First Year students in their early months at University*
> • *far better to take the same group for several tutorials..this would give us all a*

chance to get to know one another better
• *a better rapport could be built between tutor and students by giving student tutors the opportunity to take one group on a number of occasions-tutorials would be more constructive ...it would reduce the novelty of the situation and provide more realistic results.*

At the conclusion of the debriefing session, the project leader indicated that the student tutors, who had undertaken the task voluntarily, would receive in recognition of their efforts, a Certificate of Competence for inclusion in their CV and a personal copy of their videoed tutorial. Student tutors were also given a book token in recognition of their contribution.

Evaluation and dissemination

The evaluation questionnaire was administered in lecture time within 4 days of the first tutorials. Questionnaires were completed by 85 of the 157 First Year students including recent school leavers, graduate entrants and mature students. Overall the response to student-led tutorials was very positive and criticisms came from only a small minority of students. Critical responses correlated with one particular tutorial.

Just under half of the students (47%) considered that the tutorial run by the student tutor had been better than their normal tutorial, a third considered the student-led tutorial to be the same as their normal tutorials and 20% thought that it had been worse. A key advantage of student-led tutorials was a more relaxed, informal atmosphere in which students felt less intimidated and not under as much pressure to perform well and therefore more willing to contribute and participate:

• *there's a more relaxed atmosphere and you feel as if you're learning together rather than being taught*
• *students feel less intimidated and more ready to participate in discussion*
• *informality encourages participation*
• *there was more participation by the group than normal.*

Student tutors were regarded as peers and therefore were seen as more approachable. Students were more inclined to ask questions and not afraid to show a lack of understanding. Their questions were answered in ways which were sometimes easier to understand and more straightforward than when staff tutors took the tutorial:

• *it is much easier to relate to persons of a similar age and someone who has experienced the same course*
• *the concepts were explained in a way which seemed more understandable ..the language was less sophisticated*
• *a student was far more able to let us know how to go about answering a question..and help with exam technique*

> • *student tutors can understand problems experienced by First Year students and*
> *explain them*
> • *tutors tend to tell you what they want from an answer not how to reach it logically*
> *and under stress.*

It was felt by some respondents that student tutors had prepared the tutorials more thoroughly than staff tutors did and that student tutors showed more interest and enthusiasm. This is not surprising given the emphasis placed on training and preparation for the student tutors and the focus on one tutorial problem only. Inevitably the one-off nature of the pilot project for the respondents gave student-led tutorials a certain novelty value.

> • *the student seemed more clued up on the subject- no doubt as the result of*
> *studying it at the time*
> • *student tutor seemed to have done more preparation than the normal tutor*
> • *this one knew what she was talking about, was up to date and used the full hour.*

Students also noted that student tutors gave them increased confidence in their own ability to complete the course satisfactorily and enabled them to see a progression from First Year topics to more advanced courses in Honours years.

About one fifth of the respondents saw disadvantages in the use of student tutors. The main concern was that student tutors might lack the depth of knowledge of staff tutors.

> • *it may be that student tutors lack the full depth of experience necessary to expand*
> *on and answer awkward questions arising in tutorials*
> •*perhaps not as knowledgeable as the tutor would be*
> • *not as much knowledge if someone asked a question which they could not answer*
> • *students aren't 'authorities' and haven't written books yet.*

However, less than half of those who expressed such concerns indicated that this had been their actual experience in the tutorial and several were quick to point out that the student tutor had displayed very good knowledge of the subject matter.

Another perceived disadvantage stemmed from the nervousness of student tutors, their lack of teaching experience and their inability to control a tutorial group.

When asked whether the students wished to repeat this type of student-led tutorial in another Law course, 84% considered the affirmative. An even greater proportion (88%) indicated that this format should be offered to next year's students.

Finally, 60 % of respondents registered that they would be interested in volunteering to be a student tutor.

Conclusion

The originator of the student tutor project had anticipated a much larger pilot in terms of the number of student tutors involved and the number of tutorials taken. However as outlined above, the decision to limit the pilot project was taken by the Department. At times the proportion of hours spent in preparation, training and debriefing seemed far in excess of the number of tutorial hours being undertaken. Even under these circumstances, there was an over-riding commitment on the part of the course organiser to develop a detailed and comprehensive process of establishing a peer tutoring project, so that in the event of 'success' there would be a complete package on hand to sustain an expansion to the programme.

The project has been deemed highly successful by the staff and students involved. Strategies are now in place to disseminate the findings of the pilot project to other departmental staff in the hope that an expansion of the project can be undertaken in the next academic session. Many of the final comments from students were extremely positive:

> • *the tutor was very good...keen to help and give explanations*
> • *it has been one of the best tutorials and if they were always like this then I wouldn't mind going to them*
> • *the student tutors are more helpful, more relaxed and more in touch with the needs and concerns of other students*
> • *X was brilliant and conducted the tutorial with confidence and authority. I personally found her to be an inspiration!*

Adequate programme planning and tutor preparation and training are key elements in the success of this cross-age peer tutoring project. The project's positive outcome contributes further evidence to the assertion that benefits for both the tutor and the tutee can be forthcoming in peer tutoring activities.

References

1. Goodlad, S. & Hirst, B. *Explorations in Peer Tutoring,* Basil Blackwell Ltd. Oxford, 1990.

2. Whitman, N. A. *Peer Teaching To Teach Is To Learn Twice*, ASHE-ERIC Higher Education Report No 4, Association for the Study of Higher Education, Washington D.C., 1988

Paired learning: Methods, organisation and evaluation

K.J. Topping
Centre for Paired Learning, Department of Psychology, University of Dundee, Dundee DD1 4HN, UK

Tutoring systems designed for use by non-teachers which are dependent on specific educational materials or equipment are unlikely to truly empower. They will always be too expensive, too restricted in scope and interest and likely to risk creating dependency. The real challenge is to design tutoring systems which can be used by anyone, anywhere, with any material which is to hand and is of interest. The design of such systems should seek to minimise complexity, while maximising interactivity and mutual and equivalent intrinsic reward, to ensure generalisation and maintenance over time and contexts. Such systems could be used by peer tutors in schools or community, by parent tutors at home or in school, and by other volunteers anywhere the need arises.

This may sound challenging, but is certainly possible. In this paper three such systems will be described: Paired Reading, Cued Spelling and Paired Writing. In each case the method will be elaborated, its organisation in practice detailed and research evidence on effectiveness briefly summarised.

Paired Reading

Method
The tutee chooses high interest reading material **irrespective of its readability level** provided it is within that of the tutor, from school, the community library or home. Newspapers and magazines are fine. There is no requirement to finish the book, but if tutees keep changing in midstream maybe they need to take more care choosing.

Pairs commit themselves to an initial trial period in which they agree to do at least 5 minutes Paired Reading on 5 days each week for about 8 weeks. This time can be found in any part of the day and the frequency of usage enables them to become fluent in the method and is sufficient for them to begin to see some change in the tutee's reading. Different kinds of tutor can be encouraged to help, but must all use the same technique - the tutee is deliberately asked to quality control the tutoring they receive.

The usual advice about finding a relatively quiet and comfortable place applies. It is important that both members of the pair can see the book equally easily - tutors who get neck-ache get irritable! The pair should discuss the book (or whatever it is), but in Paired Reading the tutee is more likely to want to talk about a book **they** have chosen. Talk is also more necessary given the (probably) greater difficulty of the text, as a check on comprehension.

A very simple and ubiquitously applicable correction procedure is prescribed. When the tutee says a word wrong, the tutor just tells the tutee the correct way to say the word, has the tutee repeat it correctly and the pair carry on. Saying "No!" and giving phonic or any other prompts is forbidden. However, tutors do not jump in and put the word right straight away - the rule is that tutors pause and give the tutee 4 or 5 seconds to see if they will put it right by themselves. (The exception to this rule is with the sprint reader, who 5 seconds after making an error could be three lines along and have made more errors - in this case earlier intervention and a finger point from the tutor to guide racing eyes back to the error word is necessary).

Praise for good reading is essential. Tutors must **look** pleased as well as saying "good" and other positive things. Praise is particularly required for good reading of hard words, getting all the words in a sentence right and putting wrong words right before the tutor does (self-correction). Nagging, fussing and complaining are forbidden, but PR does not rely on negative commands for effectiveness - these undesirable behaviours are engineered out by engineering in incompatible positive behaviours.

So how is the tutee going to manage this difficult book s/he has chosen? Tutors support tutees through difficult text by **Reading Together** - both members of the pair read all the words out loud together, with the tutor modulating their speed to match that of the tutee, while giving a good model of competent reading. The tutee must read every word and errors are corrected as above.

When an easier section of text is encountered, the tutee may wish to read a little without support. Tutor and tutee agree on a way for the tutee to signal for the tutor to stop Reading Together. This could be a knock, a sign or a squeeze. When the tutee signals, the tutor stops reading out loud right away while praising the tutee for being so confident. Sooner or later while **Reading Alone** the tutee will make an error which they cannot self-correct within 4 or 5 seconds. Then the tutor applies the usual correction procedure **and** joins back in **Reading Together**.

The pair go on like this, switching from Reading Together to Reading Alone to give the tutee just as much help as is needed at any moment, according to the difficulty of the text, how tired the tutee is, and so on. Tutees should never 'grow out of' Reading Together; they should always be ready to use it as they move on to harder and harder books.

Of course there is little new about PR - some elements of long-standing practice have merely been put together in a particularly successful package. A few teachers have difficulty accepting the technique for philosophical reasons. Forget that, just try it. Remember PR does not constitute the whole reading curriculum, but is designed to complement it without interfering with it. Further details will be found in Topping and Wolfendale [1] and Wolfendale and Topping [2].

Organisation
PR is widely used with tutees of all reading abilities and it makes sense to try it out initially on a range of students rather than attempt to solve all your worst reading problems overnight. This will also help to avoid stigmatisation of your first effort. Choose a small group of fairly well motivated pairs to practise on, but not so small or scattered that there is no sense of group solidarity or togetherness (around 10 would be good). Ensure that the tutees have easy and frequent access to a wide range of books which they can take away.

Invite main tutors (and all other potential tutors) to a launch or training meeting, together **with** the tutees, since pairs are trained together from the outset. At this meeting, after an introduction designed to create an air of novelty and excitement (some people like to put on a little play about how NOT to do reading), training in the technique commences. Tell the group about the basic structure of the technique **and** give a demonstration of how to do it. The demonstration can be on video, live by role play between teachers or by a teacher with user-friendly tutee, or by a graduate pair from a previous programme. Demonstrate Reading Together and Reading Alone separately to start with, then in normal alternation. Take especial care to highlight the correction procedure, the 4-5 second pause and lots of praise.

Now have the pairs practise the technique, offering them necessary space and privacy. Remember that to practise Reading Together at all sensibly the pair will need a book above the tutee's current independent readability level, so it is highly desirable to have the tutees choose books for the practice before the meeting so you can keep an eye on this. Left to themselves, the tutees will choose easy books for the purpose of making a good impression! As the pairs practise, circulate to diplomatically check on technique, offering further advice, coaching or re-demonstration with the individual tutee where necessary - and don't forget the praise! Remember that you can't advise or coach unless you have tried out the technique yourself on a few tame tutees.

After the practice, feed back your observations to the group, take questions, outline the day to day operation of the project, and offer refreshments if appropriate. Pairs should keep a PR Diary, noting the date, what was read, for how long, with whom and any comments about how well the tutee did. Some tutors have trouble thinking what to write in the last column, so some schools provide them with a dictionary of praise - tutees are always happy to offer suggestions for this. The diary should be taken into school each week by the tutee to show the teacher, who should add their own positive comment and sign the card officially, perhaps also issuing a new one for the next week. This is a means for the tutee to get a double dose of praise - and is also a mutual accountability device, of course.

You will also need to advise pairs about the different places from which they may borrow books. Give pairs an easy read handout to remind them of the technique and to show to other potential tutors (this may need to be in more than one language). Some schools offer Paired Reading badges, balloons, and other such nonsense - all helping to advertise the programme. You may wish to have the pairs contract into the programme more or less formally.

When discussing diaries with tutees in the ensuing weeks, check if all is going well. If it is not, you may wish to call the pair in for a brief conference about the programme and to see if they are still 'doing it right'. If you can find the time, a visit is even better. In all cases have the pair show you how they are doing it and check the difficulty level of the books chosen (these may be consistently too hard or too easy).

After the initial period of commitment, gather the pairs together again for a feedback meeting. Tell them how you think things have gone and seek their opinions on the technique and organisation of the project. Some present will say little and some will not attend, so you might also wish to have feedback questionnaires for the participants (see Topping and Whiteley [3] for examples). You might wish to test the tutees' reading before and after the project so you can feed back the overall results to the group, but avoid giving out individual scores to tutors as one score is unlikely to accurately reflect the complexity of what has occurred. You might also want to offer the group further tangible indicators of your approval at this point.

The main purpose of the meeting is to regenerate enthusiasm and group cohesion, since you do not want anyone to think this is "the end". Encourage pairs to say where they want to go from here: go on with PR 5 days a week, go on but only 2-3 days a week, go on with reading but in a different way, or stop for a rest and perhaps start again later. Tutees may wish to go on keeping the diary and you will have to decide how often you can find time to see this in the longer run.

Effectiveness

Paired Reading has been the subject of a very large amount of research, starting in the UK and now internationally, and this has recently been reviewed by Topping and Lindsay [4].

Much of the evaluation has been in terms of gains on norm-referenced tests of reading before and after the initial intensive period of involvement. Published studies do not always reflect the reality of ordinary life in the classroom, but with PR it is possible to compare the results of 60 published (and therefore selected) studies of projects with outcome data from 155 unselected projects operated in one school district. In the published studies, involving a total of 1012 tutees, for each month of time passed the average Paired Reader gained 4.2 months in reading age for accuracy and 5.4 months for comprehension. In the 155 unselected projects, involving 2372 tutees, for each month of time passed the average Paired Reader gained 3.3 months in reading age for accuracy and 4.4 months for comprehension. The majority of studies were parent tutored rather than peer tutored.

Of the published studies, 19 included control or comparison groups, while of the unselected projects, 37 included control groups. Although the control groups often also made gains greater than would normally be expected, the PR groups on aggregate did far better, although the differential was greater in the selected projects.

But do these gains last? Previously published reports on five projects with follow-up data are available, but of the unselected projects 17 included such evidence. In the latter, up to 17 weeks after the initial project intensive period, 102 tutees in 7 projects were still gaining over 2 months of reading age per chronological month elapsed for both accuracy and comprehension. At longer term follow-up, 170 tutees in 10 projects were still gaining well over 1 month of reading age per month elapsed in both accuracy and comprehension. Thus it seems that while the initial startling acceleration does not continue indefinitely, the gains certainly do not 'wash out' subsequently, and follow-up data from control group projects confirms this (Topping [5]).

The data from the unselected projects further suggested that well-organised projects yielded better test results, that participant tutees from lower socio-economic classes tended to show higher gains, that home visiting by teachers increased test scores and that boys tended to accelerate more than girls. Also, second language Paired Readers accelerated more than first language Paired Readers in accuracy but less in comprehension (while of course accelerating a great deal more than non-Paired Readers of either type).

Taking another approach to evaluation, the subjective views of tutors, tutees and teachers in the unselected projects have also been gathered, by structured questionnaire enabling responses to be summarised (Topping and Whiteley [3]). In a sample of over 1000 parent tutors, after PR 70% considered their tutee was now reading more accurately, more fluently and with better comprehension. Greater confidence in reading was noted by 78% of tutors. Teachers reported better reading in the classroom in a somewhat smaller proportion of cases (about 8% less). Of a sample of 964 tutees, 95% felt that after PR they were better at reading and 92% liked reading more. Eighty-seven per cent found it easy to learn to do, 83% liked doing it and 70% said they would go on doing it.

Paired Reading has been used in an Adult Literacy context, with spouses, friends, neighbours and workmates acting as tutors. The advantages of being able to use more appropriate and more readily available reading material and receive tutoring on a little and often basis closely linked to everyday life are extremely important, especially for the majority of adults with literacy difficulties who cannot or will not attend a class. Scoble, Topping and Wigglesworth [6] reported the evaluation of a six-week project of this type, noting average gains of 10.4 months in reading age for accuracy and 13 months for comprehension for those students who could register on the scale at pre-test. On miscue analysis, most tutees showed a striking increase in self-correction.

Cued Spelling

Method
The basic structure of the technique comprises 10 Steps, 4 Points to Remember and 2 Reviews. The 10 Steps and 4 Points apply to every individual target word worked upon by the pair, while the 'Speed Review' covers all target words for a particular session and the 'Mastery Review' covers all the target words for one week or a longer period if desired.

The tutee will choose high interest target words irrespective of complexity (Step 1). The pair check the spelling of the word and put a master version in their Cued Spelling Diary (Step 2) and usually also add it to the top of a piece of paper on which subsequent attempts will be made. The pair then read the word out loud synchronously, then the tutee reads the word aloud alone, ensuring tutee capability of accurate reading and articulation of the word (Step 3).

The tutee then chooses Cues (prompts or reminders) to enable him or her to remember the written structure of the word (Step 4). These Cues may be phonic sounds, letter names, syllables or other fragments or 'chunks' of words, or wholly idiosyncratic mnemonic devices. Tutees are encouraged to consider and choose Cues which fit well with their own cognitive structures, ie. make sense and are memorable **to them**. Thus, although a tutor might make suggestions or stimulate imagination, the decision on Cueing rests wholly with the tutee.

Once Cues are decided upon, the pair say the Cues out loud simultaneously (Step 5). The tutee then says the Cues out loud while the tutor writes the word down on scrap paper to this 'dictation' (Step 6) - thus the tutee is provided with a demonstration or model of the required behaviour. At Step 7, the tutor says the Cues out loud while the tutee writes the word down. At Step 8, the tutee says the Cues and writes the word simultaneously.

At Step 9, the tutee is required by the tutor to write the word as fast as possible (the tutee may or may not decide to recite the Cues out loud at this Step, but may well recite them sub-vocally). At Step 10, the tutee again reads the word out loud as a reminder of the meaningful context in which the target word hopefully has remained embedded.

The 4 Points cover aspects of the technique relevant to its practical application. At every attempt at writing a target word, the tutor ensures previous attempts on the work paper are covered up, to avoid the possibility of direct copying. Every time there is a written attempt on a target word, the **tutee** checks the attempt and the tutor only intervenes if the tutee proves unable to check his or her own attempt accurately.

If tutees have written a word incorrectly, they are encouraged to cross it out very vigorously to assist its deletion from their memory. At an incorrect attempt, the correction procedure is merely that the pair return to the Step preceding the one at which the error was made. Tutors are required to praise at various junctures which are specified quite clearly. These precise details of the nature of praise and the criteria for its application are intended to promote higher frequency and regularity of praise, as well as more effective use of it.

At the end of each tutoring session, there is a 'Speed Review', wherein the tutor requires the tutee to write all the target words for that session as fast as possible from dictation in random order. The tutee then self-checks all the words with the 'master version' in the Cued Spelling Diary. Target words which are incorrect at Speed Review have the 10 Steps applied again, perhaps with the choice of different Cues. In fact, tutees make only a small proportion of errors at Speed Review and the requirement to re-apply the 10 Steps is not as onerous as it sounds.

At the end of each week, a 'Mastery Review' is conducted, wherein the tutee is required to write all the target words for the whole week as fast as possible in random order. No specific error correction procedure is prescribed for Mastery Review and it is left to the pair to negotiate for themselves what they wish to do about errors. Many pairs choose to include failed words in the next week's target words.

Organisation
Cued Spelling projects follow many of the organisational guidelines for Paired Reading projects. Tutors and tutees are trained together. A talk on the method is best accompanied with a demonstration on video, since a live demonstration of CS often lacks clarity of small detail and tends to be less successful. An additional practical demonstration of Cueing using a chalkboard and soliciting from the group different words and different cueing strategies for each word is helpful in making the point that there are no "right" cueing strategies, only effective and ineffective ones. Pairs are given a '10 Steps' chart to refer to while practising the method with the tutee's own words (chosen before the meeting), using the paper, pencils and dictionaries provided. Individualised feedback and further coaching is provided as necessary.

Cued Spelling Diaries are given to each pair, each page including space to write the master version of up to 10 words on all days of the week, together with boxes to record daily Speed Review and weekly Mastery Review scores and spaces for comments from tutor (daily) and teacher (weekly). The pair are asked to use the technique on about five words per day (implying a minimum time of 15 minutes) for 3 days per week for the next 6 weeks. The tutees are encouraged to choose words from their school spelling books, graded free writing, relevant project work or special Cued Spelling displays of common problem words, and collect these (in a CS "collecting book"), so they always have a pool of suitable words from which to choose.

Tutees are asked to show their C.S. Diaries once each week to the co-ordinating professional. Keep watch on the words chosen, since some tutees choose words they already know while others choose extremely difficult words of very doubtful utility - in this case you might need to prescribe a formula of "3 for everyday use and 2 just for fun". Participating tutees might receive a badge and tutors a higher readability information sheet with further ideas on Cueing.

Cued Spelling has been much used in a reciprocal peer tutoring format, where both members of the pair are of equal spelling ability. In this case it is especially important that the master version of the word is looked up in the dictionary **and** copied correctly into the CS Diary. Thus a tutor who is of limited spelling ability could work with a tutee of similar spelling ability, or sibling tutoring could operate between tutees of similar or different ages. In reciprocal tutoring, the fact that everyone gets to be a tutor is good for the self-esteem of both members of the pair, who of course end up learning their partner's words as well as their own.

Effectiveness
The initial reports on Cued Spelling were of a descriptive nature. Emerson [7] reported on a brief project using the technique with four tutors who tutored their own tutees at home. Results at Mastery Review were excellent. Scoble [8] reported a detailed case study of an Adult Literacy student tutored by his wife using the technique. After ten weeks of Cued Spelling, a Mastery Review of all words covered in the preceding weeks yielded a success rate of 78%. Subsequently, Scoble [9] reported on the progress of fourteen similar pairs, most of whom had done Paired Reading together first. The most long-standing student had used the method for over a year and usually achieved Speed Review scores of 100% and Mastery Review scores of 90%. Harrison [10] reported on a similar project and its extension to peer tutoring between Adult Literacy students in a class situation.

In the event, however, the most popular application of Cued Spelling then proved to be in a peer tutoring format. Oxley & Topping [11] reported on a project in which 8 seven- and eight-year-old pupils were tutored by 8 nine-year-old pupils in the same vertically grouped class in a small rural school. This cross-age, cross-ability peer tutoring project was found to yield striking social benefits and the tutees spontaneously generalised peer tutoring to other curricular areas. Subjective feedback from both tutors and tutees was very positive. The self-concept as a speller of both tutees and tutors showed a marked positive shift compared to that of non-participants, especially so for the tutees. After six weeks, a total Mastery Review of **all** target words yielded average scores of 66% correct, but a test session of up to 92 items for such young tutees was considered of doubtful reliability. Results on two norm-referenced tests of spelling were equivocal, since although the scores of both tutees and tutors were strikingly improved at post-test, so were those of non-participants in the same class.

Peer tutored Cued Spelling in a class-wide, same-age, same-ability reciprocal tutoring format was reported by Brierley, Hutchinson, Topping & Walker [12]. All pupils in the three first year mixed ability classes (aged 9 to 10 years) in a Middle school participated. Tutor and tutee roles changed each week. All the tutees were trained in a single group meeting. After six weeks, a total Mastery Review of all words covered yielded average scores of 80%. On a norm-referenced test of spelling, the average gain for all tutees was 0.65 years of spelling age during the six-week project, certainly many times more than normal expectations. Subjective feedback from the tutees was very positive, 84% of the tutees reporting feeling they were better spellers after the project. Subsequently, peer tutored Cued Spelling was initiated by a number of schools, especially in the reciprocal tutoring format, but few found time to evaluate it.

A study of parent tutored Cued Spelling with tutees of eight years of age and of the normal range of spelling ability (France, Topping & Revell [13]) indicated that the intervention appeared to be effective in differentially raising the spelling attainments of participants as compared to non-participants who were more able spellers, at least in the short term. Tutees felt Cued Spelling was easy to learn to do and that it improved their spelling along a number of dimensions. However, they said they tended to become bored with it and had difficulty finding enough words with which to use the technique.

It can be argued that any method involving extra time on task at spelling and extra valuable tutorial attention and approval related to spelling might be likely to yield differential gains. A study by Watt and Topping [14] compared Cued Spelling with traditional spelling homework (an alternative intervention involving equal tutor attention and equal time on spelling tasks), compared the relative effectiveness of parent and peer tutored Cued Spelling and assessed the generalisation of the effect of Cued Spelling into subsequent continuous free writing. On a norm-referenced spelling test, Cued Spellers gained over 2 months of spelling age for each chronological month elapsed, while the traditional spelling homework comparison group of more able spellers gained only half a month of spelling age per month. The average score for parent tutored tutees at final Mastery Review of words used in the programme was 93% correct. Parent and peer tutoring seemed equally effective.

Participating tutees returned questionnaires identical to those used by Oxley and Topping [11]. Of these, 56% found it easy to think up good Cues while the rest thought it hard, but 87% now felt happier about spelling in general and that their spelling was better when writing, while 83% felt they now did better at spelling tests. Ninety-one per cent reported a higher rate of self-correction after doing Cued Spelling and the same proportion said they liked doing Cued Spelling, while 87% said they wished to go on doing Cued Spelling. Tutors returned feedback questionnaires and 88% reported a higher rate of self-correction, confirming the feedback from the tutees, while 58% reported noticing their tutees spontaneously generalise the use of Cued Spelling techniques to other words. Three of the four teachers involved noted higher rates of self-correction of spelling in classwork and a general improvement in free writing.

Pre-post analysis of written work was based on samples of writing from Cued Spellers and comparison children. The average number of spelling errors per page reduced from 8.5 to 4.62 for the Cued Spellers and from 3.7 to 2.1 for the comparison group, who clearly had a lower error rate to start with and thus had less room for improvement. Generally, all but one of the participants and all but one of the comparison group were adjudged to have improved in quality of written work (one would of course expect children in school to improve over time), but the C.S. group recorded an average of 1.7 specific improvements per tutee while the comparison group averaged 1.25.

Paired Writing

Method
Writing can be a lonely business and a blank piece of paper waiting to be filled strangely daunting. Paired Writing is a framework for a pair working together to generate (or co-compose) a piece of writing for any purpose they wish. The guidelines are designed to structure interaction between the pair so that a higher proportion of time is spent on task - hopefully reducing dithering, head-scratching, staring out of the window and blind panic to a minimum.

There is great emphasis on continuity - the pair stimulating each other to keep going at any threatened hiatus. There is also constant inbuilt feedback and cross-checking - what is written must make sense to both members of the pair. The system is designed to be supportive and eliminate the fear of failure. Anxiety about peripheral aspects of writing such as spelling or punctuation should thereby be reduced to an appropriate level, and dealt with in an orderly way. As the "best copy" is a joint effort of the pair, criticism as well as praise from external evaluators is shared.

Peer evaluation is incorporated, relieving the supervising professional of the burden of grading innumerable scripts after the event (sometimes so long after that the feedback given is totally ineffective). Peer evaluation has been found to be at least as effective as teacher evaluation.

Paired Writing usually operates with a more able writer (the Helper) and a less able one (the Writer) in the pair, but can work with a pair of equal ability so long as they edit carefully and use a dictionary to check spellings. In this latter case, it is possible to reciprocate roles from time to time to add variety - however, this should not be too frequent and the two roles should always be kept clearly separate.

The system may be used in creative writing or English composition, or in descriptive or technical writing, or as part of cross-curricular work, employment or other life needs. A Paired Writing project may be designed to mesh in with, or follow on from, direct instruction from a professional teacher on structural aspects of the writing process or a Paired Reading or Cued Spelling project, but the method may equally be used on an ad hoc basis as the need arises once pairs are trained and practised in its use.

The structure of the system consists of 6 Steps, 10 Questions (Ideas), 5 Stages (Drafting) and 4 Levels (Editing). Helpers should not be overly didactic, nor **too** supportive. Helpers are there to help Writers to help themselves, not to do everything for them. As there are no "right answers" about what constitutes good writing, Helpers should avoid direct criticism of the Writer's efforts, but instead make comments about their own subjective reaction, e.g. "I find that bit hard to understand - can we think of a clearer way to write it?" More praise for good bits than comment on doubtful bits is the rule, and praise must be given at least at the end of each step.

Step 1 is Ideas Generation. The Helper stimulates ideas by raising various stimulus words (who, do, what, to, with, where, when, how, why, and, if, but?) with the Writer, not necessarily in that order. As the Writer responds, the Helper makes one-word notes. As this proceeds, the Helper might recapitulate previous ideas before presenting the next stimulus word. The Helper might also think up new stimulus words not listed.

Step 2 is Drafting. The stimulus notes should then be placed where both members of the pair can easily see them. Drafting then proceeds without concern for either spelling or punctuation. However, legibility is desirable, as is double spaced writing to allow for subsequent editing. Most pairs will do better with lined paper. The Writer considers the notes and dictates, sentence by sentence, what he or she wishes to communicate. Generally a pair will choose one of the five Stages of Support to operate in for the session. (Stage 1 = H writes it all, W copies it all; Stage 2 = H writes hard words in for W; Stage 3 = H writes hard words in rough, W copies them in; Stage 4 = H says how to spell hard words; Stage 5 = W writes it all).

For a 'harder' piece of writing, the pair are likely to choose a low (numbered) Stage, for an 'easier' assignment a higher (numbered) Stage. However, they might go back one stage (or more) when encountering a particularly hard bit. In any event, if the Writer cannot proceed within 10 seconds, the Helper must go back a stage on that problem word to give more support. There is a great emphasis on keeping going and not getting bogged down. Keeping going with more support is better than struggling for a long time with less support.

Step 3 is Reading. The Helper reads the Draft out loud, with as much expression and attention to punctuation (real or imagined) as possible, while the pair look at the text together. The Writer then reads the text out loud. If a word is read incorrectly, the Helper says that word correctly for the Writer.

Step 4 is Editing. The pair look at the draft together and the writer considers where s/he thinks improvements are necessary. The problem word, phrase or sentence might be lightly marked with coloured pen, pencil or highlighter. The most important criterion of need for improvement is where meaning is unclear. The second most important is to do with the organisation of ideas within the text or the Order in which meanings are presented, whether phrases or sentences. The next consideration is whether Spellings are correct and the last whether Punctuation is helpful and correct.

The Helper praises the Writer for completion of this demanding task, then marks any areas they feel the Writer has "missed", while bearing in mind the subjective nature of some aspects of "quality" in writing. The Writer then suggests changes, the pair discuss the best correction to make, and when agreement is reached the new version is inserted in the text (preferably by the Writer). Spellings over which there is the slightest doubt in the pair should be referred to the dictionary.

Step 5 is Best Copy. The Writer (usually) then copies out a 'neat' or 'best' version of the corrected draft. Sometimes the Helper may write or type or word-process the piece, however, depending on the skill and stamina of the Writer.

Step 6 is Evaluate. The pair should inspect and consider the best copy. Given the effort they have expended, they are likely to think their co-composed text is really rather good, and be happy to congratulate each other as members of a successful composing duet. However, external evaluation by more objective assessors is highly desirable. Peer evaluation is a useful mutual learning experience, and assessment by another pair can proceed by reference to the criteria encompassed in the Edit levels, again hopefully with positive comments outnumbering negative.

As with Paired Reading, there is nothing new in this, including as it does many of the traditional elements of process writing. More complex versions with more Editing options have been developed for older tutees, but these are not appropriate for those with learning difficulties.

Organisation

For training purposes (and indeed subsequently) each pair must have a system flowchart, two pens or pencils, scrap paper, easy access to a dictionary of an appropriate level and good quality paper for the best copy. Most pairs will do best with lined paper. It is recommended that the use of erasers is strongly discouraged. A coloured pen or pencil for editing might be found helpful.

At a training meeting participants should sit at tables in their pairs, with a hard copy of a chart of the Steps, Questions, Stages and Levels, which could also be projected. Talking through the chart should as always be accompanied by a demonstration of the system in operation, and the most visible way of doing this is usually by live role play between teachers writing on an acetate sheet which is continuously projected. Practice, monitoring and coaching follow. You may choose to specify some simple topic for all pairs for the practice, which should be common to all and preferably functional, e.g. 'how to use a coin-operated telephone' or 'how you should brush your teeth'. Allow at least 40 minutes and preferably one hour for the meeting.

After training, the system will need to be used as frequently as possible for the next few weeks, to ensure consolidation and promote fluency in its use and enable any problems to be picked up. An informal contract regarding minimum frequency of usage should be established - e.g. Paired Writing for 3 sessions of 20 minutes per week for 6 weeks - and this can be tied in with regular homework requirements.

Effectiveness

To date, the evaluations of Paired Writing have been solely descriptive and anecdotal. The task of evaluating quantitative and qualitative change in tutees' writing is an enormously time-consuming undertaking from a research point of view, and the difficulty of checking if any changes endure in the longer term even greater.

The objective of Paired Writing is to produce an increase in the quality and quantity of written output which generalises to the solo writing situation and endures over time. Even in cross-ability tutoring, tutor writing skills may also improve along the way. A more complex issue also arises - is the final product better than if the members of the pair worked separately? If the abilities of the two are very disparate, this may not be the case.

Most of the usage of Paired Writing since its recent inception has been on a same-age cross-ability peer tutoring basis in schools with classes of mixed ability students. In this situation, it is clearly important that the ambitious objective of joint written products being better than either member of the pair could create alone is achieved, or a reversion to traditional solo writing in isolation is inevitable given the accountability demands of the education system. Gratifyingly, in a majority of cases this is exactly what happens, and students mostly prefer the sociability and supportiveness of Paired Writing to the traditional approach. Parent tutored Paired Writing has so far been largely confined to parents worried about their child's learning difficulties, although the interpretation of learning difficulty has been wide, so that the method has been used with University students by parents worried about upcoming examination performances, for instance.

Designing tutoring systems

There is now an ever expanding wealth of knowledge and experience about systems for tutoring by non-professionals and from this it is possible to distil a checklist of engineering criteria likely to maximise success. Those educators inventing their own local procedures may find this helpful.

Objectives - what benefits the programme is expected to have should be clearly articulated, not least for marketing/recruitment and subsequent evaluation purposes. The programme must not interfere with the regular school curriculum, but should dovetail into it, while capitalising on the qualitative differences and advantages of tutoring as compared to school instruction. Keep the objectives modest for your first attempt.

Ability differential - be clear with potential volunteers (and yourself) about the degree of ceiling competence needed in the tutor and the feasible range of ability differential (if any) in the pair. If tutor competence is in doubt there must be reference to some acceptable master source to verify correctness, since over-learning of errors would leave the tutee worse off than when they started.

Flexibility - procedures should be applicable without major modification to participants of different ages and abilities with different life situations and needs, different learning styles and different ambitions, and in different physical environments. Clearly, the more specific materials are deemed to be necessary, the less these flexibility requirements are likely to be met. Likewise, the procedure should enable and facilitate the tutee to deploy a range of strategies, rather than strait-jacketing them into a single professionally preferred one. Activity should preferably be varied and multisensory, with alternation between different styles of reading, listening, writing, speaking, and so on.

Interaction - procedures should involve responsive (inter-) activity from both members of the pair, since if one declines into being merely a checker or passive audience motivation will soon evaporate. The procedure should promote a high rate of time on task, with an emphasis on keeping going - maintaining the flow of activity increases the number of learning opportunities and helps stave off anxiety.

Satisfaction - likewise, both members of the pair must gain some intrinsic satisfaction from the activity, since pure altruism will always expire eventually through boredom. Basically, it's got to be fun.

Self-management - the tutee should have a substantial degree of control over the process of tutoring and preferably over the curriculum content and materials as well. Tutee control of the amount of support offered by the tutor is especially valuable. Tutees should be able to exercise choice and initiative - deprived of the opportunity, they will never develop the skills.

Instructions - should be simple, clear and above all **specific**. Instructions are probably best given as a series of finely task analysed steps. Tutors like to be told what they have to do to be right, at least at the start. Mostly they dislike wordy educational philosophising and vague and fuzzy open-ended statements. Both tutor and tutee should be given very clear (interactive) job descriptions, since without this the process of tutoring can rapidly degenerate into a muddle. The provision of a simple visual map, chart or other cue to remind the pair of how it is all supposed to work may well be helpful.

Materials - especially for tutees with learning difficulties, the curriculum materials in use should be individualised to match the tutee's needs and interests, but are they to be completely free choice, controlled choice from ranges of difficulty or precisely specified by the professionals, or some continuum of these as the tutoring develops? Are the materials required actually available and easy for regular access by pairs? Does the tutoring procedure accommodate to progression onto increasingly difficult materials? Have you specified what the pair will need to have available by way of basic equipment (pen, paper, dictionary?), and ensured it will be available?

Error control - the tutee should not feel as if they are making many errors, since this is bad for morale. If this is not controlled via tutee-, tutor- or teacher-selected materials, careful accommodation by the tutor to the tutee's natural pacing and the provision of swift non-intrusive support must be a feature of the tutoring technique, without creating tutee dependency. Errors are potentially the major stress point in the tutoring relationship - but be alert to other possible causes of stress and fatigue in the system.

Error signalling - when an error is made, feedback should be swift that this is the case, but not so immediate that the tutee has no opportunity to detect the error themselves. Error signalling should be positive and minimally interruptive.

Error correction - a swift, simple, specific and preferably ubiquitously applicable error correction procedure must be clearly laid down, which is seen by the tutee as supportive and draws minimum attention to the error. There should be a strong emphasis on self-checking and self-correction, both higher order skills which need to be fostered. In a more general global sense, peer evaluation could be incorporated.

Eliminate negatives - "don't say don't" - prescribe positive error signalling and correction procedures which are incompatible with the negative and intrusive behaviours we all sometimes perpetrate, rather than giving tutors a list of prohibited behaviours.

Accentuate positives - be specific about requirements for praise, including what to praise (especially self-correction and initiative-taking), frequency, verbal and non-verbal aspects, and the need for variety and relevance to the task. Deploy individual token or tangible rewards only if all else fails. Some group acknowledgement of participation via badges, certificates, etc might be valuable and acceptable, and is useful advertising.

Discussion - emphasise that discussion by the pair is essential to promote and confirm full understanding by the tutee, and is genuine work, to avoid mechanical conformity to the surface requirements of the task.

Modelling - ensure the tutoring procedure includes a demonstration of competence by the tutor which may be imitated (or improved upon) by the tutee, rather than over-reliance on verbal promptings. Tutors should also be encouraged to model more general desirable behaviours, such as enthusiasm for the topic in hand. Participant pairs will also serve as models for other pairs, and the project group should deliberately be kept in contact so that the social dynamic adds a further dimension to motivation. Remember the co-ordinating professional must model continuing enthusiasm for the programme!

Training - is essential, and should be done in vivo with both members of the pair present via verbal, visual and written information-giving (bi-lingual if necessary) coupled with a demonstration, immediate practice, feedback, further coaching and subsequent monitoring. Training individual pairs is very costly, and well organised group training is as effective while also serving to develop group support and solidarity. You may need specially pre-selected materials or equipment for the training meeting.

Contracting - Specify an initial trial period and be very clear about the time costs for the pair should they participate. Remember little and often will be most effective, especially with tutees with learning difficulties. Expect pairs to clearly contract in to participation, which is of course voluntary but needs to be seen as total and not optionally partial. Ensure there is mutual feedback about effectiveness and proposed improvements by the end of the trial period. Discuss continuation options and seek contract renewal, possibly in a range of formats, by participants. At this point pairs should be increasingly confident and capable of devising their own adaptations and creating their own novelty, and should be increasingly ambitious.

Monitoring - Emphasise self-checking. Some simple form of self-recording is desirable, and both members of the pair should participate in this. Periodic checking of these records by the co-ordinating professional is a minimal form of accountability of high cost-effectiveness. This may need to be supplemented in at least some cases by verbal enquiry of one or both members of the pair and/or direct observation of the pair (and preferably other supplementary tutors) in action, in the first case either on an individual basis or in a group setting.

Turning from monitoring the process of tutoring to evaluating its products or outcomes, be clear as to the objectives of evaluation, since there is little point in doing it for its own sake - what are you going to **do** with the results? Feeding back to the participants data on their success might increase their motivation. Publicising the data might expand subsequent recruitment or attract additional funding. How should you review to what extent the curriculum content of the tutoring has actually been mastered and retained in the longer term? Criterion-referenced tests closely allied to the tutoring process are likely to give the most valid (and most impressive) results, but a norm-referenced test in the same general area is a more stringent test of generalisation of skills acquired through tutoring and might be construed as more "objective" by outsiders.

You might also solicit subjective feedback from the participants on a consumer satisfaction basis, but design any questionnaire carefully to ask very specific questions and avoid inbuilt positive bias, since in any case you will benefit from the "grateful testimonials" effect. Also remember to make it easy to score and summarise! Comparison or control groups are great if you can get them. Do try and save a little spare energy to collect longer term follow-up data on at least a sub-sample, to check on wash-out of gains. However, also ensure the evaluation procedure does not overwhelm or stress the participants - or indeed yourself!

Generalisation and maintenance - you will need to build in means for continuing review, feedback and injection of further novelty and enthusiasm if pairs are to keep going and maintain the use of their skills. Again, the social dynamic of the group is important. You are likely also to need to consciously foster their broadening the use of these skills to different materials and contexts for new purposes - all of this will consolidate the progress made, build confidence and empower the pair still further. When pairs have developed sufficient awareness of effective tutoring to begin to design their own systems, you know you have done a good job. As tutees themselves recruit a wider range of tutors, the tutee becomes even more central as quality controller of the tutoring process.

Wider alternatives

We have focused on literacy here, and this is indeed an excellent place to start, but the possibilities are endless. A great deal of work has been done on tutor and peer tutoring of mathematics, considerable attention has been paid to systems for developing tutee oracy, and interest is spreading rapidly into other areas of the curriculum such as Science (see, for example, the Paired Science pack by Croft and Topping [15]). Further guidelines for operating peer tutoring in other curricular areas will be found in Topping [16]. The basic principles for designing effective and durable systems for non-professional tutoring are applicable to a very wide range of formal and informal educational activities, both within and without educational establishments.

References

1. Topping, K.J. & Wolfendale, S.W. (eds) *Parental Involvement In Children's Reading*, Croom Helm, London; Nichols, New York, 1985

2. Wolfendale, S.W. & Topping, K.J. (eds) *Family Involvement in Literacy: Effective Partnerships In Education*, Cassell, London, 1995.

3. Topping, K.J. & Whiteley, M. *Participant Evaluation Of Parent-Tutored And Peer-Tutored Projects In Reading*, Educational Research 1990, 32 (1) 14-32.

4. Topping, K.J. & Lindsay, G. *Paired Reading: A Review Of The Literature*, Research Papers In Education 1992, 7 (3) 1-50.

5. Topping, K.J. *Short- And Long-Term Follow-up Of Parental Involvement In Reading Projects*, British Educational Research Journal 1992, 18 (4) 369-379.

6. Scoble, J., Topping, K. & Wigglesworth, C. *Training Family and Friends As Adult Literacy Tutors*, Journal of Reading 1988, 31 (5) 410-417.

7. Emerson, P. *Parent Tutored Cued Spelling in a Primary School*, Paired Reading Bulletin 1988, 4, 91-92.

8. Scoble, J. *Cued Spelling in Adult Literacy - A Case Study*, Paired Reading Bulletin 1988, 4, 93-96.

9. Scoble, J. *Cued Spelling and Paired Reading in Adult Basic Education in Ryedale*, Paired Learning 1989, 5, 57-62.

10. Harrison, R. (1989) *Cued Spelling in Adult Literacy in Kirklees*, Paired Learning 1989, 5, 141.

11. Oxley, L. & Topping, K. (1990) *Peer-tutored Cued Spelling with Seven- to Nine-year-olds*, British Educational Research Journal 1990, 16 (1) 63 -78.

12. Brierley, M., Hutchinson, P., Topping, K. & Walker, C. *Reciprocal Peer Tutored Cued Spelling with Ten Year Olds*, Paired Learning 1989, 5, 136-140.

13. France, L., Topping, K. & Revell, K. *Parent Tutored Cued Spelling*, Support for Learning 1992, 8 (1) 11-15.

14. Watt, J.M. & Topping, K.J. (1992) *Cued Spelling; A Comparative Study Of Tutor And Peer Tutoring*, Educational Psychology in Practice, 1993, 9 (2) 95-103.

15. Croft, S. & Topping, K. (1992) *Paired Science - A Resource Pack for Tutors and Tutees*, Centre for Paired Learning, University of Dundee, Dundee, 1992.

16. Topping, K.J. (1988) *The Peer Tutoring Handbook: Promoting Co-operative Learning*, Croom Helm, London; Brookline, Cambridge MA, 1988.

Note

The Paired Reading and Paired Learning Bulletins are available on microfiche from ERIC (1985 ED285124, 1986 ED285125, 1987 ED285126, 1988 ED298429, 1989 ED313656).

Student tutoring: The research background

K.J. Topping

Centre for Paired Learning, Department of Psychology, University of Dundee, Dundee DD1 4HN, UK

Student tutoring is the name given in the UK to the practice of having students from universities and colleges of further and higher education tutoring children in primary (elementary) and high school classrooms under the guidance of the classteacher. Various benefits for the student tutor, the tutored children and the classteacher have been hypothesised, assumed, claimed and anecdotally reported as resulting from this practice.

Consulting the wider international research literature indicates that the UK "model" of student tutoring is both idiosyncratic and idiosyncratically internally consistent. The latter feature doubtless reflects rapid growth in this particular type of venture in the UK in recent years as a result of funding and promotion by British Petroleum and the appointment of an extremely effective national co-ordinator.

In this paper some selected studies illuminating the psychological underpinnings of some of the hypothesised gains for tutors from Student Tutoring will be considered. Subsequently, an overview of the literature will be offered, working towards a typology of different kinds of "student tutoring" operated around the world and setting the UK model in this context. Thirdly, a brief summary of existing evaluations of the outcomes for tutors, tutees and teachers in different models will link into a select bibliography of evaluation research in this area.

Cognitive processes in Student Tutoring

A number of authors have proposed that the process of "Learning by Teaching" which characterises the tutor's role is likely to result in cognitive acceleration both before and during tutoring. Cognitive processes which may be enhanced in this way include: attention, motivation, reviewing capabilities, organisation, association, integration, exemplification, clarification and simplification (Gartner, Kohler and Riessman 1971, Barg and Schul 1980, Webb 1982).

Annis (1983) had 130 female students read a 1500 word article under five conditions: A Read, B Read in order to tutor (but did not tutor), C Read to tutor and did tutor, D Read and were tutored (separately) and E Did not read and were tutored (by C). On subsequent test results ($p < 0.05$), B & C were best but C > B, C > all others, and B & C > E. This was true for both content-specific and generalised gains. Annis proposed that tutoring involved enhanced attending, encoding and associating.

Benware and Deci (1984) compared a group of 21 students learning material for a formal examination with a group of 19 students learning the same material in order to tutor it to others. Comparisons were made of four different types of learning from the material. On rote learning, the groups performed equally well, on intrinsic motivation the tutoring group did better, on conceptual learning the tutoring group did better and on active engagement the tutoring group did better.

Lambiotte and his colleagues (1988) divided 83 students into two groups; one group utilised a "paired co-operative study script" while members of the other individually used a programmed teaching script covering the same content. In terms of rote learning, the individual study group did better, but in the development of transferable skills such as ability to communicate the content paired study proved superior.

In a related study, Stewart & Palcic (1992) had students write maths teaching scripts for elementary school pupils. One group wrote scripts for imaginary pupils, another group wrote them for real pupils, corresponded with by the students. Results showed that both sets of students became better writers, but the "real contact" improved more than the other and showed more involvement in the task, as well as preferring it to other coursework writing tasks.

These studies suggest that the interactive aspects of tutoring as well preparing for tutoring can have positive effects on higher level thinking, motivation, involvement and transferable skills. The sense of audience and purpose inherent to tutoring seem to be important in this respect. However, none of these studies dealt with Student Tutoring into schools on the UK model. It is to a typology of cross-phase student tutoring from an international perspective that this paper now proceeds.

A typology of Student Tutoring

Studies and descriptions of student tutoring into schools in the international literature show differences on a number of dimensions: tutee characteristics, tutor characteristics, curriculum, contact constellation, time, place, style, goals & outcomes for tutees and goals & outcomes for tutors.

Tutee characteristics can be further discriminated into sub-categories: learning disabled (eg Flippo et al. 1993), learning delayed (eg Sandler et al. 1970), socio-economically disadvantaged (eg Eisenberg et al. 1980), English as second language (eg Fischetti et al. 1989), ethnic minorities (eg Rhodes & Garibaldi 1990), drop-out risk (eg Fasko & Flint 1990), other "at-risk" tutees, gender groups and the gifted (eg Prillaman & Richardson 1989).

Categories of tutor characteristics have included the academically competent, the academically under-prepared, pre-service teachers (eg Rhodes and Garibaldi 1989, Bacon 1992), ethnic minorities (eg Sandler et al. 1970) and student athletes (eg Juel 1991).

The curriculum of tutoring has included reading, other literacy skills, maths, science, information technology (eg Ross et al. 1989), other schools curricular areas, specific homework (eg Cloward 1967), vocational skills, sports skills, recreational skills and cultural activities (the latter particularly in Eisenberg et al. 1980).

Contact constellations have varied greatly. Tutoring has occurred in one-to-one situations, tutors dealing with one tutee or several consecutively. Groups of between 2 and 30 are frequently found to be tutored by one Student Tutor. In the UK model, it is difficult to be specific about contact constellation, since a Student Tutor working in the classroom might work with one child or many at different times in the same session.

Tutoring occurs at many different times, including: class time, break or recess time, after school, in the evening, at weekends and during school holidays. It has occurred in many different places, including in class, elsewhere in school, at a community centre, on the university or college campus, at the tutee's home and out in various community activity settings.
The style and aims of tutoring have also varied - some programmes are intended to be remedial, some compensatory and some targeted on enrichment.

Goals and outcomes for tutees are of course important, since participation in the exercise only for the benefit of the tutors would require uncommon altruism. Reported outcomes for tutees include raised aspirations (eg Sandler et al. 1970), improved basic skills, deeper learning, improved motivation (eg Sandler et al. 1970), affective and attitudinal gains (eg Flippo et al. 1993), a reduction in tutee drop-out from school, generalised gains in achievement (eg Ross et al. 1989), improved attendance at school (eg Huisman et al. 1992) and gains in various transferable skills.

Goals and outcomes for tutors have included under the general heading of cognitive and transferable skills: better communication skills, deeper understanding, practice in applying knowledge, improved retention and greater commitment to area of tutoring. Under the general heading of affective and social gains, improved motivation, self-esteem, self-understanding, and self-confidence have all been reported, together with greater empathy with others and a greater sense of achievement. More tangible and observable gains for tutors have included reduced drop-out rates, course accreditation or credit, and payment.

Outcomes of Student Tutoring

A major review of Student Tutoring into schools in the USA was undertaken by Cahalan and Farris (1990). It was noted that 40% of tutors were volunteers, 31% were involved as a course or graduation requirement and 29% were paid. This contrasts with the UK model, in which the vast majority of tutors are volunteers and receive only travelling expenses. In the USA, around three quarters of tutees were socio-economically disadvantaged and/or members of an ethnic minority. While half the tutees were female, 70% of the tutors were female.

Tutoring provision was evenly divided between primary (elementary) and high school pupils. However, only 39% of contact occurred in school, 46% occurring on campus. One-to-one tutoring was the most common format, usually occurring for 3 hours per week during the project. In tutoring programmes, 59% of time was spent on basic skills remediation and 28% of time on homework assistance, while in mentoring oriented programmes there was much more emphasis on recreational and cultural activities.

Seventy-five to eighty per cent of programmes considered themselves successful in improving basic skills and self-esteem in tutees, while 47% claimed impact on drop-out rates. However, no supporting evidence is given and gains for tutors are not specific.

A review of the more objective evaluation research on various forms of student tutoring around the world enables crude summary categorisations of outcomes, given in Tables 1 and 2 below. Table 1 summarises outcomes for tutors; for each gain factor investigated an indication is given of which studies could be considered to have unequivocally demonstrated such gains, in which studies the evidence could be considered equivocal and in which studies no gains of that type were found despite efforts to find them. Table 2 summarises outcomes for tutees in the same way. Table 3 summarises outcomes for classteachers solely in the UK model of classroom based Student Tutoring.

It should be remembered that the types and models of Student Tutoring encompassed by these studies are many. Two studies listed in the same column of the same table against the same gain factor may have investigated very different models of operation with very different populations for very different purposes. Thus like is rarely adjacent to or compared with like. The overall patterns of outcomes certainly cannot be assumed to apply in their entirety to the UK model of Student Tutoring or any other single specific model. Future research could usefully focus on aptitude X treatment interactions - which models of Student Tutoring are most effective for which types of populations in which contexts.

Nevertheless, the general picture is very positive, relatively few studies yielding equivocal or negative results. However, positive outcomes demonstrated for tutors are mostly within the social/affective domain. Relatively few studies have explored cognitive and/or transferable skill gains for tutors. Cognitive and attainment gains are more frequently reported for tutees, especially in basic literacy and numeracy skills. However, this finding does not relate to the UK model of Student Tutoring, which does not tend to focus on basic skill remediation. There is a need to establish whether cognitive and attainment gains for tutees accrue from the UK model.

Taking all methods of Student Tutoring together, it is however clear that schools may be reassured in very general terms that gains for tutored pupils are commonly achieved, an important point for marketing and dissemination. The research on outcomes for classteachers relates solely to the UK model and includes largely subjective feedback data, but is also largely positive - again important in marketing and dissemination.

Further research is currently being undertaken in the UK to investigate cognitive and transferable skill gains for tutors in the UK model of Student Tutoring. As indicated, research on such gains for tutees from the UK model appears to be needed as a matter of priority.

Table 1

RESEARCH ON OUTCOMES FOR TUTORS

GAIN FACTOR	YES	DOUBTFUL	NO
COMMUNICATION	*Goodlad/ Hughes *Beardon *Reisner		
REINFORCE KNOWLEDGE		*Goodlad/ Hughes *Beardon	
ACADEMIC PERFORMANCE	*Reisner		
ATTITUDE TO SUBJECT	*Stewart		
LEADERSHIP	*Reisner		
SELF-ESTEEM	*Raupp *Stewart *Reisner		
SELF-CONFIDENCE	*Goodlad/ Hughes *Reisner *Beardon		
SELF-SATISFACTION	*FreskoChen *Ross *Bacon *Goodlad/ Hughes *Beardon		
SELF-UNDERSTANDING	*Flippo		
UNDERSTANDING OTHERS	*Flippo *Raupp *Goodlad/ Hughes *Beardon		
CLARIFY VOCATIONAL INTENT	*Beardon		

Table 2

RESEARCH ON OUTCOMES FOR TUTEES

GAIN FACTOR	YES	DOUBTFUL	NO
COGNITIVE/ACHIEVEMENT:			
READING	*Schwartz *Ross *Butler *Eisnberg83 *Klosterman *Juel *Reisner	*Powell *Turkel	*Eisenberg81 *Valenzuela
MATH	*Ross *Bausell *Eisnberg83 *Reisner		*Eisenberg81
WRITING	*Ross *Reisner		
GENERAL GRADES	*Flippo *Huisman *Reisner *Valenzuela	*Turkel	
ORAL ENGLISH (ESL)	*Valenzuela		
LOWER GRADE RETENTION	*Juel		
BETTER UNDERSTANDING	*Goodlad/ Hughes *Stewart		
AFFECT OUT:			
CLASS EFFORT	*Sandler	*Hughes	
ATTITUDE TO SCHOOL	*Turkel *Reisner		
ATTITUDE TO CURRICULUM	*Sandler *Flippo *Goodlad/ Hughes *Eisnberg81 *Stewart	*Hughes	

continued . . .

Table   2   (continued)

RESEARCH ON OUTCOMES FOR TUTEES

GAIN FACTOR	YES	DOUBTFUL	NO
AFFECT OUT: (continued)			
ASPIRATIONS	*Sandler *Eisnberg83 *Rhodes *Glazer	*Hughes *Jones	
MOTIVATION	*Eisnberg82 *Reisner		
AFFECT IN:			
SELF-ESTEEM	*Fasko *Eisnberg81 *Reisner		*Eisenberg83 *Hughes *Valenzuela
SELF-CONFIDENCE	*Eisnberg81 *Reisner		
OTHER BEHAVIOUR:			
ATTENDANCE	*Huisman	*Powell *Turkel	*Valenzuela
LOWER DROP-OUT	*Fischetti *Eisnberg83 *Valenzuela		
INCREASE LEISURE READING	*Eisnberg81		
IMPROVED SOCIAL BEHAVIOUR	*Valenzuela		

Table 3

RESEARCH ON OUTCOMES

FOR TEACHERS

GAIN FACTOR	YES	DOUBTFUL	NO
PUPILS LEARN MORE	*Goodlad/ Hughes *Beardon		
CLASS EASIER TO MANAGE	*Goodlad/ Hughes		*Beardon
ENJOYMENT OF LESSONS	*Goodlad/ Hughes	*Beardon	

Evaluation research on Student Tutoring - a select bibliography

Annis, L.F. (1983) *The Processes And Effects Of Peer Tutoring*, Human Learning 2, 39-47.

Bacon, C.S. (1992) *Pre-service Teachers And At-Risk Students*, Unpublished Paper, Indiana, ED351308.

Bausell, R.B., Moody, W.B. & Walzl, F.N. (1972) *A Factorial Study Of Tutoring Versus Classroom Instruction*, American Educational Research Journal 9, 592-597.

Beardon, T. (1990) *Cambridge STIMULUS*, in: Goodlad & Hirst (ibid.), Chapter 5.

Benware, C.A. & Deci, E.L. (1884) *Quality Of Learning With An Active Versus Passive Motivational Set*, American Educational Research Journal 21 (4) 755-765.

Butler, S.R. (1991) *Reading Program - Remedial, Integrated and Innovative*, Annals of Dyslexia 41, 119-127.

Button, B.L., Sims, R. & White, L. (1990) *Experience Of Proctoring Over Three Years At Nottingham Polytechnic*, in: Goodlad & Hirst (ibid.), Chapter 7.

Cahalan, M. & Farris, E. (1990) *College Sponsored Tutoring And Mentoring Programs For Disadvantaged Elementary And Secondary Students*, Higher Education Surveys - Report Number 12, U.S. Department Of Education (Office Of Planning, Budget & Evaluation), Washington DC, ED323884.

Cloward, R.A. (1967) *Studies In Tutoring*, Journal Of Experimental Education 36 (1) 14-25.

Davis, D., Snapiri, T. & Golan, P. (1984) *A Survey Of Tutoring Activities In Israel And Associated Evaluation Studies (Publication No. 96)*, Research Institute For Innovation In Education, The Hebrew University Of Jerusalem.

Deering, A.R. (1975) *High School Peer Tutoring (Homework Helpers) Program 1974-75*, Board Of Education, City of New York.

Eisenberg, T., Fresko, B. & Carmeli, M. (1980) *A Tutorial Project For Disadvantaged Children: An Evaluation Of The PERACH Project*, Perach, Weizmann Institute of Science, Rehovot, Israel.
Eisenberg, T., Fresko, B. & Carmeli, M. (1981) *An Assessment Of Cognitive Change In Socially Disadvantaged Children As A Result Of A One To One Tutoring Program*, Journal Of Educational Research 74 (5) 311-314.

Eisenberg, T., Fresko, B. & Carmeli, M. (1982) *Affective Changes In Socially Disadvantaged Children As a Result Of One To One Tutoring*, Studies In Educational Evaluation 8 (2) 141-151.

Eisenberg, T., Fresko, B. & Carmeli, M. (1983a) *A Follow-up Study Of Disadvantaged Children Two Years After Being Tutored*, Journal Of Educational Research 76 (5) 302-306.

Eisenberg, T., Fresko, B. & Carmeli, M. (1983b) *The Effect At Different Grade Levels Of One And Two Years Of Tutoring*, Perach, Weizmann Institute, Rehovot, Israel.

ERIC Office Of Educational Research And Improvement (1988) *ERIC Database: College Students Who Tutor Elementary And Secondary Students*, US Department Of Education, Washington DC.

Fasko, D. & Flint, W.W. (1990) *Enhancing Self-esteem Of At-Risk High School Students*, Unpublished Report, Kentucky, ED348593.

Fischetti, J., Maloy, R. & Heffley, J. (1989) *Undergraduates Tutoring In Secondary Schools: Collaborative Opportunities For Teacher Education*, Action In Teacher Education 10 (4) 9-14.

Flippo, R.F. et al. (1993) *Literacy, Multicultural And Sociocultural Considerations: Student Literacy Corps And The Community*, Paper Presented At The Annual Meeting Of The International Reading Association, San Antonio Texas April 26-30 1993, ED356466.

Fresko, B. (1988) *Reward Salience, Assessment Of Success And Critical Attitudes Among Tutors*, Journal Of Educational Research 81, 341-346.

Fresko, B. & Carmeli, A. (1990) *PERACH: A Nation-wide Student Tutorial Programme*, in: Goodlad & Hirst (ibid.), Chapter 4.

Fresko, B. & Chen, M. (1989) *Ethnic Similarity, Tutor Expertise and Tutor Satisfaction in Cross-Age Tutoring*, American Educational Research Journal 26 (1) 122-140.

Fresko, B. & Eisenberg, T. (1985) *The Effects Of Two Years Of Tutoring On Mathematics And Reading Achievement*, Journal Of Experimental Education 53 (4) 193-201.

Glazer, J.S. & Wughalter, E. (1991) *MENTOR In Education: Attracting Minority Students To Teaching Careers*, Mentoring International 5 (1-2) 15-20.

Goodlad, S. (1985) *Putting Science Into Context*, Educational Research 27 (1) 61-67.

Goodlad, S. & Hirst, B. (1989) *Peer Tutoring: A Guide To Learning By Teaching*, Kogan Page, London; Nichols, New York.

Goodlad, S. & Hirst, B. (eds.) (1990) *Explorations In Peer Tutoring*, Blackwell, Oxford.

Goodlad, S., Abidi, A., Anslow, P. & Harris, J. (1979) *The Pimlico Connection: Undergraduates As Tutors In Schools*, Studies In Higher Education 4 (2) 191-201.

Hedin, D. (1987) *Students As Teachers: A Tool For Improving School*, Social Policy 17 (3) 42-47.

House, J.D. & Wohlt, W. (1990) *The Effect Of Tutoring Program Participation On The Performance Of Academically Under-prepared College Freshmen*, Journal Of College Student Development 31, 365-370.

Hughes, J. (1993) *The Effectiveness Of Student Tutoring To Raise Pupils' Aspirations*, Paper Presented At The Second Scottish Conference On Student Tutoring, Glasgow April 30 1993.

Hughes, J. & Goodlad, S. (1993) *Raising Pupils' Aspirations For Science*, School Science Review 74 (268) 124-127.

Huisman, C., et al. (1992) *Student Mentoring Program 1989-1992. Evaluation Report*, Oregon Community Foundation, Portland OR, ED356701.

Johntz, W. (1973) *An Introduction To The Evaluations Of Project SEED*, Lawrence Hall Of Science, University of California, Berkeley CA.

Jones, A. (1993) *Law Students As Peer Tutors*, In: Proceedings Of A Conference On Peer Tutoring At The University of Auckland New Zealand 19-21 August 1993, Higher Education Research Office And University of Auckland.

Jones, J. (1989) *Effect Of University Student Tutors On School Student's Attitudes And Aspirations*, University of Auckland, New Zealand (Report To The Department Of Education).

Jones, J. (1990) *Tutoring As Field-based Learning: Some New Zealand Developments*, in: Goodlad & Hirst (ibid.), Chapter 6.

Jones, J. (1993) *University Students As Tutors In Secondary Schools*, In: Proceedings Of A Conference On Peer Tutoring At The University of Auckland New Zealand 19-21 August 1993, Higher Education Research Office And University of Auckland.

Juel, C. (1991) *Cross-age Tutoring Between Student Athletes And At-Risk Children*, The Reading Teacher 45 (3) 178-186.

Klosterman, R. (1970) *The Effectiveness Of A Diagnostically Structured Reading Program*, The Reading Teacher 24, 159-62.

Lambiotte, J.G., Danserau, D.F., O'Donnell, A.M. & Young, M.D. (1988) *Effects Of Co-operative Script Manipulations On Initial Learning And Transfer*, Cognition And Instruction 5 (2) 103-121.

Michael, J.R. (1989) *A Handbook For Developing A Pre-college Program And Involving College Students In A Community Service Project And A Report Of The Pre-collegiate Enrichment Program, West Georgia College*, West Georgia College, Georgia, ED332646.

Moran, J. & Oja, S. (1977) *Training Kids To Teach: Peer Teaching Program*, Institute of Technology, Minneapolis, Minnesota.

Powell, J.V., Weisenbaker, J. & Conner, R. (1987) *Effects Of Intergenerational Tutoring And Related Variables On Reading And Mathematics Achievement Of Low Socioeconomic Children*, Journal Of Experimental Education 55 (4) 206-211.

Prillaman, D. & Richardson, R. (1989) *The William And Mary Mentorship Model: College Students As A Resource For The Gifted*, Roeper Review 12 (2) 114-118.

Raupp, C.D. & Cohen, D.C. (1992) *"A Thousand Points Of Light" Illuminate The Psychology Curriculum: Volunteering As A Learning Experience*, Teaching Of Psychology 19 (1) 25-30.

Reisner, E.R., Petry, C.A. & Armitage, M. (1990) *A Review Of Programs Involving College Students As Tutors Or Mentors In Grades K-12 (Volumes I and II)*, Policy Studies Institute/US Department of Education, Washington DC.

Rhodes, E.M. & Garibaldi, A.M. (1990) *Teacher Cadets Answer The Call*, Momentum 21 (4) 36-38.

Ross, S.M. et al. (1989) *The Apple Classroom Of Tomorrow Programme With At-Risk Students*, in: Proceedings of Selected Research Papers Presented At the Annual Meeting of the Association For Educational Communicators And Technology, Dallas Texas, February 1-5 1989, ED308837.

Sandler, I.N., Reich, J.W. & Doctolero, J. (1970) *Utilization Of College Students To Improve Inner-City School Children's Academic Behaviour*, Journal of School Psychology 17 (3) 283-290.

Schwartz, G. (1977) *College Students As Contingency Managers For Adolescents In A Program To Develop Reading Skills*, Journal of Applied Behavior Analysis 10, 645-655.

Semb, G.B., Ellis, J.A. & Araujo, J. (1993) *Long-Term Memory For Knowledge Learned In School*, Journal of Educational Psychology 85 (2) 305-316.

Shafer, D.T. (1976) *Comparative Analysis Of Previous Evaluations Of Project SEED*, University of California, Berkeley CA.

Stewart, M.F. (1991) *Peer Tutoring: What's In It For You?*, School Science Review 71 (257) 140-142.

Stewart, M.E. & Palcic, R.A. (1992) *Writing To Learn Mathematics: The Writer-Audience Relationship*, Paper Presented At The Annual Meeting of The Conference On College Composition And Communication, Cincinnati Ohio, March 19-21 1989, ED347549.

Teaching And Learning Research Corporation (1970) *Final Report Of The Evaluation Of The Homework Helper Program*, Teaching And Learning Corporation, New York.

Turkel, S.B. & Abramson, T. (1986) *Peer Tutoring And Mentoring As A Drop-out Prevention Strategy*, Clearing House 60 (2) 68-71.

Valenzuela-Smith, M. (1983) *The Effectiveness Of A Tutoring Program For Junior High Latino Students*, University Of San Francisco, ED237307.

Teaching adults: Integrating theory and practice by a system of peer tutoring

S. Wilden & N. La Gro

Psychology Department, University of East London, Romford Road, London E15 4LZ, UK

Abstract

Current debates consider the impact of varying degrees of structure on approaches to co-operative learning and secondly the impact of the adopted approach on the learning of tutees. This paper aims to investigate these issues in the context of adult learners in one of the 'helping professions'. It is aimed to contribute to this debate with a particular focus on the relationship between the framework of a structured approach and learning objectives.

Introduction

The term peer tutoring is generally reserved for 'activities in which there is systematic and explicit use of students to teach students'(Goodlad & Hirst,1989). There are many variants on this approach and the learning exercise considered in this paper could be described more accurately as reciprocal tutoring or group learning. It also nests in the more general area of co-operative learning which has been described as 'structuring positive interdependence.'(Davidson,1990 cited in Topping, 1992)

Evidence has pointed to the value of using a more structured approach to peer group tasks. K. Topping (1992) considered this issue in a paper that provided an overview of the whole area of co-operative learning and peer tutoring. He noted the work of Slavin (1990) who demonstrated that group work in which students are provided with limited structure and few incentives to work together has been found to have significantly less effect on student learning.

Topping (1992) also identified broad differences between the American and British approach to co-operative learning with the Americans tending to be more "prescriptive and rigid "and

them to trust their assumptions of 'how things are', there was
also a need to move purposefully from start to finish of the
exercise in a task-centred sequence.   Adults have often made
personal sacrifices to commit time and finances when undertaking
education.   Frequently they feel a great sense of frustration
and confusion when they are presented with unclear aims,
objectives and guidelines which are antithetical to their need
to have specific indicators of progress.   Bruner, J.(1966)
situates   this   requirement   in   one   of   four   criteria   for
constructing learning:

> 'A theory of instruction must specify the ways in which a
> body of knowledge should be structured so that it can be
> most readily grasped by the learner'.(P91)

The degree to which learners are able to complete a task,
solve a problem that would otherwise be beyond them without some
instructional   underpinning   has   been   characterised   as
'scaffolding', Vygotsky (1978, 1987), Wood, Bruner and Ross
(1976).   Ellice Forman (1989) takes up the importance of
scaffolded instruction in relation to co-operative learning in
developing children's discovery and application of mathematical
concepts. Initial conclusions show that considerable gains were
achieved in cognitive development.

> "The subjects we discussed above were not only learning
> from each other, they were also actively involved in
> increasing their knowledge of geometry and in discovering
> how the shadows of geometric shapes change mean their
> distance from the course light is systematically varied".

Learning can be identified along dimensions of cognitive,
affective, social and the acquisition or development of skills.
Tough's (1979) investigation into the processes of adult
learning revealed that the subjects in his study indicated the
relationship between motivation and gains in learning.

> "more than half the person's total motivation is to gain
> and retain certain fairly clear knowledge and skill, or to
> produce some other lasting change in himself". (P6)

Comments made in the evaluation helped to identify the
learning outcomes associated with this exercise.   It appeared
that learning occurred primarily on the cognitive and social
dimensions.   The majority of students reported they achieved a
greater understanding of the relevance and impact of theories
from this approach as compared to other methods of teaching and
learning used on the course. Students pointed to the usefulness
of the work sheet and prompt questions, the fact that there was
the time to consider closely and discuss a whole interview and
that it was a more 'objective' exercise.

One argument for using a more structured approach is that the content can be clearly defined. Although the students had the opportunity to reflect independently, certain parameters had M. (1992) draw attention to the relationship between learning and practice in nursing education.

> 'In the context of empowerment and good practice in nursing, an educational process must therefore reflect the demands of practice as described and must allow the learner to develop a sense of responsibility by being responsible; the ability to initiate wisely and/or collaborate in management and evaluation of care, by 'acting out' these skills and to engage continuously in a meaningful learning process by carrying out the learning themselves'.
> P223(1992)

A central aim of the course is to foster autonomy in how students develop the capacity to integrate knowledge into their own practice. In considering adult learning and particularly experiential learning, Boud (1989, P43) identified three separate ideas around the notion of autonomy; "Autonomy as a goal" - educators aiming to support the development of people who attain their own understanding; "Autonomy as an approach to teaching and learning" and thirdly "autonomy as a necessary element in learning", ie, that students are able to make their own judgements about a body of knowledge and can make assessments about what is appropriate in a particular professional setting. Although all three are relevant, this exercise is particularly concerned with this last aspect.

The importance of providing an adult learner with a sense of autonomy and concern to give an explicit value to their experience has been central to developing an adequate theory of teaching suited to an adult age range of students. Dewey (1938) gave prominence to the value of experience in describing his conceptual framework for education:

> 'All genuine education comes about through experience'
> (P13)

> 'The central problem of an education based upon experience is to select the kind of experiences that live fruitfully and creatively in subsequent experiences'. (116-17)

Sadington (1992) also places experience centrally in a framework for adult learning:

> "The intrinsic tendency of people to draw upon their own experience for both the knowledge and skills, and the vast accumulation of experience that an adult has compared to a child, makes learner experience an important concept in

adult education theory and practice". (P37)

But autonomy and relationship to practice are not the only two required design features of the exercise. In addition to providing students with a learning exercise which allowed them to make reference to their own practice, and which encouraged Europeans more "warm and fuzzy". He highlights as a crucial issue the question of "how much structure and of what kind" to integrate into any co-operative learning activity.

It is necessary to consider the issue of structure in the context of the purpose of this particular learning exercise. The setting is a Higher Education institution and the exercise was first introduced to a group of mature students undertaking part-time study and already practising as trainees in the guidance field. The course directly relates to their professional practice and seeks to ensure students acquire the required level of professional competence which combines a mastery of skills with an understanding of relevant theoretical frameworks. The learning exercise specifically relates to interview training.

The interview training on the course requires students to become familiar with and competent in a range of skills, together with the various stages of interviews in relation to a variety of clients and settings. In addition, there is input and reflection on a range of theoretical perspectives both to the process of understanding the client and decisions on strategies to utilise within the interview. Recent research (Kidd,Killeen,Jarvis and Offer 1993) has argued that in their approach to interviewing, guidance practitioners draw in a limited way on relevant theories. This premise remains under debate but tutors at the course centre assert the importance of professional interview practice being informed by appropriate understanding of theory.

This view informed the construction of a structured learning exercise which entailed the analysis of a video of a guidance interview in a small group setting. Two groups of 8 students carried out the learning exercise, making a total sample of 16. Students were asked to work through a booklet which contained questions, tasks and the rationale for these various items and to discuss their views and interpretations in pairs and also as a whole group. The specific questions and tasks focused on the successive stages of the interview, the use of interpersonal skills and relevance of various theories. The session was structured to allow time for personal reflection and group discussion.

One of the objectives for the learning exercise was the integration of learning from both the course and the workplace.

In asking students to identify aspects of good practice in the videoed interview, the educational process was requiring them to exercise judgement based on their awareness of models and skills from classroom learning and their own observations and experience of conducting interviews in the workplace. Their view of what worked and didn't work in interviews took account of the many varied and complex interactions that were brought together in these situations; to be discovered by the reflection on 'taught' elements of the course and the reality of practitioner and client interaction. Anderson, B. and McMillan, been set. The approach to interviewing promoted by the course centre was integral to the way the questions and tasks were organised.The exercise was thus designed to ensure 'recognisable cognitive gains' accrued to the students (see Goodlad and Hirst, 1989, P82). At the same time, students had the opportunity to discuss without a tutor how they understood and viewed the interview, the relevance of theory and the use of skills.

In the evaluation 14 of the 16 students stated that the exercise had helped to develop their own interviewing practice. All students commented positively on the value of discussion with their peers, particularly on specific points and the value of seeing different interpretations. They observed that working as part of a group meant sharing information and understanding although they did not always agree on questions and/or answers and it was noted that "we have all got a similar level of understanding". Thus students had a structured space where they could explore their knowledge and understanding and where they could express themselves freely. One comment gives a more direct indication of how the exercise was experienced, "By being given very specific areas to concentrate on, a deeper analysis of skills used could directly relate to personal skills and skill shortages".In this exercise, there was the opportunity to stand back and observe and reflect in a detached manner yet work closely together with peers.

It has been cogently argued that peer tutoring has the potential to inculcate deep rather than surface approaches to learning (Goodlad and Hirst,1989). This relates both to the fact that students are actively processing information and ideas and communicating with each other while doing so. One element that is an important part of the learning is that students made visible to one another their levels of understanding and varying perspectives. There is often little opportunity to do this in a 'safe' way. In this way the learning is also transformed from a 'private to a social activity'P16, (Goodlad & Hirst,1989) .

At the same time, some students expressed the need or desire for 'expert knowledge'. The question does arise as to whether there is the need for some external reference point against which work can be assessed or checked (Topping,1992) and it also points to the fact that for many students an authority figure remains an integral part of their version of learning and teaching. In this situation, the group were required to take responsibility for their own interpretations and although the students challenged one another, a final verdict on the 'outcomes' was not part of the exercise.

Conclusion

The aim of the exercise was to use structured learning to contribute to the development of autonomous learning and reflective practice. The structured approach helped to ensure the exercise was able to meet desired outcomes at the same time as supporting independent learning. Students were motivated to consider closely examples of practice and relate them to their own development. The value for adult learners was that the learning exercise provided a forum for debate where they could share ideas and interpretations and engage in focused, yet active learning which had direct relevance to the professional setting.

REFERENCES

Anderson, B.& McMillan M. Learning Experiences for Professional Reality and Responsibility, ed Milligan, J.& Griffin, C. *Empowerment Through Experiential Learning*, Kogan, Page 1992.

Boud, D. Some Competing Traditions in Experiential Learning, Chapter 3, in *Making Sense of Experiential Learning; Diversity in Theory & Practice ed*, Weil, S. McGill, I. The Society for Research into Higher Education & OU Press, Milton Keynes, 1989.

Bruner, J. *Toward a Theory of Instruction* Cambridge, Mass, Harvard University Press, 1966 in Knowles, M. *The Adult Learner; a Neglected Species*, 4th Edition, 1990. P.91.

Davidson, N. *Co-operative Learning in Mathematics*, 1990 in Topping, K. C-operative *Learning and Peer Tutoring: an Overview*. The Psychologist, Vol. 5, No. 4 April, 1992.

Dewey, John, *Experience and Education*, New York: MacMillan 1938.

Forman, Ellice *The Role of Peer Interaction in the Social Construction of Mathematical Knowledge*, International Journal of Educational Research 1989 Vol. 13.

Goodlad, S. & Hirst, B. (1989) *Peer Tutoring: Guide to Learning by Teaching*, London, Kogan Page.

Kidd,J.M., Killeen,J.,Jarvis,S. & Offer, M. *Working Models of Careers Guidance: The Interview*, Department of Organisational Psychology, University of London & NICEC, 1993.

Sadington, J.A. Learner *Experience: A Rich Resource for Learning* in Tough, A. *The Adult's Learning Projects*, Toronto: Ontario, Institute for Studies in Education, 1979.

Slavin, R.E. *Co-operative Learning: Theory, Research and Practice*, Englewood Cliffs, New Jersey: Prentice Hall, 1990.

Topping, K. Co-operative Learning and Peer Tutoring: an Overview *The Psychologist*, 1992, Vol. 5, No 4 April,151-157.

Vygotsky,L.S. *Mind in Society.* M.Cole,V.John-Steiner,S.Scribner,& Souberman,E. (eds) Cambridge:Harvard University Press, 1978.

Wood,D.,Bruner,J.S., & Ross,G. The Role of tutoring in problem solving.*Journal of Child Psychology & Psychiatry*,1976, 17,89-100

Initial experiences of student tutoring at the Cardiff Institute of Higher Education

M.F. Wilson[a] & D. Saunders[b]

[a] Cardiff Institute of Higher Education, Llandaff Centre, Cardiff, UK
[b] Enterprise Unit, University of Glamorgan, Pontypridd, Mid Glamorgan CF37 1DL, UK

1 Introduction

Student Tutoring exists in many forms, (Saunders[1]), but in spite of all its different names, such as proctoring, peer tutoring, student tutoring, supplemental instruction and student volunteers it retains a common theme: both tutees and tutors can gain from the experience. Tutees can benefit from the help they receive with their learning and the tutor can improve transferable skills.

> "Tutoring schemes, known variously as Peer Tutoring, Cross-age Tutoring, Youth Tutoring Youth and Each One Teach One, have used students to teach students, students to teach children, non-professional adults to teach adults and children, and children to teach children."
> (Goodlad and Hirst[2])

This review involves students from further and higher education institutions giving help to pupils in local primary and secondary schools. Volunteer students assist teachers in classrooms for between two and six hours a week for 6 weeks or more. They always work under the supervision and direction of teachers helping pupils with their work and discussing the relationship of the subject being taught to everyday life (Hughes[3]). Students get involved in a wide variety of subject areas with pupils of all ages and abilities.

Many tutoring schemes are being developed nation-wide through support from private and voluntary sectors. BP Chemicals Aiming for a College Education (ACE) programme launched in 1990, is a £3m initiative to help bring about a significant increase in the number of pupils who stay on after compulsory schooling and aspire to further and higher education. Student Tutoring is one part of the ACE programme and there are now over 120 schemes in the UK. Similarly the Learning Together initiative has been spearheaded by Community Service Volunteers and Digital.

There are other advantages to the scheme. Student Tutoring can help make lessons more interesting, provide extra stimulus and individual attention to pupils of all abilities and the scheme gives students the opportunity to enhance their skills.

2   Wales' And Cardiff Institute's Involvement In Student Tutoring

Wales first became involved in Student Tutoring with the introduction of a pilot scheme at the University of Glamorgan in 1992. The scheme was received very well by teachers, pupils and students and it was decided to develop such a scheme through partnerships with other Higher Education Institutions throughout Wales.

With sponsorship from the BP (Baglan Bay) ACE programme and matchfunding from local Training and Enterprise Councils, the Student Tutoring Wales initiative was established quickly in colleges throughout North, South and West Wales. Funding was essential for administration and travel expenses incurred by students on school visits and also for the appointment of a managing agent(University of Glamorgan), which meant that information and good practice could be spread quickly to higher education partners as well as school networks.

With the help of Education Business Partnerships in Gwynedd, West Glamorgan, South and Mid-Glamorgan, over 400 students joined the Student Tutoring Wales initiative in 1993.

Cardiff Institute of Higher Education (CIHE) is one of seven HE institutions involved in the Welsh initiative. Over 200 CIHE students have been placed in 30 schools throughout South Glamorgan since February 1993. The scheme is growing in popularity with the scheme being opened up to more and more courses as interest grows and the benefits are recognised.

The feedback obtained from CIHE's evaluation and monitoring of the scheme, and from schemes nation-wide, indicates that everyone can benefit from Student Tutoring. Pupils get more individual attention and can learn from their role models about college life and courses. Teachers can benefit from being able to carry out tasks which they otherwise could not attempt without extra help. They are also made aware of up-to-date information in particular areas especially science and technology. Student Tutors can improve communication and problem solving skills (WWF[5]) and get an insight into the teaching profession.

Views from students, teachers, and pupils obtained during the monitoring of CIHE's scheme are very supportive. Evaluation questionnaires to students revealed that 95% (n=71) felt that they improved their communication skills.

"The reward for a student tutor is the satisfaction of just being able to help someone. You are also constantly adjusting your level of language, especially with young children, to be able to be understood. This can only serve to enhance communication skills."

"It has been an excellent experience working with children. It has improved my self-confidence no end and enhanced my communication skills"

"I really enjoyed helping with the children. It has been an opportunity that I have found beneficial and I'm glad I took part."

Similar questioning of teachers elicited comments such as:

"Through the student tutor's assistance, pupils have become more motivated and more inclined to finish their work." - (French teacher at a secondary school in Cardiff)

"Nicola has been a great help and has tackled a variety of tasks with efficiency and confidence. I shall be sorry to see her go and the children will miss her too." - (Primary school teacher)

Pupils also enjoyed student tutors' help.

"We are able to communicate well with the student tutors and it makes lessons enjoyable."

"We like Joanne being in the class. Now we know we can do what she does, it's not just for boys."

"We like listening to the tutors explaining about their work. They are easy to talk to and we are learning new ideas."

Student Tutoring is a very powerful mechanism as it is able to build a bridge between HE and secondary and primary sectors thus bringing pupils into contact with higher education either to acquaint them with an inconceivable concept (as a lot of pupils involved in the scheme are from a low social background) and to dismantle preconceived ideas they may have harboured. This of course works both ways. It is obviously an advantage for colleges because it provides an additional valuable learning experience to students. Colleges may also be able to improve recruitment and acquire a 'feel good' factor through helping the community.

A primary objective of the Student Tutoring Wales programme is to target what may generally be described as "under-achieving" pupils within schools which have relatively low continuation rates into Higher and Further Education. Student Tutors help to build bridges in terms of awareness raising, public relations and motivating pupils - as reinforced by the above quotes. We also emphasise the cognitive gains for tutees as demonstrated by tutoring intervention for the improvement of reading(Goodlad and Hirst[7]) and (Cloward[6]) and mathematics(Bae-Eli and Raviv[8]). Such improvement helps pupils to cross

Higher Education bridges at the next practical level: by getting better qualifications.

3 The Research

The above feedback from students as well as published literature on cognitive gains prompted CIHE to conduct research to gather 'hard' evidence to show whether student tutors improved skills while participating in this experience.

Published research makes claims about improving tutors' cognitive performance within their chosen specialisation or discipline. It is argued that this has been accomplished through learning by reviewing and summarising, making material more meaningful through recasting and reformulation, and through identifying knowledge gaps or conceptual misunderstandings(Goodlad and Hirst[2]), (Malamuth and Fitz-Gibbon[9]) and (Shisler, Top and Osguthorpe[10]). These conclusions are limited, however, in some cases the students were of secondary-school age and in other cases they were described as low-achievers who would especially benefit from repeated reviews of basic theory and method.

The current focus is on Higher Education students from a wide range of backgrounds, who would not be described as under-achievers, and who work with primary and secondary school pupils. The general hypothesis is that student tutors improve skills due to taking part in the tutoring scheme. The problem comes in stating and quantifying which skills. Indeed, this is a proverbial can of worms because there is no universally accepted skill classification to work to. It was necessary to first identify the skills that students appeared to improve. A comprehensive list of skills was produced from workshop sessions with students and from BTEC Common Skills and GNVQ Management Skills:

- team-work;
- dealing with people;
- communicating with others;
- analysing and solving problems;
- student skills;
- finding and organising information and
- managing oneself.

The research in progress is investigating whether student tutors 'change' - in terms of developing social skills, and at more invisible levels in terms of cognitive ability and even personality dispositions. It is hypothesised that the most obvious evidence of change and development will be observed for specific skills such as team-work and problem solving whereas the most difficult and subtle measurement of change will be with 'personality'. This reasoning is based on the work of Allport[11] who argued for the existence of relatively transient and changeable trait labels in addition to consistent underlying cardinal traits which essentially determine personality.

The psychometric tests that are to be used target achievement motivation (Smith[13]), locus of control (Trice [14]) , and perceptiveness (Smith[12]).

Two other sets of data are included in the research. These will be used in the analysis to indicate any significant factors that affect changes in skills. First, entry data, i.e. age, sex, educational qualifications, and ethnicity, will be collected for both experimental and control groups. Second, tutoring data is included only in the student tutor post-questionnaire. Items such as school type, subject area, and contact time will help to point to areas which appear to maximise skills improvement.

4 The Methodological Problems

A before-and-after survey design incorporating self-administered questionnaires was deemed appropriate as the research is attempting to measure change brought about by student tutoring. It is therefore essential to establish baselines for later comparison.

The self-administered questionnaire technique(Oppenheim[15]) was adopted in preference to interview methodology which while invaluable for generating detailed data would be too time consuming for both interviewees and interviewers (a trial sample of 200 tutors is envisaged).

A crucial inclusion within the design of the research programme is the control group of students who do not engage in tutoring but who have similar background characteristics to the student tutoring 'experimental' groups. It is accepted that perfect matching is not possible, but that an approximate balancing of groups is feasible.

The Problem of Interpretation: Confounding variables
The skills sections for pre and post questionnaires are the same for both the experimental group(student tutors), and the control group, thereby attempting to establish that differences could be attributed to the experimental variable and not to other activities that students are involved in.

There are numerous confounding variables which may emerge during the tutoring period:

- the students are six weeks older;
- they have had more teaching at college;
- they may have had practice in completing questionnaires;
- communication skills may have been learnt through a module before or during their tutoring experience;
- governmental factors affecting the college, courses or student life;
- financial factors;
- outside activities such as coaching and youth groups;

- satisfaction or dissatisfaction with the scheme;
- mood at time of completing questionnaires.
- underlying achievement motives may be responsible for change and development, rather than tutoring per se.

Some confounding variables can be addressed by using the control group and every effort will be made to account for other variables. (Smith[13]) points out that "a subjects level of achievement motivation may substantially influence the responses to experimental situations".

According to (Morris and Garden[16]) "internal scorers share a tendency to perform somewhat better academically than their extroverted and external counterparts." It is for these reasons that achievement and locus of control measures have been included in the research design, in order to check on confounding variables.

Some confounding variables can be addressed through the use of matched subjects within a control group: gender, age, entry qualification and subject specialisation within Higher Education being obvious examples. We conclude this discussion by highlighting a more problematic concern which applies to a wide range of peer tutoring research. When Higher Education students become tutors they do so - with some notable exceptions(Hughes and Metcalfe[4]) - as volunteers. Student tutoring may therefore attract a particular kind of student who may have specific dispositions: intuitive examples include greater altruistic tendency, increased social confidence, or more motivation towards study and work.

It is therefore difficult to conclude with any degree of certainty whether tutoring per se has a particular effect on students, because such students may already have been progressing in a particular direction and would have improved in various ways. Previous authors who have investigated supplemental instruction within US Universities(Rye, Wallace and Bidgood[17]) have observed an overall increase in examination and coursework marks for those students who act as supplemental instructors, as compared with those who do not. The obvious is overlooked: the more motivated students will volunteer for any initiative linked to their studies, and the more motivated students tend to get higher grades at the end of the course.

One solution is to match subjects for ability as well as levels of motivation towards academic study, and to ruthlessly allocate them to tutoring or control groups. For a variety of reasons associated with ethics and the importance of using volunteers this is not possible within the present research programme. Another solution is to use volunteers as their own controls, and to examine the relative benefits of tutoring associated with varying degrees of motivation or orientation. It is this strategy which is to be pursued within the CIHE programme.

Smith[13] points out that a subjects level of achievement motivation may substantially influence the responses to experimental situations. If tutoring is to be viewed as an experiment, then higher levels of achievement will be positively correlated with increased perceived gains from student tutoring. Another possible correlation lies with internal-external locus of control and tutoring gains. Morris and Garden [16] argue that internal scorers share a tendency to perform somewhat better academically than their extroverted and external counterparts. It is therefore hypothesised that those tutors who have more confidence and belief in their abilities to determine and shape their own learning outcomes will be more likely to show an improvement in a variety of tutoring skills.

The CIHE research project will be completed in the 1994-95 academic session. A pilot programme has been completed during this academic session, indicating that student tutors have increased the targeted skills whilst a control group of students not involved in tutoring (but matched for academic performance and subject specialisation) actually decreased their skills scores within the six week period. The sample sizes are however limited to 20 students within each group, and to date no significant conclusions can be reached. It becomes crucial that the tutoring and control groups are matched as closely as possible which necessitates the targeting of relatively large cohorts for popular subject-specialisms.

References

1. Saunders, D. Peer Tutoring in Higher Education, Chapter 2, *Studies in Higher Education 17*, 211-219, 1992.

2. Goodlad, S. and Hirst, B. *Peer Tutoring: a Guide to Learning by Teaching*, Kogan Page and Nichols, London and New York, 1989.

3. Hughes, J. *Tutoring: Students as Tutors in School*, London: BP Educational Service, 1992.

4. Hughes, J. and Metcalfe, R. *Tutoring and Proctoring* in Saunders, D. *The Complete Student Handbook*, Blackwell, Oxford, 1994.

5. *Supplemental Instruction: Report on WWF Involvement*, World Wildlife Fund For Nature (1991).

6. Cloward, R.D. Studies in Tutoring, Chapter 1, *Journal of Experiential Education 36*, 14-25, 1967.

7. Goodlad, S. and Hirst, B. *Exploration in Peer Tutoring*, Blackwell, Oxford.

8. Bae-Eli, N. and Raviv, A. Underachievers as Tutors, Chapter 3, *Journal of Educational Research 75*, 1982, 139-143.

9. Malamuth, N.M. and Fitz-Gibbon, C.T. *Tutoring and Social Psychology: a theoretical analysis.* CSE Report No 116, Los Angeles: Centre for the Study of Education, UCLA Graduate School of Education, 1978.

10. Shisler, L., Top, B.L. and Osguthorpe, R.T. Behaviourally Disordered Students as reverse-role tutors: increasing Social Acceptance and Reading Skills, Chapter 2, *BC Journal of Special Education 10*, 101-119, 1986.

11. Allport, G.W. *Personality and Social Encounter: Selected Essays*, Boston, Beacon Press, 1960.

12. Smith, D. J. Effective Governance Questionnaire, 1993.

13. Smith, J. M. A Quick Measure of Achievement Motivation, Chapter 12, *British Journal of Social and Clinical Psychology*, 1973, 137-143.

14. Trice, A. D. *An Academic Locus of Control Scale for College Students. Perceptual and Motor Skills*, Volume 61, 1043-1046, 1985.

15. Oppenheim, A. N. *Questionnaire Design, Interviewing and Attitude Measurement* (new edition), Pinters, London, 1992.

16. Morris, L. W. and Garden, R. L. Relationship between locus of control and extroversion-introversion in predicting academic behaviour. *Psychological Reports*, 1981, 48, 799-806.

17. Rye, R.D., Wallace, J. and Bidgood, P. Instructions in learning Skills : an Integrated Approach, *Medical Education 27*, 1993, 470-473.

SECTION D:

Collaboration Amongst Children

Children learning about friendship in the context of an English reception classroom

A. Avgitidou

University of Sussex, ICAPE, Education Development Building, Falmer, Brighton BN1 9RG, UK

Abstract

This research explores young children's friendships in the context of their peer culture as constructed by children themselves in the setting of an English reception classroom. Learning about friendship is perceived as a dynamic, dual process: children construct their rituals and concerns as well as apply and make use of them in their specific friendships. Clinical interviews and daily observations of children's classroom interactions for a period of seven months provide a description and an understanding of children's own views of their specific friendships and detailed information about their actual friendship characteristics. Peer culture is presented as contextualised by the adult world and developing among children in their classroom.

1 Introduction

This paper provides a description and analysis of the processes and socialising agents of children's learning about friendship in the context of an English reception classroom. It focuses on "interactive learning" within the "peer culture" context. The meaning and use of these terms concerning children's learning about friendship are explored. By interactive learning this paper refers to the processes of learning emerging from or constructed within interaction and exchange between peers. The process is interactive; children are active constructors of their environment [4] and they learn about friendship within their interactions with peers and adults; this accords with Vygotsky's view of socialisation on two levels, first between people (interpsychological), and then inside the child (intrapsychological) [6]. Within this process, Corsaro & Rizzo [2] suggest childhood socialisation as a social and collective process.

---

[1] I am grateful to the Greek States Scholarship Foundation for their research grant for the completion of my Ph.D. I would like to thank Dr. Peter Kutnick, Dr. Barry Cooper, Dr. Harry Torrance and Dr. David Stephens for reading earlier drafts of the paper.

"The approach is essentially interpretative, stressing that children discover a world that is endowed with meaning and help to shape and share in their own developmental experiences by their interactive processes (Cook-Gumperz and Corsaro, 1986)", [2, p. 880].   Peer culture provides a context for understanding children's active construction of their own world in relation to the adult world. Peer culture is defined by Corsaro & Eder [1] as : "a stable set of activities or routines, artifacts, values, and concerns that children produce and share in interaction with peers" (p.197). These sets of activities and routines are, therefore, recognisable (stable) in the peer culture. However, peer culture is perceived by Corsaro & Eder [1] as something negotiable between peers and continuously changing. Therefore, construction of the peer culture is a developing process.

This paper explores ways within which friendship is established as a peer culture concern, and ways it is related to other main peer concerns in the classroom. Multiple types of friendship activity are observed at anyone point of time and at different time periods within the year. Shared activity is seen as a peer culture concern and a developing friendship characteristic. In addition, processes within which children's experiences in the adult world and social life are shaped outside of school are related to the content and processes of the peer culture (see further discussion in Denzin, [3]). This exploration is in accordance with the view of children as active reproducers of their own world [5,7]. Certain adult values or norms may therefore be reflected in children's peer culture; however, their meaning and use in terms of friendship vary according to the classroom context and children's concerns.

This ethnographic case study provides an in depth exploration of the actual characteristics and social processes of friendship. The reported findings are derived from interviews with children over a two year period, observations of friends' interactions during the first year in school, and teacher's and mother's interviews. First and second interviews with children took place at the beginning and end of the school year respectively. Third interviews were conducted at the end of the following school year.

Looking for a playmate; Looking for a friend: Developmental changes

a. Looking for a playmate: Implications for friendship development.
It is not clear from my observations if children start to interact with a child with the clear intention to initiate a friendship or shared play at the beginning of the year. However, children do try to find someone to play with and share an activity. The fact that shared play is one of children's main concerns is evident in children's first interview as the category 'shared activity' is mentioned by all children and is employed as a basic reason for liking, playing, working and being friends with another child. Playing with someone is perceived as liking and accepting them. Liking and accepting someone

additionally forms a motive for selecting one child as a playmate-friend and not another. The following children's answers in their first, as well as second interviews are illuminating:

Helen, 1st interview: (Do you think Lucy likes you?) "Yes, because she always plays with me.

Lucy, 1st interview: (Do you think Kathy likes you?) "Yes, because she read a long book to me" (shared activity).

It is interesting that, further to liking, shared activity is perceived as a necessary prerequisite for the maintenance of friendship.

Juliet, 2nd interview: (You are not friends with Mary?) "No". (Why is that?) "No, we first played in the beginning but not anymore".

It is important to note that children refer to quantitative differences in the way they refer to shared play. Children frequently responded:

"He always plays with me", "She sometimes plays with me".

The significance of shared play is supported when children make positive attributions of someone (e.g. nice) justified by the fact that he or she plays with the self: " He is nice, he plays with me all the time".

Children's answers emphasise a motivation to play or be friends with someone based on shared play, liking and complementary behaviour. A model of cognitive interconnections emerges from children's perceptions:

Plays with me = reciprocates play = likes me = I play with him or her = I reciprocate play = I like him further, = is my friend, which leads to a spiral. It is important that in the first interview, the spiral revolves around play and not around friendship.   Later, the spiral begins to revolve around friendship, because of the experiences children have within the development of their peer relationships.

b. Partner versus activity oriented interactions.

An observed tendency in established friends' interactions is playing in certain areas of the classroom and gradually constructing certain games and ways of playing within these activities. However, friends' play is not activity - oriented but friend - oriented. In my observations, children chose an activity not because of its content but according to the position of their friend and later according to the shared interests of their friendship.   Although, children gradually develop their own favourite games, the motive of proximity and shared activities with the friend is more important for children than the actual content of the activity. In latter observations and as relationships develop, continuity of interactions and shared play between friends further emphasise that activity choice is partner oriented. This is important to note here because the basic and most significant reason that children provide for friendship / best friendship selection is shared activity and play with someone. In their third interview during the follow up year, many friendship choices depend on a) personal liking ("Because I like him) which shows that selection is much more conscious than before when it was dependant on shared play and the other's liking, b) the other's psychological characteristics like being helpful and nice as well as to attributions of the nature of the relationship ("He's always been nice to me"), and c) extension of interaction outside of school which for children shows the other's special liking and a level of intimacy outside the classroom context ("Because he invites me over to his house", "Because today Mark is coming to my brother's birthday").

c. Children constructing the nature of their friendships: Shared activity becomes a friendship ritual.

Relating to questions "what do you usually do with your friend?" or "what kind of games do you play together?" children refer to their shared favourite activities and friendship 'rituals'. 'Rituals' are repeated patterns of activity or interaction in classroom daily activities which have a specific meaning for the friends in the context of their relationship. For example, certain favourite activities (playing at the sand corner) which both friends play together daily, or sitting next to the friend at milk-time, or selecting the same colours or shapes for drawing have a specific meaning for friends and become friendship rituals. A ritual of Helen's and Lucy's friendship, telling jokes, is described by both of them in their second interviews as something which is characteristic of their interactions and meaningful for both of them.

Helen, 2nd interview: (Do you ever say special things or secrets to Lucy?) "Only jokes". (What kind of jokes?) "What did the man say with the three heads? Hello, Hello, Hello", smiling at me. (Does Lucy ever tell you any jokes?) "Yes". (Do you make the jokes up?) Helen nods yes. "Kathy told us Hello, hello, hello, and now she is our friend". Helen's last comment shows that something which is shared between friends as funny and meaningful, may cause friendly behaviour towards someone else who knows and uses this ritual when relating to the friendship dyad.

Lucy, 2nd interview: (Do you ever say jokes to each other?) Lucy nods yes smiling. (What kind of jokes?) "Why can't the orange get up the hill? Because she ran out of juice instead of petrol", smiling. (Did you make it up?) "I made it up". It is interesting that even after a year the same best friends refer to the same jokes when talking about what they do with their friends. This ritual, telling jokes, is then part of the history of their best friendship and has a special value as it is constructed and maintained between them.

Mothers also refer to their children's shared activities with friends. John's mother explains about his relationship with Nick at school: "I think they are very alike. When I talked to the teacher, she said they are very much the same, and *they tend to play the same things in the classroom.* They want to talk about things and in the classroom *they tend to go for the same things* and if they are not pushed on to different things, they tend to sit there, and you know they need a lot of stimulation. *They are both very proud of what they are doing* and they both talk a lot".

d. Affirming friendship as a peer culture concern.

The fact that children build on their interactions and behaviour on the concept of friendship developmentally is evident in children's second interviews. Children reverse the model *he plays with me so he is my friend* to *he is my friend and therefore I play with him.* They, additionally, decide about the nature of their interactions with someone based on the friendship criterion: e.g. he is my friend and therefore I am nice to him. An example of this change is shown in Nick's second interview when he talks about his best friend, John.

(Do you have a best friend in your classroom?) "John".

(Why is he your best friend?) "Because he always helps me doing some things, like pick me up when I'm not very good at the playground, when I fall over, John pulls me up, he helps me".

(And do you do the same for him?) "Yes!" (quick and spontaneous).

(Why do you do the same Nick?) "Because he is my friend, so I **always** help him".

Another connection which shows the significance of the friend rather than the one of the playmate is the fact that children nominate their best friend as the one who they play with most, they like most and they work with most. Nick, 2nd interview: (Who is your best friend?) "John, because he plays with me". (Who do you like most in your classroom?) "John because he plays with me all the time". (Who do you like to play with most?) "John, because he wants to play with me". (Who do you work with most?) "John, because he always comes to my house". In this way, children, in their second interviews, relate everyday patterns of activity as play with, like, and work with, to their best friend relationship.

e. Children's concerns in their peer culture in relation to their social experiences.

It is interesting to note that 'being nice' and kind is highlighted as a friendship value consistently from children, mothers and teachers, who virtually create a milieu within which children learn about 'being nice' to their friends. Although, a reference to 'nice' was found in the content analysis of the first and second interviews, it is more evident in children's third interviews, showing that this perception was encouraged through time. In addition, the teacher emphasises the fact that children should "be nice to each other" and that there should not be any "fighting" and "bullying". These are some of the main rules of the school and were also included in the classroom rules which children decided about together with their teacher in their first year.

Kathy's explanations of being "nice" are presented because she refers to most of the meanings 'being nice' has for children. It is interesting to see that further to showing concern or being polite to someone, 'nice' is related to classroom rituals and concerns as acceptance in play and doing 'nice drawings'. This reveals children's active reconstruction of an adult value, 'nice', and its integration in their peer world:

Kathy, 3rd interview: (Why is Anna your friend?) "Because she is nice to me when I hurt myself". (Why is Samuel your friend?) "Because he is nice to me and he is funny". (What do you mean he is nice to you?) "Well, he's nice because he lets me play with him". (Who is your best friend?) "Amanda, because she's ever so kind, she does nice things like drawings". (What do you like best about her?) "Cause she is nice" (Can you explain this to me?) "Well, because she's nice she does lots of things and uses nicer colours". (How were you going to be friends again if you had an argument?) "We would be nice to each other and we would be friends again".

Mothers explain "nice" behaviour similarly mainly when I ask them (a) how they contribute to their child's effort to get along with others, or when I ask them (b) what they would do if their child had a complaint about their best friend: Kathy 's mother (a) : "I think making an effort to make sure she mixes with other children....take her to the park where she meets other people, just make sure she is nice to them".

John 's mother (a) : "I try to teach him to be nice. I think sharing and things like that. 'She's nice', 'she helped me with that' (quoting her child's comments), he likes that".

Therefore, "nice" behaviour is expected from children and is reinforced by adults both at home and at school. Children reproduce this model of being nice in relation to their friendship choices and development. "Nice" forms a stereotype in the nature of English children's friendships. However, children adjust it to their peer concerns and rituals. "Nice" is seen not only as someone being polite and not fighting but also as one playing with the self, accepting in play, being funny and helping you in your school work.

Conclusion

This paper noted that certain patterns and rituals develop within specific friendships and acquire specific meaning for the participants. Peer culture integrates an active reconstruction of the adult world values. However, it has a unique and context-specific character. Although children are seen to have highly sophisticated perceptions of their own friendships, they are not adequately capable of reflecting upon the social processes of building up a close friendship and more they do not have the meta cognitive abilities to relate their use of rituals to the wider peer culture context. For these reasons, a contextual interpretative approach has been used to provide a detailed description as well as an understanding of the qualities of children's early friendship characteristics. The implications of an awareness of the peer culture and its influence on children's socialisation is important because it stresses the significance of peers in learning and the contextual opportunities offered in the process of learning about social relationships.

References

1. Corsaro, W. A. & Eder, D. Children's peer cultures, *Annual Review of Sociology*, 1990, **16**, 197-220.

2. Corsaro, W. A., & Rizzo, T. A. *Discussione* and friendship: socialisation processes in the peer culture of Italian nursery children, *Annual Sociological Review*, **53**, 879-894.

3. Denzin, N. K., *Childhood Socialisation: Studies in the development of Language, Social Behavior, and Identity*, Jossey-Bass Pu., U.S.A., 1977.

4. Piaget, J. *The Language and Thought of the child*, World, Cleveland, OH, 1930.

5. Valsiner, J., (ed.) *Child Development within Culturally Structured Environments*, Vol. 2: Social co-construction and environmental guidance in development, Ablem Publishing Corporation, U.S.A., 1988.

6. Vygotsky, L. S. Genesis of the higher mental functions, Chapter 3, *Learning to think*, ed. Light, P., Sheldon, S. & Woodhead, M., pp 32-41, Routledge, Great Britain, 1991.

7. Winegar, L. T. & Valsiner, J. (ed.) *Children's Development within Social Context*, vol. 2: Research and Methodology, Lawrence Erlbaum, U.S.A., 1992.

The conditions of acceptance of joint cognitive tasks by preschool children

O.B. Chesnokova

Department of Developmental Psychology, Faculty of Psychology,
Moscow State University, Stroiteley Street 6-5-43 117311 Moscow, Russia

Abstract

The aims of this study were firstly, to investigate the influence of social conflict on the joint solving of cognitive tasks; and secondly to examine how children perceive the necessity to combine their efforts in order to solve a cognitive task under social conflict conditions. Same-sex triads of 6-year-old children were successively given three types of cognitive tasks: one type did not provoke social conflict, whilst the other two did. Measurements were made of the correctness of solutions to the cognitive tasks and the interaction of each child with the other members of their triad. The findings argue for the creation of different models of joint cognitive activity.

Introduction

The problem of the role of social interaction in the development of cognition remains an urgent one today, and there is a noticeable trend towards an exchange of influences between theoretical studies and teaching practice. One may distinguish four main directions of theoretical and experimental development. The first is the extension of J. Piaget's ideas about the influence of peer interaction on the development of different characteristics of operational thinking. The second is the examination of the age periods in which this influence is at its peak. The third direction is the analysis of the factors (both personal and contained in the situation itself) that mediate the influence of joint activity on cognitive development (e.g. Resnick, Levine & Teasley [1]). The fourth one is the study of the mechanisms of this influence. Proposed mechanisms have included cooperation (e.g. Cooper, Marquis & Edwards [2]; Slavin [3]), imitation (e.g. Bandura [4]) and socio-cognitive conflict (Perret-Clermont [5]; Doise [6]).

Whichever mechanism is held to be explanatory, investigators have generally come to the same conclusion: that social interaction aimed at solving cognitive tasks favours the cognitive progress of those involved. The aim of our study was to clear up what determines the *joint* character of the activity (i.e. when a task being worked on by several children at the same time begins to be adopted as a joint activity). Investigation of this brought us to consideration of a broader problem: the creation of a model of joint cognitive activity that takes into account different versions of the relationship between the social and the cognitive.

The joint character of cognitive activity may be determined by the following factors:

1. The requirement to do anything (e.g. to solve a task) together; this may coincide or not with the objective necessity for joint work.
2. The requirement to have a common product (e.g. working out a common method of solving a task).
3. The availability of a common means for the solution of a task (e.g. one measuring instrument).
4. The distribution of complementary functions (operations) between the partners.
5. The need for one of the children to argue with another at a certain step if the task is to be solved successfully; it may be supposed that this situation of socio-cognitive conflict can be described by different models of the joint character of activity.

In our study we decided to investigate the joint intellectual activity that resulted from the operation of the first and last factors.

Method

Subjects

Ten same-sex triads of children aged 6 years old took part in the experiment. We specifically used triads because under these circumstances opposition between a majority and a minority may appear.

The triads were composed in such a way that none contained a child who had been rejected by the other two children. In addition, children were individually pre-tested before the experiment, using a task which required them to identify one appointed contour among a set superimposed onto each other in a random order. Each triad consisted of children with nearly equal ability to solve this task.

Experimental Tasks

Children were given three types of cognitive task in succession, each one to be carried out by all three members of a triad. Each task consisted of two elements. First, each child had to choose and identify his or her part on a common picture containing parts belonging to the other children. Secondly, each child had to circle with a pencil of the appointed colour his or her part in a composite picture that included parts belonging to the other children.

To begin with, it was suggested to children that they solve these tasks together. However, the solution of each task depended in different ways on social interaction, and in particular on varying degrees of necessity for each child to argue a solution. The first task type contained no conflict situation. A composite picture consisting of three parts was presented. Each of the children had to recognize and circle his or her part in the composite picture. All the parts were non-overlapping. The second task type provoked a conflict between the children by dint of the fact that the picture on one child's card partly coincided with the picture on another child's card. The third type provoked a still stronger social conflict. The conditions of the second task type were repeated, but in addition by utilization of a specially designed folder with a plastic window, only two of the three children participating was given the opportunity to recognize their parts. The third part simply disappeared (i.e. it came down into the folder).

For each task the procedure was as follows. Each child in the triad was given a transparent card on which his or her part of a composite picture was represented. They were given one minute to memorize it, during which time they could examine each other's cards as well as their own. After this, all the transparent cards were fitted on top of each other in the folder, forming a composite picture, visible in a special window. The children had to identify their own parts in this composite picture. Next the children were given the same composite picture on a

single sheet of paper. Each child was given a different coloured pencil and asked to circle the part corresponding to his or her original card. After this, the composite picture was removed from the folder and the children were instructed to choose their cards. The triad was again given a single sheet of paper displaying the composite picture, and each child was again asked to circle the part of the picture corresponding to the part shown on their card. This allowed comparison to be made between each child's identification and circling of his or her part whilst inserted into the folder (the "before" picture and situation) and after taking the card out of folder (the "after" picture and situation).

In the tasks of the third type, two of the children were given cards of the standard size whilst the third child was given a noticeably smaller card that would disappear into the folder. In this case, the part depicted on this card was absent from the composite picture and only two of the children were able to recognize their original parts in the "before" situation.

Scoring
Analysis focused on three aspects of each child's performance: a) their verbal interaction with other members of the triad and with the experimenter; b) whether or not they correctly recognized their own part in the composite picture (i.e. the card given to them at the beginning of each task) in the "before" situation and identified that card as their own in the "after" situation; c) whether or not they correctly circled their own part in the composite picture represented on paper in the "before" and "after" situations. For each task, a child received up to two appraisal points (depending on the quantity of mistakes) for the "before" and "after" situations. We used chi-square to carry out a comparative analysis of the results of the three task types, and the sign test to analyse differences in results between the "before" and "after" situations for each task.

Results and Discussion

Unfortunately , space restrictions prevent discussion of all the results obtained. However, the following points were noted:
1. The first task type (no conflict) gave a higher success rate, the results differing significantly from those of the second and third task types, where there was conflict (chi-square = 4.3; p < .05). There was no difference between the results of the second and third task types (chi-square = 2.7 and 2.65; p < .1).
2. Comparison of the results in the "before" and "after" situations showed significant differences only in the non-conflict task (sign test, T=22 > n-t ; p < .05).

The psychological trends so revealed were explained by us as follows. The cognitive demands of all three task types remained the same, but the degree of social conflict increased. Therefore the character of the interaction between the children changed depending on the type of task and was determined by different factors. In the first task type, the children solved both the cognitive and social elements. Joint activity took the form of group discussion, either of differences and similarities between the cards, or of the question of what should be circled and in what sequence. The availability of cards in the "after" situation allowed mistakes committed in the "before" situation to be corrected by superposition of one's card onto the composite picture. In the second task type, the social element was more of a priority for some children. Each child had the choice of either recognizing the existence in their part of the picture of features common to the other children's parts and circling these twice; or deciding that the overlapping part could only be owned by one of the partners and entering into a social conflict. In the third task type, the child whose card disappeared either entered into an ownership conflict and circled parts of the picture that were not his own, his part simply being absent from the composite picture; or recognized this objective fact and tried, for example, to complete his part by after-drawing.

The availability of the transparent card in the "after" situation meant that it was possible to check the correctness of the solution of the cognitive task, but only in the first task type. In the second and third task types involving social conflict, the children were not guided by this checking method (although verbally the cognitive task could be solved correctly either jointly or individually). In fact, in the third task type, the availability of the card in the "after" situation only strengthened the conflict.

It is also of interest to note here that the outcome of social conflict in the third task type depended on who had the card which had disappeared i.e. the intellectual leader, or a child with the habit of dominating socially without taking into consideration the results of the cognitive task.

Conclusions

We have shown that a cognitive task solved by several children at the same time becomes a joint task whether or not it provokes social conflict. However, social conflict is an important factor in in bringing about conditions that will stimulate children to search for methods to work together. The results obtained have raised problems that can be solved only through studies of a greater scale and with many more factors. In particular, we need to:
1. Create a description of different models of joint activity in the solution of cognitive tasks (involving both the character of the tasks and other factors).
2. Analyse the objective factors that determine different kinds of joint solution.
3. Identify which factors are responsible for making a child come to the realisation that it is necessary for solution of the cognitive task to work together with his or her peers; and how these factors relate to each other.
4. Examine how the objectively given joint task is subjectively perceived and experienced by children.

References
1. Resnick, L.B., Levine, J.M. & Teasley, S.D. (eds). *Perspectives on socially shared cognition*, American Psychological Association, Washington, 1991.
2. Cooper, C.R., Marquis, A. & Edwards, D. Four perspectives on peer learning among elementary school children, *Process and outcome in peer interaction*, eds E. Miller & C. Cooper, pp 267-299, Academic Press, New York, 1986.
3. Slavin, R.E. *Learning to cooperate, cooperate to learn*, Academic Press, New York, 1983.
4. Bandura, A. *Social learning theory*, Englewood Cliff, New York, 1977.
5. Perret-Clermont, A.-N. *Social interaction and cognitive development in children*, Academic Press, London, 1980.
6. Doise, W. Regulations sociales des operations cognitives, *Relations interpersonnelles et development des savoirs*, eds R.A. Hinde, A.-N. Perret-Clermont & J. Stevenson-Hinde, pp 419-438, Delval, Cousset (Suisse).

Child's play: Creative writing in playful environments

P.G. Johnson, C.K. Crook & R.J. Stevenson
Department of Psychology, Durham University, South Road, Durham DH1 3LE, UK

Abstract

This study examines the use of the computer as a tool to facilitate the writing processes of eight-year-old children. Children were recruited to a computer club where they engaged in writing activities with a view towards producing a Journal. Children using word processing wrote longer more complex manuscripts compared with those produced in school settings. Analyses of composing and conferencing sessions, indicate that peer interaction can expand evaluative perspectives by providing a sense of "audience". The implications of these findings are evaluated in relation to substantive theoretical and methodological issues underlying the social organization of writing environments.

Introduction

This study represents the first phase of a project which purports to examine the ways in which writing activities and interactions are embedded in and structured by the cultural contexts in which they occur. Vygotsky argued for the importance to educators of the relation between the contexts in which children participate and the concepts they acquire (Vygotsky, 1986). A framework that emphasizes intra-psychological functioning as a result of participation in a socio-cultural world forces us to examine more closely the state of research involving contexts, including those that make use of cultural artifacts, such as computers. The findings from many studies involving computers and writing are equivocal (see Snyder, 1993 for review). A growing theme in the literature reflects the view that word processing, is a variable device to be interpreted diversely across contexts and cannot be evaluated in isolation. Studies that have considered the total learning context of the writers (e.g., Snyder, 1992b) found that computers served as   catalysts for social interaction among students and teachers thus emphasizing   the importance of the whole social context in shaping the writing process. This orientation invites us to pay attention to certain aspects of context and underlies the strategy to construct a context and articulate the activities within it.

Constructing a context

Two lines of research influenced our initial decision to create a context rather than draw on naturalistic observations of existing situations where computers are used in school settings. Scholars refer to the limitations of naturalistic studies of this kind. They argue that how the new technology is used is strongly influenced by preexisting pedagogical practices (e.g., Michaels, 1985). While the data may reveal much about the particular form, content and practices of education conforming to current expected societal ideas, it may well inhibit ideas for creating propitious environments for computer use.

A second line of research involves the creation of a writing activity system based on a collaborative culture which emphasizes the role of play and imagination in learning and writing development. Inspiration for this approach is drawn from the theoretical frameworks of both Piaget (1932/1965) and Vygotsky (1933/1967) who see play as having an important role in fostering rule systems implicit in the process of learning and cognitive development. This framework provides the rationale for our attempt to construct an educational context in which collaboration, play and imagination have a central role. These theoretical issues also framed the questions we wanted to ask. The first addresses the computer's potential to contribute to an environment that is playful, and therefore, more akin to children's immediate concerns. The second reflects the need to characterize particular qualities of playful interaction and its effect on the writing process. Finally, we ask in what ways do texts produced in this writing activity system compare with those written in the formal school setting?

The Context

Our approach was to create a context for writing that incorporated elements more closely resembling playground activities than those of school classrooms. Within this play-world, children acted out their roles as writers persisting in coordinated action in pursuit of a common goal. Five children of mixed ability, 8 years old, were drawn from a local school to use resources located within a university. In contrast to school where scarce resources limit access, each child was given individual access to a PC, loaded with a simplified version of Word for Windows. The children met voluntarily for 1-2 hours weekly after school during the summer term. Data was collected using observation, field notes and videotapes.

Tasks and goals

The overall purpose in setting up this writing activity system was made clear to the children at the outset. The group's goal was to assist in producing a Journal to be sold in school to assist the funding of new equipment. The success of the enterprise required, both that participants become reasonably confident about writing with computers, and that they assume the role of editors with responsibility for supporting, monitoring and critiquing each other's work during composing and conferencing sessions. To maximise achievement, our writers had to accomplish a series of writing tasks. These writing activities were organized into a hierarchical system of increasing levels of difficulty, beginning with a simple word substitution exercise, proceeding on to a task requiring words to be moved around text, advancing to an autobiographical writing task. Each subgoal was designed to advance mastery of keyboarding skills towards a final writing task involving the adventures of an imaginary figure known as Professor Brilliance. The ultimate goal of the programme was to create a context for writing which encouraged collaboration and within which children were motivated to become active in their own development.

As this discussion progresses, it should become clear that the context we are describing provides a structured environment that functions on two levels: (1) at the level of the computer club in which a group of children choose to participate in shared playful activity towards a common goal; and (2) at the level of a series of disciplined individual writing activities of which acceptance is necessary for the success of the enterprise as a whole.

It is precisely this interpenetration of play and discipline which structures the activity and sustains the social group. Within this context the origin of the discipline comes from the activity rather than the authority invested in any particular figure.

Measures

The most crucial problem posed by this type of research is how to make public "what is going on" in the context of a dynamic socio-cultural system. The question of interest is not individual performance on particular tasks but, rather how participants work together to support individual development in the writing process. In evaluating individual development in different contexts, the most appropriate unit of measurement was deemed to be the written product. In this respect, the children's word-processed stories about the imaginary "Professor" were compared to samples of their own hand-written texts produced in the school context.

Results & Discussion

In presenting this analysis, we disclaim any expectations that our writers, over the course of one short term, would make great developmental leaps in the quality of their writing. However, all the children wrote considerably more with word processing than they did with pencil and paper in the classroom (Table 1). This increased productivity points to the persistence which characterized the children's attitude towards writing in this context and reflects the constraints inherent in writing activities as they are organized in school.

TABLE 1. Comparison of word-processed (WP) texts with school-written pen and paper (PP) texts

Subjects scores		No. of words	Av. sentence length	Holistic quality
Andrew	WP	614	13.74	5
	PP	120	9.73	3
Gillian	WP	531	11.44	5
	PP	134	12.23	4
Catherine	WP	360	12.70	4
	PP	87	9.08	4
Victoria	WP	160	9.70	3
	PP	119	8.00	3
Natasha	WP	361	11.59	5
	PP	130	11.23	4

Children Together

During initial writing tasks children often asked each other how to perform procedures and frequently displayed a sense of frustration with the computer. "This computer is a spoil-sport. It won't do what I want it to do" or "I can't find D...where's D gone to now?". The autobiographical task prompted questions about each other's eye and hair colour, and offers of support with ideas based on knowlege and past experience of one another. For example:

V: I haven't any hobbies
A: You have
V: I can't think of any
A: You have. I saw you playing football in the yard yesterday
V: Oh, I'll put that down shall I?

They vied with each other in telling jokes, or joined together in playing imaginary musical instruments with appropriate sounds and accompanying arm gestures. These playful exchanges also punctuated their writing: "How much have you written?" was a question that called for comparing lengths of texts between thumbs and forefingers.

The children frequently expressed curiosity in each other's activities, leaning over one another, and picking up on each other's behaviours. For instance, Gillian found that by holding down a key, she could produce a sound effect e.g., whoooooosh". The other children speedily followed her example and soon they all began to experiment with producing sounds from static words. In this fashion the children were able to share their adventures with writing.

Conferencing and Critiquing

In the previous examples, we saw children engaging in spontaneous, pleasurable activity, sharing their feelings and binding themselves together as a group. These patterns of behaviour that constituted the playworld also served as a powerful springboard into the conferencing sessions where children defined themselves as individuals.

In this section, we see the pattern of action drifting towards a more serious intent. Conferencing sessions provided the opportunity to listen and comment on another's work. For instance, Andrew's narrative included references to Richard Starkie (otherwise known as Ringo Starr - the Beatle's drummer) and Donald Campbell's attempt to break the world's waterspeed record in his craft, Bluebird:

N: I didn't understand that about Bluebird
T: What was Bluebird, Andrew?
A: He (Donald Campbell) tried to break the land speed record but crashed at 300
C. I didn't know who Richard Starkie is
T: Me neither
A: Richard Starkie was the Beatles' drummer and he changed his name to Ringo.
T: You could make that clear. A lot of people won't know that.

Andrew clearly took these comments seriously and successfully incorporated some explanations in his revised draft.   At other times there was scope for negotiation in defence of one's own product. According to Gillian's account, the professor had taken three years to invent his time machine and then "didn't know which buttons did which things because he hadn't labelled them while he was making this machine". Having pressed one of the buttons, the machine and its inventor had travelled back in time "to the first second of life" where he had met God.   God had declared "...I think I'll make the solar system now". When Gillian had finished reading out her story, the following comments were made:

A: Surely, the professor would have known which buttons to press if he had invented the machine.

G: Well he didn't because he had forgotten. It took him three years to invent the machine.
C: God would not have invented the solar system after inventing the earth. Surely, the solar system would have been invented before the earth
T: Well, Gillian   (no reply)

While Gillian was able to respond to the first of these comments, she failed to make any change to her final draft. In essence, this exchange forced her to confront the need for a major re-organization and adjustment of her knowledge of the world. These critiques provided the opportunities for reflection on the distinction between writer and reader. More importantly, this continual movement between an imaginary world and a rule-governed world provide the basis of learning and development. Britton (1985) observed that: "In taking part in rule-governed behaviour...the novice, the individual learner, picks up the rules by responding to the behaviours of others, a process precisely parallel to the mode by which the rules first came into existence".

Conclusion

The research presented in this paper invites a conception of collaborative action in its broader, more "social" sense, and of the computer as playing a pivotal role in a merry-go-round of interaction. Moreover, computers were viewed in the same way as any other tool to a child - as an instrument of play, providing scope for experimentation with the sounds and meaning of language. Although there was no formal assessment as in school-sponsored writing tasks, the children constantly evaluated themselves and each other in their need to explore the essence of what constitutes good literature. In this study, the computer played a fundamental constituting role in creating a learning environment in which a community of writers played with and against each other as authors.

References:
Britton, J. Research currents: Second thoughts on learning, Lang. Arts, 62, 1985
Michaels, S. Classroom processes and the learning of text-editing commands. Quar. Newsletter of the Laboratory of Comparative Human Cognition, 1985, 7, 3, 69-79.
Piaget, J. (1932/1965). The moral judgement of the child. New York: Free Press.
Snyder, I.A. (1992b). Writing with word processors: the computer's influence on a classroom context. Journal of Curriculum Studies (in press).
Snyder, I.A. Writing with word processors: a research review. Educational Research, 1993, Vol 35, No.1, 49-68.
Vygotsky, L.S. Thought and Language. Cambridge, MA: MIT Press, 1986
Vygotsky, L.S. (1933/1967). Play and its role in the mental development of the child. Soviet Psychology, 12, 6-18 (stenographic record of a lecture).

Developing pupils' social skills for learning, social interaction and cooperation

P. Kutnick

Faculty of Education, Roehampton Institute, Froebel Institute College, Grove House, Roehampton Lane, London SW15 5HT, UK

Abstract:

The paper tells of the need for, generation of, and results from a classroom based programme for the development of social skills. The programme is based upon a developmental model of close social relationships, integrating sensory-affective schemes with communication and joint problem-solving. Integrating this developmental/relational model is effective in promoting social skills with teacher labelled 'antisocial' infants and promoting social and cognitive skills amongst normal junior aged pupils.

1. Introduction:

A programme to develop pupils' social skills was designed and initiated upon the request of a local Head teacher who was concerned about 'antisocial' behaviour amongst the infants (aged 5 to 7 years) in her school. At the same time, another Head requested a programme to create conditions to enhance children's work in small groups on microcomputers in a local junior school (pupils aged 7 to 12 year). The requests were answered in two ways. First, it was established that there were a variety of programmes which support specific social skills and could be applied in primary schools, although no holistic programme existed. Second, it was also established that co-operation amongst pupils helps to overcome many of the identified problems, although research in primary schools finds little effective use of co-operation within classrooms or group work (Galton [2]).

Evidence from psychological and educational research suggests that the rationale for a holistic programme to develop social skills may be pieced together. Such a programme could enhance social skills and co-operation and promote cognitive and school development. Research underlying the holistic programme includes: a) Successful 'co-operative group work' programmes have been organised to overcome bullying and integrate the full spectrum of pupils into class work Smith et al. [8]. b) Experimental classroom co-operation studies show that teachers must provide appropriate interpersonal 'goal structures', learning tasks and supportive classroom context. Most experimental co-operation studies draw upon specific social psychological theories but have a mechanistic bias although Kutnick & Brees [4] drew upon trust and sensitivity exercises to encourage close peer relationships and co-operation. c) Understanding of cognitive development has progressed beyond stage identification to emphasise the importance of joint resolve of conservation problems (Light & Littleton [5]), and social facilitation (Monteil [6]) such that pairings of children will be effected by the pupil's emotional and social responses to their 'working conditions'. d) A variety of social skills have been used to enhance classroom co-operation and support intellectual and social development including: effective communication (Webb [10]), sensitivity to the needs and feelings of others with whom the pupil works (Pfeiffer & Jones [7]), and the ability to share perspectives for the joint/social resolve of new and difficult problems (Damon & Phelps [1]). Yet, little effort has been made to integrate these skills in a meaningful way.

2. Development of close relationships and learning:

A review of children's social relationships shows early close relationships support learning and social competence. These relationships are based upon a trust/dependence similar to attachment and are further developed in co-ordination with the child's cognitive capacities of communication and rule understanding (Kutnick [3]). From this information a developmental model of close relationships can be constructed: the model effectively integrates the diverse approaches described above into a coherent social skills programme. In the model early relationships develop from schemes which promote an affective tie between child and specific others, to a realisation of dependence, to communicative understanding of rules (especially respect for others) and ability to change and develop new perspective and rules. What is unusual about the model is the separate identification that close relationships may develop between the child and adult as well as the child and peers. Educators of young children should note that pupils may readily form close relationships with adults but may not have the ability to transfer close relationships to peers due to a culturally restrictive lack of opportunity/experience (see Figure 1).

Figure 1: Developmental model of close relationships.

RELATION STRUCTURE	PERSONAL RELATIONSHIPS	
	Adult-based	Peer-based
Sensori-affective schemes	(sensori-affective contacts)	(sensori-affective contacts)
Development of dependent relationship	adult oriented attachment	peer-oriented attachment
Early rule application	unilateral respect of knowledgeable (and powerful) other	sharing of experience and information
Concrete rational rule application	legitimisation of expert	mutuality and joint resolve of problems
Reflective rule application	collaboration	negotiation/co-operation

Adapted from Kutnick [3], Ch. 3

The model suggests that effective and close social relationships are based on a trust/dependence which sensitivity exercises may facilitate, followed by increased communication skills to extend affective ties and understanding of interaction, and the promotion of problem solving skills.   Focus on close relationships in the developmental model is particularly important given the realisation that the most effective instances of learning take place in these relationships (which is often dominated by the child's relationships with adults).   Such a programme focuses on close relationships amongst classroom peers, develops over time and is obviously experiential in nature.

3. Has the developmental plan been effective?

Table 1: Average ratings and changes in behaviour for infants in the social skills programme (ratings made on a 1 to 5 point scale; 1 indicates anti-social performance, 5 indicates highly social performance).

Rated Behaviour	Average score before programme	Average score after programme	Change rated as improvement, decline, no change
General knowledge	2.625	2.375	no change
Interaction with peer when confronting a classroom problem	2.000*	2.125	improvement
Communication with teacher	2.500	2.376	no change
Concentration on educational tasks	2.125	1.750	decline
Pay attention in class	2.125	2.250	improvement
Interaction in working group	1.375**	1.500**	improvement
Solitary/social when working in class	1.625*	2.500	from solitary to sociable worker
Dependence on teacher	2.250	2.375	improvement
Popularity with peers	2.000**	2.125**	improvement
Bold/shy with peers	2.000	2.000	no change
Co-operative with peers	2.250**	2.750	improvement
Adjustment to social demands of playtime	1.750**	2.000	improvement

* and ** denote .01 and .001 level of difference between the children who received social skills training and the other children in their classes.

Social skills training in the infant school: Eight children participated in the programme which took the place of 'remedial' lessons (which the pupils would have been assigned) during the autumn term, one hour per week. Pupils' anti-social behaviours were identified on a 12 item rating scale concerning learning and social skills by teachers who rated all members of their classes.

At the end of the term all pupils were re-rated by their teachers. Table 1 displays areas of improvement by the eight children which included working and playing with peers and their relationship with teachers. When comparing these children's behaviour to the rest of their classmates, behaviour was significantly different in six areas at the start of the term and only two at the end. Within those two areas of difference (popularity with peers and ability to work with peers in the classroom) there was an improvement in the children's behaviour. The social skills programme was not successful in all areas of behaviour (decline in concentration and general knowledge), although these declines may be explained as a result of any one child acting persistently anti-social within this small group. An additional, but not statistically substantiated, sign of improvement came in a follow-up visit to the school approximately nine months later. The special needs co-ordinator was asked about the current behaviour of the eight pupils and she responded that they were no longer the cause of concern for their teachers.

Social skills and cognitive development in a junior school: This study was undertaken with two, parallel Year 5 classes over the course of a spring term. At the start of the term each teacher completed an 11 item rating scale for every child in their class. Classes were divided into small groups and pupils undertook the simulation 'Water Game ' [9] on microcomputer; a cognitive problem solving task that required social interaction. Pupils' interaction and game results were recorded by an observer. During the term, one class (experimental) undertook the social skills programme during physical education sessions (twice per week) while the other class (control) maintained its ordinary classroom and physical education routine. At the end of the term teachers re-rated their pupils' behaviour and the small groups were asked to play the 'Water Game' again. Table 2 presents outcomes from the analysis of classroom behaviours: Pupils who undertook the social skills programme showed significant pro-social and pro-learning changes, especially when compared to the control class. With regard to the pro-social skills, pupils in the experimental class improved on: positive interaction with peers when confronting a classroom problem, working productively within classroom groups, maintaining a sociable presence (as opposed to solitary) when working in class, popularity with peers, and ability to co-operate with peers. Teacher rated improvements of learning skills for the experimental class showed: improved concentration on tasks and attention paid to teacher. The second sitting of the microcomputer 'Water Game' showed a significant improvement in understanding and ability to handle the programme (cognitive understanding) by the experimental class who increased litres carried by each pupil from 72 to 129. The control class only managed an average improvement from 102 to 118 litres. While working on the microcomputer subtle differences in the conversation and actions of the children in the experimental class were found. Compared to the start of term, children in the experimental class became more focused in their communication. They spent less time asking general questions, making general responses and directing others in keyboard use. They increased time spent on keyboard use, supporting skills necessary to move the litres of water. The experimental class significantly decreased 'superfluous conversation' which may have threatened or put down other members of the group. The control class improved their keyboard use but increased superfluous conversation as well. One interpretation for the difference in performance between the two classes on the microcomputer task is that the experimental class was able to draw upon 'elaborating skills' (see Webb [10]) while providing a supportive (non-threatening) atmosphere.

Table 2: Average behavioural ratings and amount of water carried (game score) of experimental and control classes in the junior school (before, after and change scores).

Rated Behaviour	Class	Average score before the programme	Average score after the programme	Significance of change for experimental or control class
General knowledge	Exper.	2.567	2.533	NS
	Control	2.100	1.867+	
Interaction with peer when confronting a classroom problem	Exper.	3.667	4.100	Exper.>
	Control	4.067	3.900	Control **
Communication with teacher	Exper.	2.800	2.933	NS
	Control	2.333+	2.533	
Concentration of educational task	Exper.	3.000	3.400	Exper.>
	Control	2.700	2.633++	Control **
Pay attention in class	Exper.	2.133	2.367	Exper.>
	Control	2.467	2.267	Control **
Interaction in working group	Exper.	2.633	3.133	Exper.>
	Control	2.667	2.467++	Control **
Solitary/social when working in class	Exper.	3.267	3.500	Exper.>
	Control	3.067	3.200	Control *
Dependence on teacher	Exper.	2.867	2.866	NS
	Control	2.400++	2.400++	
Popularity with peers	Exper.	2.467	2.900	Exper.>
	Control	2.500	2.400++	Control **
Bold/shy with peers	Exper.	4.067	3.333	Exper.<
	Control	3.467	3.400	Control **
Co-operation with peers	Exper.	2.500	3.667	Exper.>
	Control	2.267	2.333++	Control **
Litres of water carried	Exper.	71.689	129.414	Exper.>
	Control	101.517	118.286	Control **

+ and ++ denote levels of difference (.05 and .01 respectively) between the two classes based on the raw data collected at the start and end of the term.
* and ** denote significant levels of difference (.05 and .01 respectively) in the amount of change within each class over the term.

4. Conclusion:

The studies reported were undertaken in response to requests by two primary Head teachers for programmes to enhance the social and learning skills of their pupils. A review of research established need for the development of social skills in primary schools. The review also noted that many 'piecemeal' programmes existed but these programmes focus on specific social skills and do not take account of the development of close relationships in children. Integrating a range of social skills into a non-linear developmental sequence modelled on close relationships was effective in promoting social skills with teacher labelled 'antisocial' infants and promoting social and cognitive skills amongst junior aged pupils. The social skills programme, while following a developmental path and having been based on close relationships that support social and learning development, is something that teachers will need to consider in relation to the time given to the National Curriculum. If teachers wish to improve social and learning skills in their pupils they cannot simply match interesting and curricularly meaningful work to their pupils' levels of ability. Time, effort and legitimacy must be given to social skills in the classroom. Finally, we must not draw conclusions that are too grand from the programme described; while having been planned in a developmental manner distinct from other programmes, more time should be given to assessing immediate impact on pupils and teachers while also initiating long-term follow-ups to ascertain whether these skills are retained by pupils.

References:

1.   Damon, W. & Phelps, E. Critical distinctions among three approaches to peer education, *International Journal of Educational Research*, 1989, **13**, 9-19.
2.   Galton, M. Grouping and groupwork, *The social psychology of the primary school*, eds C. Rogers & P. Kutnick, Routledge, London, 1990.
3.   Kutnick, P. *Relationships in the primary school classroom*, Chapman, London, 1988.
4.   Kutnick, P. & Brees, P. The development of co-operation: explorations in cognitive and moral competence and social authority, *British Journal of Educational Psychology*, 1982, **52**, 361-5.
5.   Light, P. & Littleton, K. Cognitive approaches to group work, *Groups in schools*, ed P. Kutnick & C. Rogers, Cassell, London, 1994.
6.   Monteil, J-M Towards a social psychology of cognitive functioning, *Social representation and the social representation of knowledge*, eds M. von Granach, W. Doise, & G. Mugny, Hubert, Berne, 1992.
7.   Pfeiffer, J.W. & Jones, J.E. *Handbook of structured exercises for human relations training*, University Associates, La Jolla, Calif, 1974.
8.   Smith, P., Cowie, H. & Berdondini, L. Co-operation and Bullying, *Groups in schools*, eds P. Kutnick & C. Rogers, Cassell, London, 1994.
9.   Water game, CWDE Software, London, 1989.
10.   Webb, N. Peer interaction and learning in small groups, *International Journal of Educational Research*, 1989, **13**, 21-39.

A dialogue between a psychological and sociological perspective on classroom learning

S.E.B. Pirie[a] & T. Wood [b]

[a] *Mathematics Education Research Centre, Oxford University, 15/28 Norham Gardens, Oxford OX2 6PY, UK*

[b] *Department of Curriculum and Instruction, Purdue University, West Lafayette IN 47907-1442, USA*

Abstract

The mathematical learning of one elementary pupil, Sam, is examined through a dialogue between two different theoretical positions. Events in Sam's learning are described and interpreted and the influence of the classroom context and social interaction are discussed.

Introduction

At present, the relationship between the nature of social interaction and cognition is not clearly understood, e.g. Forman, Minick, & Stone [1], Light & Butterworth [2], particularly within the setting of school classrooms, e.g. Pirie & Kieren [3].

In this paper, we examine the mathematical learning of one elementary pupil, Sam, through a dialogue between two different theoretical perspectives. On the one hand, we attempt to characterize how mathematical understanding is constructed by an individual across time, e.g. Pirie & Kieren [4]. On the other, we try to illustrate the role that social interaction and classroom environment play in the process, e.g. Wood [5]. To do so, we draw on our collaborative microanalyses of a sequence of videotaped mathematics lessons collected over four months in a second-grade classroom.

Our two perspectives have as a common ground a constructivist philosophy, but our individual theoretical constructs are drawn respectively from psychology and sociology. We hold in common a view that learning is an individual constructive activity that may occur in situations in which understanding is of central interest. In addition, we hold the position that knowledge is socially constructed and meanings are negotiated and validated between participants. For one of us, the central analyses will be illustrative of a cognitive perspective and emphasize growth and development in understanding. For the other, a social perspective will be considered and the focus will be on the interaction and the meaning that is constituted between the participants.

Background

The episodes under consideration are drawn from a second-grade classroom from a research and development project in the United States, c.f., Wood, Cobb, Yackel, & Dillon [6].   In this project, instructional activities were developed to provide problematic situations for students to solve in collaborative pairs followed by whole-class discussion. The classroom reflects one teacher's interpretation of the researchers' views and the manner in which she put this into practice. As an underlying aspect of the theory, some such as Edwards & Mercer, [7], hold the view that the classroom environment which is established greatly influences the opportunities children have for learning. They also suggest that the nature of the patterns of interaction which are established create different obligations and expectations for behavior.

In this particular class, the teacher and students have established social norms in which conflict or different points of view are encouraged and mutual respect for the ideas of each member of the class is emphasized. The teacher views her role as one in which her obligation is to create trust and respect for others' ideas and act to develop in her students the necessity to be self-directing and self-reliant.

In correspondence, the students' view their role as one in which they are responsible for communicating to others their mathematical thinking and for trying to understand the thinking of others. More specifically in this class, they are expected to think about what one another says, decide if they did it in the same or a different way, and then decide if they agree or disagree with the solution. In addition to their responsibility of trying to understand what the other person is thinking, they also are expected to ask questions if they do not understand. In the case of a disagreement, they are expected to acknowledge this and to give reasons for their decision. Thus, the children's mathematical ideas and their personal constructions are not only made public but are subject to critique by their peers. Therefore, meanings that become accepted as taken to be commonly held are subject to a process of critical analysis and validation by all the members of the class. This particular aspect is what defines an inquiry mathematics class.

Mathematical Topic   It should be noted that, unlike the majority of classrooms in Britain and the United States, those involved in the project are not directly taught the standard algorithms for adding and subtracting multi-digit numbers. Instead, the children are encouraged to construct their own efficient nonstandard algorithms for solving the problem-centered activities. In the case of Sam's class, the students have been solving problems involving 2-digit addition and subtraction during the second half of the school year.

Sam

In our case of Sam, the following episodes from the whole-class discussions are given as evidence for the manner in which he made a connection from his informal ways of understanding place value to the more formal mathematical ways of symbolizing meaning. This connection evolved in the course of his interaction with the other students during the class discussions in which he presented and refined his ideas. In the process of meeting his obligations to present his own ideas and yet to make sense of others' ideas, he developed multiple images for place value. In order to accommodate the page limitation here and yet present the discourse, the dialogue has often been carefully edited to maintain the essence of the episode.

Episode 1
Background The children are solving problems referred to as "Balances" in which the goal is to balance both sides of a pan scale by making the amounts equal. These problems are presented as a drawings of boxes on a pan scale. The problem is: Two boxes with the number 7 written in each, three boxes with 10 in each on one side of the scale, and an empty or blank box on the other side.
Record During the class discussion, Sam offers the following for the problem given above:
Sam: 10, 20, 30, (holding up his hands and opening and closing his fingers for each 10). 31, 32, 33, 34, 35,   36, 37 (counting on his fingers). And that was 37. I   went 38, 39, 40, 41, 42, 43, 44.
Tch: That's another way to do it, isn't it?
Analysis Here we offer the manner in which Sam solves the problem by first counting groups of ten and then ones.   The example also reveals the expectation that in this mathematics class there are many alternative ways to solve the same problem. And, additionally, the teacher's question models her expectation that those listening are involved in deciding whether Sam's way is a valid alternative solution.

Episode 2
Background In this class discussion the children are solving 2-digit addition/subtraction problems using the Candy Shop. The Candy Shop reflects

an idealized realistic context problem in which children are solving problems involving the buying and selling of candy. Fortuitously, the candies are packed with 10 in a roll.

Record The problem under discussion is: This many peppermint candies are in the Candy Shop (a picture shows 9 loose candies and 4 rolls). Ms. Wright makes 49 more candies. How many candies will be in the Shop now?

Dan: 49, 59, 69, 79, 89, 90, 91, 92, 93, 94, 95, 96, 97, 98.

Tch: Linda, do you have a question?

Lin: When he counted them here, there's 49 (points to the first roll. 50, 60/He went 59, 69, 79, 89, 90, 91, 92, 93, 94, 95, 96, 97, 98.

Tch: Can he do that?

Lin: No.

Tch: Why not?

Lin: It's a tens.

Tch: Think you can help? (to Sam).

Sam: Yeah! He went/he pretended that the other 49 was there. And he just started at 49 and went to 59, 69, 79, 89. And he counted it.

Analysis This episode indicates that Sam, listening and attempting to meet his obligations in the class, understands another's solution method. Although this is not the way in which he previously demonstrated his solution to a 2-digit addition problem, he is able to tell Linda the strategy Dan used to solve the problem.

Episode 3

Background On this day the children are again using the "Balances" to solve 2-digit addition problems using the Balances as a context. The problem is: A large box with 52 written in it. Above this box is an arrow pointing to a smaller box which has the number 20 written in it. This is a convention of the drawing which has been established early on in the class to mean a piece has fallen off or has been removed from the large box. On the other side of the scale is an empty box.

Record On this day, the children are giving numbers sentences written both horizontally and vertically when giving their answers. Linda has just used a vertical number sentence, but given an explanation involving counting back by tens. The teacher now asks:

Tch: Who gave us the number sentence written in the other direction? Sam?

Sam: Um. I know another way to do it with Linda's number sentence.

Tch: Okay.

Sam: 5 take away 2 would equal 3 (points to 5 - 2). And 2 take away 0 would equal 2 (points to 2 - 0. Then looks expectantly at the teacher.)

Tch; (long pause). Seems to work doesn't it?

Sam: (shakes head yes).

Tch: Did you want to tell us anything about what you did, though?

Sam: Me? We went 52. I took away 10. I took away 10 off my fingers/then I took away 10 more. And that would be 20. So I took away 52 from 10. That's be 42, and 10 more would be 32.

Tch: Okay. That's another one that works isn't it? Any questions about that?

Analysis This is a pivotal incident for Sam. Although the problem seems relatively straightforward to the teacher, to Sam his solution is a new insight. The realization that numbers written in a vertical format carry the meaning for all the various images that he has built up for adding and subtracting 2-digit numbers is a powerful insight for Sam. Now rather than counting tens, drawing rolls of candy, or using his fingers, the number symbols carry the meaning for these acts. The next episode further substantiates this event.

Episode 4

Background On this day Eliz is trying to solve a 2-digit problem which she has written as a vertical number sentence. The problem is $33 + 27$.

Record Eliz first has added 30 and 20 to get 50, and then the ones to get 10. At this point, she is unclear as to the answer. The teacher asks:

Tch: Who can talk about that? If we add 7 and 3 together, we get 10 not zero.

Sam: ...if 7 plus 3 equals 10, then you gotta do something with the 1 off the 10.

Tch: What are you going to do with it? (pause). You're saying 3 plus 7 is 10 and you've got to do something with the 10.

Sam: Yeah. there's like a 50. Then you can add onto the 5 and make it a 60.

Tch: Oh (surprised tone) You're saying then that you take the group of 10 you put it with the 3 and 2 that made 5 and that makes it 6. So then you have 6, zero, 60.

Sam: Yeah.

Tch: Can you do that Eliz?

Eliz: I don't understand because he had a 10. But on here there would be 5 not 6.

Sam: Here's what I'm trying to say. I took the 5, and then 7 plus 3 would equal 10. (He writes the vertical sum 5 10.) So then, I would take this 1 off, take the 10 off (he crosses off the 1 leaving the 0) that 1 with a 10, and add it onto the 5 and make a 6 (he crosses out the 5 and writes 6 above it). And make 60.

Analysis In this incident Sam's explanation indicates that for him the numbers written in a vertical format can be used to solve the problems.   His explanation to Eliz is evidence that he understands and can give meaning for his actions.

Summary

Through discussions involving a wide variety of contexts including using concrete materials and idealized realistic contexts, Sam developed an understanding of addition and subtraction of two-digit numbers. These strong images that were formed enabled Sam to move from informal thinking about whole numbers as evidenced by his counting-based solutions to formalizing with symbols to solve problems written in vertical format. The teacher's questions, "Can you think of another way to do it?" and, "Is there another way to do it?" helped to create opportunities for Sam to form these images during the class discussion.

In addition, the particular expectations and obligations for participating in mathematics in this class created opportunities for Sam to move from intuitive understanding to formal understanding of additive situations involving multi-digits. The social obligations that were constituted reflected two aspects of the students' responsibilities in the class--to help others understand their thinking and to try to understand and critique others' thinking. This duality not only encouraged individual constructive mathematical activity, but also created a collaborative community in which this could be accomplished.

References

1. Forman, E., Minick, N., & Stone, C. A. (eds). *Contexts for Learning: Sociocultural Dynamics in Children's Development,* Oxford University Press, Oxford, 1993.
2. Light, P., & Butterworth, G. (eds). *Context and Cognition: Ways of Learning and Knowing,* Lawrence Erlbaum Associates, Hillsdale, NJ, 1993.
3. Pirie, S., & Kieren, T. Creating constructivist environments and constructing creative mathematics, *Educational Studies in Mathematics*, 1992, **23**, 505-528.
4. Pirie, S., & Kieren, T. Beyond metaphor: Formalizing in mathematical understanding within constructivist environments, *For the Learning of Mathematics*, 1994, **14**,(1), 39-43.
5. Wood, T. Patterns of interaction and learning in mathematics classrooms. *Cultural Perspectives on the Mathematics Classroom,* ed S. Lerman, Kluwer, Dordrecht, in press.
6. Wood, T., Cobb, P., Yackel, E., & Dillon, D. (eds). *Rethinking Elementary School Mathematics: Insights and Issues.* Journal for Research in Mathematics Education, Monograph No. 6, National Council of Teachers of Mathematics, Reston, VA, 1993.
7. Edwards, D., & Mercer, N. *Common Knowledge,* Methuen, London, 1993.

A case study approach to studying collaboration in primary science classrooms

E. Scanlon, P. Murphy, B. Hodgson & R. Whitelegg
Institute of Educational Technology, The Open University, Walton Hall, Milton Keynes MK7 6AA, UK

Abstract

The research focus in the Collaborative Learning and Primary Science (CLAPS) project is to examine the cognitive benefits children gain from learning in groups in the context of curriculum moves towards investigative learning in science. In this paper we describe our methodology and some episodes from the first phase of our data collection which highlight the importance of the resolution of conflicts which arise, the role of variables and some gender effects.

1 Why study collaboration in primary science classrooms?

We wish to examine the cognitive benefits children gain from learning in groups undertaking investigative learning in science. The aim of this work is to investigate the processes which operate in groups in primary classrooms tackling investigative science tasks and the way in which these processes can support the children's science learning. Psychologists have been studying the effectiveness of group processes in supporting learning, and a mass of evidence has been collected which suggests, although somewhat equivocally, in general that children working together on a problem benefit more (individually) than children working alone. Richard Joiner [1] concludes from a review of studies of peer interaction that learning is facilitated but only when both participants have some understanding of the task and when participants share decision making. However there is a difference of opinion on the way in which this enhanced learning in groups arises. One controversial question is the role played by conflict in such learning. Joiner stresses the importance of the resolution of conflict.

The domain of primary school science is particularly interesting for considering ways in which collaboration may or may not support learning. The advent of the National Curriculum for England and Wales in the late eighties was the culmination of activity aimed at increasing the amount of science included in the primary curriculum. Simultaneously there has been an increasing focus on the study of how children learn science and what strategies teachers can use to support their learning. The most popular view on the process by which children develop their science learning is that of the "constructivists" (e.g. Driver et al., [2]). Most science educators who hold a constructivist view of learning still see learning as an essentially cognitive phenomenon. Consideration of students' interests and attitudes is minimal and often related to issues of access rather than engagement with tasks. We believe it is important to consider the interplay between the cognitive and affective aspects of learning in terms of how students involve themselves in, and perceive challenge in tasks and reflect on and collaborate during their learning. In a *social* constructivist perspective of learning the notion of the child as agent is significant but so also is the learning context in terms of the interactions with significant others and with significant features of tasks. The child draws on the gamut of experiences from school and elsewhere in making sense of situations. Hence the nature of her experiences, her views of their relevance and application and her understanding of what is appropriate behaviour for herself, in her view and others, will all influence how she perceives and reacts to tasks and others involved in them. The cognitive and affective aspects of knowing are thus intimately intertwined.

One characteristic feature of children's experience is manifest in their different gender identities. There is a vast literature which establishes the influence differential experience has on the affective domain. It is clear from this literature that children's cognitive responses are mediated by affective characteristics i.e. children's expectations of themselves and others affects their self images, values and confidence in themselves and their abilities. In social interactions in science practical activities, certain significant gender effects have been noted which might influence the potential for learning in collaborative settings. These include, for example, girls and boys different approaches to practical contexts in terms of learning styles (Cohen, [3]), confidence (Murphy, [4]), apparatus handling (Whyte, [5]) and the nature, patterns and purpose of their discourse (e.g. Randall, [6]) and their perception of what is relevant in a task and what therefore constitutes an appropriate solution (Murphy, [7]).

The focus on investigative learning in science grew out of the social constructivist notion that learning occurs through cooperative action. Thus the transmission of teaching and learning was associated with the acquisition of inert concepts that were viewed as self contained abstract entities whereas social constructivism was associated with the notion of knowledge as a tool ie where concepts are progressively developed through action (Brown, Collins and Duguid, [8]). Hence to develop useful robust knowledge an investigative approach was needed which involved children in defining problems, developing strategies, collecting and interpreting data and evaluating actions. In this view of investigative activity, science concepts and procedures are essential elements of any solution. The significance of this for research is two fold. If collaborative and investigative activity are considered to be essential elements for science learning then it is necessary to explore the quality of children's collaborations in this context. Furthermore, if investigative activity depends on both the procedural and conceptual understanding that children have any research that considers how conceptual development can be enhanced must pay attention to children's procedural competency and how this mediates their conceptual development (Murphy, [9]). In all this the teacher plays the key role in manipulating the learning environment and selecting and structuring tasks to achieve the best learning effect for all children so their agenda must also be considered. Teachers in general value group work but again the quality of this group work has been challenged by research (Alexander, [10], Galton and Williamson, [11]).

2 Data collection

We have filmed numerous instances of collaborative learning in the context of normal classroom science learning situations in two primary schools. We first collected observations of single lessons focussing on one collaborating group. We trialled the use of radio microphones with these groups of children and developed and trialled some questionnaires and interview schedules for use with children and teachers. Then, for an in depth case study, we decided to focus on group working in a Year Five classroom in one of our schools where we had made snapshot observation in the two preceding terms. We followed two groups of children in their science activities over an extended period of five weeks working on the topic of water. Previously the teacher had frequently switched the composition of the groups on a week by week basis. For the five weeks work on water, two groups were selected by the teacher to work together throughout the five week period, partly because of his concern that mixed gender groups should develop ways of working together, and partly because, having tried a variety of groupings he felt confident in his knowledge of the individual children's strengths and weaknesses in group working. Children in these target groups had been observed in at least one other group working situation.

To investigate the effects we have identified, we planned to collect data that took account of the teachers' perspective on children's science achievement and group work, children's understanding of science, their learning and preferred ways of working, and to provide an analysis from our own perspective based on research into learning in science and collaboration. In order to achieve this we chose to video activities selected by teachers and children as part of ongoing classwork in science and to focus on groups identified by teachers as collaborating well. While doing this we have needed to interview teachers about their approach to science generally, their approach to specific tasks, their views of what would be achieved and of what was achieved and for what reasons, and their reasons for grouping children and their views of the success and failures of particular situations. Also we needed to interview children about their intentions and actions and to probe, where appropriate, their procedural decisions and conceptual understanding. We have used small activities with children to elicit some of their starting point ideas. We used a questionnaire for all children in the class to ascertain attitudes to groupwork and group compositions. Using this and video snippets, we probed target children's feelings and attitudes to groupwork and its effects on their learning.

Two episodes from the data collection
Two episodes which illustrate some important features which have emerged from our preliminary analysis of this phase of data collection are decribed below.

Resolution of conflicts The episode is taken from the work of four boys on how to change a slope to make a toy car travel further. While the children are planning their work they have a difference of opinion about what would affect the distance travelled by the car. Two boys disagree about whether a steeper slope causes the car to go further and do not resolve their disagreement.

B: The steeper the hill, the shorter it will go. You could say, the longer the slope the car would have more time to build up and would be able to go further.

D &M :   No.. but why?

B: Do you agree with that, J?.. The longer the slope the further it goes because it has more time to build up.

D: I reckon it would..its cardboard remember

J: I don't think so... I think if it's the longer kind of wood ...wood, it won't go as far.

B: Why...yes it will because the car will have more time to build up its speed so it will go further.

J: That's only if it's steep, if it's about that height, it's not going to go very far is it?

B: The steeper the hill the shorter it will go.

J: If it's about up to ...about up to..like that

M: If it's like that
B: You don't seem to understand... if it's like that it won't go,
            but if it's like that it will go furthest. Shall we just leave it
            at that. The steeper the hill, the shorter it will go.

The fact that the conflict is unresolved leads to problems with the
direction that the group takes. It becomes clearer later that the
children are focussing on two different variables - one is trying to
consider whether the length of the slope will affect distance
travelled while another is concentrating on its steepness. As a result
the children decide on a combination of their individual hypotheses
using two different lengths of wood and decide to make the slope
both longer and higher. Although the teacher tries to encourage
them not to do both experiments the children continue to try to
pursue both .

Gender effects   In one group of two boys and one girl the following
incident was observed. The teacher had provided a scenario to
stimulate children planning an investigation with dissolving. The
scene involved a girl suggesting that if her dad put the sugar into
his tea as soon as it was poured instead of five minutes later it
would dissolve quicker and not need so much stirring. The children
were to choose what to find out about. The scenario focussed on the
dependent variable time of dissolving and temperature as the
independent variable. The everyday setting however talked only of
time and stirring. No explicit mention of temperature was made
except at the point where the problem was framed. In the following
dialogue an apparent conflict arises between the girl and one of the
boys
G: I think we should do two tests ...
B: No not just straight and five minutes. We shoud have
            three... one waiting ten minutes
G: We're not asked to do that...I think we should do one test
            straight away and then one after five minutes
B: That's a rubbish idea.

The girl's suggestion of what to test pays close attention to the
context set in the stimulus material. The boy however focusses on
the task highlighted in the same material (which was to find out
how the time taken for sugar to dissolve depends on the
temperature of the liquid) and has ignored the context as irrelevant.
A consequence is that the boy and girl cannot communicate as they
are unaware of the source of their difference i.e. different
perceptions of what is relevant and hence of the tasks. Similarly the
male teacher does not consider the girl's focus appropriate. The
effect on the girl and boy is that they consider that neither is
prepared to listen to the other. This is evident in a later situation
which arises in another task two weeks later. Yet we have seen both
the boy and girl in other group settings working with the same
gender understand and hear another's point of view and attempt to
accommodate.

Conclusions We are finding many interesting sequences in the data we have collected. Data like this suggests to us that our decisions to focus on group composition, to look at its effects across tasks and over time and to consider the same child in different group settings are proving fruitful. The preliminary observations we have made here suggest that the complete analysis will throw light on the role of unresolved conceptual conflict as a mechanism for learning, the issue of how group composition influences the group behaviour, and in particular the ways in which gender affects the collaborative learning processes.

Acknowledgements Our thanks are due to Kim Issroff and Sue Browning for help with data collection, and the teachers and pupils in the schools involved in the study for allowing us to observe them.

References
1.   Joiner, R. *A dialogue model of the resolution of inter-individual conflicts: implications for computer based collaborative learning,* Unpublished Ph. D. thesis. Open University, 1993
2.   Driver, R., Guesne, E. and Tiberghien, A. (eds) *Children's ideas in science,* Milton Keynes: Open University Press, 1985.
3.   Cohen, R. *Conceptual styles and social change,* Acton, MA: Copley Publishing, 1986
4.   Murphy, P. Gender and practical work, In Woolnough, B. (ed) *Practical Work in Science,* Milton Keynes: Open University Press, 1991
5.   Whyte, J. *Girls into science and technology,* London: Routledge, 1986
6.   Randall, G. Gender differences in pupil-teacher interaction in workshops and laboratories, In Weiner, G. and Arnot, M. *Gender under scrutiny- New enquiries in education,* London: Hutchinson; Open University Press, 1987
7.   Murphy, P. Gender and assessment, *Cambridge Journal of Education,* 23, 330-6, 1991
8.   Brown, J.S., Collins, A. and Duguid, P. Situated cognition and the culture of learning, *Educational Researcher* 18 (1) 32-42, 1989
9.   Murphy, P. Insights into pupils responses to practical investigations from the APU, *Physics Education,* 23, 330-336, 1982
10.   Alexander, R. *Policy and Practice in Primary Education,* London: Routledge, 1992
11.   Galton, M. and Williamson, J. *Groupwork in the Primary Classroom,* London: Routledge, 1992

SECTION E:

General Applications
in Interactive Learning

New technology and team training

N. English[a]* & A. Guppy[b]

[a] Cranfield University, Cranfield, UK
[b] Cheltenham and Gloucester C.H.E., Cheltenham, Gloucestershire, UK

Abstract

This paper considers the use of error analysis and interaction process analysis (IPA) as a methodology for assessing the effect of communication on military team performance. A trial conducted by the DRA Centre for Human Sciences (CHS) assessed combat team performance before and after one week of training in a networked simulator system. This paper focuses on the reduction of "process loss" within teams and the extent to which these skills can be trained within Distributed Interactive Simulation. The methodologies, preliminary findings and the potential for future team training will be discussed.

1. Introduction

Faced with economic, political and environmental pressures the forces are turning more and more to indoor simulation to supplement field training. During 1993/94 research undertaken at the Centre for Human Sciences has addressed the issues of collective training utilising networked simulation systems.

The focus of this research has been state of the art simulation systems supported by technology known as Distributed Interactive Simulation (DIS). This technology enables simulation systems to support collaborative training of teams with the capacity to provide enhanced feedback facilities only available using this type of simulation. The system supports the full visual and audio recreation of the exercise enabling the crews to view their actions after the exercise has taken place whilst simultaneously hearing a communication replay.

Networked simulators present an ideal arena for the study of team training. They present a controlled yet realistic environment in which to study tasks similar to those conducted on the job and with teams that are not artificially

* Seconded to Psychology Division, DRA Centre for Human Sciences, Farnborough GU14 6TD, UK

created for the purpose of research. The data collected from these systems is unique in that previous training can be reconstructed to allow analysis slow time.

Performance in the Army is frequently a function of teamwork. Teamwork is generally required due to the high workload involved in a task. For instance in the case of vehicle crews it would be impossible for one person to simultaneously drive, load, fire, navigate and make command decisions regarding other vehicles within a troop.

Various models exist to explain the factors that affect team performance (McGrath, Hackman, Gladstein, Morgan and Salas [1]). A majority of these models identify three components; input, process and output components. Much research has addressed the relationship between input and output factors, however, little empirical work has been carried out to assess the implications of the group processes that occur in between. It is well recognised that the team output need not equal the sum of its parts indeed the output can be considerably diminished. This phenomenon has been termed "process loss". One factor that can promote process loss is communication.

This research addresses the affect of team communication processes on overall performance. The methodologies, preliminary findings and implications for future combat team training are addressed in the following sections;
a)   A methodology for assessing communication skills of a military team; interaction process analysis.
b)   A methodology for assessing team performance; error analysis.
c)   Combining error analysis and communication analysis.
d)   Preliminary Findings
e)   The potential implications of this research on future combat team training.

2. A methodology for assessing communication within teams.

The trial involved training teams of tank troops over a one week period. The troops were trained in a networked simulator environment. A troop consists of 3 tanks. Each tank contains four crew members; a gunner, loader, driver and commander. This research utilises both inter and intra team data.

The analysis of the communication data requires the slow time recording of the following components of communication;
a)   Who sent the communication
b)   To whom the communication was sent

c)   Content of the communication
d)   Time of the communication

Each interaction can then be coded using Interaction Process Analysis (Bales 1950 [2]). IPA is a well recognised technique and as such will not be outlined in detail in this paper. IPA basically classifies communication according to 12 mutually exclusive categories, for example; gives orientation, asks opinion, gives suggestion etc. The subsequent analyses of the coded communication data includes;

a)   An analysis of the interaction profiles of the crew or of individual crew members. These profiles demonstrate the frequency of certain types of communication for each crew member, the whole crew and the troop.
b)   An analysis of sequences of communication between crew members and between vehicles. For instance, whether orders given by the commander tend to be followed by requests for further clarification or repetition.
c)   An analysis of several indexes of communication problems as proposed by Bales. For instance, problems with evaluation, decision making, control, tension reduction etc. These indices are based upon the expected frequency of certain types of communication. This uses a symmetrical pairwise structure within the twelve categories. For instance, the "gives orientation" category and the "asks for orientation" category would be classed as a pair.

In addition to the standard IPA analysis outlined above, the relationship between communication profiles and particular tasks/errors can be assessed as can the **content** of communication during particular tasks or events. This analysis will be discussed further in the section on combining IPA and error analysis.

3. A methodology for assessing team performance

Quantifying performance output for military teams is more complicated than for individual soldiers. The sphere of performance within a team is multidimensional, the performance of a task may be a function of the crew, the troop leader, the troop sergeant the troop corporal or of the troop as a whole.

Traditionally defining optimum performance within a military operational context was largely subjective. This has been justified by the premise that tactically correct performance is an ill-defined concept which is both mission and terrain specific. However error analysis can be utilised to produce a behavioural checklist which could enhance the objectivity of this performance assessment.

Error analysis is a technique that enables the systematic study of human errors and their causes. The analysis of errors enables reasons to be identified which contribute to a troop's failure to accomplish a mission. This allows future training to focus on the deficiencies that were identified. The technique was used to develop a behavioural checklist. The methodology of the process of development will now be outlined.

In order to utilise error analysis for the purpose of performance appraisal several stages of development are required. Assuming a task analysis is available, the first stage is to interview Subject Matter Experts's (SME's) in order to determine examples of both competent and poor performance of the tasks. This follows a critical incident technique as proposed by Flannagan 1954 [3]. Having identified examples of poor behaviour it is necessary to identify all possible errors that could lead to the failure of a sub-task. The task analysis can assist in this process of defining several error trees since the identification of actions required to perform the task implicitly provides the stages at which potential errors could occur. Having identified the errors for each task, a checklist can be produced for a particular mission, presenting each error in chronological sequence. The checklist is presented in a negative form in order for the assessor to concentrate on the errors made. It will also reduce the time required to record the data.

The implication of this method of performance assessment and the potential to automate it within networked simulation systems are considered in English & Guppy 1994 [4].

4. Combining Error Analysis and IPA Analysis.

The aim of this research is to consider tank troop performance as a function of communication. The methodology suggests performance can be assessed by way of an error checklist and communication data through the use of IPA. The data can then be combined in the following methods in order to address the initial aim.

a)   An analysis of the relationship between low and high error crews and their interaction profiles. This will give a crude measure of types of communication associated with low error crews.

b)   An analysis of crew communication profiles and sequences with reference to specific tasks ie, tactical movement, engagements etc. This analysis will highlight the differences between the communication profiles before, during and after significant events or errors eg. before and after an engagement.

c)   An analysis of the communication content of the Commander and its relationship to errors made. The communications are coded on the basis of the focus of his attention on the available resources. For instance; proportion of time spent on micro-management tasks eg. directing the driver compared with time involved in macro-management tasks eg. problem solving.

5. Preliminary Results

The preliminary results presented in this paper are limited to the initial stages of the analysis; the interaction profiles of crews have been considered against the total frequency of errors. The conclusions are currently based on one tank troop and represent trends from a one week training period within a network simulation system.

Performance data: errors.

Preliminary results suggest training within networked simulator environments to be beneficial to overall team performance. The results suggest crews made significantly fewer errors after one week of training within the simulator system ($p = .01$). The number of errors were reduced in all areas of performance including; ground appreciation, mutual support, tactical movement and target acquisition.

Group process data: Interaction Process Analysis

The following results are trends suggested by the changes in communication profiles of crews after 1 week of training ie. associated with an improvement in performance. Also considered are trends that appear in the profiles of crews making the most and least errors. The communication profiles of crews with superior performance were characterised by;
a)   Less overall communications.
b)   A larger proportion of orders.
c)   A larger proportion of orientation information provided both within teams and between teams.
d)   Crew members request less orientation information.
e)   Communications tended to included specification of addressee ie. "go right driver" or "drive right" rather than just "go right".

A User-evaluation Survey

A user-evaluation survey was also conducted during the CHS trial, these results concur with the preliminary findings of this study in demonstrating the benefit of networked simulation for team training. The results suggest a marked improvement in perceived team skills. Ninety-two percent of the trainees considered that their troop worked better as a team. More specifically 66% considered that the troop communicated better as a team as a result of using the networked simulators.

6. Implications for Team Training

This paper examines the use of new technology for team training. The type of networked simulation systems discussed in this paper are likely to play an increasing role in team training in the future. The systems can support instructor training, team training, and enhanced performance measurement and feedback facilities. The system can also support future research into all aspects of team performance.

The aim of this research is to contribute to team training within the military utilising the technology of networked simulation. It is a common misconception that team skills are learned as a by-product of training in groups ie. within networked simulators. This misconception results in little if any explicit training in team skills. Therefore, guidelines are required that suggest how to implement the new technology within the current training programme in order to gain the most team training benefit.

Training in team skills is currently recognised within other industries eg. civil aviation. Team training programmes such as Cockpit Resource Management (CRM) aim to train the effective use of all resources available to the flight crew. Several components of current CRM training are centred around communication eg. briefing, inquiry, assertion, communication and acknowledgement of decisions, communication of workload distribution and the management of emergencies.

The networked simulator systems discussed here potentially provide a powerful training tool for CRM type training as well as for the more acknowledged use as a tool for standard collective training. CHS have developed a tool to enable the creation of training material that will support the recreation of actual behavioural examples of "effective" and "ineffective" team behaviour. This material could be used to initially train instructors and later for trainees. It is anticipated that further research is required to develop and validate a CRM type training package for use within the Army. It is expected that this approach could be applicable across all services.

REFERENCES
1.   Salas, E. et al. Toward an Understanding of team performance and training, Chapter 1, *Teams Their Training and Performance*, ed R. W. Swezey & E. Salas, pp 3-29, Ablex Publishing Corporation, 1992
2.   Bales, R. *Interaction Process Analysis: A Method For The Study Of Small Groups*, Cambridge, MA: Addison-Wesley, 1950.
3.   Flannagen, J. The critical incident technique, *Psychological Bulletin,* 1954, **51**, 327-358.
4.   English, N. & Guppy, A. Error analysis; a methodology for assessing combat team performance. CHS working paper no. 94c.

Interactive learning approaches to road safety education: A review

H.C. Foot, J. Thomson, A.K. Tolmie & B. McLaren

Department of Psychology, University of Strathclyde, Turnbull Building, 155 George Street, Glasgow G1 1RD, UK

Abstract

Research on child development suggests that children's understanding flows from their experience and behaviour. Within the field of road safety education this thinking places the focus squarely on the need for practical, action-based training as a pre-requisite for more sophisticated conceptions of the traffic environment. Interactive learning which offers practical road-side training and a range of group-based classroom exercises promises a new approach for use with young children.

Introduction

A central aim of road safety education in the UK is to teach the Green Cross Code. The Code was conceived as a simple, general-purpose strategy that children could learn without too much difficulty and that would be applicable to a wide variety of road crossing situations. In fact, it quickly became apparent that the Code was rather too difficult for younger children to learn, and so a simpler version, (Stop, Look, Listen, Think) was introduced for use with the under 7s. The Green Cross Code has long held a pre-eminent position in British road safety education and, in fact, much road safety material takes the teaching of the Code as its primary goal (Thomson [1]).

Children and the road crossing task

First attempts to analyse the road crossing task and its underlying functional processes were made by Older and Grayson [2] and Avery [3]. Later, more detailed analyses have attempted to outline both the functional processes involved in road crossing and their development. For example, Thomson, Tolmie, Foot & McLaren [4] have identified a range of fundamental skills required in order to interact safely with traffic. These include:

(i)   detecting the presence of traffic (involving visual search and attention)

(ii)   visual timing and gap selection (involving estimates of time-to-contact of approaching vehicles)

(iii)   coordinating information from different directions (involving memory, and ability to divide attention)

(iv)   coordinating perception and action (whereby pedestrians must relate the time available for crossing to the time required and knowledge of their movement capabilities)

Given that even a 'simple' road requires competence in these primary perceptuo-cognitive skills, it is crucial to know how these skills develop in childhood and what level of skill can be expected in children of different ages. Not only is there little recognition of the sophistication of the skills needed to interact with traffic (Ampofo-Boateng & Thomson [5]), but no effort has been made to teach any of these skills within existing road safety programmes in the UK. Similarly no serious attempt has been made to increase children's strategic competence as their experience and exposure to traffic changes, though this has long been advocated (e.g. Sheppard [6]). Instead, the Green Cross Code is taught as a sort of universal 'golden rule' that is assumed to apply to most, if not all, road crossing situations. It is seldom recognised that the Code is an elementary strategy that becomes unsuitable when more complex traffic situations are encountered. As a result, even adults tend to assume that the Code is the 'right' way to cross - in spite of the fact that adults invariably develop quite different strategies for interacting with traffic and seldom behave in accordance with the percepts of the Green Cross Code (Thomson et al [4]).

The teaching of road safety

Numerous methods of teaching have been attempted but, in practice, the vast bulk of road safety education takes place in the classroom. The material is thus almost exclusively verbal: that is, children learn by being told what to do rather than by actually doing anything. The approach is thus almost entirely centred on the acquisition of knowledge and the development of appropriate attitudes rather than tackling behaviour directly. There is very little practical training in the UK at the present time and certainly none of the elaborate traffic parks or gardens that have been established in other European countries. Similarly, almost no attempt is made to provide children with guided roadside experience, although recent efforts have been made to establish a national traffic club in which children would receive roadside training from their parents (e.g. Downing [7];   West, Sammons and West [8]). This situation exists even though a major European review conducted over 15 years ago advocated the development of practical training methods in the strongest terms - advice that was acted upon by other European countries (OECD, [9]).

The shift of focus from the acquisition of knowledge about road safety to children's actual behaviour at the road-side is firm acknowledgement that practical methods of instruction in pedestrian skills are most likely to be effective. The evidence suggests that knowledge does not automatically translate into behaviour at the roadside and skills such as timing and judgement simply cannot be taught by methods other than practical training. There is also evidence that practical training can be introduced for children as young as four or five years of age (Rothengatter, [10]) whereas other methods of training and the use of the Green Cross Code are not suitable for children under the age of seven.

Powerful support for practical training with young children also comes from developmental theory and research which, almost with one voice, argues for the natural progression of understanding from action to concept (Piaget, [11]; Vygotsky, [12]). Given that sophisticated pedestrians have both practical skills and broader-based conceptions of the traffic environment which guide the deployment of these skills, the implication is that methods of instruction will be effective when they work consistently with this progression from action to concept rather than when they work against it. Explicit training in particular road-side actions should provide the necessary basic information about the relationship between action and environment in a form which children will adopt and use for themselves.

Practical training and interactive learning

Action-based developmental theories of Piaget and Vygotsky have an inherently interactive character. For Piaget the most important element in promoting development is the experience of conflict between ideas and experience or between one's own ideas and those of others as revealed during dialogue. Progress and understanding are held to occur through the internal resolution of externally induced conflict. Piaget particularly emphasises the role of peer discussion in this process because peers speak the same language, are more likely to find the same aspects of experience to be salient, are more likely to question and challenge each other and debate competing perspectives. Adult-child interaction is more likely to result in the adult putting forward his/her own view for the child to accept and the child acquiescing with or without understanding.

For Vygotsky the central mechanism of learning is the guidance of action, especially via 'corrective' dialogue and within the child's existing capabilities. Inevitably, therefore, the interactant through whom the guidance is mediated is more likely to be an adult or expert peer. Despite obvious differences both theories emphasise the importance of social interaction, and of interactive learning, and they can clearly operate as alternative, complementary mechanisms within interaction.   Classroom experience presents the close juxtaposition of teacher-led instruction alternating with periods of group-based activity, offering the opportunity in rapid succession for expert guidance and help followed by group discussion and debate.

In terms of interactive learning approaches these models suggest the appropriateness of tutoring or peer tutoring on the one hand, and collaborative learning on the other. Peer tutoring meets the basic requirements of Vygotsky for an asymmetrical relationship in which the teacher or expert child instructs and guides the learning of the tutee or naive child and advances that child's understanding within his or her 'zone of proximal development' (Foot, Shute, Morgan and Barron [13]). Collaborative learning satisfies the symmetrical conditions suggested by the Piagetian ideas for individuals of roughly comparable knowledge and ability working together in small groups to establish a joint solution to a specified problem.

Peer tutoring is particularly useful in situations where there is a need for supplementary bolstering of adult instruction (Damon [14]). It is, therefore, an excellent way for children to exchange skills and information and to learn rules and procedures which they must follow in performing skills and tasks involving a sequence of operations. Children can, of course, benefit from the experience of imparting competence to others. On the other hand, the acquisition of basic reasoning and problem-solving skills occurs best in a collaborative rather than a tutoring relationship (Sharan [15]). Genuine collaboration fosters the all-important acquisition of basic thinking skills.

Applications of interactive learning methods to road safety

The need for road safety education to impart both skills and the conceptual framework for the deployment of those skills has already been mentioned. The implication is that such education could benefit from carefully structured implementation of some of the principles of interactive learning. In particular we advocate a complementary programme of adult-child interaction and peer collaboration. Adult-child interaction could be employed in the development of the skills required to interact safely with traffic using a hierarchical progression from simple tasks such as finding a safe place to cross to more complex action plans for exposure to different kinds of traffic situations.

This programme of guided participation could be backed up by related group work in an appropriate classroom context with the aim of clarifying the connection between events (e.g. different road users' actions) and identifying the underlying principles.

These two strands together would, over time, promote the development of a sophisticated model of traffic to guide practical action. The practical experience gives context to conceptual understanding which in turn provides the rationale for practical action.

Road-side training   Road-side training programmes need to adopt a structured learning approach focussing on the types of errors most commonly made by young children and designed to help children discover the basic principles for themselves.   The group training of children at the road-side affords ample opportunities for the benefits of interactive learning to accrue.

Classroom based training   Once children have been exposed to the practicalities of the road-side, there is much work that can be carried back into the classroom.   The actual situations they have been confronted with can be translated into a range of classroom exercises, some addressing traffic situations similar to those they have experienced, others extrapolated from them.   This supporting programme of collaborative group work would be aimed at developing further the conceptual framework for safe road behaviour.

The advantage of classroom exercises to complement road-side practical training is, first, that they can be developed to present challenges and group activities to children in many different structured ways, and, second they can be used to encompass a much wider range of potential crossing situations than practical road-side training can possibly achieve.   They help therefore in developing understanding and in generalising the skills which children learn at the road-side.

References

1. Thomson, J.A.   *The Facts about Child Pedestrian Accidents*, Cassel, London,   1991
2. Older, S.J.   & Grayson, G.B.   Perception and decision in the pedestrian task, *Department of the Environment Report 49UC.*   Crowthorne: TRRL, 1974.
3. Avery, G.C.   The capacity of young children to cope with the traffic system: a review, *Traffic Accident Research Unit Report.*   Department of Motor Transport, New South Wales, Australia, 1974.
4. Thomson, J.A., Tolmie, A., Foot, H.C. & McLaren, B.   Child development and the aims of road safety education - a review and analysis, *Department of Transport Report*, 1994.
5. Ampofo-Boateng, K. & Thomson, J.A.   Child pedestrian accidents: a case for preventative medicine, *Health Education Research: Theory and Practice*, 1990, **5**, 265-274.
6. Sheppard, D.   Teaching pedestrian skills: a graded structure.   *Safety Education*, 1975, **133**, 5-7.

7. Downing, C.S. Improving parental road safety practice and education with respect to pre-school children, *Road Safety: Research and Practice*, ed. H.C. Foot, A.J. Chapman & F.M. Wade, Praeger, Eastbourne, 1981.
8. West, R., Sammons, P. & West, A. Effects of a traffic club on road safety knowledge and self-reported behaviour of young children and their parents. *Accident Analysis and Prevention*, 1993, **25**, 609-618.
9. OECD. *Special Research Group on Pedestrian Safety. Chairman's Report and Report Subgroup II: Road Safety Education*, TRRL/OECD, Crowthorne, 1978.
10. Rothengatter, J.A. *Traffic Safety Education*, Swets & Reitlinger, Lisse, 1981.
11. Piaget, J. *The Language and Thought of the Child*, Meridian Press, New York, 1955.
12. Vygotsky, L.S. *Mind in Society: The Development of Higher Psychological Processes*, Harvard University Press, Harvard, Cambridge, 1978.
13. Foot, H.C., Shute, R.H., Morgan, J.M. & Barron, A-M. Children's helping relationships: an overview, Chapter 1, *Children Helping Children*, ed H.C. Foot, M.J. Morgan & R.H. Shute, pp 3-17, Wiley, Chichester, 1990.
14. Damon, W. Peer education: the untapped potential. *Journal of Applied Developmental Psychology*, 1984, **5**, 331-343.
15. Sharan, S. *Cooperative Learning*, Erlbaum, Hillsdale,New Jersey.

Peer tutoring: Toward a new model

A.J. Gartner

Peer Research Laboratory, The Graduate School and University Center, The City University of New York, 33 West 42 Street, New York NY 10036, USA

Abstract

Research on peer tutoring indicates that gains for tutors often outdistance those of the students receiving help. Learning through teaching poses an opportunity to reformulate and extend the use of peer tutoring. This paper discusses a new tutor-centered model aimed also at removing the negativity and stigmatization often associated with receiving help. In addition, a contrast between traditional models of tutoring programs and the new model is presented, along with a discussion of how to implement the tutoring strategy in the school.

Introduction

Research on peer tutoring indicates that the intervention is relatively effective in improving both tutees' and tutors' academic and social development and their attitudes toward school (c.f., Cohen, Kulik & Kulik [1], Bloom [2], Ashley et al. [3], Hedin [4], Goodlad & Hirst [5], Greenwood, Delquadri & Hall [6], Benard [7], Swengel [8]). However, some studies caution that effectiveness may be moderated by similarity in age and achievement level of tutors and tutees (DePaulo et al. [9]) and academic deficiency of tutors (Willis & Crowder [10]).

The literature also shows that the gains for tutors often outdistance those of the students receiving help (Cloward [11]). As a result of their efforts to help others, tutors reinforce their own knowledge and skills, which in turn builds their self-confidence and self-esteem. There are gains for tutors in reviewing and consolidating prior learned knowledge, filling in gaps, and reformulating their knowledge into new conceptual frameworks.

Tutoring develops a sense of individual responsibility, an understanding of individual differences and needs, skills to deal with others, and a sensitivity toward the learning process. Learning through teaching is the significant mechanism here, although not to be dismissed is the impact that comes from helping others, what is known as the "helper-therapy principle" (Riessman [12]).

The New Tutor-Centered Model

The Peer Research Laboratory has been designing a new model to address the issue: If the tutor role is effective, why not give all students the opportunity to be a tutor? This model differs from usual tutoring approaches where, generally, more proficient students tutor the less proficient.

A second thrust is to make the tutoring process a central instructional strategy, integrated fully in everyday classroom work, in contrast to current practice that employs tutoring mainly as a peripheral and remedial activity rather than using it also for enrichment and an expansion of learning.

These goals have several implications. If every student is to be a tutor, they must be well prepared to perform this task. Thus, in-depth training is essential, both pre-service and on a continuous basis. This provides tutors with the opportunity to learn and refine their tutoring, communication, and problem-solving skills, understand different educational approaches, and how to be a role model. They meet together to share their feelings about the tutoring process and expand their comprehension of learning through teaching. Included here are different learning strategies, the significance of indirect and informal learning, the relationship between cognitive and social development, the importance of individualization and attuning the material to the learner's interests and learning styles, the use of pacing, repetition, and reinforcement.

In the new model, the tutoring process is viewed as developmental, where tutors have had the experience of being a tutee as part of their apprenticeship for becoming tutors. For example, in an elementary school, whole classes of heterogeneous 6th graders tutor, one-to-one, a whole 2nd grade class; the 2nd graders, in turn, may tutor kindergartners. In cross-age tutoring schemes, students in junior high school may tutor elementary school youngsters, while junior high school students are tutored by high school students, who may themselves be tutored by college level students.

In this model, both tutors and tutees gain greater understanding of the subject matter that is being tutored. Second, they learn how to tutor. Third, they learn how to listen and communicate effectively. Fourth, and perhaps most important, they learn about learning. To strengthen the tutee-to-tutor conversion, a crucial ingredient in the new model, and to build a sense of shared ownership of the program, tutees meet with the tutors to reflect on their joint tutoring experiences, as givers and receivers of help.

Tutees benefit from the tutor-centered program by improving their motivation to learn through participatory sharing with the tutors; by having well-trained and supervised tutors to heighten their learning; and increasing their self-esteem as they recognize the value of being tutored as preparation for their tutor role in the future. In essence, receiving tutoring serves more than the goal of learning the lesson.

A Comparison: The Old and New Models

Old	New
More proficient student is tutor	Everyone is a tutor
Remedial help	Reinforcement/enrichment
Tutee dependency	Conversion of tutee to tutor
Learning by receiving	Learning by teaching
Emphasis on tutee improvement	Emphasis on tutor development
Incremental improvement	Leap in learning
Limited use of student resources	Increase of help-giving resources
Add-on, peripheral activity	Central educational strategy
Little impact on school culture	Change in school climate

Putting Theory into Practice

For the new model to work, clearly, district and school administrative support, as well as that of the school-based management team are crucial (Gartner [13]). The support of the teachers is essential too, particularly because of the shift in their role to facilitators and managers of the learning process. To do this, they need to be oriented, trained and encouraged to put the program into place. The Peer Research Laboratory has worked with a number of New York City schools in collaborative efforts to provide the training, support, and resources necessary to implement the new model on the elementary, intermediate, and high school levels. For example, at one elementary school, with more than 500 low-income, largely Asian students, whole classes of students are tutors to younger students. In spreading the tutor role, all students in the school, regardless of academic ability, and including special education students, have the opportunity of learning through teaching.

In cross-age tutoring schemes, teachers have to develop a working relationship. As pairs of teachers work together, time is set aside for the teachers to meet to decide on the curriculum to be tutored, plan logistical arrangements, and evaluate program components. Part of the new model includes the establishment of teacher support groups, where all the participating teachers in a school meet together regularly, either before or after school, to not only receive ongoing training and support, but also to break down teacher isolation; this has led to the development of innovative teacher partnerships.

Making More Intensified Use of Students as Tutors

Following are examples of other programs where the Peer Research Laboratory has applied the new tutoring model.

• In an alternative dropout-prevention high school program, student tutors who successfully had completed the course in which they were to tutor assisted "at-risk" peers. To eliminate the "hierarchical" structure that generally exists between tutors and tutees, which makes the tutee feel dominated, inadequate, or dependent, the experimental program introduced three features: 1) tutees were involved in activities to promote joint ownership that included weekly group meetings with tutors for planning, training, and assessment; 2) tutees were given a chance to become tutors the following semester provided they passed their tutored course with at least a 75% grade and were regular group attendees; and 3) tutees were provided a stipend for participation in the group meetings, but not for receiving tutoring. The program was implemented in three experimental and three control groups, randomly selected from among six inner-city high schools. The control group members participated in a traditional tutoring program.

The findings for tutees in the experimental program included:
a. Involvement in greater number of tutored courses;
b. Higher program involvement;
c. Higher rate of completion in tutored courses;
d. No significant differences in attitudinal measures with respect to school, teachers, self, locus of control (probably because initial scores were already high allowing little room for growth);
e. Significantly higher grade point averages.

In the new tutoring model, tutoring was more collaborative and less tutor-directed. Tutee interactions with tutors were more extensive and personal. The data are interpreted to suggest that relaxation of artificial barriers to full and equal participation in tutoring allows greater benefits for tutees and tutors.

• In a current pilot project, high school students participate in an academic course with a world-citizen curriculum and are paired with newly arrived immigrant students, who are flooding the New York City schools. The program is designed to further the tutors' understanding of cross-cultural and multi-cultural studies, through structured interaction with their tutees, as well as to train them to be effective tutor/mentors. Students receive credit for both the coursework and for the tutoring activities, which take place during class time. The tutees, at the same time, are introduced in the course to their new environment--both school and community--helped to "navigate the institutional system," learn about what is expected of them from administrators, teachers, and other students, and benefit from the skilled attention and assistance of their tutor/mentors.

● Tutoring provides the practicum component of a high school psychology course in another program. Students are paired for the semester with elementary school students as the field requirement that provides them with practical experience complementing what they are learning in class.

● Finally, in a program that took place in four diverse high schools, students received community service credit for tutoring elementary/junior high school students, during the school day. Tutors were recruited from high-, middle-, and low-achieving high schools, all in close proximity to the receiving schools, in order to minimize travel time. All the tutors received in-depth training to enhance their tutoring skills and tutored under adult supervision. Results of this study showed that regardless of the achievement levels of the tutors, their effectiveness was consistently high across the program.

Conclusion

The critical importance of youth having the opportunity to participate in meaningful roles such as youth-helping-youth is a salient factor in preventing social problems, including substance abuse, teen pregnancy, and delinquency. The need exists to expand the opportunity to have all students experience the helping role.

At the same time, education is under attack in our society and resources are shrinking. An underutilized and powerful peer approach expands the resources available to provide education--the students themselves. Student-centered learning has been demonstrated to be highly beneficial in a number of studies, with positive effects on both cognitive outcomes as well as student self-esteem and empowerment. Students, as the most important constituency in the learning process, largely have been ignored. Their active involvement is required to change the culture and ethos of the school--where students can experience a sense of community and ownership of the education endeavor.

The peer participatory approach, whether it be tutoring, cooperative learning, peer mentoring, peer mediation, or some other strategy, is valuable for students, in terms of effective instructional practices, as part of a larger effort to restructure schools as learning communities, and in promoting heightened respect for the capabilities of all students.

References

1. Cohen, P.A., Kulik, J.A. & Kulik, C.-L.C. Educational outcomes of peer tutoring: A Meta-analysis of findings, *American Educational Research Journal*, 1982, **2**, 237-248.
2. Bloom, B.S. The search for methods as effective as one-to-one tutoring, *Educational Leadership*, 1984, **41**, 4-17.
3. Ashley et al. *Peer Tutoring: A Guide to Program Design*, Ohio State University Center for Research in Vocational Education, Columbus, 1986.
4. Hedin, D. Students as teachers: A Tool for improving school climate and productivity, *Social Policy*, 1987, **17**, 42-47.
5. Goodlad, S. & Hirst, B. *Peer Tutoring: A Guide to Learning by Teaching*, Nichols, New York, 1989.
6. Greenwood, C.R., Delquadri, J.C. & Hall, R.V. Longitudinal effects of classwide peer tutoring, *Journal of Educational Psychology*, 1989, **81**, 371-383.
7. Benard, B. *The Case for Peers*, Northwest Regional Educational Laboratory, Eugene, OR, 1990.
8. Swengel, E.M. Peer tutoring: Back to the roots of peer helping, *The Peer Facilitator Quarterly*, 1991, **8**, 28-32.
9. DePaulo et al. Age differences in reactions to help in a peer tutoring context, *Child Development*, 1989, **60**, 423-439.
10. Willis, J. & Crowder, J. Does tutoring enhance the tutor's academic learning? *Psychology in the Schools*, 1974, **11**, 68-70.
11. Cloward, R.D. Teenagers as tutors of academically low-achieving children: Impact on tutors and tutees, Chapter 7, *Children as Teachers*, ed V.L. Allen, pp 219-229, Academic Press, New York, 1976.
12. Riessman, F. The helper-therapy principle, *Social Work*, 1965, **10**, 27-32.
13. Gartner, A.J. *A Peer-Centered School*, Peer Research Laboratory, New York, 1992.

Student tutors' perceptions of their cognitive and transferable skill development

S. Hill
Centre for Paired Learning, Department of Psychology, University of Dundee, Dundee DD1 4HN, UK

Abstract

This paper presents the results of a national survey of the cognitive and transferable skills of student tutors in relation to their involvement in a student tutoring programme. In such programmes, higher and further education students tutor primary or secondary school pupils in the presence of the classroom teacher.

Prospective student tutors were asked to complete a questionnaire indicating the extent to which they believed they had developed a range of cognitive and transferable skills. They were also asked to provide personal and demographic information.

The results of this pre-tutoring survey revealed that the vast majority of the student tutors rated quite highly the extent of their cognitive ability development in the subject they expected to be tutoring.

In addition, the vast majority rated the extent of their development of transferable skills quite highly. This result in particular is encouraging in view of the increasing desirability of such professional transferable skills in the current employment market.

The baseline prevalence of these cognitive and transferable skills has been established by this pre-tutoring survey. The extent of the student tutors' development in these skills as a result of their school tutoring experience will be evident from results of the post-tutoring survey.

Introduction

Student tutoring refers to a method of teaching/learning whereby students from further and higher education establishments tutor pupils in primary or secondary schools in the presence of the classroom teacher. Such schemes have been in operation in the UK since 1975, when 'The Pimlico Connection' (Goodlad et al 1979 [1]), was introduced. This involved students from Imperial College London tutoring pupils at Pimlico Comprehensive School.

The main rationale for such schemes is to raise school pupils' aspirations and motivation to continue their education at a higher level by the positive role model provided by the student tutors.

However, the student tutors themselves have the opportunity to develop their understanding of the tutored subject, by applying their knowledge in practical contexts, and to develop many of the professional 'transferable' skills increasingly in demand by employers, e.g. communication, interpersonal and organisational skills.

This paper reviews the results of a pre-tutoring survey of higher and further education students involved in student tutoring schemes throughout the UK, co-ordinated by the Community Service Volunteers (CSV) agency.

The CSV student tutoring programme, 'Learning Together', was developed with the support of the Lord Mayor of London's Appeal and was implemented for the first time in the academic session 1992-93. With support and funding from its Principle Partners, it has continued to grow and expand, and during its first year of implementation was involved in the establishment of over 100 student tutoring schemes nationwide. In addition, CSV appointed Regional Co-ordinators to manage the operation of Learning Together schemes in 11 regions nationwide.

The Centre for Paired Learning at the University of Dundee is one of four locations in the UK which are currently involved in the student tutoring evaluation and research programme established by CSV Learning Together and supported by British Telecom.

The research being carried out in Dundee is a national evaluation of student tutors' perceptions of their cognitive and transferable skill gains as a consequence of their school tutoring experience. With the help of CSV Regional Co-ordinators, a large questionnaire survey of student tutors has been undertaken. This paper describes the first part of this survey, providing a measure of the baseline prevalence of such abilities and skills in student tutors.

Method

A comprehensive list of cognitive abilities and transferable skills was produced by searching through and synthesising information from relevant literature sources (School of Computing and Information Studies, University of Central England, 1990 [2], Personal Skills Unit, University of Sheffield, 1993 [3]).

Consultation with students from Dundee University who had recently participated in a student tutoring programme refined the list of cognitive and transferable skills to those most relevant to tutoring. A draft pre-tutoring questionnaire was developed and piloted with the Dundee students.

Changes suggested by the Dundee students were incorporated, and a revised version of the questionnaire was subsequently distributed for comment and revision by CSV Regional and National Co-ordinators. A final version was agreed and distributed to the 11 regions nationwide in time for completion by the student tutors at their pre-tutoring training sessions i.e. the questionnaires were completed before the students commenced any tutoring.

The final version of the pre-tutoring questionnaire was divided into 3 parts. The first part asked the student tutors to provide personal and demographic details. Part 2 asked them to estimate the extent to which they believed they had developed certain cognitive or 'intellectual' abilities in relation to the subject they expected to be tutoring. Students were asked to complete this section only if they already knew which subject they were going to tutor. Finally, part 3 asked them to estimate to what extent they believed they had developed certain transferable skills. All students were asked to complete this section.

The respondents were not required to provide their name and were reassured that all information supplied would remain confidential. They were asked to supply their date of birth only for the purposes of identifying pre and post-tutoring questionnaires from the same individuals.

Returns of the pre-tutoring questionnaire were manually coded for region, institution of origin, and the term in which the students began tutoring, i.e. the Autumn or Spring term. They were then checked for duplicate date of birth identifier codes. Questionnaires originating from each institution that had duplicate dates of birth were further identified by gender, if this was possible, and then by subjects studied/tutored, where these had been specified.

In this way, all pre-tutoring questionnaires were uniquely identified to enable cross-matching with post-tutoring questionnaires from the same individuals. The questionnaires were then processed by an Optical Mark Reader.

Results

TABLE 1
Distribution and Return of Pre-tutoring Questionnaires by Region

REGION	AUTUMN		SPRING		OVERALL	
	Dist.	Ret.	Dist.	Ret.	Dist.	Ret.
Bath	20	5	87	42	107	47
Birmingham	140	140	109	105	249	245
Bradford	43	43	0	0	43	43
Bristol	110	51	0	0	110	51
Leeds	0	0	0	0	0	0
London SE	51	40	31	27	82	67
London SW	138	127	10	10	148	137
London N	0	0	0	0	0	0
Manchester	100	83	53	27	153	110
Northern Ireland	88	88	0	0	88	88
Sheffield	105	105	17	17	122	122
Total	795	682	307	228	1102	910

Return Rate = 910/1102 = **83%**

TABLE 2
Where subject to be tutored was studied

(Responses only from students who knew which subject they were going to tutor = 482/910 students)

Where studied	Percentage of students
University/college only	21.4
University/college and secondary school	62.0
Secondary school only	10.4
Not at all	6.2

TABLE 3

Extent of Cognitive Ability Development

(Responses for students who completed Part 2 on 'Intellectual Abilities' = 477/910 students)

EXTENT OF DEVELOPMENT
(% of students)

COGNITIVE ABILITY	Not at all	A little	Some	A lot
Recall of subject	.8	3.4	36.5	59.3
Understanding of subject	0	3.4	36.7	60.0
Accuracy with subject	.4	11.5	54.5	33.5
Speed and fluency with subject	.6	11.7	55.1	32.5
Gaps in knowledge of subject	4.6	41.5	48.0	5.9
Confidence in knowledge of subject	.6	9.4	51.2	38.8
Understanding how others learn subject	2.5	29.8	49.6	18.1
Communication of subject facts and principles	.2	11.3	54.1	34.4
Practical demonstration of subject skills	.3	25.7	53.0	31.0
Application of knowledge in new situations	.2	13.2	59.1	27.5

TABLE 4
Extent of Transferable Skill Development

(Responses for students who completed Part 3 on 'Transferable Skills' = 894/910 students)

EXTENT OF DEVELOPMENT
(% of students)

TRANSFERABLE SKILL	Not at all	A little	Some	A lot
Selecting, retrieving, organising and summarising	.3	7.6	47.0	45.1
Managing workload, priorities and time allocation	2.0	10.4	42.7	44.9
Communicating information/ideas orally	1.9	15.8	49.6	32.8
Listening, questioning and clarifying effectively	.8	14.0	51.8	33.4
Communicating information/ideas in writing	.7	9.6	44.6	45.1
Collaborating with others in a group situation	2.0	13.0	42.8	42.2
Leading others in a group situation	7.9	26.0	47.7	18.5
Identifying problems	1.3	12.0	55.3	31.4
Planning actions and identifying problem solutions	2.8	19.4	52.5	25.4
Improvising, innovating and being flexibly creative	4.8	23.4	45.1	26.7
Evaluating and interpreting results and outcomes	1.8	12.1	48.7	37.4

TABLE 5

Current year of study of student tutors (respondents = 908/910 students)

Year	Percentage of Students
First	19.8
Second	49.4
Third	22.5
Fourth	6.4
Other	1.9

TABLE 6

Results for comparison of current year of study of students and their responses to the extent of their development in each ability/skill listed

Kruskal-Wallis One Way Analysis of Variance by Ranks

COGNITIVE ABILITY	Value of chi-square (df = 4)	Significance
Recall of subject	3.574	ns
Understanding of subject	12.438	$p<.02$
Accuracy with subject	14.346	$p<.01$
Speed and fluency with subject	20.607	$p<.001$
Gaps in knowledge of subject	3.129	ns
Confidence in knowledge of subject	15.530	$p<.01$
Understanding how others learn subject	5.564	ns
Communication of subject facts and principles	18.714	$p<.001$
Practical demonstration of subject skills	6.504	ns
Application of knowledge in new situations	4.092	ns

TRANSFERABLE SKILL	Value of chi-square (df = 4)	Significance
Selecting, retrieving, organising and summarising	11.013	$p<.05$
Managing workload, priorities and time allocation	13.554	$p<.01$
Communicating information/ideas orally	4.684	ns
Listening, questioning and clarifying effectively	4.086	ns
Communicating information/ideas in writing	32.884	$p<.001$
Collaborating with others in a group situation	4.755	ns
Leading others in a group situation	4.994	ns
Identifying problems	0.947	ns
Planning actions and identifying problem solutions	5.066	ns
Improvising, innovating and being flexibly creative	3.547	ns
Evaluating and interpreting results and outcomes	2.601	ns

Discussion

Table 1 shows the distribution and return figures for the pre-tutoring questionnaire. Only 2 regions, Leeds and London North, were unable to distribute any pre-tutoring questionnaires. The majority of other regions distributed most of the questionnaires in the Autumn term, since most students commenced tutoring at this time. The drop in distribution figures for the Spring term reflects a drop in the number of new students commencing tutoring. The exception here is Bath, where most students commenced tutoring in the Spring term.

Most regions achieved almost 100% return rate for the pre-tutoring questionnaires. This was mainly due to the students being asked to complete and return the questionnaires at their pre-tutoring training sessions, which are generally well attended. It also avoided the difficulty of postal returns.

The results from Parts 2 and 3 of the questionnaire, percentage ratings for the extent of the students' development in each cognitive and transferable skill, are shown in tables 3 and 4 respectively.

Given that the majority of the students who knew which subject they were to tutor had studied this subject at university/college (83.4% of all students responding to this question - see Table 2), then one might expect them to rate the extent of their cognitive abilities with this subject highly ($84 \rightarrow 97\%$ of students responding to this section rated the extent of their development in all but two of the cognitive abilities as 'some' or 'a lot' - see Table 3).

The two exceptions were firstly, the extent to which the student tutors believed they had 'Gaps in knowledge of subject', which the majority of students (89.5%) rated as 'a little' or 'some', and secondly, the extent to which they had an 'Understanding of how others learn subject'. A sizeable minority of students (32.3%) rated the extent of their development in this area as 'not at all' and 'a little'. This second result is interesting and one which might be particularly affected by tutoring.

Table 4 shows the students' ratings for the extent of their development of certain transferable skills. Again the majority of the students rated the extent of their development in many of these skills as 'some or 'a lot'. However, a sizeable minority rated 'Leading others in a group situation' and 'Improvising, innovating and being flexibly creative' as 'not at all' or 'a little' (33.9% and 28.2% respectively). A change in the first of these results, 'Leading others in a group situation', might be anticipated following the students' school tutoring experience.

Although the vast majority of students rated their pre-tutoring development level in many of the abilities and skills quite highly, any possible ceiling effect will be discernible from the post-tutoring questionnaire, which has an additional question relating to perception of tutoring effect, if any, for each ability and skill. This will provide a further measure of the extent to which tutoring has enhanced these abilities and skills.

Differences in the student tutors' responses according to their current year of study were investigated using the Kruskal-Wallis one-way analysis of variance by ranks procedure, which produces a statistic with a chi-square distribution (see Tables 5 and 6). This revealed several significant differences, particularly in the students' ratings of their cognitive abilities.

Understanding, accuracy, speed and fluency, confidence and communication of the subject they were to tutor, all revealed significant differences according to the current year of study of the students (see Table 6).

Similarly, the students' ratings for the extent of their transferable skill development revealed differences in selecting and retrieving information, managing workload and time, and communicating information or ideas in writing, according to their current year of study (see Table 6).

A further analysis of these differences in ratings will be reported elsewhere. However, it is interesting to note that the students' current year of study does appear to be related to their ratings for quite a number of cognitive abilities and transferable skills. Whether this relationship changes following tutoring remains to be seen, but a more detailed analysis of the precise nature of any differences will be undertaken with reference to the post-tutoring data.

References

1. Goodlad, S., Abidi, A. Anslow, P. & Harris, J. The Pimlico Connection: undergraduates as tutors in schools, *Studies in Higher Education*, 1979, **4(2)**, 191-201.

2. *A Study of Personal Transferable Skills Teaching in Higher Education in the UK*, Final Report, School of Computing and Information Studies, University of Central England, (1990).

3. *A Conceptual Model of Transferable Personal Skills*, Personal Skills Unit, University of Sheffield, (1993).

Student tutoring and student mentoring

J.C. Hughes

International Mentoring and Tutoring Project, BP Oil International/Imperial College, Britannic House, 1 Finsbury Circus, London EC2M 7BA, UK

Abstract

Student tutoring involves volunteer students from colleges and universities helping in local schools on a sustained and systematic basis. Student tutors act as a resource to the teacher and work one to one or with small groups helping school pupils with their work and relating the subject to the outside world. Student mentoring operates in a similar manner but the contact is normally on a one to one basis outside of the classroom. Student tutors can provide school pupils with a positive role model to help increase aspirations and motivation to stay-on in education and training. Student mentors are more than just role models and could be said to be providing the message; 'be as you can be' rather than just 'be as I am'. This article provides an overview of world-wide activity and focuses on a student tutoring scheme called the Pimlico Connection at Imperial College in London.

1. The Problem

The UK has a staying-on rate in full-time 16-18 education and training of less than 50%. The problem is not confined to the UK with a similar drop-out problem in many areas of North America. Many of our young people leave education and training at the first available opportunity; they are not aware of the potential benefits of staying on in post-compulsory education and they simply do not see it as something that is relevant or accessible to them. There is an urgent need to increase our participation rates if we are to meet the needs of industry and society as a whole but also to offer access to education and true equality of opportunity to all of our young people. Science and Engineering has a further problem in that children often think of an 'engineer' as someone who works in a dirty factory or a scientist as a mad, balding, boffin.

2.   Towards a solution: Student Tutoring/Mentoring.

Student tutoring involves volunteer students from colleges and universities acting as a resource to the teacher in schools local to their institution. This contact is on a sustained and systematic basis to provide attitudinal gains to student tutor and pupil alike. This contact between college student and school pupil takes place on an in-classroom basis.

Student mentoring operates in a similar manner but the contact is normally outside of the classroom with a higher level of commitment on behalf of the student mentors and their protégés.

Student tutoring is a specific example of the wider term of peer tutoring: that being the system of instruction in which learners help each other and learn by teaching. Peer tutoring covers an extensive area that includes in school cross-age or same-age scheme, cross phase schemes from High School to Elementary School as well as adult to adult initiatives.

3.   Student Tutoring in the UK

In 1990 a project commenced at Imperial College, funded by BP, to which the author was appointed as the BP Fellow for Student Tutoring. The project led to a massive increase in the number of schemes nation-wide from 5 universities and colleges involved to 170 by the beginning of 1994. In 1993 the International Mentoring and Tutoring Project was set up to support the demand from universities outside of the UK to set up their own student tutoring programmes. Many of the new schemes have a component of assessment built into the coursework so that the skills acquired by the student tutors can be recognised. But one of the underlying outcomes in nearly all schemes for both the UK and elsewhere is the provision of positive role models to children and an attempt to help them with their learning. In all of the schemes in the UK the college is sending its students into local schools for the equivalent of an afternoon a week for between 10 and 20 weeks. In the student tutoring scheme at Imperial College known as The Pimlico Connection some 1300 volunteer students have assisted nearly 15000 children since 1975. In the academic year 1992/93 there were nearly 160 students active once a week for 15 weeks in 18 local primary and secondary schools with a new initiative with the Science Museum where student docents support school visits.

4.   The Difference between Student Tutoring and Student Mentoring

Mentoring and Tutoring are phrases that can mean different things to different people. Within the USA the two terms do not have a consistent interpretation but broadly could be differentiated as follows:

Mentoring involves a 1:1 or often a 1:small group relationship that has as an aim to provide affective changes in the mentee/protegee. The idea of a positive role model is common and the objective is often to increase staying-on rates or decrease attrition; sometimes in particular 'at risk' groups. Mentoring, however, involves providing more than just a social role model with the mentor sometimes providing in depth guidance.

Tutoring has more academic connotations and is often school based though rarely (in the USA) does this include in-class support. Most of the tutoring in the USA operates on a withdrawal system; with college students working with the school pupils in the library or cafeteria. In New Zealand, Australia, India and Europe the tutoring operates within the classroom.

5.   Student Tutoring in the USA

The USA has the longest history of running student tutoring/mentoring schemes. In a national survey carried out in 1990 there were over 1700 student tutoring/mentoring type schemes in operation across the USA [Cahalan & Farris (1990)] with little differentiation between the terms mentoring and tutoring. Cahalan & Farris (1990) use the term 'tutoring and mentoring' programmes to refer to college sponsored students working with pre-school, elementary, or high school pupils to help the pupils improve their academic skills and motivate them to continue their education. In 1988 there were more than 63,000 college students, primarily volunteers, working with nearly 200,000 school pupils with about a third of all colleges involved. The majority of the pupils reported that they acquired increased self confidence as well as a greater enthusiasm to learn with more self motivation. The college student tutors reported having an increased commitment to community service, exposure to new cultural environments and improved academic record. Highly structured programmes were found to be the most effective. A second USA survey [Reisner et al (1990)] reports that tutoring and mentoring services have positive effects on:

- test scores, grades, and overall academic performance of disadvantaged elementary and secondary pupils,
- the pupils' motivation and attitude towards education,
- the pupils' familiarity with an environment other than their own,
- the pupils' self-esteem and self-confidence,
- student tutors' leadership and communication skills,
- students' commitment to community service,
- students' self-esteem and self-confidence.

Reisner et al's (1990) view is that the positive effects are most likely to be demonstrated when there is a high degree of structure to the programme and when the schemes include the following:

- defined time from tutors and mentors, often three hours a week.
- systematic screening of prospective tutors and mentors and matching with younger pupils.
- thorough training and monitoring of tutors.
- a close relationship between the college and participating schools.

6.   Other International Developments

With support from the International Mentoring and Tutoring Project the number of countries running student tutoring schemes continues to rise. This new project supports student tutoring initiatives world-wide - there are now developments in India, Belgium, Netherlands, Eire, USA, Australia, New Zealand, Tanzania, South Africa, Russia and Singapore. The aims, as with the programme in the UK is to increase the profile of the benefits of education but is often specifically focused, particularly in third world countries, on the need to increase the number of trained technicians. The developments are too new for any systematic evaluation but there is evidence that the findings are similar to those reported from Imperial College in London.

7.   Benefits of Tutoring.

The benefits of running a tutoring scheme are well documented (Goodlad and Hirst, 1989; Beardon, 1990; Hughes, 1991 (a), Hughes, 1992) To summarise:

Students: get practice in communication skills

gain insight into how others perceive their subject

feel they are doing something useful

gain self-confidence

get to know people with different social backgrounds

have their subject knowledge reinforced

Teachers: find lessons more enjoyable

feel pupils learn more

find teaching more enjoyable

Pupils: find lessons more enjoyable

feel they learn more

find lessons more interesting

find lessons easier to follow

8.   Help in Starting a Tutoring Scheme

If you would like a copy of the free booklet on Tutoring do not hesitate to contact me.   There are extensive international resources published by BP Educational Service available for schools, colleges and universities world-wide.

This is an edited version of a paper accepted for publication in the Journal of At-Risk Issues in the USA.

References

Beardon, T. (1990). *Cambridge STIMULUS*, in Goodlad & Hirst (1990).

Cahalan, M and Farris, E (1990). *College Sponsored Tutoring and Mentoring Programs for Disadvantaged Elementary and Secondary Students,* Higher Education Surveys Report, Survey Number 12, US Department of Education.

Goodlad, S & Hirst, B. (1989). *Peer Tutoring: A Guide to Learning by Teaching.* Kogan Page, London.

Goodlad, S & Hirst, B. Eds, (1990). *Explorations in Peer Tutoring,* Blackwell, Oxford.

Hughes, J. (1991(a)). *Wicked Brilliant Radical: Pimlico Connection Annual Report*,Imperial College, London.

Hughes, J. (1991(b)). *Tutoring: Students as Tutors in Schools.* BP Educational Service, London.

Hughes, J. (1991(c)). *Tutoring Resource Pack.* BP Educational Service, London.

Hughes, J. (1992). *My Happiest Moments at Imperial: Pimlico Connection 17th Annual Report,* Imperial College, London.

Reisner, E., Petry, C., Armitage, M., (1990). *A Review of Programs involving college students as tutors or mentors in grades K-12,* Policy Studies Institute, Washington.

Interactive learning in an organisational intervention

B. Kennedy

Department of Psychology and Sociology, James Cook University, Townsville, Australia 4811

Abstract

In Organisation Development, staff participation is critical to long-term success. On the basis of a soft systems analysis, Structured Interactive Group Learning was successfully used to simultaneously facilitate development and overcome deficits in staff collaboration skills in a small non-profit organisation.

Introduction

Facilitating self-perpetuating improvement is a common dilemma for the Organisation Development (OD) practitioner. French and Bell[1] identify solving problems *for* an organisation as a major trap (for the OD practitioner) and argue that it results in decreased effectiveness. In listing OD pitfalls, Kast and Rosenzweig[2] mention over-dependence on the consultant and lack of internal resources to continue action without the consultant. In a more comprehensive context, Argyris[3] identifies three primary tasks for an intervention: ensuring that information is valid and useful, and that there is both free choice and internal commitment. He notes that "one of the most frequent manipulations attempted by clients is to demand that the interventionist shortcut the three primary tasks and get on with change" (p.28). Once the trap is recognised, the issue is positive avoidance. While the OD literature abounds with techniques, they presuppose appropriately developed client skills in analysis and communication. This paper reports work in a small non-profit organisation in which staff skills for collaboration were inadequate.

The organisation was dedicated to the retraining of long-term unemployed people. Recently stabilised after an organisational crisis, Government-driven requirements instigated radical changes in the services to be offered. The intervention was initially framed as systematic training and development (after Goldstein[4]). Needs analysis confirmed the manager's perception regarding skill deficits, and revealed further problems including lack of (shared) clarity of organisational objectives, operational structures and procedures, staff relationships, and inability to deal with externally imposed changes.

Avoiding the expert trap

The approach to avoiding the expert trap is summarised using Soft Systems Methodology (SSM) (Checkland & Scholes[5]). While 'hard' systems approaches direct choice of the best alternative to achieve a specifiable objective, SSM suits situations in which problems and solutions are ill-defined. Figure 1 illustrates a model of a traditional intervention approach constructed according to SSM conventions .

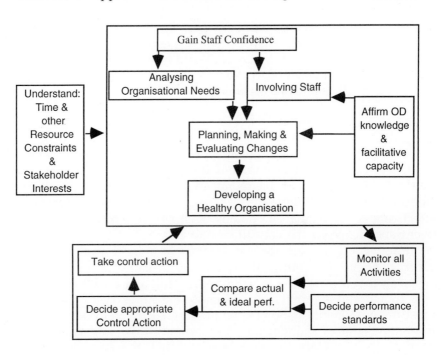

Figure 1. An SSM model of a traditional intervention approach.

The mismatch between staff skills and the activity "involving staff" rendered this model unsuitable. The two logical alternatives were: (i) abandon the participative approach and direct both the content and process of change or (ii) train staff in participation skills before proceeding to facilitate change.   The first was rejected according to the action research philosophy and the second requires more time and funding than were available. Hence the problematic situation was reframed. The resulting *root definition*, system and model (after Checkland[5], Davies & Ledington[7]) were as follows:

An interventionist and staff owned and operated system to take immediate action while ensuring that staff will become participatory without becoming expert-dependent by analysing the needs, choosing immediate action requirements and using interactive group learning. The system is made meaningful by the belief that full staff participation is required if the organisation is to achieve long-term gains, immediate action is required and staff are not yet able to participate meaningfully. The system operates within the constraints that time and other resources for the intervention are scarce and staff must maintain normal activities while the intervention occurs.

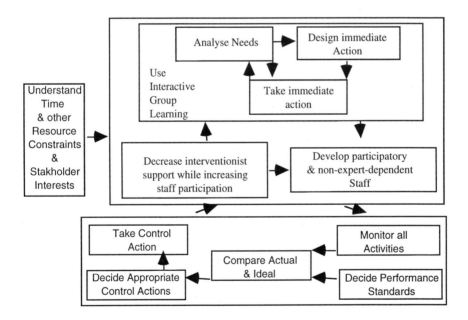

Figure 2: A system for avoiding the 'expert' trap in an action research intervention

The next step was to consider methods for each of the activities, choosing those most consistent with the situational variables, activity interactions, and the entire problem situation as depicted by the model. For example, job analysis is a prerequisite for job enrichment which, according to the needs analysis, was appropriate. Full participation in job analysis was desirable but not feasible given resource constraints. Therefore, staff involvement was minimal. Rather than imposing what appeared appropriate in terms of enrichment, this was facilitated by structured learning activities and constituted an early, primarily interventionist-directed activity. As Structured Interactive Group Learning (SIGL) progressed in a variety of contexts, job re-design became staff-directed. Participative decision making was also desirable but was initiated months later, building on the foundation of earlier SIGL and thus required substantially less interventionist-direction.

The dynamics of using SIGL to circumvent the expert trap were conceptually simple. At no stage were staff relieved of 'ownership' of organisation functioning and problem solving. Every activity was structured so that staff had broad input and partial responsibility. Over time, staff responsibility increased against a carefully balanced decrease in interventionist input. The issue of balance was critical. Had expectations of staff been too high, this may have increased stress to such an extent that motivation would wane and lead to dysfunctional responses (Stewart[6]). The converse leads back to the expert trap. SIGL was the mechanism for equipping staff with the required skills. It was initially applied with an emphasis on the 'structured', concrete, least emotive issues (e.g. reorganising the filing system). As staff skills increased, these were employed in SIGL to deal with less concrete, more emotive issues, (e.g. philosophy of training) gradually reducing imposed structure on the interactive group learning. Figure 3 summarises the relevant dimensions.

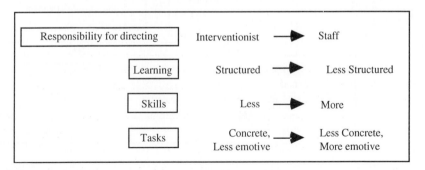

Figure 3. Trends in relevant factors over time.

Figure 4 represents the intervention and structuring process over time. The lines dividing each rectangle indicate the relative input of those two factors over time.   They have not been mathematically derived, but serve to illustrate the general principle. Some general characteristics of the lines are relevant: the removal of the starting point from zero (activities were never totally structured by the interventionist), the steeper incline in the middle of the intervention (corresponding to one week of intensive whole-of-staff activity) and the comparatively steeper rate of increase thereafter.

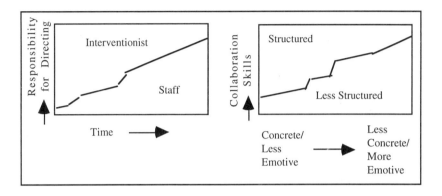

Figure 4. Interactions between some dimensions

In practice, the task of using SIGL to achieve organisational tasks and sequence skills acquisition simultaneously in time to deal with more difficult issues, was complex.   This presupposed a 'possible-future' plan of tasks and skills required and the need to sequence tasks and learning to provide the basis for staff to use informed free choice in subsequent action.

For example, a required objective was certification as an Approved Training Organisation (ATO). Among the many changes required to become an ATO was a transformation of training and documentation practices. This necessitated changes in knowledge, skills and organisational culture. Hence it was necessary to make staff aware of their deficits, while maintaining their confidence in their ability to develop as trainers. Early activities (unrelated to training *per se*) were carefully structured to ensure success and develop confidence, and emergent issues were used to expand their perceptions of training. For example, a particular incident led to a negotiated decision to abort a planned session and conduct impromptu training in task analysis. Subsequently, decisions were made about its use in planning courses. Later work involved sub-groups working together to transfer the learning into work practices, in the process of which, new issues emerged. (It was the first centre in the state to achieve ATO status.)

Conclusion

Structured interactive group learning was crucial in both developing the requisite collaborative skills in staff and in ensuring that the ownership of organisational operations and problems remained with the staff. It was implemented in a context of simultaneously decreasing interventionist input while increasing staff direction of the process. Followup indicates that the intervention was successful in terms of achieving the results desired by the organisation (the *raison d'etre* for the intervention), establishing an organisational culture of learning about its own organisational learning (a bonus in terms of the organisation's expectations) and avoiding the 'expert' trap in conducting an action research intervention (a small innovation in OD).

References

1 French, W.L. & Bell, C.H. Jr. (1984) <u>Organisation development. Behavioral science interventions for organisation improvement.</u> 3rd. Ed. New Jersey: Prentice Hall.

2 Kast,F.E. & Rosenzweig,J.E. (Ed) (1984) <u>The nature of management.</u> Chicago: Science Research Associates.

3 Argyris,C. (1970) <u>Intervention theory and method: A behavioural science view.</u> Reading, Mass: Addison-Wesley.

4 Goldstein, I.L. (1986) <u>Training in organisations - Needs assessment, development and evaluation.</u> (2nd Ed) California: Brooks/Cole Publishing Company.

5 Checkland, P.B. & Scholes, J. (1990) <u>Soft system methodology in action.</u> Chichester:Wiley.

6 Stewart, V. (1992) Human capital issues in organisational change. <u>Asia Pacific Journal of Human Resources.</u> <u>30</u>, 1, pp 53-64.

7 Davies, L. & Ledington, P. (1991) <u>Information in Action: Soft Systems Methodology.</u> London: Macmillan Education Ltd.

Psychology and environmental sciences via experiential learning

B. Kennedy
*Department of Psychology and Sociology, James Cook University,
Townsville, Australia 4811*

Abstract

This pilot project introduces a psychological perspective on individual differences and group dynamics to a research methodology subject in environmental science. In accordance with calls by industry for the development of transferable skills, it aims to enhance student capacity to work effectively in teams.

Introduction

The impetus for this interdisciplinary project arose from a recognition in Environmental Science that in addition to learning content and method, students need to develop 'transferable' skills. The importance of transferable skills was confirmed by a survey conducted by the Business and Higher Education Round Table in 1992 which showed that employers valued communication skills highest of twelve skills expected of new graduates; capacity for cooperation and teamwork was valued third.

EV3003 is a third year research methodology subject in the Department of Tropical Environmental Science and Geography at James Cook University and is taken primarily by students with a background in one of the natural sciences. The subject aims to develop (in students) the ability to conduct research in teams. Content covers research methodology and an introduction to individual differences and group dynamics. Working in teams, under supervision, students conduct and report a field research project. Strategies include lectures, interactive learning, field work and student seminars in which teams present their research.

Rather than expecting students to learn to work effectively in groups simply by conducting research projects in teams, this subject provides an appropriate psychological framework for developing knowledge about group functioning.   Teaching and learning strategies and assessment were linked to the focus on team work. The subject was jointly designed as a pilot project. Few students had any prior learning in psychology. Students were required to keep and submit for assessment a project note book using a reflective practitioner (Schon[1]) approach. The subject outline booklet provided both a prose version of marking criteria (adapted from Gibbs[2]) and examples of entries relating to both content and process of learning.

Teaching individual differences and group dynamics

In undergraduate psychology, individual differences and group dynamics are typically taught at a theoretical level.   To achieve teaching objectives, this subject required an applied approach suited to non-psychology students.   In organisation development and human resource management, this type of activity includes techniques such as team building, communication training etc. using experiential/ interactive methods.   One instrument used widely in both private and public sectors in Australia and America is the Myers Briggs Type Indicator (MBTI). In this subject, the MBTI was used in conjunction with a more social-psychological introduction to group dynamics and communication.

The MBTI is based on Jung's notion of individual preferences for ways of perceiving information and making decisions.   It proposes individual differences on four basic dimensions and considers the implications of sixteen permutations of these preferences. The first dimension (Judging - Perceiving) relates to a tendency to place more emphasis on either making decisions or collecting more information. The model proposes two preferences each for Judging and Perceiving.   Decisions may be made predominantly on the basis of logic (Thinking) or according to the human values in the situation (Feeling).   Information may be gathered via an emphasis on facts as perceived by the physical senses and sequential processing (Sensing) or wholistically via parallel processing (iNtuition). These are all influenced by a focus on the external world of people and events (Extroversion) or the internal world of thoughts and feelings (Introversion). The model specifically does not propose that individuals will only behave in accordance with their preferences, but rather it indicates their preferred mode of operation.

In interpersonal interactions, an understanding of conflicts can often be framed in terms of the different orientations indicated by preferences. For example, a J preference often leads to a push for closure, sometimes on the basis of inadequate information while a P preference often results in a reluctance to make a decision and take action until more information is acquired. An individual with a T preference may make a decision according to the logic of a situation while an F preference emphasises the likely effect of the decision on the people in the situation. Individuals with an S preference are often good at dealing with facts and details but may overlook context and long term consequences while an N preference usually translates into a future orientation concerned with the big picture and may pay insufficient attention to details. These are highly relevant to individuals operating in a team and to raising self awareness.

All students took the MBTI, received an individual profile, attended a debriefing session (which explained the theory) and participated in structured interactive learning activities to explore the preferences. Links between individual differences, self awareness of these differences and team functioning were made overt.

A mini-lecture concerning the attributes and functioning of effective groups was presented and supported by interactive group learning. Working in their research teams, groups made decisions about: group goals, management of leadership, procedures and power in decision making and conflict resolution (after Johnson & Johnson). The strategic approach to planning was introduced with research teams beginning to structure their project accordingly.

An introduction to communication was taught inductively working from a structured one-way/two-way communication exercise (Johnson & Johnson[3]) to a minimally facilitated whole-class construction of a model of communication (after Adler & Towne[4]) which integrates the impact of attitudes, values and feelings, processes of encoding and decoding, verbal and other channels of communication, types of interference in the communication process and the importance of feedback between sender and receiver.

These sessions were held early in the semester. At the end of semester, a debriefing session was conducted to integrate this learning with student experience and to gather evaluative feedback about the teaching/ learning process.

Student Reaction
Analysis of student feedback was incomplete at the time of writing. Some students feel the process of learning about individual and group factors was extremely valuable and a few rejected its

appropriateness in a science subject. While the impact is evident in the notebooks, a majority appear not to be conscious of having used information presented in the psychology component. There is a consensus that the subject is worthwhile but needs fine-tuning.

The areas of highest agreement are related to the subject as a whole. The subject workload was perceived to be too high for its assigned point value and most students objected to having the four contact hours scheduled on the one day. The room was seen to be unsuitable for group work (over the break, fixed seating had been installed to replace movable chairs). Most students had major difficulties scheduling group meeting times due to clashes between university timetables (this is complicated by commitments to part-time work which many students find necessary to survival). These issues appear to have coloured summative feedback more than reflections recorded in log books. Students did recognise the importance of gaining experience in team research projects for future employment prospects. Some students however, retained unrealistic perceptions of the similarity between student and employee teams on the basis that at work, it would be much easier to arrange team meetings, projects would be socially significant and social loafing would not be a problem since those who did not contribute would lose their job rather than being 'carried' by other team members.

Some negative feedback has focussed on the notion of involving a psychologist in a science subject, the use of interactive learning rather than lectures containing facts, the use of a psychological inventory and the skills of some group supervisors. Some positive feedback has identified the value of acquiring frameworks for thinking about group, individual and communication processes, advantages of interactive learning in class, providing a time-effective means of establishing relationships between members of the research team, and the change of pace in having a science subject taught in a different way.

The notebooks have proved to be beneficial for both teaching and learning. They provide a valuable insight into the effect of specific teaching activities and supervisory practice on student behaviour and learning. Some students have indicated that although they initially did not like the idea of the notebook, they came to value it as a means of monitoring both project progress and the development of their own thinking over the semester. It is particularly interesting that a previous attempt to use notebooks in a first year science subject achieved little, while in this subject, the majority of students have put considerable effort into them and demonstrated the ability to learn from reflecting on experience.

Some quotes serve to illustrate the variety of learning students have written about in their notebooks:

Structured interactive learning: "these kinds of prac sessions are very different from the prac sessions I am used to . I had some trouble coming to terms with these new thought processes. I have begun to realise that my thought processes are very channelled by doing a Science degree . . ."   ". . . didn't see the relevance of the survival exercise until the results - nearly everyone did better as a group."   ". . . learned that just listening to someone telling you something is not always the best way to learn how to do something, rather one must interact with the speaker to ensure that the right meaning of the information is received."

Communication: "New learnings: be more precise and concise about what I am trying to say. Get to the point and don't wander on other ideas. Must listen to people in an open minded manner so that there is no offensiveness or bitterness." "Two way communication is consistently better than one way communications." "I think I'll start listening more to people's feedback when we're in a group instead of worrying about what's for dinner"

Science/psychology interface: ". . . perhaps I'm realising there is a certain learned skill in creating an effective questionnaire. Not just "a bit of common sense". Personally I feel that I'm developing more respect for the so-called "soft sciences" than I had at the start of the year." ". . . not used to lectures that are not straight forward as most science lectures are." ". . . talked to working scientists about group approach and psychology - they said there is generally a lot of pettiness in group projects and that understanding others interests is vital"   ". . . also if you can see from what point of view others are making decisions, then you can accommodate these ideas into the larger plan." "As a group of scientists we are not really a very interactive group, I think the reason for this is that we are so used to being fed factual information whereby responses are minimal."

Miscellaneous: "Consensus seems to be working quite well, but it takes time!!! ". . . it is these sorts of mistakes that waste time and therefore in the real world, money, and any sort of inefficiency means that you don't make a very good employee. So it's really important that I get this sort of thing under control before I enter the workforce" "In reflecting on what I have learnt during this course I find I have learnt not only material given at lectures but also everyday situations . . . Basically this course has taught me how to work in a group - the difficulties that arise as well as the positive benefits of working together.. . . "

Conclusions and Future Directions

While some adjustment to workload is appropriate, it is also evident that inefficient group management was a major contributor to perceived overload. This will be positively addressed by alterations to both the content and process of teaching next year.

Problems students experienced in adapting to interactive group learning requires further investigation given the increasing emphasis on using group techniques to teach higher numbers of students (e.g. see Gibbs). While prior learning in methodology varied considerably, most students in EV3003 have a background of lecture based teaching and learning with surface learning (Ramsden[5]) the predominant style. The experience in this subject suggests that more preparation may be required to effectively introduce interactive group learning into a learning sub-culture characterised by emphasis on large volumes of information (which students perceive to be facts) to be surface learned to complete degree requirements.

Transfer of learning from sessions dealing with group functioning to the processes of independent group management was inadequate. This suggests a need for some mechanism to structure transfer. Consideration will be given to the teaching of group management and providing a framework for supervisors to overtly deal with team processes as well as research issues.

Data gathered in June will be used to restructure EV3003 for 1995. A related project has been proposed to extend this pilot into the conduct of fourth year projects in both Environmental Studies and Psychology. It is envisaged that this project would produce curriculum materials and guidelines relevant to other disciplines in which students need to develop skills for working in teams.

References

[1]Schon, D. (1987) <u>Educating the Reflective Practitioner.</u> San Francisco: Jossey-Bass.

[2]Gibbs, G. (1992) <u>Teaching More Students.</u> Oxford Brookes University: Oxford Centre for Staff Development.

[3]Johnson, D.W. & Johnson, F.P. (1987) <u>Joining Together.</u> (3rd Ed) Englewood Cliffs: Prentice Hall.

[4]Adler, R.B. & Towne, N. (1990) <u>Looking Out, Looking In: Interpersonal Communication.</u> (6th Ed) Fort Worth: Holt, Rinehart & Winston Inc.

[5]Ramsden, P. (1992) <u>Learning to Teach in Higher Education.</u> London: Routledge.

Peer interaction and communication skills in children with moderate learning difficulties

S.J. Lamb & D.J. Wood
ESRC Centre for Research in Development, Instruction and Training, Department of Psychology, Nottingham University, Nottingham NG7 2RD, UK

Abstract

The paper reports the outcomes from the initial phase of a long-term intervention study aimed at assessing the effects of communication tasks on the communicative abilities and aspects of academic achievement of children with moderate to severe learning difficulties. The research aims to expand on work which demonstrates that children's use of certain aspects of spoken language can be made more effective with the aid of practice and feedback and that such improvement in communication skills may influence learning. Profiles of achievement of 80 children are being developed and early analysis demonstrates significant relationships between communicative competence and reading comprehension. The overall pattern of relationships is described. Reading accuracy, gender and communication skill are significant predictors of reading comprehension. Communication skill is directly effected by age and reading comprehension. These relationships are discussed with respect to this population of children.

1 Introduction

The aim of the research reported in this paper is to explore the relations between communication skill and reading ability in children with moderate to severe learning difficulties being educated in special schools. This work constitutes the initial stage of a long-term study designed to assess the effects of school-based interventions using structured communication activities on the learning skills and academic achievement of this population of children.

The work has been informed by two related lines of enquiry. The first influence comes from work in Scotland which demonstrated that children's ability to use spoken language, specifically information transfer, can be developed by practice and feedback (Brown, Anderson, Shillcock and Yule[1]). They argue that pupils approaching the end of their secondary education and still performing poorly on communication tasks either have not had sufficient exposure to situations demanding informative speech, or have not benefited from these experiences by developing appropriate skills. By providing children with a range of tasks which offered opportunities for them to develop their spoken language, Brown *et al* showed that pupils could make swift progress over a relatively short period of time.

The second motivation comes from work by Ann Brown and her colleagues in the USA. This group have produced evidence of long-term gains in children's reading comprehension skills and several aspects of academic achievement using a technique known as "reciprocal teaching" (Brown and Palinscar[2]). This technique is based on a strategy whereby the teacher models, explains and negotiates learning with the pupil. The children involved in the initial studies were receiving remedial support for reading. The teacher and a group of pupils take turns to lead a dialogue centred on key features of a text which they have either listened to the teacher reading or read silently to themselves. The leader of the discussion opens by asking a question and closes the session by generating a summary and predicting future content. During the dialogue members of the group attempt to clarify any comprehension problems that arise. In this way, the adult models expert reading behaviour, and is able to scaffold the weaker reader, fading into the background when the children are competent to take control of their own learning. The reciprocal nature of the process encourages participation and shared responsibility between the teacher and children for understanding the text. Using this method over a range of classroom activities significant improvements are made in pupils' reading comprehension, an effect that is maintained for up to a year after intervention. The gains were also generalised to other areas of the curriculum, in particular science and social studies (Brown and Campione[3]).

These studies demonstrate that by improving children's communication through the nature of their interactions in the classroom, practise on tasks which demand communicative skill and co-operative teaching strategies, gains are made in their communication and learning skills. The majority of the research, however, concerns children struggling in mainstream education. This study aims to explore these issues with children presenting more severe learning difficulties.

It is hypothesised that children with learning problems lack specific skills in "self-regulation" (Brown *et al* [2]) which result from, and lead to, language and communication difficulties. By providing children with experiences aimed at developing their communicative competence, it is predicted that significant gains will also be made in their learning skills and academic achievement. Very little is known about the abilities of this population of children and consequently there are no norms by which to monitor progress. The work reported in this paper constitutes the initial stage of the research which is to develop a profile of children's abilities in language, communication and selected areas of the curriculum. This will provide insight into the nature of these children's learning skills and also data from which the effects of a long-term intervention study may be measured.

2 Method

Subjects
A total of 98 children are completing a battery of tests. These include an intelligence test, assessments of their reading and mathematical abilities and a communication skills task. The subjects come from two Nottingham schools catering for children with moderate learning difficulties and all speak English as their first language. 15 children have not scored highly enough to be given a reading age based on the norms of the test and are not reported in this paper. Two outliers have also been removed. The number of subjects described in this analysis is therefore 81, comprising 29 females and 52 males, ranging in age between 11 years, 6 months and 16 years, 5 months.

Measures
Reading ability This was assessed using the Individual Reading Analysis and the New Reading Analysis (Vincent and de la Mare[4,5]). The test was administered according to the criteria in the assessment manual with the exception of the comprehension measure which was adapted to suit the particular needs of this group of children.

Communication skill Communication skill was assessed using a task taken from Concept 7-11 (Schools Council[6]). Pairs of subjects sit facing each other across a table divided by a low screen preventing them seeing each other's materials. Both subjects have a similar booklet containing five diagrams of increasing complexity, drawing paper and a red and blue pen. The children take it in turns to describe the first diagram in their booklet for their partner to draw. When the instruction follower (I.F.) thinks that they have completed the diagram, they pass it over the screen to the information giver (I.G.) The I.G. compares this diagram with the original and reconstructs the description if the match is not acceptable. This continues until the experimenter and the I.G. agree to accept the I.F.'s diagram. The children then swap roles. Both children are encouraged to ask each other questions.

The activity continued in this way until both subjects had described and drawn five diagrams. As long as the children were still able to concentrate and succeed at the task, the experimenter gave both children another booklet each with more complex diagrams and the procedure started again. The activity continued until either the experimenter thought that the tasks were getting too hard, and the children were beginning to struggle to concentrate, or the final pair of booklets (booklets 9 and 10) had been completed. The experimenter intervened where necessary to keep the children on task. The performance of each pair of children was video-taped.

The highest level of complexity reached was taken as a measure of communication skill.

Intelligence An abbreviated version of the Wechsler Intelligence Scale for Children, Revised (WISC-R; Wechsler[7]) is currently being administered according to the WISC-R manual. Scores from the mathematical subtest of the WISC-R will be used as an indicator of mathematical ability.

4 Results

It is the intention of this paper to provide a summary of the data analysis completed up to date and to report the overall pattern of relations between certain variables. Full details of the complete analysis can be found in Lamb, Wood and Leyden[8].

We await data from the WISC-R test and consequently measures of intelligence and mathematical ability do not feature in the following analysis. In addition to the measures of communication and reading ability two other variables have been included; season of birth and school. Children born in the summer may have experienced up to two terms less than their peers in a reception class. It is increasingly thought that this may have implications for academic achievement and referral to special education (Williams, Davies, Evans & Ferguson[9]). 'School attended' was used as an indicator of socio-economic status since the catchment areas of the two schools used in the study are dissimilar. School A draws from a generally middle class area, whereas school B's catchment is predominantly working class.

Table 1 shows the means and standard deviations (in brackets) of the reading and communication measures split by gender and by season of birth. 'Summer born' describes those children born between May and August. 'Not summer born' constitutes children born in the months between September and April.

Table 1. Descriptive statistics

	age	reading accuracy	reading comprehension	communication (range 1-10)
female *n=29*	13.9 (1.15)	7.6 (1.07)	7.9 (0.83)	7.0 (1.92)
male *n=52*	14.1 (1.44)	7.5 (1.32)	8.5 (0.97)	7.7 (1.94)
summer born *n=42*	14.0 (1.29)	7.7 (1.13)	8.5 (0.96)	7.9 (1.71)
not summer born *n=39*	14.1 (1.50)	7.3 (1.30)	8.0 (0.88)	6.8 (2.03)

Bivariate correlations demonstrated that reading accuracy and season of birth are significantly and positively correlated with reading comprehension (reading accuracy: $r=0.486$, $p\leq0.001$; season of birth: $r=0.275$, $p\leq0.01$). Significant positive relationships also exist between communication and age ($r=0.439$, $p\leq0.001$), reading comprehension ($r=0.345$, $p\leq0.01$) and season of birth ($r=0.28$, $p\leq0.01$). All other correlations fail to reach significance.

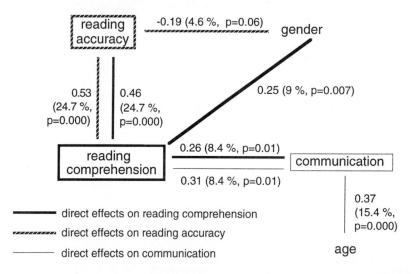

Figure 1: Structural path analysis showing direct effects of independent variables on reading and communication. Values given are: Beta (% variance uniquely explained, probability level).

Multiple linear regressions were used to determine the predictors of reading comprehension, reading accuracy and communication. The effects reported here comprise only those which directly explain unique proportions of variance (see figure 1). Although significant zero-order correlations exist between season of birth and both reading comprehension and communication, season of birth is not a significant predictor in any of the regression equations. The difference between the pattern of zero-order coefficients and the pattern of beta coefficients in the regression equation is due to correlations between season of birth and the other predictor variables. Reading accuracy, gender and communication all directly contribute to better performance in reading comprehension. That is, children with good word recognition skills, males and good communicators demonstrate superior performance at reading comprehension. Reading accuracy has a stronger effect than either of the other two variables.

The effect of gender on reading accuracy is approaching significance. However, this result lies in the opposite direction to the effect of gender on reading comprehension; girls are more accurate than boys in their reading.

Age and reading comprehension are found to be significant predictors of communication skill. Older children and those with good reading comprehension skills all appear to be communicating more successfully in the task. The direct effect of age is the strongest predictor.

5 Discussion

The predictive nature of communication skill on reading comprehension demonstrated by the data from this study is consistent with the premise underlying the work of Ann Brown and her colleagues in Illinois. Their claim is that children who use spoken language effectively to describe, question and clarify, are able to achieve higher levels of reading comprehension. This supposes reading comprehension and communication abilities are associated. The present study supports this assumption and justifies the intervention to follow. However, whilst communication skill predicts reading comprehension, it does not predict reading accuracy. This could be due to the nature of the communication skill required for successful completion of the current task. In the present study, communication skill describes the ability to transfer information and negotiate meaning. Other aspects of communicative competence include having confidence to initiate interactions between yourself and the teacher and knowing to request help when in difficulty. It is these latter skills which may be of more use for children facing problems in decoding the written word and which have not been addressed by this study.

One of the most surprising results emerging from the data is the conflicting pattern of effects of gender on the two aspects of reading ability. Boys are performing better than girls on tasks of reading comprehension, yet girls demonstrate superior reading accuracy. In the normal population, the incidence of specific learning difficulties in reading is higher in boys than it is in girls (Rutter and Yule[10]). This would suggest that the children in the present study are reflecting a similar pattern of reading accuracy skills to the normal population. Children with poor word recognition and decoding skills are likely to develop compensatory strategies for reading the written word (Stanovich[11]). These strategies may include techniques such as paying particular attention to the meaning of the text and making use of other cues such as the picture. The data may be reflecting successful application of these compensatory strategies by boys.

However, despite this similarity to the normal population, other aspects of the analysis suggest that these children are quite different from the norm. A striking feature is the result that age is correlated with neither reading accuracy nor reading comprehension. This is contrary to expectation. As children get older their reading becomes more accurate and they show greater maturity in their comprehension abilities. However, within this group of children there is no such relationship.

The preliminary profile of the abilities of these children has served two functions. Primarily it has provided evidence that a relationship does exist between communication skill and reading ability which provides a firm grounding for the intervention work to follow. The aim is that children will learn to use effective communication and will be encouraged to regulate and monitor their learning behaviours. According to Brown et al [2] this type of support will have ramifications for children's learning skills throughout the school environment. Secondly, the analysis has illustrated that this is a group of children presenting a wide range of difficulties and an unusual pattern of behaviours. This may have something to do with the criteria for admission to the special schools. Although the schools officially cater for children with general learning disability, in reality the schools provide for children with a wide range of difficulties including specific learning difficulties, behaviour problems and severe learning difficulties. This may account for the rather unusual pattern of relationships portrayed in the data. Future work must be aware of these interesting quirks and take into account the heterogeneous nature of the population.

References

1. Brown, G., Anderson, A. Shillcock, R. & Yule, G. *Teaching Talk*, Cambridge University Press, Cambridge, 1984.

2. Brown, A.L. & Palinscar, A.S. Guided co-operative learning and individual knowledge acquisition, *Knowing, Learning and Instruction; Essays in Honour of Robert Glaser*, ed L.B.Resnick, pp 393-451, Hillsdale, NJ, Lawrence Erlbaum Associates, Inc., 1989.

3. Brown, A.L. & Campione, J.C. Communities of learning and thinking, or a context by any other name, *Developmental Perspectives on Teaching and Learning Thinking Skills. Contributions to Human Development*, ed D.Kuhn, vol. 21 pp 108-126, Basel, Karger, 1990.

4. Vincent, D. & de la Mare, M. *New Reading Analysis*, Macmillan Education Ltd, Basingstoke, 1985.

5. Vincent, D. & de la Mare, M. *Individual Reading Analysis*, Macmillan Education Ltd, Basingstoke, 1985.

6. Schools Council Publications *Concept Seven-Nine; Unit 3 Communication*, Leeds, E.J.Arnold, 1972.

7. Wechsler, D. *Manual for the Wechsler Intelligence Scale for Children-Revised*, New York, Psychological Corporation, 1974.

8. Lamb, S.J.,Wood, D. & Leyden, G. Children with learning difficulties: a profile of abilities and implications for intervention, *in preparation*.

9. Williams, P., Davies, P., Evans, R, & Ferguson, N. Season of birth and cognitive development, *Nature*, 1970, **228**, 1033-1036.

10. Rutter, M. & Yule, W. The concept of specific reading retardation, *Journal of Child Psychology and Psychiatry*, 1975, **16**, 181-197.

11. Stanovich, K.E. Matthew effects in reading: some consequences of individual differences in the acquisition of literacy, *Reading Research Quarterly*, 1986, **21**, 360-407.

Temporal effects of cooperative contact on children's attitudes toward disability

P. Maras

Centre for Group Processes, Department of Psychology, University of Kent, Canterbury CT2 7LZ, UK

Abstract

A quasi-experimental study was conducted that looked at temporal effects of contact on non-disabled (ND) children's attitudes to disability. They were involved in an integrated programme with schoolchildren with severe learning disabilities (SLD). The ND children's social orientations to disabled peers changed over time and implications for collaborative working are discussed.

Introduction

In recent years there have been moves aimed at the educational integration of children with disabilities (DES [1]). There is growing debate about the appropriateness of integration for all (Hornby [2]). It has been reported that attitudes towards disabled people are frequently negatively biased (Wright [3]) and research reflects a general consensus that lack of contact can result in negative attitudes to, and unrealistic perceptions of disability (eg. Brinker & Thorpe [4]; Esposito & Reed [5]). Some studies have focused on processes underpinning attitudes arising out of integrated contact (Fortini [6]; Hazzard [7]; Lewis & Lewis [8]). Lewis and Lewis utilise the intergroup perspective of Allport [9] who suggests that the effects of contact are enhanced by institutional support, common goals and the perception of communality between groups. This view has come to be held by an increasing number of others (eg. Cook [10]; Pettigrew [11]). Recently, two contrasting models of intergroup contact have emerged which offer very different strategies for optimising the effects of contact (Hewstone & Brown [12]; Brewer & Miller [13]). Brewer and Miller see the breaking down of group or category boundaries as essential to personalization and reduction of categorical biases. Hewstone and Brown propose that maintaining group boundaries can be beneficial for aiding positive generalization beyond the contact situation. Early work on attitudes to disability showed trends toward contact improving attitudes (eg. Chesler [14]). More recently researchers have begun to pay attention to how the contact experience should be structured (eg. Acton & Zarbatany [15]; Donaldson [16]; Voeltz [17]), and the efficacy of cooperative learning (Armstrong, Johnson & Balow [18]; Johnson & Johnson [19]); Bryan, Donahue & Pearl [20]; Foot, Morgan & Shute [21]).

Research reported here examined ND children's attitudes over a period of time when children with SLD were integrated into their mainstream school. A main aim of the research was the measurement over time of changes in children's attitudes to SLD as a function of structured, collaborative contact. The principal hypothesis was that participating children would show more positive attitudes towards their disabled peers than those not participating.

Design 2 x (3): Participation (Experimental *vs* Control) & Time (t1 *vs* t2 *vs* t3).

Method

Participants
28 girls, 22 boys (mean age 8.8). Experimental group (26), Control group (24).

Procedure

The integration programme 20 SLD children participated. Sessions took place one afternoon a week and ND children were given information about SLD.

Stimuli Photographs (SS) of ND, physically disabled (PD), learning disabled (LD) and hearing impaired (HI) children were utilized, all were unknown.

Measures & Tasks: To explore how the children organized their perceptions of DIS they sorted the SS into piles (categorisation). They then used five different sized balloons to assess amounts of physical and psychological attributes (stereotypes) of pairs of SS (evaluation measure). Finally, the children used a five postboxes measure to indicate how much they would like to play with SS 'always' 'alot', 'sometimes', 'not much' 'never' (sociometric preference).

Results

Categorization
Multi-dimensional scaling was applied. Data from t1 & t3 are presented, distance between plots shows mow much children categorized SS as similar (figure 1).

Experimental group At t1 SS were sorted on gender and DIS dimensions. At t3 DIS remained salient but more differentiated whilst gender became less salient.

Control group At t1 Control children sorted on two dimensions - gender and disability. In contrast to the Experimental group this remained the same at t3.

Key
F female; M male; (HI) hearing impaired
(LD) learning disabled; (PD) physically disabled

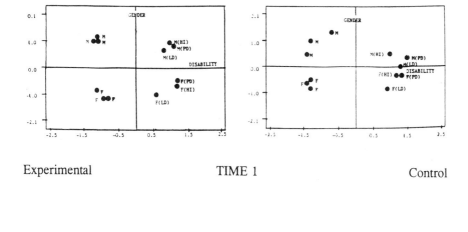

Experimental   TIME 1   Control

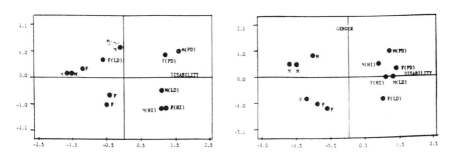

Experimental   TIME 3   Control

Figure 1: MDS plots of sorting standard stimuli at times 1 & 3

The evaluative measures: running, hearing & thinking
There was a highly significant main effect of stimulus photographs evaluated with
ND being rated more favourably than DIS. Of most interest, are interactions
involving Contact, particularly Contact x Time x SS, these show differential
changes in attitude to particular stimulus groups over time (figure 2).

Running There were two-way [Contact x Stimulus ($F(3,129)=3.24$; $p < .05$)]
and a three-way interactions involving Contact [Contact x Stimuli x Time
($F(6,222)=3.8$; $p < .01$)].   There was virtually no difference at t1 in
Experimental and Control groups. Ratings of Experimental group show a marked
rise at t2 and are significantly higher for DIS at t3. Positive effects in LD and
reflected in HI are indicative of a reduction in stereotypes of both HI and LD.

Hearing There are interactions [Contact x Stimulus ($F(3,129)=2.76$; $p < .05$); Contact x Stimuli x Time ($F(6,222)=2.89$; $p < .05$)] and again, there is little difference between the groups at t1. Ratings in the Experimental group become greater over time for LD and PD whilst the Control group show little difference over time. In this instance contact seems to be changing stereotypes about LD and PD children's hearing, whilst retaining a realistic picture of the HI children.

Thinking A Contact x Time interaction was identified [$F(6,56)=6.56$; $p < .01$)]. Experimental children rate DIS significantly lower than those in the Control group at t1, but higher at t2. At t3 there is little difference in the groups ratings of HI and LD, though children in the Experimental group rate PD higher.

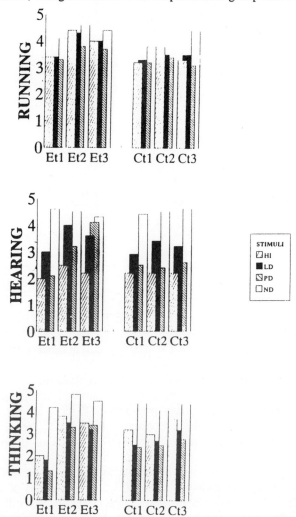

Figure 2: Experimental (E) & Control (C) groups evaluations at times 1, 2 & 3

Sociometric preference In line with past research there was a significant interaction between sex of participating child and gender of stimuli [$F(2,35)=72.03$; $p < .001$] which was revealed in a consistent and strong same sex preference. More relevant are the interactions involving Contact, Stimuli and Time [$F(6,222)=9.11$; $p < .001$]. Contact as a whole had a main effect (3.2 *vs* 3.9), this was qualified by Time and type of stimulus.

Discussion

The study has interesting implications for both Hewstone/Brown and Miller/Brewer's models. Categorization is fundamental to both. For the former it is an essential precursor to generalized positive attitude change; for the latter it is only when categorization is eliminated that positive outcomes occur. At the start of the programme both Experimental and Control groups categorized on the same dimensions. After only three months of structured, collaborative and planned contact the Experimental group had ceased to use gender but continued to use disability, though in a more differentiated way, whilst Control children persisted in using the categories of gender and disability. There were also highly significant changes in the Experimental group's evaluations of running, hearing and thinking over time. On the first two ratings of LD and PD children were significantly higher at t2 and t3. Findings on the measure thinking were slightly less clear, perhaps reflecting the abstract nature of the concept being rated. Also, the Experimental group knew that they would be involved in the programme and expressed uncertainty about participation. This may be reflected in the low ratings of thinking at t1. The increase in ratings over time is a particularly hopeful finding as a number of the SLD children were in wheelchairs and had PD as well as LD. This increase was reflected in the sociometric data and bode well for integrated contact - the evaluative measures were abstract constructs, playing is one of the most salient activities for children. The quasi-experiment lends support for integration when contact is organized in a planned and structured way. Findings have important implications. Numbers of children in the programme were small, children and teachers were prepared and supported, the collaborative work was carefully planned and implemented, and there is a strong ethos of support for integration in the schools. These are all factors identified as important for successful contact (Allport [9]). In conclusion, anecdotal evidence suggests that mainstream teachers and children had very mixed feelings about participating in future integrated projects. Findings suggest that future research should focus on both preparing mainstream children and teachers for integration and on the effects of attitudes on children with disabilities integrated into mainstream schools.

References

1. DES (1981) *The Education Act* London, HMSO.
2. Hornby, G. (1992) Integration of children with special educational needs: Is it time for a policy review? *Support for learning, 7,3*, 130-4.

3.   Wright, B. (1988) Attitudes & the fundamental negative bias: Conditions & corrections In H. Yuker (*ed*) *Attitudes toward persons with disabilities* Springer.

4.   Brinker, R. & Thorpe, M. (1984) Integration of severely handicapped students & the proportion of IEP objectives achieved. *Exceptional children, 51,* 168-175.

5.   Esposito, B. & Reed, T. (1986) The effects of contact with handicapped persons on young children's attitudes. *Exceptional Children, 33, 3,* 224-229.

6.   Fortini, M. (1987) Attitudes & behaviour toward students with handicaps by their nonhandicapped peers. *American Journal of Mental Deficiency, 92,1,* 78-84.

7.   Hazzard, A. (1983) Children's experience with, knowledge of & attitudes towards disabled peers. *Journal of Special Education, 17, 2,* 131-9.

8.   Lewis, A. & Lewis, V. (1988) Young children's attitudes after a period of integration, towards peers with severe learning difficulties. *European Journal of Special Needs Education, 3, 3,* 161-72.

9.   Allport, G. (1954) *The Nature of Prejudice* MA: Addison-Wesley.

10.   Cook, S. (1978) Interpersonal & attitudinal outcomes in cooperating interracial groups. *Journal of Research & Development in Education, 12,* 97-113.

11.   Pettigrew, T. (1971) *Racially separate or together?* New York: McGraw.

12.   Hewstone, M. & Brown, R. (1986) Contact is not Enough: An Intergroup Perspective on the Contact Hypothesis. In M. Hewstone & R. Brown (*eds*) *Contact & conflict in intergroup encounters* Oxford: Blackwell.

13.   Brewer, M. & Miller, N. (1984) Beyond the contact hypothesis In Miller & Brewer *Groups in contact: The psychology of desegregation.* Academic Press.

14.   Chesler, M. (1965) Ethnocentrism & attitudes toward the physically disabled. *Journal of Personality & Social Psychology, 2, 6,* 877-82.

15.   Acton, H. & Zarbatany, L. (1988) Interaction & performance in cooperative groups: effects on nonhandicapped students' attitudes toward their mildly mentally retarded peers. *American Journal of Mental Retardation, 95* 16-23.

16.   Donaldson, J. (1980) Changing Attitudes Toward Handicapped Persons: A review & analysis of research. *Exceptional Children, 46, 7,* 504-14.

17.   Voeltz, L. (1984) Effects of structured interactions with severely handicapped peers on children's attitudes. *American Journal of Mental Deficiency, 86,* 380-90

18.   Armstrong, B., Johnson, D. & Balow, B. (1981) Effects of Cooperative vs Individualistic Learning Experiences on Interpersonal Attraction between Learning-Disabled & Normal-Progress Elementary School Students *Contemporary Educational Psychology 6,*102-9.

19.   Johnson, D. W. & Johnson, R. T. (1981)   The Integration of the handicapped into the regular classroom: Effects of cooperative & individualistic instruction. *Contemporary Educational Psychology 6,* 344-53.

20.   Bryan, T., Donahue, M. & Pearl, R. (1981) Learning disabled children's peer interactions during a small-group problem solving task. *Learning Disability Quarterly, 4,* 13-22.

21.   Foot, H., Morgan, J. & Shute, R. (1990) (*eds*) *Children Helping Children* Chichester: John Wiley & Sons

Do pairs of people cross cue each other so as to generate new information and produce more accurate memories?

P.R. Meudell

Department of Psychology, University of Manchester, Manchester M13 9PL, UK

Abstract

This paper addresses the issue of whether two collaborating people can generate new information not accessible to either member of the pair. In order to investigate the issue, people were tested on a public event questionnaire tapping their memories for *when* the events took place. All subjects made an initial recall attempt and then some were tested again on their own whilst others were tested as collaborating pairs. Since it was known what events people could date on their own, the emergence of new memories in pairs could be ascertained: concordant with previous work, the results showed no new memories emerged. However, since assigning the date to an event is a graded response, it was also investigated whether pairs of people got *closer* in time to when the events took place compared to individuals. The results showed that there was a tendency for this to occur: on second recall collaborating pairs had a smaller error in dating their inaccurate memories than did individual controls.

Introduction

The experimental psychology of memory has concentrated almost exclusively upon the individual learning and remembering in isolation yet collaboration in recall is a relatively frequent occurrence. Following Bartlett [1] and more recently the work of Stephenson [e.g. 2] we have begun to investigate the nature of the cognitive and possible social processes that might operate when two people collectively try and remember a mutually experienced event.

Meudell, Hitch and Kirby [3] set themselves two questions. First, did pairs of people recall more than a single individual and second, did pairs of people generate new information not available to either member of the pair. They reported 4 experiments which all used the same sequential paradigm where every subject recalled on their own initially: some were then retested for their recall (of the same material) on their own once more whilst others were formed into pairs and recalled collaboratively. This design enabled the identification of what individuals could recall on their own and, thus, what *new* information emerged in pairs. If the amount of new information in pairs was greater than that shown in retested individuals (called reminiscence controls) it was argued the facilitatory effects of social interaction on memory would have been demonstrated. In fact, although pairs always recalled more than a single person, in *none* of the 4 experiments did this effect materialise: Meudell et al.[3] concluded social interaction did not facilitate memory through the generation of new information.

One problem with the Meudell et al.[3] study was that the measures of memory used all involved an all or none response - people could either recall an item or they could not [4]. Perhaps the great benefit of social interaction in memory might come not from the production of new items in a quite discrete way but, if a graded response were available, somehow for collaborating pairs being able to get a more accurate memory than could any individual.

It is the purpose of this report to investigate memory for the time at which events took place. Since dating events allows a more or less continuous response, use of our sequential design allowed both the evaluation of whether new dates appeared in pairs and also whether pairs got *closer* to the actual date than did individuals.

Method

Subjects
Forty eight undergraduate students from the University of Manchester took part in the study and their ages ranged from 18 - 40 years. Sixteen subjects were randomly assigned as reminiscence controls and these individuals recalled on their own on both occasions: 32 people, randomly determined, recalled on their own initially and then were assigned as collaborating pairs for their second test (16 pairs in all).

Materials
A 20 item questionnaire was devised that sampled current affairs from the period 1982 to 1992: the subjects' task was to assign the year that the event took place. Pilot studies generated the 20 "dating" questions such that the mean score was about 6 items (thus allowing for improvement without ceiling effects in pairs), with no questions always being answered correctly by all pilot

subjects and none which no subject could answer.

Design and Procedure
All 48 subjects were first tested individually. They were asked to complete the 20 item questionnaire on their own and to provide an answer to all questions guessing if necessary. After completion of the questionnaire, all subjects were then given the Minnesota Paper Form Board test as a "filler" task. After 15 minutes, subjects were asked to stop working on this task. Sixteen subjects then completed the events questionnaire once again on their own (reminiscence controls) whilst 16 pairs of subjects collaborated over the questionnaire to produce one agreed set of dates for each of the 20 questions. The pairs were tested in separate rooms. Neither reminiscence controls or pairs knew in advance about the second test and pairs were told to talk over their memories for each tested event to try and achieve an agreed date. No time limit was set either for controls or for pairs.

Scoring
The number of correct dating responses was found for first and second recalls. On second recall the number of *new* correct dates was obtained (new dates being responses that were incorrect for on first recall for but correct on second: for pairs this required both partners to be incorrect on first recall). On both recalls, the mean overall error (in years) in dating events was also found as was the mean year error in dates that were given incorrectly.

Results and Discussion

The number of correct responses on *first* recall for reminiscence controls and those who subsequently formed pairs was 6.2 and 6.4 respectively. These two means did not differ significantly, $t(46)=0.30$. Across all questions, the mean total error in years was 2.1 for controls and 2.2 for pairs and these two means did not differ, $t(46)=1.0$. Reminiscence controls and pairs were thus matched on initial levels of recall and on levels of dating error.

On second recall, the pairs of subjects recalled the dates of 9.4 events correctly whilst reminiscence controls identified 5.9: these two means differed significantly, $t(30)=4.1$, $p<0.001$. People recalling in pairs therefore knew the dates of more events than did a single person. Is this higher score for pairs merely due to the pooling of their separate memories or does it include additional new dates not available to either member of the pair when recalling in isolation?

The mean number of new dates identified on second recall was 1.9 for pairs recalling jointly and 1.5 for reminiscence controls: these two means were not significantly different, $t(30)=0.8$. Relative to individual controls therefore, pairs did not generate new information on second test. In the absence of additional new information by pairs, their overall performance advantage must relate simply to the independent pooling of their separate memories: the social interaction appears not to be facilitative of emergent memories. This result, of course, parallels those reported earlier by Meudell et al.[3] where all or none measures using a variety of stimulus materials also failed to demonstrate additional new information in pairs.

Do pairs of people get nearer to the correct date even if they do not produce more correct answers? The mean error in (years) on second recall was 0.9 years for pairs whilst that for reminiscence controls was 1.5 years. A *t* test on these data showed that these two means were significantly different, t(30)=2.7, P<0.02. This might suggest that pairs do indeed get closer to the actual date than individuals. However, on second test, pairs also get more items correct overall than do individuals and so it might not be surprising that pairs overall error score is lower - they have more zero errors as a result of the higher number of correct responses. A more appropriate measure is therefore the mean year error on second test for *incorrect* dates. That is, both people may be *wrong* about the dating of a particular event but, because of cross cuing, the pair might be able to get closer to the correct time than could individuals. The mean error score for pairs and reminiscence controls on second recall for incorrect dates across the sampled periods is shown in Table 1.

	| Year Event Took Place:				
	'82/3	'84/5	'86/7	'88/9	90/91/92
Pairs	1.5	2.1	1.7	1.1	0.8
Inds.	2.2	2.3	1.9	1.5	1.5

Table 1. Mean error in assigning dates when date is incorrect for pairs and for individuals (Inds.) on second test.

A 2 x 5 (2 subject groups by 5 time periods) analysis of variance was carried out on these data. There was a borderline effect of groups, F(1,30)=3.71, p<0.10>0.05 such that there was a tendency for pairs to make less error on their incorrect responses than did reminiscence controls. There was a significant difference between the accuracy of dating across the sampled time periods F(4,120)=12.2, p<0.001 and the linear component of this analysis was highly significant, F(1,120)=55.4, p<0.001, suggesting that that on the whole subjects found it easier to date more recent than more distant events: however, there was no group by time period interaction F(4,120)=1.2, so the pattern of error across time periods was the same for both pairs and reminiscence controls.

As they stand therefore these results give little substantial support for the notion that, even if they do not gain new items of information *per se*, pairs can generate more accurate memories than do individuals.

However, the issue of whether pairs get closer to the actual date through collaboration can also be attacked from a slightly different perspective by a consideration of how pairs might actually set about collaborating to produce their incorrect dating responses. One simple (and non-facilitatory) activity that they might engage in could be a simple *averaging* of their separate responses. We can directly investigate this from the data by the following means. On those occasions when a pair were wrong about the date of a particular event on second recall, we could look back to the *initial* (and separate) dating responses for each member of the pair. From these two first recalls we can thus predict, on the basis of a putative simple averaging procedure, what date the pair *should* produce on their second test. If, at the end of their discussion, they just took the mean of their initial responses, the actual error in dating a memory in a pair should not be significantly different from this predicted value. On the other hand, if pairs do more than simply average their first responses so as to get closer to the real date than either member alone could achieve, then their actual joint performance should show less error than their predicted error. For reminiscence controls, the predicted error for second dating attempts is simply the magnitude of the error that they made to the test question on first the trial.

	Individuals	Pairs
Actual Error	1.9	1.4
Predicted Error	1.7	2.7

Table 2. Mean absolute actual error in years for incorrect responses on second test and predicted absolute error (both pooled over time periods) for pairs and reminiscence controls.

A 3 way analysis of variance (2 groups x 5 time periods x actual vs predicted error) was carried out on these data. No effects were significant although the interaction of actual vs predicted error by pairs vs individuals bordered on significance, $F(1,30) = 3.98$, $p<.10>0.05$. Table 2 shows the relevant data. There is thus some suggestion that whilst pairs' predicted performance overestimates their actual error, the opposite is true for individuals.

In summary, there is no suggestion whatsoever that pairs generate new correct dates and so there is no evidence at all for social interaction facilitating memory through the emergence of novel *items* of information [5]. The intuition that many share that pairs do produce new information might arise from a mis-attribution effect. Thus, if Person A recalls a,b,c,d about an event and person B recalls a,b,x,y,z then A leaves the interaction with the "new" information x,y,z and B leaves with the "new" information c,d. However, the information is new to each person as an individual but not to the pair and there are no emergent memories.

Tantalisingly, pairs do show a tendency to get *closer* to the actual date than do individuals and pairs also show a trend to perform better than that predicted on the basis of the partners merely averaging their individual knowledge. If it is indeed true that pairs can get closer to a more accurate memory, its basis remains unknown as does the answer to the question as to whether the process is unique to the temporal context measure of memory employed in this experiment: accordingly, we plan to follow up this study using graded responses of "content" memories.

References

1. Bartlett, F. C. *Remembering*, Cambridge University Press,   Cambridge, 1932.

2. Stephenson, G. M., Brandstätter, H. & Wagner, W. An experimental study of social performance and delay on the testimonial validity of story recall, *European Journal of Social Psychology*, 1983, *13,* 175-191.

3. Meudell, P. R., Hitch, G. J., & Kirby, P. Are two heads better than one? Experimental investigations of the social facilitation of memory, *Applied Cognitive Psychology*, 1992, *6,* 525-543.

4. Meudell, P.R. Remembering in a social context: experimental methods for the evaluation of collaborative recall, *Psychological Research: Innovative Methods and Strategies*, ed J.H. Haworth, Routledge, London, In Press.

5. Meudell, P.R., Hitch, G.J. & Boyle, M.M. Collaboration in recall: do pairs of people cross cue each other to produce new memories? *Quarterly Journal of Experimental Psychology*, In Press.

The learning cascade - Strategies for stimulating cross-phase peer education

J. Potter

CSV Education, Community Service Volunteers, 237 Pentonville Road, London N1 9NJ, UK

Abstract

"Each one teach one" is the theme for CSV's approach to peer education. In this paper a strategy is set out to cascade peer education from adults and university students into schools, and from school students and pupils to younger pupils both within and between schools. *CSV Education* has developed a number of nationwide pilot projects to promote this strategy and is evolving systems of evaluation. The paper ends with an invitation to academics to identify further areas in which research might prove beneficial to both practitioners and supporters.

1. Introduction

My contribution to this conference is as a practitioner rather than a researcher. As Manager of CSV Education, my task is to create opportunities for young people in education to learn to be effective citizens through community service that responds to real needs. The work covers activity from the infant classroom to the university campus and appropriate challenges are set at each stage.

CSV has shown that learning through community service is a powerful tool that strengthens the whole and taught curriculum. The majority of students learn best through practical activity that (a) meets real needs and (b) offers an opportunity for reflection and the acquisition of knowledge and skill. Many schools have used the cross curricular elements, particularly of Citizenship education, as the context for this learning. Research in the United States has demonstrated the cognitive and affective gains that flow from service learning.

Peer education has become a key element in our work in universities, colleges and schools. Our experience is that this approach raises standards, develops skills and increases motivation and maturity among tutors and tutees alike.

2. The Cascade

Dr Alec Dickson, founder of both VSO and CSV, has given us the simple slogan 'Each One Teach One'. For many years he has been an exponent of peer education and, in particular, of what is now usually called student tutoring. He points out that 'in the United States literally millions of college students have helped in tutoring programmes in local schools.

'Early on it was recognised that the multiplication factor was of enormous importance. That is that those who have been tutored should in turn help others, younger or less advantaged than themselves. The programme took on the dimension of a *cascade*, with a ripple effect all the way down the age ranges. In Mineapolis earlier this year (1993) I watched a 12 year old tutor a 7 year old. "I knew I mattered when they called me "Mr", exclaimed the 12 year old. When the programme ended and the older child said that they wouldn't be meeting again, the 7 year old flung his arms around the neck of his tutor and cried, "But you're my special friend." That scene might have been repeated in every school in America - and why not in Britain too?"[1] It is our aim at CSV to realise Alec Dickson's vision through our Education programme.

3. An Effective Strategy

An effective strategy requires three things[2]
1.   there has to be a clearly perceived need
2.   there have to be people who are ready to do something about it
3.   there have to be the resources to take action

CSV's approach to cascading peer education has taken account of each of these factors.

A widely perceived need: The debates over education in recent years have focused on four needs: (1) The need to ensure that more young people stay in education after the age of 16; (2) The need to ensure that more support is put into all education and in particular into teaching maths, science and languages; (3) The need to ensure that we educate for capability as well as for knowledge and analytic skills; (4) The need to foster the motivation as well as the ability of students and pupils

Peer education makes a significant contribution to all these widely perceived needs. The value of evaluation and research is to demonstrate how these needs are most effectively met by this approach.

People ready to do something about it: Over the past five years there have been increasing numbers of educators and other stakeholders who have not only seen the need but been ready to do something about it. Student tutoring, whereby university and colleges students, spend an afternoon a week assisting school pupils with their studies under the supervision of teachers, admirably illustrates this sea-change in attitudes.

Student tutoring had taken off in the United States in the 1960s, but it was not until 1975 that the first British scheme was launched from Imperial College by Dr Sinclair Goodlad as a course project for twelve engineering students. The Pimlico Connection was born. By 1989 there were five tutoring schemes in the UK. In the following year BP in partnership with Imperial College appointed John Hughes as the BP Fellow in Student Tutoring and began a major piece of development work nationwide.

In parallel with this development, CSV renewed its interest in tutoring and, in partnership with BP and four other major companies, established a nationwide tutoring programme, *CSV Learning Together..* Since then the growth of scheme has been phenomenal. There are now over 5000 students involved in regular tutoring working from over 160 universities and colleges throughout the country. In Scotland and Wales there are national schemes co-ordinated by BP; in England and Northern Ireland *CSV Learning Together* is now the lead organisation, following the move of John Hughes to manage the *BP International Student Tutoring and Mentoring Project.*

Resources to Take Action: The generation of financial and other resources to promote student tutoring has been central to *CSV Learning Together.* The then Lord Mayor of London, Sir Brian Jenkins, made *CSV Learning Together* the focus of his Appeal.   CSV, with the active support of BP, sought four additional Principal Partners from among major companies with a commitment to education. British Telecom, National Power, NatWest Bank and Royal Mail each responded warmly and very positively to the invitation to join that small, but crucial group of key players who would together set the pace for other sponsors. Each partner contributed a minimum of £200,000 to the work. In addition to the core contributions from the Principal Partners the Appeal received contributions from over four hundred individuals and institutions.

Dinners, receptions and launches were held throughout the country to ensure that student tutoring had the active support of universities, schools, business partners and agencies such as Training and Enterprise Councils and Education Business Partnerships.

Resources have been found for CSV Learning Together to support 11 new student tutoring co-ordinators in key regions in addition to providing start-up grants to a number of other institutions.

The first lesson from our partnerships is that much more can be achieved through co-operation than can ever be achieved by an individual agency on its own.

The second lesson from our partnerships stems from the fact that each partner has specific interests and needs, and it is vital that its contribution reflects those interests. For example, BP see its *Aiming for a College Education* initiative as a part of its broad international strategy of community involvement. Royal Mail and National Power in addition to regional interests are, as a part of their company's restructuring, keen to offer their employees a chance to gain fresh experience by working with education through the Voluntary Sector. We have had two National Power employees and, since the programme started, eight Royal Mail employees seconded to the *CSV Learning Together* programme. We are also working with the Birmingham Education Business Partnership. NatWest has provided a secondee to manage a special programme on Financial Literacy. British Telecom has a powerful commitment to education and has joined us as a Principal Partner with a commitment to both funding projects and resourcing further research on issues that have to date had relatively little attention in the UK.

4. The Benefits of Student Tutoring

An effective strategy is built on the mutual benefit of all concerned. Everyone gains from student tutoring. In my workshop I will give further details of the evaluation programmes that support tutoring. The papers from my colleagues on student tutoring will also report on the evaluated benefits of the initiatives. What follows is a brief summary of the general findings.

There is no question that schools benefit from student tutoring Teachers report regularly that they find:

❏ Lessons more enjoyable
❏ Lessons easier to handle
❏ More learning activities are made possible
❏ More opportunities for oral and practical work
❏ Free classroom assistance
❏ More efficient learning.
❏ The chance to learn more about FE/HE students and courses.

The pupils benefit in many ways. They:

❏ receive more individual attention
❏ find lessons more fun and interesting
❏ learn more than usual
❏ enjoy sympathetic help from another young person
❏ increase their aspiration to further training and education
❏ meet with positive role models

The students also gain from the experience of tutoring. They have reported the following benefits:

❏ The feeling that they are doing something useful
❏ Enhanced problem-solving and organisational skills
❏ Reinforcement of their grasp of their subject
❏ Reflection on their subject
❏ Enhanced sense of personal adequacy
❏ Experience of being productive
❏ Insight into the teaching/learning process
❏ Meaningful use of their studies
❏ Increase in self-confidence
❏ Valuable community service
❏ Enjoyment!

The universities and schools have also reported benefits from the scheme.

5. Evaluation and Research

A basic evaluation programme was laid down by the original Pimlico programme which is till followed by CSV Learning Together. Details of this will be available at the workshop. CSV has undertaken further research with support from BT. It will address two questions: *What objective evidence (as opposed to subjective reports from participants) is there that student tutoring*
- ❏ *raises pupils aspirations?*
- ❏ *improves student tutors performance in their own subjects or in other ways?*

Dr Keith Topping will address this issue in his seminar earlier in the day from the point of view of the national survey commissioned by CSV/BT. I shall report in my workshop on further work undertaken by Birmingham University, London University and Cambridge University.

Evaluation must also be looked at from the point of view of quality management of the tutoring process. I shall explore this matter briefly in the workshop and will draw on work done by Strathclyde Education Authority.

6. Embedding and Ownership

The success of a tutoring initiative depends ultimately on two things: (1) the benefits derived from the work and (2) the extent to which local partners in the initiative accept continuing responsibility for the scheme. HE institutions have formally to recognise the value that tutors gain from their work. In many cases tutoring is becoming an accredited option within course work. Schools need to accept responsibility for developing tutoring as an educational strategy for the work of the school as a whole. Agencies such as TECs and EBPs need to recognise and support local and regional initiatives. It is CSV's aim to ensure that tutoring becomes a valued and normal part of educational provision.

7. Cascading Peer Education

CSV's strategy is to cascade tutoring through the *CSV Learning Together* initiative. Schools that value their student tutors are encouraged to enable their own students to tutor others. They are also encouraged to use other adults as tutors and mentors in a strategic rather than ad hoc fashion. CSV has pioneered a further strategy for involving significant numbers of adult volunteers in primary schools under the leadership of an Honorary Coordinator. The initiative is being promoted nationwide under the title, *No Limit*.[3] Employees, retired people and local volunteers are involved in addition to student tutors.

CSV has pioneered three further pilot projects: (1) a cross-phase initiative from a girls' comprehensive into a local primary school. The project involved 49 year 11 girls in regular tutoring support with their primary school partners. The both parties gained greatly from the experience and the benefits of student tutoring were replicated. (2) A Lunchtime Link project at three London Comprehensive schools whereby Sixth formers have helped recently-arrived refugee pupils with their English one lunch-time a week. Training was jointly organised by the CSV project co-ordinator and by the Islington Home Tutors scheme. (3) CSV's final peer education programme is a nationwide cross-phase peer education initiative on the prevention of HIV/AIDS, *PeerAid* .

8. *PeerAID*

In the summer of 1992 CSV in partnership with the *Ibis Trust* set up a three -year nationwide project to work with young people in school to prevent the spread of HIV/AIDS. The project was inspired by pioneering work at the Luton Sixth Form College. Young people are given basic training so that they themselves can become the educators among their peers. Older students work either with their same age group or with younger students. In some cases students work with groups *in schools other than their own*. The details of the approach vary, but the central message is the same: *Young people take responsibility for developing a health project with and for their peers.*

CSV/Ibis has developed the scheme in seven centres nationwide. In each centre the students themelves will equip the next generation of students to become peer educators.

All the projects will be evaluated at different levels, incorporating some monitoring designed by the young people themselves - pupils in Matlock have already started to devise a method of assessing the number of people they are reaching through *PeerAID*. Evaluation will look at the process as well as the outcomes, to include:

- ❑ assessment from individual audiences for peer-led sessions and activities
- ❑ extended interviews with parents, and with staff and students who are directly involved
- ❑ assessment of peer educators in terms of knowledge, communication and skills development
- ❑ overall evaluation and comparisons of project centres on results and effectiveness
- ❑ observation and comment on the number, range and scope of activities undertaken.

Each individual project has been evaluated against the criteria for success identified by the school(s) concerned. In this way a range of prospective processes and outcomes have been addressed by the scheme as a whole. The evaluation strategy will be explored in greater depth at the seminar. The results of the evaluation will be available at the end of 1994, but the response to date has been very positve.

The aim is to disseminate a range of models of good practice through conferences and workshops and the work will lead to a resource pack to be produced in the year 1994-5 to support the nationwide dissemination of further projects. We plan to: (1) Seek funding to establish the national co-ordination and support of the initiative on a long-term basis. (2) Look at ways in which this particular approach to peer education can be taken up around other health and relational issues.

9. Further Research

At the seminar I shall: (1) update participants on recent CSV evaluation and research on both student tutoring and *PeerAID;* *(2)* raise some of the general questions prompted by attempts to evaluate the impact of cross-phase peer education; and (3) invite participants to explore further possibilities for relevant research and evaluation in the field of cross-phase peer education.

References

1 Dickson A, "A Future for Community Service?' (*Community Action,*Nov 93)

2 Fullan M (1991)   *The New Meaning of Educational Change* (Cassell Educational, London)

3. *No Limit: A Blueprint for Invovling Volunteers in Schools* (CSV/Esso 1994)

Working with groups on sensitive issues

M. Robson
School of Education, University of Durham, Leazes Road,
Durham DH1 1TA, UK

Introduction

The aim of this paper is to examine some of the ways that a facilitator may help a group of people work on sensitive issues. The nature of the sensitive issues are not discussed but could include anything which is felt to be difficult to work on within the group. They could include such things as helping people explore sexual abuse to helping people learn to use a computer. The emphasis of this paper is to examine methods of creating safety and investigating the balance between challenge and support.

Creating Safety

The work of such people as Bowlby has shown us how important it is for children to feel secure before they are able to venture out and explore the world. Bowlby (1988) regarded the provision of a secure base as a central feature of good parenting and argued that its provision was essential if children or adolescents were to be empowered to venture into the world. He likened it to the needs of a military officer:

> " For it is only when the officer commanding the expeditionary force is confident his base is secure that he dare press forward and take risks."

The same needs for safety are around when adults engage in new learning, either of new facts or new learnings about themselves.

Every invitation to learn is an invitation to take a risk. As McGuiness (1993) argues:

> "Every invitation to learn is an invitation to change; it is an invitation to leave the familiar, the mastered, the comfortable and the position of competence we have now, and move to a new place, where, for a time we feel unfamiliar, not in control, uncomfortable and incompetent"

It asks that we move from a place where we feel safe, comfortable and secure to become, voluntarily, incompetent and uncomfortable. We need to move from a position of safety through a period of uncertainty when we are de-skilled and vulnerable to position of safety. Hence it is important for the facilitator to create an environment in the group where it is safe to learn and to be 'voluntarily incompetent'. The safety of the environment is important **especially** in groups looking at sensitive issues.

If we, as facilitators, accept the need to create a safe environment, the next question is how. In this we need to consider both the physical setting of the room in which the group meets as well as the emotional climate.

Physical Setting
The physical setting can either threaten or sustain the population within. Thus care needs to be taken with the choice of location. Is the room too open to public view, or conversely, too separate from the rest of the institution? Is it warm and comfortable? Do the chairs move to give people the opportunity to decide an individual distance between themselves and their neighbours? Does the arrangement of the furniture allow people to hide (e.g. behind desks or tables) or leave them too exposed? The creation of a physically safe environment can be fundamental in the creation of an emotionally safe one.

Emotional Climate
The crucial nature of providing a nurturing emotional climate has been highlighted by Rogers (1973)

> " I have come to trust the capacity of persons to explore and understand themselves and their troubles, and to resolve those problems, in any close continuing

relationship where I can provide a climate of real warmth and understanding"

How can we do this? Perhaps the first step is to make the creation of safety overt. This can be done by finding out what the group needs and what the group can offer using a variety of means such as:-

    I) making connections in group by getting to know each other
    II) by opportunities being created to:-
        i) Identify own needs
        ii) Identify groups ability to support each other

Another element may be the modelling of the 'core' conditions by the facilitator. These 'core' conditions are ones identified by Rogers when he began to look closely at the conditions that facilitated client change. He published a paper describing the necessary and sufficient conditions for therapeutic personality change (Rogers, 1957), and he argued that these conditions are necessary in the creation of any safe environment.

In this paper he listed six conditions, three of which are generally known as the core conditions.

The first condition is that the facilitator be genuine or congruent. That is they should be honest, open and should not attempt to put on a facade. The second condition is that of unconditional positive regard. This is a prizing of the group members without condition or possessiveness. It is to recognise that each group member is a separate person with their own identity and experiences, which may be quite different from those of the facilitator. The final condition is known as empathy. This is the ability of the facilitator to completely understand the group member's world from the group member's point of view. The facilitator should try to understand the group member's feelings and the group member's mood and will convey this understanding by their verbal responses, their tone of voice and their non-verbal responses.

Another element in the creation of emotional safety is that of the facilitator taking responsibility for safety <u>and</u> sharing this with the group. Once the issue of safety has been made overt, the facilitator needs to stress to the group that s/he is not able to guarantee the safety, but that each member needs to bear responsibility both for their own safety and the safety of others. Discussions can arise about what is needed and how this can be provided and the group can enter into negotiations.

Challenge and Support

In order to enter into any new learning we need a balance between challenge and support. If the challenge is too great or the support insufficient, then learning is unlikely to take place. One explanation of why this occurs may be the need to retain self esteem. McGuiness (1989) argues:

> "..when our self-esteem is attacked our defence of it is virtually a reflex action. Such an attack has been compared to having one's supply of air cut off - the desperate battle to get air is paralleled psychologically by the ferocity and tenacity with which we defend our self esteem."

Snygg and Combs (1959) argue that:

> '...the single most important motivation of all human behaviour is the establishment, the maintenance and the enhancement of self esteem'

Self esteem, or how we value ourselves, is made up from two elements - self - image (the answer we have for "who am I") and our image of the ideal self (who is valued here?). All of us find ourselves in different environments and in each environment we experience the same process - 'Who am I?' (self-image) and 'What kind of person is highly valued here?' (ideal self). Self esteem is measured by the size of the gap between the match of the two concepts. The challenge in creating a safe learning environment is to attempt to provide an opportunity for a match between ideal self and self-image.

The challenge in creating a safe and supportive learning environment is to attempt to provide an opportunity for a match between ideal self and self-image. This may be achieved by such things as by trying to value each member of the group and by displaying the core conditions. A good match needs to be created between group members and kind of persons valued in the group.

Support versus challenge

Often, in order to learn from our experiences, we need to explore them and challenge them. To do this, we need an environment which focuses high support with high challenge. The illustration below has been adapted from Inskipp (1993) .

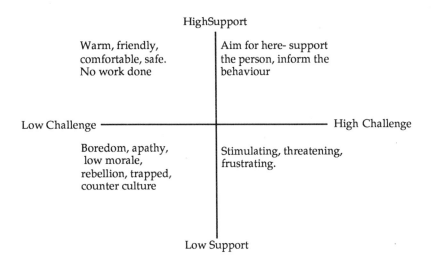

The balance of support and challenge may vary throughout the groups life and circumstances and there may be times when high support and low challenge is necessary in order to allow members a space to 're-energise'.

The balance can be achieved in several ways. It may be necessary for the facilitator to have the courage and expertise to recognise and accept and give permission for 'difficult issues' to be raised,   but within the safety of 'an appropriate level'. This level will depend upon the purpose of the group, the time it has together, and the resources of the group.

The facilitator also needs to create a 'container' for the group by such mechanisms as boundaries of group, in terms of time, content and framework for the day etc. The offering of choice and real options are also a necessary part of empowering a group in this context.

Also important is the offering of support <u>after</u> the session - not necessarily by the facilitator, but to:

i) acknowledge support may be needed.

ii) be very definite about where it can be sought e.g. Rape Crisis, CRUSE etc.

The facilitator also needs to be constantly aware of what's going on in the group and to individuals and offer lots of opportunities for people to say how they feel and what they need.

Conclusion

This paper has examined some of the broad issues which need to be considered when facilitating groups looking at sensitive issues. Although the focus is 'sensitive issues', it is hoped that the humanistic philosophy upon which this is based will be found to be relevant to all group facilitation. The tenet upon which this paper is based is that people, in McGuiness's (1993) words:

> "...will perform tasks more completely, will learn more effectively, when they perceive themselves as possessed of inviolable dignity and worthy of unconditional respect."

References

Bowlby, J. *A Secure Base* London, Routledge, 1988

Inskipp,F. *Counselling: the Trainer's Handbook*, National Extension College Trust Ltd., 1993.

McGuiness, J. *A Whole School Approach to Pastoral Care* London, Kogan Page, 1989.

McGuiness, J. The National Curriculum: the Manufacture of Pigs' Ears from Best Silk *British Journal of Guidance and Counselling*, 1993, Vol. 21, No. 1, January, pp 107-111.

Rogers, C.R. The Necessary and Sufficient Conditions of Therapeutic Personality Change, *Journal of Consulting Psychology*, Vol. 21, 1957.

Rogers, C.R. My Philosophy of Interpersonal Relationships, *Journal of Humanistic Psychology*, Spring 1973, Vol. 28, No. 5, pp3 - 15.

Snygg, A.W. & Combs, D. *Individual Behaviour.* New York: Harper Row, 1959.

An investigation of factors essential for visually impaired graduates seeking equitable employment

A.W.N. Roy[a] & G. Dimigen[b]

[a] *Further and Higher Education Service, Department of Education, Training and Employment, Royal National Institute for the Blind*
[b] *Department of Psychology, University of Glasgow, 56 Hillhead, Glasgow G11, UK*

Abstract

The present study investigated factors which affected the employment prospects of visually impaired graduates. It was found that students who had a combination of good technical skills, wide social network, structured career path, postgraduate studies and work experience were more likely to gain employment.

Introduction

According to the Royal National Institute for the Blind (RNIB), over the last decade the number of visually impaired students entering further and higher education has increased more than tenfold (Roy[7]). The reasons for the dramatic increase of visually impaired students are manifold. First of all, the number of all students has increased considerably over the last ten years. Secondly, career expectations of visually impaired school-leavers have changed. Five years ago Bush-LaFrance[2] reported that blind and partially sighted school leavers had significantly lower career aspirations than their sighted peers. However, a more recent British study (Dimigen et. al.[4]) found that this is no longer the case. Changes in the educational system have encouraged blind and partially sighted pupils to achieve higher academic qualifications and to have similar career aspirations as their sighted classmates. Thirdly, provision for disabled students in general, and for the visually impaired in particular, have improved with the introduction of the Further and Higher Education Act, 1992 (Dryden[5], Roy and Dimigen[8]). Visually impaired, full-time students can claim extra allowances to pay non-medical personal helpers and purchase technical equipment (Skill[9]). Fourthly, the technology for accessing course material has become more sophisticated and more widely available, i.e. portable tape-recorders, computers, scanners and closed circuit television. And lastly, as more visually impaired students enter further and higher education, they act as role models for other blind and partially sighted pupils and adults.

Graduated students also expect improved employment prospects compared to those offered to school-leavers. However, the employment opportunities in Great Britain for the visually impaired are still rather poor. According to the RNIB Needs Survey[1] only 25% of visually impaired people are in employment, 17% of blind and 31% of partially sighted people. When visually impaired people do gain employment, they are often under-employed , i.e. working part-time or below their qualifications. According to the same Needs Survey, university graduates do not fare much better. Visually impaired people are clearly underrepresented in the professional classes (14%) as compared to the general population (34%).

In general little is known about the employment prospects of visually impaired graduates. Thus the present study interviewed employed and unemployed visually impaired graduates to investigate whether the following factors affect employability: level of disability, qualifications and technical skills, career choice, social and career support, and communication skills.

Method

Subjects

A total of 34 subjects participated in the study. All subjects were visually impaired and had graduated from an institution of higher education. The subjects' demographic background, their education , level of impairment and length of unemployment are reported in Table 1. From Table 1 it can be seen that 16 of the subjects were in employment, 18 were unemployed. The length of unemployment since graduation varied from 5 years to zero. The age range was considerably wide, the oldest subject being 54 years of age, the youngest 22. More male than female graduates were interviewed. The majority of subjects were single. The level of visual impairment was assessed in two ways: (a) according to the official registration based on the medical diagnosis, (b) according to the functional level of the subjects' eye-sight , i.e. "totally blind" subjects, "P1 partially sighted" subjects (those who had some sight, but used predominantly non-sighted methods for studying or working), and "P2 partially sighted" subjects (those who, although visually impaired, used predominantly sighted methods for their work). The majority of graduates were registered blind but had some residual vision. Most of the subjects had been integrated pupils at a mainstream school for at least some time during their primary or secondary education. The majority of graduates had obtained Higher- or A-level grades. Half of the employed and a quarter of the unemployed graduates had done a postgraduate course.

Table 1: Demographic background of the subjects

Characteristic		Unempl.	Employed	Total
Number of subjects		18	16	34
Age (in years):	Mean	30.22	30.75	30.47
	Range	22-54	23-45	22-54
Gender:	Female	7	6	13
	Male	11	10	21
Marital status:	Single·	13	6	19
Married/ live-in partner		5	10	15
Registration:	Blind	14	14	28
Partially sighted		2	2	4
Unregistered/unknown		2	0	2
Vision level:	Totally blind	5	5	10
P1 partially sighted		4	5	9
P2 partially sighted		9	6	15
School type: Special school only		6	4	10
Integrated school only		10	9	9
Special & integrated school		2	3	5
Time of unemployment	Mean	18.5m	7.6m	13.41m
post graduation:	Range	4m-60m	0m-24m	0m-60m

m = month

Procedure

The graduates were recruited from RNIB's database. Most subjects were interviewed at home, a few at their place of work. Most of them lived in Strathclyde Region, in the Midlands, and in the London area. Interviewers used a semi-structured questionnaire developed in a pilot study by Pimm[6]. The questions covered topics such as interviewee's disability, educational background, practical skills, social network, assessment of his/her communication ability, and his/her attempts to find employment. The majority of interviews lasted between 1 and 2 hours.

Statistical analysis

The responses to the questions between the employed and the unemployed graduates were compared either (a) by the Fisher Exact Probability test or (b) by Mann Whitney U test.

Results

Table 2 displays an excerpt of the results from the interviews. Column one of the table records the items in abbreviated form. Column 2 displays the probability levels based on either the Fisher Exact Probability test or the Mann Whitney U test, depending on whether the data was nominal or ordinal. In addition to the usual levels of 1 % and 5% (in bold), the 10% level of confidence is mentioned as well to indicate trends in the results. Column 3 displays the direction of the results. "E" stands for employed graduates, "U" for unemployed ones.

Most of the comparisons in Table 2 favoured the employed group, although only a few were statistically significant or showed a statistical trend. The employed graduates had started their studies more with a vision of what they wanted to do after graduation. They had pursued this career vision more consistently throughout their undergraduate/ postgraduate course, and they had gained some work experience in that area before applying for employment. They were in general somewhat more proficient in technical skills, such as in braille and in word-processing. Compared to the unemployed, the employed seemed to have a greater social network that supported them in their search for job vacancies.

The two groups did not differ from each other in the level of disability, except for one characteristic. The employed graduates suffered more from a degenerative condition. For five of the partially sighted subjects in this group their sight had not yet stabilised but was worsening (e.g. three suffered from retinitis pigmentosa). It is interesting to observe that the employed group did not look less impaired than the unemployed group. Thus the obvious degree of disability was not a decisive criterion in obtaining a job.

Discussion

The present study endeavoured to identify factors that enhanced or hindered the employment prospects of visually impaired graduates, despite the great individual differences perceived in this group. A further complicating factor was that although 80% of the employed were happy to have a job, half of them were already looking for other employment. This was due to the fact that a number of graduates with a job were under-employed, i.e. in temporary jobs or in a position below their qualifications.

It appeared that employment of graduates was determined by a combination of interacting factors. One of these factors that improved employment prospects was the students having a clear idea of their future

**Table 2: Comparison of items between employed and unemployed
graduates**

Items investigated	p≤	Direction
Level of disability		
1. Visual condition: degenerative (stable)	.10	E>U
2. Sightedness: totally blind (partially sighted)	n.s.	E>U
3. No additional disabilities	n.s.	E>U
Education/academic qualifications/technical skills		
4. Higher -, A-level grades	n.s.	U>E
5. Postgraduate degree	.10	E>U
6. Vocational (non-vocational)	n.s.	E>U
7. Read Braille	.10	E>U
8. Type Braille	**.05**	**E>U**
9. Use of computer to write curriculum vitae	n.s.	E>U
10. Use of computer writing reports	**.05**	**E>U**
11. Use of scanner	n.s.	E>U
12. Use of closed circuit television	n.s.	E>U
Career vision/career support		
13. Pursue career path	.10	E>U
14. Employment applications in specific area	.10	E>U
15. Career vision pursued in study	n.s.	E>U
16. Work experience	.10	E>U
17. Special assistance for visually impaired students	n.s.	E>U
18. Help to look for jobs from peers	.10	E>U
19. Help to look for jobs from DRO	n.s.	U>E
20. Help to look for jobs from the RNIB	n.s.	U>E
Social network/communication skills		
21. Last week how many days did you go out?	.10	E>U
22. No. of people you went out with last week	**.05**	**E>U**
23. Socialising in pub	**.05**	**E>U**
24. Socialising in voluntary group	.10	U>E
25. Communication: succinct (repetitive)	n.s.	E>U
26. Communication: relevant (irrelevant)	n.s.	E>U

n.s. = not significant   DRO= Disablement Resettlement Officer
E , U = employed, unemployed graduates

career and pursuing this idea throughout their studies. For example, a
number of employed graduates had studied psychology at undergraduate
level and had followed this up with a postgraduate degree in social work.

In general it was found that postgraduate studies improved employment prospects. This may be due to the fact that postgraduate students become more specialised in their subjects and also tend to gain more work experience thus making themselves more attractive to future employers. Work experience on its own was shown to be a very significant factor as the student could demonstrate to the prospective employers how efficiently they could carry out the work.

Technical skills, for example fluency in braille, knowledge of word-processing and general computer skills were also shown to enhance employment prospects. Specialised equipment such as scanners, closed circuit television, etc. help to access information more quickly and efficiently. To provide blind and partially sighted students with access to such equipment, the RNIB has recently set up Resource Centres at various universities (Dimigen and Roy[3]). This is specially important for visually impaired students as, in the future, universities are planning to introduce compulsory information technology courses for sighted students.

One of the most important factors leading to employment was advice and information from a wide social network. Those graduates who were more outgoing were also more likely to become employed than those who tended to stay more at home. It seems that by meeting more people the students were more likely to hear of job vacancies and target their applications more appropriately to the specific requirements of the job.

The present investigation, although the first of its kind, was a small-scale retrospective study with a case-study approach. This has its merits as well as its drawbacks. It has shown the general trends affecting employment of visually impaired graduates. However, a large-scale, questionnaire-based, prospective study is needed. This study should follow up school-leavers through their studies and their first years after graduation.

References

1. Bruce I., McKennell A. & Walker E. *Blind and partially sighted adults in Britain: the RNIB survey*, Volume 1, London, HMSO, 1991.
2. Bush-LaFrance B.A.C. Unseen expectations of blind youth: educational and occupational ideas. *Journal of Visual Impairment and Blindness*, 1988, 82, 132-136.
3. Dimigen G and Roy A.W.N. The development of a technology centre for visually impaired university students. *New Beacon*, 1994, 920:10-12.

4. Dimigen G., Scott F, Thackeray F., Pimm M. and Roy A.W.N. Career expectations of British visually impaired students of school-leaving age. *Journal of Visual Impairment and Blindness*, 1993, 87:209-210.

5. Dryden G. Implications of the 1992 Further and Higher Education Act, Chapter 1, *The Visually Impaired: Curricular Access and Entitlement in Further Education*, eds D.T. Etheridge & H.L. Mason, pp 6-16, David Fulton, London, 1994.

6. Pimm M. A pilot study of the factors that may influence the employability of visually impaired graduates. *Unpublished Hon. Thesis.* University of Glasgow, 1993.

7. Roy A.W.N. Statistics on numbers of blind and partially sighted students in Great Britain. *Unpublished manuscript,* 1994.

8. Roy A.W.N. and Dimigen G. The history of access to education for visually impaired people in Britain. *(in press)*

9. Skill *Skill Information Sheet 2.* London: National Bureau for Students with Disabilities, London, 1993.

Learning through relationships: A re-evaluation of Waldorf education

A. Soutter

School of Psychology, University of Luton, Park Square, Luton LU1 3JU, UK

Abstract:

Waldorf education is the system which most closely follows Vygotsky's ideas although it is based on intuition rather than research. All teaching is firmly embedded in a social context with new information being given in story form by a teacher who has a strong and long lasting relationship with each pupil. The teacher models learning and creativity, conflict resolution and co-operation for the child. It is a system which emphasises the social context of learning.

Introduction :

The Waldorf school movement is the largest non-denominational system of education in the world yet it is almost completely ignored in academic publications. No doubt this is due to the intertwining of educational and religious values in the descriptions of the method given by Rudolf Steiner and his followers. However if one hurdles over the linguistic barrier and looks at what happens in the classroom, it becomes apparent that this is the method which most closely follows Vygotskian principles in its emphasis on learning as a social process.

The Classroom:

A Waldorf school is distinctive in that all teaching is through relationships illustrating the Vygotskian view that any function in the child's cultural development appears twice or on two planes.

First it appears on the social plane and then on the psychological plane [1].Thus in the early school years the social is emphasised and each class of children is accompanied through the first eight years of their school life by their own class teacher with whom it is expected that they will have a loving relationship.

This relationship has much in common with the parent/child bond through which much early learning takes place and by emphasising its affectional character Steiner attempts to overcome the problems which many researchers (Tharp & Gallimore [2]; Wood [3].) have found in the classroom application of Vygotsky's principles. When many pupils are involved it is difficult to have a clear view of each learner's relationship to the task. However when a teacher has the same group for eight years it is a measure of his competence that he becomes familiar with each individual's learning style and so is likely to be able to give the sort of help which extends the capabilities. It can be as Vygotsky [4] says, 'instruction' that 'moves ahead of development' and 'wakens a whole series of functions that are in a stage of maturation lying in the zone of proximal development.'

The teacher presents all new information in the Main Lesson during the first two hours of the morning. It is always embedded in a story so that even the cold hard facts of the sciences are presented imaginatively. .Although in this way the teacher extends the child and takes them on, it is in the process of recall that the effective use of the zone of proximal development is best seen.

Rather than ask a series of questions to check that the new knowledge has been absorbed, the Waldorf teacher uses a questioning style which is more often seen in the home (Edwards & Middleton [7]). She avoids using the type of specific questions with only one right answer which often inhibit children [3]. Firstly she does not question the children until the next day to give them time to digest the new knowledge. Then she encourages them to retell the story, only interrupting to draw inferences about characters and motivation. Because all the stories have a strong affective component she is able to involve each child personally by reminding him of his feelings. As Edwards and Middleton [7] found in their study of remembering in the home, the major grounds for remembering episodes are to do with affective reactions.

In every Main Lesson the teacher is recalling at the same time as the pupils and often to their delight she will have forgotten small details which they remember. Having elicited the previous day's portion of the story, the teacher will further model recall by relating the next episode, without the use of books or notes. This fits in with Vygotsky's view that one cannot look at the child's learning in isolation but at the whole social situation of child, teacher and peers. He said that 'instruction is possible only where there is a potential for imitation'[4].

The relationship between the teacher and pupils is not the only one valued. The relationships between the children are also very important. These are strengthened by the use of peer tutoring in all areas, which is set up to value the different gifts which different children possess. The class as a whole is brought into harmony by playing music, singing and reciting together as it is assumed that by modulating ones pitch and speed to blend with others one learns about equality in practical terms. Children are never let out into the playground without saying a verse together first to bring them together as a group. The creativity of play is valued and prepared for.

Creativity:

In his attitude to creativity, Rudolf Steiner [6] mirrors Vygotsky's ideas very closely. In his three papers on imagination, "Imagination and Creativity in Childhood", "Imagination and Creativity in the Adolescent" and "Imagination and its Development in Childhood", Vygotsky [7] puts forward the view that imagination develops out of children's play to become a higher mental function in adolescence and the basis of artistic and scientific creativity in adulthood. He draws on the work of Ribot to show that imagination develops more quickly than reason in childhood, then levels off at adolescence when the two qualities may unite or else in many people imagination declines and thinking becomes prosaic.

In a Waldorf school these ideas are put into practice with an understanding that imagination is an important foundation stone for later forms of intellectual modes of thought. Just as Vygotsky talks about the importance of unstructured toys like sticks as being perfect for stimulating creativity in the young child [9], so Steiner says that a realistic doll or a perfect model house leaves no room for something to be added by the imagination [8]. The nursery section of a Waldorf school consequently has rag dolls, big squares of light fabric which can serve many purposes, assorted logs, shells and other natural objects so that all kinds of play can take place. Playgrounds for all ages are in as far as possible grassy areas with many trees and shrubs to break them up into interesting niches for interesting games. In the class teacher period the stimulation of the imagination is from the word pictures built up in the children's heads by the stories and by the creation of a beautiful environment in which to learn.

Literacy:

When the children begin formal teaching in literacy, the form these lessons take is very much that recommended by Vygotsky [9]. He pointed out that in teaching reading and writing it is usual to emphasise the mechanics at the expense of living written language. He said that it must not be taught simply as a motor skill because it has so much cultural significance that the children need to find a path into this complex symbolism from an understanding of the derivation of the symbols. Such a path is followed in a Waldorf school where each of the letters are presented to the children in a story ; if then as Edmunds explains [10] 'out of the story a picture is selected, say of a wave, and then the child runs waves, paints and draws waves and eventually comes to a flowing w and finally to the crystallised hieroglyphic **w** he has been led along the path of experience to a conclusion.'

Vygotsky saw written language as being part of a continuous process of understanding and using symbols which develops from gesture to drawing to writing [9]. By revealing the letter embedded in a picture which illustrates a story this symbol is given a social context and is not taught in the disembedded way which Vygotsky criticises in the Montessori method. He points out [9] that though the children do learn their letters in a Montessori school they are able to make very little use of their writing skills. In a Steiner school, on the other hand children write quite creatively from the beginning because they are using writing as people have through history, as their own aid to memory in the text books they make for themselves.

The difference between Steiner's and Vygotsky's views on literacy is one of timing. Vygotsky was working in Russia where children typically come into school at the age of seven already able to read. Steiner however did not feel that instruction should even begin until the changing of the teeth at about seven. At first sight this seems a bizarre indicator of reading readiness but if one realises that it is the most easily observed measurement of skeletal age, it becomes logical. Reading readiness is largely a matter of physical maturity, especially the ability to finely co-ordinate one's eyes and the ability to say all the sounds used in the language. By delaying the teaching of reading and writing, Waldorf schools avoid labelling as failures children who are simply immature.

To Rudolf Steiner, temperament was an important influence on learning and he proposed that children could be divided into four types corresponding to the old idea of the four humors: the melancholic, sanguine, phlegmatic and choleric. Although this seems an unscientific notion, in practical terms it means that all lessons have to be taught in such a way as to engage the interest of four very different types of children and the teacher is aware of differences in learning styles. Vygotsky [4] pointed out that because all children have had different social experiences they are not identical in their approach to learning, although there may be similarities at certain stages of development.

Both Vygotsky and Steiner were interested in remedial education and rehabilitation. Since both recognised the importance of speech in this process because of its role in integrating the personality and structuring the thinking [12 & 4] and since both emphasised the social context of learning their recommendations were similar. It is interesting to compare Kovcheq, a Vygotskian remedial school in Moscow [13] with a Waldorf Camphill [12]. Both see themselves as learning environments in which the prime concern is for the inner world of the child so they are based on loving relationships. In both settings there is an emphasis on the integration of the children with special needs with their 'normal' peers and a valuing of all strengths and abilities. The difference is that Camphills are farming communities in which every aspect of life is part of the therapy which is of course a Vygotskian notion.

Conclusion:

Does such a system work? This is very difficult to say because so little research has been done on Waldorf education. It is difficult to compare results in public examinations since pupils who would not be entered in other schools, are encouraged to have a try in a Waldorf school. Preliminary results of a study on bullying in Steiner Schools [11] show an almost complete absence of physical bullying, and an expressed enjoyment of school. The pupils seemed to feel valued once they had been allowed into the class group but breaking in was not easy. Once the novelty value of a newcomer wears off they may be very isolated for quite some considerable time. This is a disadvantage of a group centred system.

Waldorf education is very much based on learning through relationships; the relationships of teacher and child, teacher and teacher, child and child are all valued as part of the learning environment. In many ways Steiner was taking a Vygotskian standpoint but there are important differences in their perspectives. Steiner's is a stage theory based on observation and intuition rather than research. It is part of a much wider philosophy, anthroposophy, which focusses on the relationship of humanity to the spiritual world. It is a pity that this has discouraged research on an interesting system of education.

REFERENCES:

1. Vygotsky, L.S. The genesis of higher mental functions, in *The Concept of Activity in Soviet Psychology.* ed J.V.Wertsch,pp144-188, Sharpe, New York,1981.
2. Tharp, R. & Gallimore, R. (eds) *Rousing Minds to Life: Teaching, Learning and Schooling in Social Context.* Cambridge University Press, New York, 1988.
3. Wood, D. Aspects of teaching and learning, in *Children of Social Worlds,* eds Richards, M. & Light, P. pp 191-212, Polity Press, Cambridge, 1986.
4. Vygotsky,L.S. *The Collected works of L.S. Vygotsky: Vol1. Problems of General Psychology.* trans. N.Munick.Plenum, New York, 1987.
5. Edwards, D. & Middleton, D. Conversational remembering and family relationships: how children learn to remember. *Journal of Personal and Social Relationships* , 1988, **5**, 3-25.
6. Steiner, R. *The Education of the Child* , Rudolf Steiner Press, London, 1965
7. Smolucha F. A reconstruction of Vygotsky's theory of creativity. *Creativity Research Journal* , 1992, **5** (1), 49-67.
8. Steiner, R. *The Kingdom of Childhood.* Rudolf Steiner Press, London 1961.
9. Vygotsky L.S. *Mind in Society.* Harvard University Press, London, 1978.
10. Edmunds, F. *Rudolf Steiner Education.* Rudolf Steiner Press. London 1982.
11. Rivers,I. and Soutter,A. Bullying and School Ethos.Paper presented to *British Educational Research Association Conference* , St Anne's College Oxford, September 1994.
12. Pietzner,C. (ed) *A Candle on the Hill.* Floris books.1990
13. Daniels,H. and Lunt,I. Vygotskian theory and special education practice in Russia. *Educational Studies* 1993 **19** (1) 79-89.

SECTION F:

Process Variables
in Interactive Learning

Task difficulty and effectiveness of group work

P. Bishop

Department of Psychology, Aberdeen University, King's College, Old Aberdeen AB9 2UB, UK

Abstract

A study was carried out to examine if task difficulty affected learning in group work on a information processing task. It was found that there did not seem to be a difference in learning between the two levels of difficulty but that the children's initial ability seemed to determine amount of learning.

1 Introduction

Recent research with children has shown group and paired work to have a beneficial effect on learning of information processing tasks such as Siegler's[3] balance beam task. Tudge [4] found that children working with more capable children improve more than children working on their own subsequent post-test scores. Howe et al [2] found that children working in groups showed superior learning if they worked in groups with differing initial abilities.

Although the usefulness of group learning has been shown on these and other tasks the effect of task difficulty on improvement has not been fully investigated. Ferretti & Butterfield [1] found that on the balance beam task children's performance, characterised by rules, was dependent on the disparity in product difference between the two sides of the balance, the larger the product difference the better the child's performance. The children performing better on problems which were perceptually clearer. It could be hypothesised that the difficulty children have with smaller product differences would have an effect on learning.

In this study an attempt was made to examine if two different levels of task difficulty, operationally defined by product difference, would have an effect on the effectiveness on learning through group work in children.

2 Method

Design
The experiment was made up of 3 phases. Firstly all the children were pre-tested on a workbook. For the second phase 48 children were split equally into three conditions. 1: the children worked with children who had scored the same in the pretest in groups of four. 2: the children worked with children who scored differently in the pre-test again in groups of four, two children with the same rule were paired with two children with a different rule. 3: children worked alone. The children were then post-tested 3 weeks later on a workbook similar to that of the pre-test.

Subjects
The children were from a middle class school in Aberdeen. They were taken from two age groups: Primary 3 (7-8 yrs) and primary 5 (9-10yrs). There were 42 children in the younger group and 43 in the older group.

The Apparatus and Materials
Balance Beam   The main piece of apparatus used was a wooden balance beam with five pegs on each side. This was used by the children in the middle phase of the experiment and by the experimenter for demonstration purposes in the first and third phases.

The Workbooks   These were made up of 36 pages with a diagram of the balance on each page. Marked on the diagrams was a configuration of weight at various distances. Each configuration was one of the balance scale problems of Siegler [3]. In the workbooks there were two sets of 4 of each of Siegler's [3] 5 Balance scale problems. In the first set the difference between the product moments on each side of the balance was 1 or 2, for example, for a simple distance problem one weight was put on the 2nd peg on the left side of the balance and one weight on the 3rd peg on the right side. In the second set the product difference was 10 or 11, for example for a simple distance problem 5 weights were put on the 2nd peg on the left side and 5 weights were put on 4th peg on the right side. There were two different workbooks with different problems, one for the pre-test and one for the post-test.

Procedure

The Pre-test   The pre-tests were carried out as paper and pencil tests(following Ferretti & Butterfield [1]) using the workbooks. The children were tested in their classroom. After each child was given a workbook, the experimenter described the relation between the diagrams in the book and the wooden balance. The children were then asked to go through the book marking in pencil the answers to each of the items . The children were told to spend as long as they wished on each item but were told not to go back to items that they had already done but to keep going forward through the book. This took around 15 minutes. When the children had finished they were asked to go through the workbook and check that they had answered every item. The work books were then collected in and scored according to the scoring system below.

The Second Phase In conditions 1 and 2 the children were taken in groups of four from their classroom to a room within the school. They were seated around a table on which was the wooden balance and told that they were going to do some work together . The children were then each given a work booklet containing 11 items which they had given answers for in the pretest (these booklet were created by removing set items from each of the children's pre-test booklets so that each child had their answers for each of the items). The children were also given a check list which they were told to go through for each item in the workbook. This check-list told them to, set up the wooden balance as it was in their books , then they were to agree on what the balance would do if the catch was released and then release the catch on the balance to see if their answer was correct. The children were told to go through their workbooks following the check-list for each item. From then on the children were on their own.   Once the children had finished the first 11 items then they were given another set of 6 items which they had not seen before and were told to go through the set as they had done before following the check-list. They were again left on their own. The phase was finished when the children completed this set of items. The sessions last around 25-30 minutes.

In Condition 3 the children were taken individually to the testing room where they were given two workbooks, identical to the ones given to the groups. The children were then told to put the weights on the balance as shown in their books and predict what would happen if the catch was released. They then released the catch. This was done for each of the items in the workbooks.

Post Test Phase The procedure for this phase of the experiment was the same as the pre-test.   The only exception being that the items in the workbooks were different. These new items followed the same rules as the items in the pre test as regard both product difference and problem type.

The Scoring   The children's pre- and post-test answers were   scored following a variation on Siegler's [3] criterion which is shown below.   The two sets of items were scored independently of each other so each child had a score for each level of the product difference of the items.

Rule 1   3/4 for the simple weight and complex weight problems and below 3/4 on the simple and complex distance items.

Rule 2   3/4 answers correct for the conflict weight and 3/4 answers correct on the simple weight and distance.

Rule 3   3/4 correct on the conflict weight and distance and 3/4 correct on the simple problem but less than 2/4 on the conflict balance problems.

Rule 4   3/4 correct on all problem types no child used this rule.

(Rule 3 was introduced because there was a large number of children who seem to fit this pattern.   There were no children who fitted the criterion of Siegler's rule 3).

3 Analysis

The post-test responses were scored and the frequencies of children advancing in rule, staying at the same rule or regressing for each condition is shown in Tables 1   for the lower product differences and Table 2 for higher product differences.

Table 1 Percentages of change from pre- to post-test for lower product difference. Chi-squared $=16.76$, $p< 0.004$

condition	Improvement	no improvement or regression
1	44	56
2	56	44
3	7	93

Table 2 Percentages of change form pre to post-test for higher product difference. Chi-squared $=8.35$, $p> 0.138$

condition	Improved	No improvement or regression
1	37	63
2	50	50
3	20	80

To examine if the improvements   which were made in the group conditions were dependent on the product level a Cochrans Q was carried on each of the conditions separately and together. This was not significant for either of conditions.

Also the effect of the children starting rule (pre-test rule) on frequency of improvement was examined in the group work conditions. Again the results of the two levels of product difference were analysed separately. The percentages of change are shown in for the lower product differences are shown in table 3 , the higher in table 4.

Table 3 The amount of pre- to post-test change dependent on pre-test rule for the lower product level in percentages. Fisher exact probability $p < .0253$

Pre-test rule	Improved	No improvement or regression
1	62	38
2 and 3	15	85

Table 4 The amount of pre- to post-test change dependent on pre-test rule for the higher product level in percentages. Fisher exact probability $p < 0.001$

Pre-test rule	Improvement	No improvement or regression
1	92	9
2 and 3	16	84

4 Discussion

One general point from the above results is that although the expected difference in benefit between the Individual and the group conditions was present in the lower product level, it was not present in the higher product level. The higher product difference replicated Tudge's [4] results by failing to find a difference in learning between the individual and group conditions. This suggests that the group work effect was nullified by the relative lack of difficulty of the higher product differences.

Another finding that contradicts other research is the lack of difference between the two group condition. Other researchers(Howe et al[2]) have found that children learned more in groups of differing initial ability due to the increased conflict in these groups. The lack of difference in the present study could perhaps be explained by the closeness of the children's abilities in the "different"(2nd) condition , the children differing only on one of their rules. It may have been the case that the levels of conflict may have been similar in each group condition. Preliminary analysis of the video tapes suggest this may be the case especially in the feedback phase of the interaction (when the children released the balance).

The analysis of levels of difficulty did not produce a difference in learning between the two levels. In fact the percentage of children who advanced at both levels simultaneously rather than on one of the levels was 55% for the lower product difference and 55% for the higher product difference collapsed across the two group work conditions. This may indicate that the levels of difficulty did not have an effect on learning in the group work conditions.

The effect of starting (pre-test) rule on children's progress is of interest. The likelihood of advancing appeared to be related to the initial rule of the child in both product levels. To move from rule 1 to 2 the children needed only to take into account another dimension: distance. Whereas to move to the higher rules the children needed to integrate the two dimensions in the complex problems, perhaps a more difficult skill. It could be considered that group work would facilitate better the first skill over the second. Previous research has shown (Howe et al[2]) this "glass ceiling" effect where children of higher levels initially (though not actually at ceiling) benefit less than other children at lower levels from group work. This could be due to the fact that this form of interaction is effective at producing changes in perspective but not in the learning of more complex integration rules.

In conclusion it could be suggested that though there was not any difference in the learning between the two levels of difficulty there was a difference in learning dependent on the children's starting rule.

References

[1] Ferretti R.P., & Butterfield E.C., Are children's rule-assessment classifications invariant across instances of problem types, *Child Development*, 57, 1419-1428

[2] Howe, C.,Tolmie, A., & Rodgers, C. The acquisition of conceptual knowledge by primary school children: Group interaction and the understanding of motion down an incline, *British Journal of Developmental Psychology*, 1992, 10, 113-130

[3] Siegler R.S. Three Aspects of Cognitive Development, *Cognitive Psychology,* 1976, 4, 481-520

[4] Tudge,J Vygotsky, the zone of proximal development and peer collaboration, Chapter 6, *Vygotsky and Education,* ed L.C. Moll, pp 165-172, Cambridge University Press, New York 1990

Social position and cognitive activity in second language production

P. Chambres
LAPSCO, U.R.A. C.N.R.S. 1719, Université Blaise Pascal, 34 Avenue Carnot, 63000 Clermont-Ferrand, France

Abstract

The principal aim of this study was to show that one must take the social environment into account when studying cognition. The experimental investigation of this perspective revealed that the cognitive activity produced by subjects in second language communicative interaction was determined, to a significant extent, by the social position of the subjects. A theoretical explanation, referring to the working self-concept, is discussed. The data underline that we have to study the learning situation, not only with a cognitive and didactic perspective, but also with a socio-cognitive approach. The social situation appears as an important source of variation of the cognitive activity.

1 Introduction

A substantial body of research has shown that, in experiments where subjects are required to accomplish an intellectual task, their cognitive performance is influenced by the social aspects of the situation (Monteil[1] & [2], Chambres[3]). For instance, in the Mann and Grabe experiment reported by Garner[4], children were better at correcting mistakes in a text when they were assigned the role of detective than otherwise. Thus, *Certain social factors have an impact on individual cognitive activity.* One of these factors seems particularly important in interactive situations: it is the social position of the subject (Chambres[5]). According to Zuengler[6], being dominated leads to limits on the "right to talk," and consequently reduces the opportunity to learn. The feeling of superiority *might facilitate the access to control strategies and to specific language knowledge* (Bialystok[7]).The following hypotheses summarize our objectives: (1) A subject who believes that she/he is more competent than her/his partner should perform better than her/him, even if he/she is actually of the same level of competence *(Experiment I)*. (2) It should be possible to compensate the negative influence of an "inferior" position in a specific comparative dimension by a "superior" position grounded in a second dimension *(Experiment II)*. (3) The social value of the second comparative dimension used modulates the compensation effect expected. More precisely, we should have a compensation effect only for a high social value of the second comparative dimension. *(Experiment II)*.

2 Experiment I

The experiment was carried out with 16 ninth grade French pupils (fifteen years old). The subjects were randomly assigned to a specific social competence position. One of them was told he was significantly better in English than his/her partner. Then, children, working in pairs and talking in English, were asked to exchange information in order to complete a map of an English town. They could not see the map of their partner. Finally, subjects, completing an empty map, were told to recall all the information they could remember about the town and they were exposed to a recognition task.

Results
The *Subjects in superior position in English started the communication more frequently* than the subjects in the

inferior position (100% vs 0%; $X^2=12.25$, p<.0005). They tended to produce more words (197.12 vs 138.37;   t=1.926 p<.037). The diversity of their vocabulary was greater (9 vs 5.62; z=-2.209, p<.015). They produced more semantic units (31.25 vs 21.87; t=2.743, p<.008), and more sentences (14.29 vs 8.60; t=1.762, p<.05). They also *tended to produce better recognition performances* than inferior subjects (38.25 vs 31.25; t=1.552, p<.072). Subjects assigned to a position of superiority were led to perform better than subjects assigned to an inferior position. Nevertheless, comparative situations are often more complicated in the sense that people frequently compare themselves to others using several comparative dimensions at the same time. The following experiment was to study the influence on cognitive activity of a social position stemming from two comparative dimensions.

3 Experiment II

This time, subjects were assigned simultaneously to an English position and a geometry position (high social value subject matter) or a drawing position (low social value subject matter). The procedure was very similar to the procedure of the first experiment.

Results

Interaction analysis *Subjects in superior position in English started the communication more frequently* than subjects in the inferior one (84.38% vs 15.62%; $X^2=27.56$, p<.0001). *They tended to ask more questions* (13.62   vs 10.81; F(1/56)=3.467, p<.067). There was a significant interaction between the position in English and the position in the second dimension (F(1/56)=6.581, p<.013). The number of questions asked by subjects superior in English and superior in the other dimension was significantly higher than the number produced by the subjects of the other groups (F=6.14, p<.0162).

Language production analysis Subjects in superior position tended to produce more words than subjects in inferior position (236.25 vs 203.22; $F(1/56)=3.447$, $p<.068$). There was a significant interaction between the position in English and the position in the second dimension ($F(1/56)=9.095$, $p<.038$). The number of words produced by subjects superior in English and superior in the other dimension was significantly higher than the number produced by subjects of the other groups ($F=13.54$, $p<.0005$). The results are quite similar for the diversity of the vocabulary, the number of semantic units and the number of sentences produced.

Memory performances analysis The recall is better for subjects who worked in the geometry environment than for subjects who worked in the drawing situation (geometry $=6.5$; drawing$=3.56$, $F(1/56)=7.69$, $p<.0075$). There is a significant two-way interaction effect for the recognition score ($F(1/56)=5.536$, $p<.021$) which mainly shows that subjects were better when they worked in the superior position in geometry and in the inferior position in English, or in the double superior position (English and drawing).

4 General discussion

Bearing in mind that the position of each subject was not a real position (in each dyad, subjects had the same level within the two comparative dimensions), the findings clearly show that *what subjects believed about their own position relative to the partner in the communication was a significant determinant of their cognitive performance.* Subjects were particularly efficient when allocated simultaneously to a superior position within the English dimension and within the second dimension. To put forward a first explanation, it seems pertinent to refer to the working self-concept. "The working self-concept is a temporary structure consisting of elements from the collection of self-conceptions, organized in a configuration determined by ongoing social events." (Markus & Kunda[8]). The working self-concept is dependent on the social situation. More interestingly, the working self-concept is a determinant of the performance of the subject (Ruvolo & Markus[9]). There is a kind of interface between the working self-concept and the cognitive abilities. According to Boekaerts[10], the self-concept may stimulate or impede ongoing behavior, determining how many resources must be expended to achieve the task. It is reasonable to go further, putting forward the idea of the existence of specific connections between certain types of self-conceptions and specific cognitive activities, and/or specific connections between certain characteristics of the situation and specific cognitive activities. These connections would be elaborated through the subject's experiences. So, the effect of a particular social position could differ as a function of the subject's personal history. In any manner, this position will be a significant determinant of both self-knowledge access, and cognitive processes' access. It is like a priming effect.

Conclusion

Taking into account the results of this study, it can be argued that second-language proficiency is facilitated by certain social characteristics of the situation in which, for instance, referential communication takes place. What subjects think about themselves and about the partner in a communicative interaction on different comparative dimensions is, to a large extent, a determinant of the quantity and the quality of what is produced. The theoretical explanations of this phenomenon, evoked previously, remain to be examined. Nevertheless, it already means that from a pedagogical perspective *it is particularly important to consider the social factors of the situations in which subjects have to learn or to produce in a second language.* More precisely it means that we have to study the learning situation not only with a cognitive and didactic perspective, but also with a socio-cognitive approach where the social situation appears as an important source of variation of the cognitive activity.

References

1. Monteil, J. M. (1991). Social regulations and individual cognitive function: effects of individuation on cognitive performance. *European Journal of Social Psychology*, **21**, 225-237.
2. Monteil, J. M. (1992). Toward a social psychology of cognitive functioning: Theoretical outline and empirical illustrations. In M. Von Cranach, W. Doise, & G. Mugny (Eds.), *Social representations and the social bases of knowledge* (pp. 42-55). Berne: Hubert.
3. Chambres, P. Social comparison and knowledge construction. *Learning and Instruction*, 1993, **3**, 23-38.
4. Garner, R. *Metacognition and reading comprehension*, Ablex Publishing Corporation, Norwood, 1987.
5. Chambres, P. The influence of an expert social position on learning: the role of the metacognitive activity, *Revue Internationale de Psychologie Sociale*, in press.
6. Zuengler, J. Performance variation in NS-NNS interactions: Ethnolinguistic difference, or discourse domain? *Variation in second language acquisition: psycholinguistic issues*, eds Gass, S., Madden, C., Preston, D., & Selinker, L., pp. 228-244, Multilingual matters Ltd, Clevedon, 1989.
7. Bialystok, E. The competence of processing: Classifying theories of second language acquisition. *TESOL Quarterly*, 1990, **24** , 635-648.
8. Markus, H., & Kunda, Z. Stability and malleability of the self-concept. *Journal of Personality and Social Psychology*, 1986, **51**, 858-866.
9. Ruvolo, A., & Markus, H. Possible selves and performance: The power of self-relevant imagery. *Social Cognition*, 1992, **10**, 95-124.
10. Boekaerts, M. (1991). Subjective competence, appraisals and self-assessment. *Learning and Instruction*, 1991, **1**, 1-17.

Learning from peer feedback marking: student and teacher perspectives

N. Falchikov

Department of Social Sciences, Napier University, Colinton Road, Edinburgh EH10 5DT, UK

Abstract

The importance of providing quick and helpful feedback to students is widely recognised, but, in an expanding educational system, is becoming more and more difficult to achieve. However, students have been found to benefit from an increased involvement in the assessment of their own work and the work of others. The paper describes a study of Peer Feedback Marking (PFM) which required students to provide feedback to their peers, in addition to awarding them a mark. Marks awarded by peers and the teacher were found to be very similar, as might have been predicted from earlier studies of peer assessment [6] [7]. The paper then compares the kinds of feedback supplied by students and by teachers. While many similarities were found, some interesting differences emerged. The paper discusses these findings and identifies some of the lessons to be learned from these studies.

1. Introduction

Feedback has been described by Brown and Knight as a "crucial issue" [3, p.17] and one which needs to be explicitly "designed in" to the learning process. Feedback is widely recognised to be very important in terms of formative assessment (e.g. Denvir, [5]). Moreover, justification of one's own strategies and reasoning serves as a spur to reflection, and also shifts the focus of assessment to a more "student centred" approach (Hoyles, [8]). Traditional feedback mechanisms which rely heavily on lecturer marking time are becoming less tenable as higher education expands. However, devolving some responsibility for assessment to students is accepted as a means of enhancing the learning process [1]. Peer assessment has a long history as a mechanism of involving students in the assessment process, and over twenty years ago, Korman and Stubblefield [9] reported that peer ratings were the best predictor of intern performance. Similarly, Linn et al [10] concluded that peer evaluation "offers a view of the student not often available, since students know themselves and their peers from a different perspective" (p.100), yet found that peer evaluations "provided ratings that were highly related to those of the grading system" (p.100). D'Augelli [4] assessed interpersonal skills and concluded that, "the convergence of peer and observer ratings suggests the former may be accurate indices of interpersonal behavior" (p. 179). Similarly, Boud and Tyree [2] used peers to assess participation in class. Peer-teacher correlations were found to be positive and highly significant. Thus, peer assessment appears to be a useful, reliable and valid exercise.

Both Falchikov [6] and Magin and Churches [11] report that students perceived the scheme of self and peer assessment to be beneficial to them. However, some students expressed a dislike of awarding a grade to their peers, particularly in the context of a small, well established group.

Earlier studies by the author [7] attempted to capitalise on the benefits of peer assessment while minimising the problems. In these studies, the emphasis was on critical feedback, rather than on the awarding of a grade, though this was required also. Results indicated a close correspondence between lecturer and peer marks. Students valued feedback and rated Peer Feedback Marking (PFM) as conferring more benefits than the more usual, lecturer marked method.

2. The present study

Participants in the current study were first year students taking a "Foundations of Social Science" module. Small groups of students were required to carry out a practical survey and then deliver a short talk to the rest of the group. They were informed that they were also required to carry out the assessment of the oral presentations. Before the first presentation, students were asked to identify the criteria of a good presentation. Copies of a peer assessment form were circulated, each simply asking students to identify the "Best feature" and a "Weakness" of each presentation. After each presentation, assessment forms were completed and an overall mark awarded. Written feedback was also provided independently by the lecturer, using the same form.

Treatment of results

Mean peer marks were calculated and compared with lecturer marks. Feedback statements made by both lecturers and students were inspected and counted, and comparisons made between the number of "positive" and "negative" feedback statements offered. Statements were then subjected to a content analysis using the following categories:

A	Amount of information (appropriate or not)
C	Content
D	Delivery and oral presentation
I	Quality of information
M	Methodology
P	Amount and quality of preparation

St   Structure
SM   Support Materials (handouts, overhead slides)
T   Teamwork (were all group members involved?)
U   Understanding
Z   Zero response or "nothing"

Sample ratings were carried out by two raters and the degree of agreement between the two found to be 89.6% Disagreements were discussed and categories clarified. For example, it was agreed that, in order to assign the category "Understanding", the understanding had to be explicitly referred to in the feedback rather then implied. All ratings were subsequently carried out by one rater.

Comparisons were made between lecturer feedback and student feedback, and between feedback supplied by the three lecturers involved in running the tutorials sessions at which presentations were made. Relationships between marks awarded by peers and types of feedback were inspected.

3. Results

Comparison of peer and lecturer marks

Mean peer marks and lecturer marks awarded were compared and found to be identical at 62.6%, with standard deviations of 4.92 for students and 4.67 for lecturers. In 55% of cases students awarded a higher mark than the lecturer (over-marking) and in 45% the reverse occurred (under-marking). Mean over-marking was by 4.5% and mean under-marking by 4.6%.

The balance of "Positive" and "Negative" feedback offered by students

Overall, students identified 1.91 "Strengths" per rater and 1.39 "Weaknesses" in the presentations made by their peers. This balance in favour of "Positive" feedback was echoed by two of the three lecturers involved in the scheme (see Table 1 below).

Categories of feedback offered by lecturers and students

Lecturer differences relating to amounts of feedback offered and categories of feedback favoured are summarised in Table 1 and peer ratings in Table 2.

While some differences between the three lecturers are apparent, they appear united in their emphasis on methodological issues when identifying strengths.

Given that each lecturer was responsible for the discussion of criteria with her or his tutorial group prior to the presentations, a relationship between frequently used categories of feedback provided by lecturers and students might be predicted. By comparing feedback categories in Tables 1 (teacher ratings) and 2 (peer ratings), it can be seen that, for group 2 and lecturer 2, "Delivery", "Methodology" and "Support Material" appear in the frequently used strength categories for both. Similarly, "Methodology" appears in both sets of frequently identified weaknesses. For group 3 and lecturer 3, "Methodology" and "Support Materials" are often mentioned strengths, together with a zero response for weaknesses. However, for group 1 and lecturer 1, "Delivery" strengths and weaknesses constitute the only point of overlap.

Table 1:   Lecturer differences (numbers of groups in parentheses)

Lecturer	Total no. strengths identified	Total no. weaknesses identified	Freq. used weakness categories	Freq. used strength categories
1 (n = 8)	19	13	D (26.3%) SM (26.3%) U (26.3%)	D (38.5%) M (30.8%) P (15.4%)
2 (n = 5)	11	10	D (45.5%) M (18.2%) SM/St/T/U (9.1% each)	M (60.0%) A (20.0%) SM (20.0%)
3 (n = 7)	15	11	M (46.7%) R (13.3%) SM (13.3%)	M (27.3%) P (18.2%) Z (18.2%)

Table 2:   Peer rated strengths and weaknesses: the 3 most frequently used categories (percentages of total ratings in parentheses)

	Strengths		Weaknesses	
Group 1	P	(36.0%)	D	(39.8%)
	D	(26.0%)	Z	(18.1%)
	I	(15.0%)	I	(9.6%)
Group 2	D	(31.4%)	A	(21.1%)
	SM	(20.0%)	D	(21.1%)
	M	(17.1%)	M	(17.5%)
Group 3	D	(28.2%)	D	(28.6%)
	M	(12.8%)	Z	(18.6%)
	SM	(12.8%)	I	(11.4%
			SM	each)

The relationship between peer assessment marks and feedback categories

For group 1, mean peer marks ranged from 57% to 70%. A strong inverse relationship between total number of weaknesses per rater and rank order of marks ($r = -0.82$), and a moderate positive relationship between total number of strengths and rank order ($r = 0.65$) was found. The mean number of zero weaknesses per rater was calculated and found to be directly related to mark awarded ($r = 0.65$). Similarly, a positive relationship between mean number of

"Delivery" statements and marks was found in the strengths set (r = 0.82), together with an inverse relationship in the weaknesses set (r = -0.93).

In group 3, mean peer marks ranged from 50% to 70%. Large correlations were found between total numbers of strengths and weaknesses identified per rater and rank order of marks (r = 0.71 for strengths and -0.94 for weaknesses), but no relationships between "Delivery" statements.

In group 2, mean peer marks were very bunched, varying only between 60% and 63%. Relationships between marks and feedback categories (as for groups 1 and 3) were sought in group 2, but, unsurprisingly, no sizeable correlations were found.

4. Discussion

In the present study, comparisons of mean peer and lecturer mark indicated remarkable similarity. These results compare very favourably with the widely differing marks awarded by experienced external and internal examiners in a recent study by Newstead & Dennis [12], and support the prevailing view that peer assessment is a useful and valid methodology.

Perhaps the most striking observation to be made is the presence of "Delivery" statements in either first or second position in all student rating lists. Student feedback is replete with statements relating to the way in which presentations were made. The act of making an oral presentation can be a stressful experience for students, so it is, perhaps, understandable that they should put so much emphasis on this aspect. However, lessons can be learned by lecturers. It is too easy for us to forget that a poorly delivered, however brilliantly structured and conceived lecture is likely to be "lost" to many students. We could do well to heed this message, and, in our own way get "back to basics". Moreover, as potential employers signal their wishes to engage students who have a wide range of personal transferable skills which include the good oral communication ability, we should create more opportunities for students to practice and improve these skills.

On the whole, teachers and students provide rather different kinds of feedback. While students focus on practical issues such as preparation and delivery, and the amount and quality of information included, teachers tend to focus on methodological issues. Explicit references to "understanding" come largely from lecturers. It is possible that these differences may reflect different approaches to studying, with student feedback suggesting a surface approach and lecturer feedback a deep one. Conversely, they may indicate an "hierarchy" of feedback, with "Delivery" being an initial hurdle, through which one must pass before being able to attend to more detailed and complex issues.

Both lecturers and students experienced greater difficulty in providing critical and helpful feedback and suggestions for improvement than in identifying good features of presentations, particularly in "good" presentations. However, it is the former category that is most useful to students. Thus, lecturers using peer feedback marking in the future might do well to spend more time at the outset discussing the issue of strategies for improvement. This important issue might also benefit from attention by staff developers.

Results from the present study tend to support the view that students are "cue sensitive" in terms of assessment, in that correspondences between an individual lecturer's main areas of concern and those of students in his or her tutorial groups were hinted at. Again, we should be mindful of this, and "use" the information gained to alert ourselves to our own "hobbyhorses".

References

1. Boud, D. (Ed) *Developing student autonomy in learning* (2nd. ed) , Kogan Page, London, 1988
2. Boud, D.J. and Tyree, A.L. Self and peer assessment in professional education: a preliminary study in law, *Journal of the Society of Public Teachers of Law,* 1979, **15(1)** 65-74
3. Brown, S. & Knight, P. *Assessing Learners in Higher Education*, Kogan Page, London & Philadelphia, 1994.
4. D'Augelli, A. R. The assessment of interpersonal skills: a comparison of observer, peer and self ratings *Journal of Community Psychology,* 1973, **1,** 177-179
5. Denvir, B. Assessment Purposes and Learning Mathematics Education, Chapter 4.6, *Developments in Learning and Assessment*, ed P. Murphy & B. Moon, pp 277-289, Hodder & Stoughton, London, 1989.
6. Falchikov, N. "Product comparisons and process benefits of collaborative self and peer group assessments", *Assessment and Evaluation in Higher Education,* 1986, **11(2)**, 146-166
7. Falchikov, N. Peer feedback marking: assessment of an oral presentation, submitted for publication.
8. Hoyles, C. What is the point of Group Discussion in Mathematics?, Chapter 2.4, *Developments in Learning and Assessment*, ed P. Murphy & B. Moon, pp 121-129, Hodder & Stoughton, London, 1989.
9. Korman, M. and Stubblefield, R.L. Medical school evaluation and internship performance, *Journal of Medical Education,* 1971, **46**, 670-673
10. Linn, B.S., Arostegui, M. and Zeppa, R. Performance rating scale for peer and self assessments, *British Journal of Medical Education,* 1975, **9**, 98-101
11. Magin, D.J. and Churches, A.E. What do students learn from self and peer assessment? *Australian Journal of Educational Technology,* 1988,
12. Newstead, S. & Dennis, I. Examiners examined: The reliability of exam marking in psychology, *The Psychologist*, 1994, **7(5)**, 216-219.

Assessment issues in group work

D. Garland
Plymouth Business School, University of Plymouth, Drake Circus, Plymouth PL4 8AA, UK

Abstract

The concern of this paper is with the assessment of small group work in Higher Education. A number of assessment issues are investigated and common problems identified. Several strategies for assessing individual performance of group members are proposed and discussed as a means of possible solutions to the problems identified. The paper concludes by highlighting some of the issues which still need to be addressed in this area.

Introduction

For the purposes of this paper 'group work' is defined within the context of Higher Education and refers to academic work set formally by tutors which involves the interaction of students in small groups of two or more. Marks allocated for the work will normally contribute (if only in some small part) to the final individual academic qualification for which each student is working.

A number of factors contribute to the increasing use of small group work in Higher Education. These include the growing awareness of the importance of team working skills, the educational benefits from the pooling of expertise, a greater emphasis in participative learning and the pressure of larger number of students. Several issues arise from the increasing use of group based learning:

(i)   helping students to learn about the processes of working in small groups.

(ii)   helping staff to make effective use of group work.

(iii)   assessing group working skills as well as the outcomes of group learning.

(iv)   assessing individual performances of group members.

(v)   use of peer and self appraisal.

A particular 'thorny' problem for Higher Education is that of the assessment of group work, as employers now demand not only 'good' individual degree classifications from prospective graduate employees, but also a higher level of interpersonal and group working skills. This paper investigates a number of assessment issues and attempts to address the urgent need to find a solution(s) to the assessment of group work which is seen to be fair and equitable by all concerned.

Assessment Issues

1. Group work as a 'time saving' mechanism

Resourcing pressures have led many tutors to turn to group based learning as a coping/survival strategy to help deal with their increasing workload and assessment burden. From an administrative perspective, group work looks very efficient, but often little account is taken of the 'hidden workload' associated with group work involving, eg. the amount of time taken in setting up and monitoring the work, dealing with student queries and the assessment process itself which may take a number of different forms. Group work, properly conducted, is a time-consuming exercise and may require more staff time rather than less.

2. Perception of the educational benefits of group work

Many tutors recognise the educational benefits associated with group work, eg: the pooling of student expertise, the ethics of sharing creative ideas, higher productivity, the gaining of self knowledge and the development of interpersonal and group work skills through feedback and guidance.

Students often have a different perception, not appreciating the benefits of formative assessment. The "lazy tutor" may be much maligned by students often concerned for their individual degree classification. Towards the end of the group work, and with the benefit of hindsight, students recognise a significant qualitative improvement in learning and then highly rate this mode of learning.

The reaction of the students may be associated with the culture of the department concerned, whether group work is a new idea, or whether interest in the method has been seen for a number of years.

3. Reliability and Validity

A major concern with assessment of any kind is the reliability and validity of the method(s) employed. The traditional individually assessed examination paper has long been utilised and accepted as a "fair" method of individual assessment. Many tutors, however, question the consistency and reliability of the marking of large quantities of examination papers over a period of time. Sometimes more than one tutor may be involved and issues of inter-rater reliability arise. Recent research (Franklyn-Stokes and Newstead[1]) has also highlighted that a significant percentage of undergraduates admit to cheating in one form or another.

It would seem that the traditional examination paper, although still a popular mode of assessment, may not be as reliable and valid a measure as is commonly perceived. Well designed group work, however, builds upon student interaction in a positive way and may even be seen as an "antidote to plagiarism"

4. Common problems associated with the assessment of group work

(i) What should be assessed?

- Product/Outcome?

- Process?

- Both?

It appears that some tutors feel more comfortable in assessing the product. The argument is that the assessment of group process is implicit in the assessment of the product of the group work, which is tangible, and which they feel confident and competent to mark. Much of the process of group work is unseen by the tutor, and therefore, any attempt to understand, or allocate a mark to the process cannot and should not be attempted by tutors - (a behavioural approach to group work?)

Other views are that either process alone or both product and process should be assessed. If staff do not feel competent to assess group process, training is another issue which needs to be investigated. Whatever is decided the question of how to assess in a fair and equitable way remains.

(ii) Who should assess?

Possibilities include tutor assessment, student self-assessment and peer group assessment. Either one or a combination of the former may be used.

(iii) How to assess group work?

A variety of methods are available(see Habeshaw[2] for a useful review), the merits and disadvantages of some of the main methods used are discussed overleaf.

- **Tutor Assessment - Overall group mark**   All members of the group receive the same mark for the final product or outcome. This method is commonly utilised, with no attempt being made to take account of individual contribution and effort.   The method therefore makes no attempt to take account of the "social loafer" or "free rider" - the student who is friendly enough with his peers at the social level, but who does not take on his fair share of the work. It seems most students choose to work with friends and prefer to accept the same mark for all the group members regardless of individual input rather than cause illfeeling between friends, unless really provoked.   A related difficulty with the overall group mark method is the exceptionally bright student whose mark may be pulled down by the remainder of the group.

Possible ways of differential marking:

- **Declaration of contribution**   The group has to submit a signed declaration stating that all members named have made a contribution to the final product. As long as the member is named on the declaration a mark is awarded. It is unlikely the remainder of the group will allow a "social loafer" to sign the declaration. When/if this happens, the tutor may find him/herself in the position of being both judge and jury. 'Evidence' of individual contribution may be provided in the form of eg: logs and minutes of meetings, tools commonly used for monitoring group process.

- **Discretionary redistribution of overall group mark**   The overall group mark decided upon by the tutor is given to the group to distribute among members. The contribution of each member is assessed by the group and the marks are allocated according to the perceived worth of each members contribution.

  A problem may arise if students choose to 'opt out' and divide the marks equally between members. Some control of this mechanism can be brought about by members stating the criteria of assessment at the commencement of the work, and by limiting the range of movement of mark for any one member. (eg a maximum of 15% in either direction).

- **Discrete divisioning of group work** The overall group work is divided into a number of discrete components, with each group member either choosing or being allotted a particular component to complete. Each of the discrete components (eg individual chapter of a report) would then be marked separately, normally by the tutor, and marks allocated to individual students on the basis of their individual contribution in the overall group work.

  This method is open to criticism in that:

(a)   it may undermine the co-operation and interaction of group members thereby inhibiting the learning process.

(b)   rather than being group work, discrete divisioning of group work is a collection of individual pieces of work amassed together and presented as group work.

- **Peer group assessment** - The supporters of this method suggest that the group members are the **only** people who can monitor the process. The tutor cannot be present at all meetings of group members.

A variety of different peer assessment methods are available. For example, each group member might be required to rate other group members in terms of key aspects of their contribution to the work of the group (Conway[3], Goldfinch[4]). A common finding is that students often show initial reluctance at being asked to criticise and evaluate each other, and are concerned about the weighting issue of such a method of assessment.   Factors to consider when introducing peer group assessment includes (i) training of students in the techniques of peer group assessment.   (ii) how far the process/outcome should be open/confidential.   (iii) whether the measures utilised should be qualitative/quantitative/holistic/on-going. (iv) what should be evaluated - amount of time/perceived effort put into the group work or the quality of the effort. (v) whether there should be a debrief .

It has already been noted that students tend to avoid confrontation with others, unless sufficiently provoked. A further question to consider about peer group assessment is what does it actually achieve, apart from extra work for both staff and students! It is suggested that introducing peer group assessment may act in some part as a deterrent to the 'social loafer'. Students also seem to feel they have had the opportunity to influence the marking scheme.

- **Self Assessment** Various self assessment forms are available and are considered particularly useful for formative assessment. It may be helpful if the self assessment forms are completed in conjunction with the tutor, as the method may otherwise be unreliable. Some students may be overly self-critical.

Concluding Comments

It has become apparent that it is difficult to isolate assessment from other issues in group work. However, a number of conclusions may be drawn.

- Group work needs careful planning, factors to consider, as well as alternative assessment strategies, include number of students involved, resources available (human, financial, physical), the learning objectives and timescale of the group work. Group work is not necessarily a time-saving mechanism.

- Assessment strategies need to be linked with the learning objectives of the group work. Both need to be clear to students, including the educational benefits.

- Staff need to feel and to be competent in dealing with group work.

- Methods of differential marking may go some way to solving the problem of how to assess individual performance in a fair and equitable manner.

- In order to increase reliability and validity further it may be useful to utilise a variety of assessment procedures in one module.

Some issues still to be addressed:

- Group work is not general across institutions. It is a mistake to assume that staff and students have a common understanding of what group work implies. Further consideration therefore needs to be given to (i) Training of staff, in all aspects of group work. (ii) Alternative approaches to introducing group work into the curriculum. (iii) Ways of developing students' group work skills during their period of study via a developmental/staged programme.

References

1.   Franklyn-Stokes, A and Newstead, S, *Undergraduate Cheating - Studies Across Disciplines and Institutions.* Paper presented at the British Psychological Society Annual Conference (1993). London.

2.   Habeshaw, S, Gibbs, G and Habeshaw, T, *53 Interesting Ways to Assess Your Students.* Bristol: Technical and Educational Services, 1993.

3.   Conway, R, Kember, D, et al, Peer Assessment of an Individual's Contribution to a Group Project. *Assessment and Evaluation in Higher Education.* 18.1. (1993): 45-56.

4.   Goldfinch, J and Raeside, R, Development of a Peer Assessment Technique for Obtaining Individual Marks in a Group Project. *Assessment and Evaluation in Higher Education.* 15.3. (1990): 210-231.

The effects on students of structured cooperative learning

R.M. Gillies & A.F. Ashman

Graduate School of Education, The University of Queensland, St Lucia 4072, Brisbane, Australia

Abstract

This study examined group factors which facilitate changes in group cooperation and learning outcomes in structured and unstructured work groups of primary-age children. The study had two foci. The first was to determine if there were differences in the cooperative behaviours and interactions of the children in the structured and unstructured groups, while the second, was an investigation of small group interactions and achievement in these groups over time.

1 Introduction

Interest in cooperative group work in schools has grown in recent years as a result of studies which have found that cooperative learning strategies have been successful in promoting numerous skills across a range of curriculum areas (Johnson & Johnson[4]; Sharan & Shaulov[7]). However, while the benefits of cooperative group work have been well documented, only recently has attention been given to variables that mediate cooperation and achievement. Researchers have found that placing children in small groups and telling them to cooperate will not necessarily lead to cooperation (Johnson & Johnson[4]). Positive interdependence and interpersonal and small-group skills are essential to the development of cooperation (Johnson & Johnson[4]). When groups are structured so that these conditions are met, students help each other and work together to attain mutual goals (Hertz-Lazarowitz[3]; Sharan & Shaulov[7]) and, in return, they exchange information, provide help, and ask questions and it is these interactions which are believed to contribute to academic success (King[5]; Sharan & Shachar[6]).

However, not all types of group interactions are beneficial. For example, explanations in response to a request for help can promote achievement while non-explanatory help is often unhelpful (Webb[8]). The manner in which help is requested and given provides information about what is taking place in the group but it may not completely explain students' behaviours or lead to increased understanding of academic content and high achievement. Ability and gender composition may also affect the interaction among group members and how much each student learns (e.g., see Webb[8]).

While researchers have elaborated on a number of factors which affect peer group interactions and learning, there are several reasons why cooperative group work is not widely implemented. First, classroom teachers may not facilitate effective group work because students are not given instruction or training in how to cooperate and work to attain the group's goals. Second, students may be assigned to work groups in which the mix of ability, gender, and personality does not promote cooperation. Third, authentic measures of academic outcomes may not be included, and, finally, children often tend to work in groups for short periods or change groups frequently thus minimising any obvious effects of group interactions over time.

The study reported here examined the effects of training children to work cooperatively in groups to determine the nature of group behaviours. The study involved structured groups and unstructured groups. Two general research questions were addressed: What are the effects of structured and unstructured group conditions on interactions and learning outcomes? Does the nature of the interaction and group cohesiveness vary over time in structured and unstructured cooperative groups?

2 Method

Participants
This study was conducted in 10 classes across 8 schools and involved 192 children in Grade 6 who were identified as having high (32 males, 16 females; mean age=134.4 months), medium (47 males, 57 females; mean age 134.3 months), or low ability (17 males, 23 females; mean age=134.2 months) based on their performances on the ACER General Ability Test F (described below). Stratified random assignment was then conducted within each class so that each work group consisted of one high-ability student (in the top quartile of the ACER test), two medium-ability students (in quartiles 2 and 3), and one-low ability student (in the bottom quartile). Each work group was gender-balanced.

Instruments
ACER General Ability Test F (GAT Test F) This group-administered

general ability test (de Lemos, 1982) comprises 76 items covering verbal comprehension, verbal reasoning, quantitative reasoning, and figural reasoning. Students' stanine scores were used because they they reduce the likelihood of overestimation of small unreliable differences as may occur in finer scales such as IQ points and percentiles.

Observation schedule   A schedule was adapted from two coding procedures developed by Sharan and Shachar (1988) and Webb (1985) to compile information on student behaviour states and constructive (verbal) input during recorded sessions. Four Behaviour State categories were used representing student activity as follows: (a) Cooperative behaviour, broadly defined as all positive task-orientated activity; (b) Non-cooperative behaviours, broadly defined as negative social behaviours; (c) Individual non-task behaviours and confusion broadly defined as negative individual acts; and (d) Individual behaviours referred to the states in which the individual was task-orientated but worked alone. Momentary time sampling was used to code behaviour states.

The second part of the Observation Checklist identified student interactions which occurred in the group activity. Eight interaction (Constructive Input) variables were identified: (a) Non-specific verbal, defined as the frequency of participation in group interactions and included all interactions which could not be coded into any of the following categories; Giving help was classified according to (b) unsolicited help-explanations, (c) terminal responses, and (d) other help which could not be categorised as either an explanation or a terminal response; and Solicited responses to (e) requests for help- explanations, (f) terminal responses, (g) no response (ignored), and (h) all other help which could not be categorised into either of the previous categories. Constructive inputs were tallied and coded according to frequency.

Learning outcomes probes   These were designed to assess students' levels of thinking about the social studies activities and consisted of a series of question stems which were based on Bloom's taxonomy of educational objectives (1976). The questions were designed to tap basic recall of details or facts and were built from the stem "What is...?" while higher order questions required the children to investigate and analyse different information and arrive at an answer or a solution to the problem and using the stem, "Examine the..." The purpose of this assessment was to determine whether the children had learned to construct new meanings and gain a deep understanding of the unit of work (following their group experience).

Analysis of the children's language   Eight language categories were identified and grouped under headings: inclusive, exclusive, and group maintenance language. Inclusive language included: a willingness to listen to others; acknowledge other's contributions ; and, language that recognised the group as a unit (e.g., use of "we"). Exclusive language included all comments that used "I" in an authoritative manner, and all negative or disparaging comments directed at others in the group. Group maintenance language included all language that was not included in one of the two preceding categories.

Procedure
Before the investigation began, the first author met with classroom teachers individually to discuss the testing (using the GAT Test F) and the assignment of students to groups, the procedure for establishing the structured and unstructured conditions, and the planned small group activities for the social studies.

Structured condition   The children participated in two initial training sessions which were designed to teach the children the procedures they were to follow during the group activities. In the first session children were introduced to group procedures and information on the social studies unit, the types of activities involved, and the resources available. The second session focused on teaching the interpersonal and collaborative skills which are believed to facilitate group learning.

Unstructured condition   Two training sessions were also conducted to introduce the children to the social studies unit, the activities, and the resources. The children were told to cooperate and work together and they were given the same length of time as their peers in the structured groups to discuss how they were going to proceed.

3 Results

The Behaviour State and the Constructive Input data for the structured and unstructured conditions were analysed in a Group x Ability x Gender x Time multivariate analyses of variance (MANOVA) with a repeated measure on the last variable. The significant multivariate effects were found for Group (Hotellings T^2 of 10.72, F=149.26, df 12/178, p<.001), Time (Hotellings T^2 of 0.31, F=4.55, df 36/534, p<.001), and Group x Time interaction (Hotellings T^2 of 0.16, F=2.35, df 36/534, p<.001) permitting an examination of the univariate results. The univariate results for Group, Time, and Group x Time are given in Table 1.

Learning outcomes   The pre- and post-test learning outcomes data were analysed in a three-way MANOVA (Group x Gender x Time) with a repeated measure on the last variable. Although there was no main effect for Group, there was a main effect for Gender (F=4.53, 1/116 df, p<.05), and Time (F=154.59, 1/116 df, p<.001) and, differences between groups over time were also found (F=28.86, 1/116 df, p<.001). These findings suggest that there was a change in the learning outcomes over time and that this change was dependent on the group condition. An examination of the pre-test learning outcomes showed that although the children in each condition had obtained comparable results (Structured group: males' mean=3.22, females' mean=2.66; Unstructured group: males' mean=3.13, females' mean=2.70), the children in the structured groups obtained higher post-test results than their peers in the unstructured groups (Structured group: males' mean=4.47, females' mean=3.67; Unstructured group: males' mean=3.66, females=3.13).

Analysis of the children's language The language children used in groups was also observed and classified according to three language categories (inclusion, exclusion, maintenance) and t-test statistics were calculated to compare students in Structured and Unstructured conditions. Significant differences were found between the groups on inclusion (t=8.85, p<.001) and exclusion (t=2.67, p<.05) but not for maintenance (t=1.10, p>.05) which confirmed the use of more inclusive and less exclusive language in the structured group when compared to the unstructured group.

4 Discussion

The present study was a 12 week investigation of small group interaction and achievement among 192 grade 6 children. The results show that the children in the structured condition were consistently more cooperative, responsive to the needs of their peers, and provided significantly more explanations to assist each other than the children in the unstructured condition. In addition, the children in the structured groups used inclusive language ("we" and "us" rather than "I"), expressed an understanding of the group as a unit, and the need to help and support each others' learning. Furthermore, they made their own group decisions and preferred to use each other as a resource than to rely on help from their teachers. Similar findings have been reported by others (e.g., Johnson & Johnson[4]) and have been identified as behaviours characteristic of independent, autonomous, and intrinsically motivated learners (Sharan & Shaulov[7]). The study demonstrates the easy with which classroom teaching-learning patterns can be changed to assist the acquisition of classroom content.

Table 1: Summary of the Univariate-F tests for Group[a], Time[b], and Group x Time[b]

Variable	Group F		Time F		Group x Time F	
Cooperation	204.21	***	0.68		1.86	
Noncooperation	85.24	***	3.48	*	3.67	*
Independent	23.24	***	1.77		3.50	*
Nontask	84.00	***	0.82		2.13	
Nonspecific Verbals	9.66	**	1.84		1.73	
Unsolicited Explanations	80.77	***	2.60		0.68	
Unsolicited Terminal	10.53	**	7.51	***	3.43	
Unsolicited Other Help	184.27	***	5.11	**	0.60	
Solicited Explanations	1179.56	***	0.79		0.60	
Solicited Terminal	0.87		9.26	***	2.00	
Solicited No Response	0.12		9.58	***	1.84	
Solicited Other Help	10.22	**	13.94	***	6.99	***

*   p<.05   ** p<.01   *** p<.001   a df 12/178   b df 36/534

References

1.   Bloom, B. *Human characteristics and school and learning*, McGraw Hil, New York, 1976.
2.   deLemos, M. *ACER Intermediate Test F.*, Australian Council of Educational Research, Hawthorn, Australia, 1982.
3.   Hertz-Lazarowitz, R. Cooperation and helping in the classroom: a contextual approach. *International Journal of Research in Education*, 1989, 13, 113-119.
4.   Johnson, D.W. & Johnson, R.T. Cooperative learning and achievement. Chapter 2, *Cooperative learning: Theory and research*, ed S. Sharan, pp. 23-37, Praeger, New York, 1990.
5.   King, A. (1990). Enhancing peer interaction and learning in the classroom through reciprocal questioning. *American Educational Research Journal*, 1990, 27, 664-687.
6.   Sharan, S. & Shachar, H. *Language and learning in the cooperative classroom*, Springer-Verlag, New York, 1988.
7.   Sharan S. & Shaulov, A. Cooperative learning, motivation to learn, and academic achievement. Chapter 8, *Cooperative learning: Theory and research*, ed S. Sharan, pp. 173-202, Praeger, New York, 1990.
8.   Webb, N. Student interaction and learning in small groups: a research summary, Chapter 6, *Learning to cooperate, cooperating to learn*, eds R. Slavin, S. Sharan, S. Kagan, R. Hertz-Lazarowitz, C. Webb, & R. Schmuck, pp 147-172, Plenum, New York, 1985.

Task design: A neglected variable in the study of group work

C.J. Howe & A.K. Tolmie

Centre for Research into Interactive Learning, Department of Psychology, University of Strathclyde, 40 George Street, Glasgow G1 1QE, UK

Abstract

This paper presents two studies relating to conceptual change after group work in primary school physics. Both studies compare group tasks where: (1) problem materials were and were not structured to facilitate critical testing; (2) learners were and were not given instructions to abstract rules which summarised their conclusions. Attesting to the significance of task design in the study of group work, the results show that both manipulations were important, with an influence exerted on the extent of learning and the process by which learning was achieved.

1   Introduction

In recent years, there has been a shift in studies of group work and learning. While in the past the emphasis was on how learners fare after group or solitary experiences, the interest nowadays is how to make groups as effective as possible in contexts where they are typically deployed. Nevertheless, while this shift is welcome the studies are still rather limited, with the constraints on effectiveness construed along a narrow range of dimensions. The focus has been on group composition, in particular whether the members should or should not be friends, whether they should or should not have equal knowledge and ability, and whether their activities should or should not be supported by an identifiable 'expert'. There is little explicit recognition that the way tasks are structured might also be important. This is despite the fact that most published studies have a history of pilot work where task parameters are tweaked, and moreover that classical social psychological research indicates 'task demands' to be a major factor in group productivity (see Brown [1]). Although productivity and learning are not of course identical, the possibility of parallels would seem worth exploring.

The force of the point came home to us through a study concerned with conceptual change in primary school physics (Howe, Tolmie & Rodgers [2]). This study was part of a series (see also Howe, Rodgers & Tolmie [3]) addressing the significance of group knowledge composition, specifically whether the difference vs. similarity of members' prior conceptions is relevant to learning. The results from half the groups endorsed the message from the series as a whole: more learning takes place when prior conceptions are different. However, the results from the other half indicated no difference between differing and similar groups, and task design seemed likely to be responsible. In particular, given the knowledge composition of the maverick groups, an alternative task would have been required to make the differences explicit, and subsequent research (Howe, Tolmie & Mackenzie [4], Howe, Tolmie, Anderson & Mackenzie [5]) has shown the exploration of difference to be crucial. It has proved to be the mechanism by which groups generate a substantial pool of ideas, a pool which plays a central role in precipitating growth.

In view of our research, it was natural to think first of the constraining influence of task. However, the corollary quickly followed and we began to wonder whether by manipulation of task design we might be able 'shape' groups productively. This was appealing because the learning observed in our research, although robust and statistically significant, was still within limits and open to improvement. Thinking how to proceed, we felt that the correct strategy would be to build on rather than replace our existing task structure, which involved group members predicting key events, testing predictions empirically and interpreting test outcomes. In particular, we felt that modifications within that structure were needed which would encourage more careful *monitoring* of proposed ideas. We identified two modifications that appeared potentially helpful. The first related to the key events which initially involved isolated objects. To highlight which ideas were relevant and which were not, a series of objects might have been preferable, chosen to vary along one dimension while holding the others constant and thereby allowing some *critical testing*. The second modification related to the interpretation of outcomes which originally emphasised the current event rather than the task as a whole. Repeated instructions to *abstract rules* across test series might have encouraged the co-ordination and weighing up of the ideas being proposed.

2   Method

Recognising the potential contribution of critical testing and/or rule abstraction, we designed two studies to explore them further. The first study was concerned with floating and sinking, the second with heating and cooling. The studies began with pre-tests which were administered in individual interviews to children aged 8 to 12. Subsequent to the pre-tests, the children were placed in groups of 4, with all groups containing children whose conceptions were different. Groups were assigned to work through different versions of a predict-test-interpret task, with the versions designed to allow exploration of critical testing and rule abstraction. Post-tests were administered in individual interviews at an interval after the group tasks. The studies have been separately described in Tolmie, Howe, Mackenzie & Greer [6] and Howe [7], where full procedural details are given. What the present paper attempts to do is synthesise across the studies and draw conclusions for task design.

143 primary school children were pre-tested for the floating and sinking study, and 100 for the heating and cooling. The floating and sinking pre-tests began by asking the children to predict whether small objects, e.g. a plastic button, would float or sink in a tank of water and to explain why they thought this. Then the children were told about real-world instances of floating and sinking, e.g. icebergs on the sea, and invited to explain why things turned out as they did. The

heating and cooling pre-tests involved showing children containers which varied in thickness, material, surface area and colour, and asking them to predict whether liquids held in them would heat/cool quickly or slowly and to explain why this would be. The pre-tests also included items where the children were invited to account for real-world instances, e.g. the cooling of hotwater bottles.

In both studies, pre-test responses were noted *in situ* and scored subsequently for conceptual level. Although many responses contained both predictions and explanations, the latter were seen as more directly reflecting conceptions, and hence were the focus of scoring. In the floating and sinking study, the emphasis was on children's conceptions of the relevant factors. Thus, explanations were scored on a scale from 0 to 4 according to the appropriateness of the factors mentioned. A score of 0 was given to explanations that omitted physical factors, e.g. *Things float when they want to,* a score of 4 to explanations that included relative density, e.g. *Things float when they're lighter than the same volume of water.* In the heating and cooling study, both factors and processes were scored. Factor scoring involved calculating the proportion of explanations in which thickness, material, surface area and colour were each mentioned and used relevantly. Process scoring involved assigning each explanation a score from 0 to 3 depending on the apparent knowledge of the heat transfer process. Failure to mention a process led to a score of 0, appreciation of conduction, convection and/or radiation to a score of 3.

As mentioned already, the children were grouped into 'differing' foursomes subsequent to pre-testing. Once the groups had been formed, each was assigned at random to work on one of a range of task designs. The designs differed over the steps taken to promote critical testing and/or rule abstraction. One design, the *Random,* was equivalent to our earlier studies in taking no special steps. The only difference from the earlier studies was the presentation of objects in unordered sets, e.g. a block, a key and a ball for floating and sinking, rather than in isolation. A second design, the *Critical Test,* was designed to promote critical testing by presenting objects in controlled sets, e.g. wooden, plastic and metal boxes for floating and sinking, identical in shape, size and weight. A third design, the *Random + Rule Generation,* focused by contrast on rule abstraction. Objects were presented in unordered sets but there were periodic instructions to write down, e.g. *The thing that is important for floating and sinking.* A fourth design, *Critical Test + Rule Generation,* deployed both controlled sets and instructions to write down rules, while a fifth *Critical Test + Rule Selection* used controlled sets but invited groups to tick the most important statement in a pair, e.g. *How heavy an object is doesn't matter to floating and sinking* vs. *An important thing for floating and sinking is how heavy an object is.*

The floating and sinking study utilised the *Random* design, the *Critical Test,* the *Critical Test + Rule Generation* and the *Critical Test + Rule Selection,* with 8 groups working on each design. The heating and cooling study used the *Random* design, the *Critical Test,* the *Random + Rule Generation* and the *Critical Test + Rule Generation,* this time with 6 groups working on each design The floating and sinking study was conducted first, and at the time it was unclear which would be preferable, the open-ended format of rule generation or the prechosen options of rule selection. As the results came down in favour of the former, we decided to exclude rule selection for heating and cooling and explore rule generation more thoroughly. Whichever design was used, the group tasks were presented between 2 and 5 weeks after the pre-tests. The tasks were described in workbooks but introduced by researchers who monitored the initial discussion to ensure grasp of the procedure. In total, the tasks lasted between 60 and 90 minutes, and were videotaped throughout. The videotapes were coded subsequently for dialogue relating to the generation and monitoring of ideas.

With the floating and sinking study, all group participants were post-tested about 4 weeks after the tasks. A randomly chosen 25% received a further post-test about 7 weeks after the first one. With the heating and cooling study, there was a single post-test to all group participants between 3 and 8 weeks after the tasks. In both studies, the post-tests were equivalent in structure to the pre-tests and presented in an identical fashion. They did, however, contain some novel items. Post-test responses were scored in the same fashion as pre-test, and measures of learning were computed for each study. For floating and sinking, the measures of relevance to this paper are first post-test factor score less pre-test (pre- to first post-test factor change) and second post-test factor score less first (first to second post-test factor change). For heating and cooling, the measures of relevance are post-test factor score less pre-test (pre- to post-test factor change) and post-test process score less pre-test (pre- to post-test process change).

3   Results

Table 1 presents the mean values of the two floating and sinking measures as a function of task design. It is clear from Table 1 that although pre- to first post-test factor change was progressive, it was modest in absolute terms and more or less equivalent across designs. ANOVA revealed no significant differences as a function of design. First to second post-test factor change was, however, more variable. With the *Random* and *Critical Test + Rule Generation* designs, factor change was progressive and this time considerably greater than between pre- and first post-test. With the *Critical Test + Rule Selection* design, factor change was also progressive but no different from pre- to first post-test. With the *Critical Test* design, there was regression to pre-test level. ANOVA revealed significant differences between the designs (F = 3.82, p<0.05), with follow-up Scheffé tests indicating more progress with the *Random* and *Critical Test + Rule Generation* designs than with the others. This cannot be attributed to the use of a 25% subsample for the second post-test since analysis of pre- to first post-test factor change for this subsample revealed no differences from the other participants.

Table 1.   Mean conceptual change in the floating and sinking study

Group Task	Pre-test	Pre- to 1st Post-test Factor	1st to 2nd Post-test Factor
Random	1.72	+0.07	+0.69
Critical Test	1.84	+0.12	-0.07
Critical Test + Rule Generation	1.78	+0.09	+0.28
Critical Test + Rule Selection	1.92	+0.10	+0.06

Although there was only one post-test in the heating and cooling study, its administration could occur up to 8 weeks after the group tasks. Thus, it was reasonable to look for parallels of the floating and sinking results, and these to some extent were found. The parallels were not so much with factor change. Here, as Table 2 shows, there was little difference between task designs over pre- to post-test factor change, a conclusion confirmed by ANOVA. The only feature reminiscent of the floating and sinking data was a tendency for the *Critical Test* children to lag behind. Where the parallels with floating and sinking occurred was with pre- to post-test process change. Here there was a statistically significant difference between designs (F = 9.96, P<0.01), with Scheffé tests showing the *Random* and *Critical Test + Rule Generation* designs once more in the ascendance. Indeed, the results from the *Critical Test + Rule Generation* design were particularly impressive, for not only was the progress greatest here in absolute terms. It was, in contrast to all the other designs, closely associated with understanding of factors, signifying a relatively co-ordinated approach to learning. The correlation between factor and process change was +0.51 (p<0.05) for the *Critical Test + Rule Generation* design while the corresponding values for the other designs were non-significant.

Table 2.   Mean conceptual change in the heating and cooling study

Group Task	Factor Pre-test	Pre- to Post-test Factor	Process Pre-test	Pre- to Post-test Process
Random	0.28	+0.24	0.31	+0.42
Critical Test	0.28	+0.15	0.42	+0.24
Random + Rule Generation	0.29	+0.22	0.50	+0.27
Critical Test + Rule Generation	0.33	+0.22	0.41	+0.53

The reason for the close association between factor and process change with the heating and cooling *Critical Test + Rule Generation* design (and the high level of process change) became clear from the dialogue. High correlations between variables (r = +0.89 to +1.00, p<0.01) indicated that processes were called upon to resolve disagreements over factors. Process knowledge benefited directly from this, with the effects being fed over time into understanding of factors. The dynamics were somewhat different with the *Critical Test + Rule Generation* design in the floating and sinking study, almost certainly reflecting limited process knowledge (see Howe [8] for further evidence here). However, there were signs of an equally co-ordinated approach to knowledge, with learning being dependent on children distilling their discussions into adequate rules. This co-ordination was in marked contrast to the *Random* design which in both studies resembled the *Critical Test + Rule Generation* in terms of pre- to post-test change. Consistent with our earlier work, the best predictor of learning here was the sheer volume of conceptually-based dialogue. Total factor discussion was correlated +0.77 (p<0.05) with first to second post-test factor change in the floating and sinking study. Moreover, although there were no clear predictors of pre- to post-test factor change in the heating and cooling study, the total amount of task related dialogue was correlated +0.47 (p<0.05) with pre- to post-test process change. No other dialogue variables were associated with learning.

In sum then, while the *Critical Test + Rule Generation* design resulted in an co-ordinated approach suggestive of monitoring, the *Random* design replicated the 'scatter gun' approach that we have observed elsewhere. The other task designs by contrast elicited neither approach and as can be seen from Tables 1 and 2, this was to their detriment. The problem with the *Critical Test* design was that the controlled sets of objects served to focus the discussion on particular factors. Without the compensating experience of rule generation/selection, the range and extent of factor discussion was correspondingly reduced (to a significant degree with floating and sinking, $F = 3.44$, $p<0.05$). The point is, then, that even if critical testing enhances monitoring, it does so at the expense of the 'pool of ideas' that our earlier work has shown to be crucial. With the *Critical Test + Rule Selection* design in floating and sinking and the *Random + Rule Generation* in heating and cooling, shortage of material was not the problem. On the contrary, these designs produced more conceptually-based discussion than any others, but the discussion was not always used in an effective manner. With *Critical Test + Rule Selection,* the closure achieved through choosing rules served to trivialise the discussion. Thus, the children learned most if they ignored the selection exercise, as evidenced by a negative correlation (-0.75, $p<0.05$) between the appropriateness of rules and first to second post-test change. With *Random + Rule Generation*, the production of rules without the constraints of critical testing was just too difficult. There was too much to consider. Thus, the dialogue variables that were strong positive predictors of progress with *Critical Test + Rule Generation* were strong negative predictors with *Random + Rule Generation,* indicating once more that the problematic exercise was best ignored.

4   Conclusions

In the event neither critical testing nor rule abstraction proved unequivocally helpful. The *Critical Test* and *Random + Rule Generation* designs which had one of these features were inferior to the *Random* which had neither, as was the *Critical Test + Rule Selection* design which had both. A case could be made for the superiority of the *Critical Test + Rule Generation* design, in that it triggered a more co-ordinated approach to learning. This was undoubtedly more efficient in processing terms, and was also a step towards an approach which Howe *et al.* [5] show to be crucial at older age levels. Nevertheless, with the present age range, the *Critical Test + Rule Generation* design did not result in more progress than the *Random.* Yet despite the equivocal results, the studies allow conclusions of theoretical, practical and methodological significance. On the theoretical side, the results from the *Critical Test + Rule Generation* and *Random* designs show that group work can trigger learning by different routes. Indeed, it could be argued that the route followed under the former was consistent with a Vygotskyan model while the route followed under the latter was essentially Piagetian. From a practical perspective, the results indicate that seemingly small changes to a predict-test-interpret structure can have major consequences for the effectiveness of group work. This must be taken as a warning to educators. Finally and relatedly, the fact that the changes influenced both the process and outcome of learning gives strong endorsement to the significance of task. Thus, unless future methodologies consider task structure in addition to group composition, our ideas about the optimisation of group work are likely to be limited.

References

1.   Brown, R. *Group Processes,* Blackwell, Oxford, 1988.
2.   Howe, C.J., Tolmie, A. & Rodgers, C. The acquisition of conceptual knowledge in science by primary school children: group interaction and the understanding of motion down an inclined plane, *British Journal of Developmental Psychology,* 1992, **10,** 113-130.
3.   Howe, C.J., Rodgers, C. & Tolmie, A. Physics in the primary school: peer interaction and the understanding of floating and sinking. *European Journal of Psychology of Education,* 1990, **5,** 459-475.
4.   Howe, C.J., Tolmie, A. & Mackenzie, M. Computer support for the collaborative learning of physics concepts, *Computer-Supported Collaborative Learning,* ed C. O'Malley, Springer, Berlin, Forthcoming.
5.   Howe, C.J., Tolmie, A., Anderson, A. & Mackenzie, M. Conceptual knowledge in physics: the role of group interaction in computer-supported teaching. *Learning and Instruction,* 1992, **2,** 161-183.
6.   Tolmie, A., Howe, C.J., Mackenzie, M. & Greer, K. Task design as an influence on dialogue and learning: primary school group work with object flotation. *Social Development,* 1993, **2,** 183-201.
7.   Howe, C.J. Conceptual change in science: optimising the design of group tasks, Paper presented at InTER Seminar on 'Collaborative Learning', Moat House, Oxford.
8.   Howe, C.J. *Theory and Concept in Children's Thinking: the Case of Everyday Physics,* Harvester Wheatsheaf, London, Forthcoming.

References

Interactive learning: Does social presence explain the results?

P. Huguet,[a] P. Chambres[a] & A. Blaye[b]

[a] *Laboratoire de Psychologie Sociale de la Cognition, C.N.R.S.-U.R.A. 1719, Université Blaise Pascal, 34 Avenue Carnot, 63006 Clermont-Ferrand, France*
[b] *U.F.R. de Psychologie, Université de Provence, 29 Avenue Robert Schuman, 13621 Aix en Provence, France*

Abstract

Studies conducted in the area of interactive learning showed marked facilitative effects of working in pairs, relative to working alone, on children's paired performance with a complex, computer-based task. However, as in most of research on interactive learning, the possible cognitive influence of more basic social variables embedded in collective working were relatively neglected in these studies. The present investigation was thus conducted to explore this influence. The results suggest that coaction and social comparison may have partially affected children's behavior in the previous studies. It means that we should pay more attention to such variables in future research on interactive learning.

1 Introduction

Hundreds of social psychology experiments (see Guerin [1] for a recent review) have demonstrated that performing tasks in presence of spectators, or others working simultaneously on the same task on which the subject is working (with or without receiving explicit social comparison information) influence performance, sometimes facilitating and sometimes impeding it.

Although many reviews of the so-called "social facilitation" (Zajonc [2]) phenomenon have been published over the years, this phenomenon has not received any extended theoretical and empirical attention in the complex area of interactive learning. This is surprising since variables such as audience, coaction, and social comparison, which appeared as important factors in both motor and cognitive task performances (see also Chambres [3], Monteil & Huguet [4] for findings in the area of social comparison) are necessarily involved in social relationships studied by interactive learning researchers. Thus, as suggested recently by Blaye, Light, and Rubstov [5], closer attention to the social nature of interactional learning situations with reference to well-established frameworks in social psychology could offer an important area of investigation which we might expect to see developed in coming years.

The present investigation is an explicit, limited step in this direction. It was conducted to complete recent studies (Blaye, Light, Joiner & Sheldon [6]; Littleton, Light, Joiner, Messer & Barnes [7]), in which the question of social presence conceived as a separate source of variation in interactive learning had been discussed. In these studies, children worked "alone" or with a collaborating partner on a complex, computer based-problem solving task. The results indicated marked facilitative effects of working in pairs on children's paired performance, and (but only in Blaye & al's study) on their subsequent individual performance. However, as noted by Littleton et al. [7], in Blaye et al.'s [6] study, the subjects in the individual condition worked alone in presence of the experimenter. Thus, "the paired condition differed from the individual condition not only in terms of the availability of a collaborating partner but also in terms of the presence of a classmate in the testing room" (p. 314). In order to remove this potentially confounding factor, in the study conducted later by

Littleton and colleagues, there were always the same number of children present during testing. However, in Littleton et al.'s investigation, pair members always came from the same school class and, in most cases, they had been classmates for several years. Since social comparison information based on past peer interactions was then available to the subjects in this second study, it remains unclear whether cooperative working more than social comparison explained the observed performance outcomes. Unfortunately, the possible impact of comparison (which is generally more salient in coaction situations than in audience situations) during testing was neither controlled nor discussed by Littleton et al. Yet, given the procedure used in this second study, the cognitive impact of coaction *per se* (embedded in the co-working activity) could not be evaluated.

Thus, in the present study, children were led to perform the same task as the one used by Littleton and colleagues, and the influence of both social presence and social comparison in task performance was estimated. Given the possible role of subjects' past experiences at school regarding the impact of actual social presence and social comparison situations (see Monteil & Huguet, [8]), two separate groups of children, high- vs low-achievers, were selected as participants in this study.

2 Empirical investigation

Method
Participants were 80 male and female children (10 to 12 years old; 40 high- vs 40 low-achievers) from French State Middle Schools. They were led to perform the task in their classroom environment, either alone (i.e., without both the experimenter and peers) or in presence of a peer-coactor with receiving social comparison information. The task was to solve, in 20 min, a complex computer-based problem couched in an adventure

game format which made heavy demands on children's information-handling and planning skills (see Littleton & al.'s paper for a full description of the task). Task performance was measured by the computer, in terms of both quantitative and qualitative aspects of the task (see the next section and Littleton et al. 's paper). As in the previous studies with this type of task, the children were introduced to the problem solving session via a practice task, lasting about 10 min, in the course of which the main features of the problem and the interface were presented. In the co-action conditions, appropriate feedback from the practice task led the subjects to anticipate performing much better versus equally well versus much poorer than the coactor. Moreover, in order to prevent the emergence of additional effects due to subjects' previous experiences with the coactor, and to facilitate the social comparison manipulation, each subject worked in a separate room. Of course, the coactor was not introduced to the participants until the end of the problem solving session.

Results

The data were analyzed in 2 (Academic Level, high- vs low-achievers) x 4 (Social Presence, alone vs coaction with receiving a negative comparison feedback vs coaction with receiving a neutral comparison feedback vs coaction with receiving a positive comparison feedback) analyses of variance (ANOVAs).

Consistent with our expectations, such analyses showed significant coaction and social comparison effects on most of the dependent measures. This is the case for the Level of Success in the problem solving, F (3, 70)=3.457, p <.02. Subjects in the positive comparison condition performed higher than subjects in the three other conditions (Contrasts method, F =9.765, p <.002), which did not differ. A similar pattern was observed for the Number of Slips-Oversights, F (3, 70)=3.707, p <.01, the Number of Information Searched before the subjects' first action, F (3,

70)=4.832, *p* <.004, the Subjects' Time Allocation to Search Information before the first action, F (3, 70)=6.323, *p* <.0007). In addition, Total Time Allocation to Search Information was higher for subjects in both the positive comparison and the alone conditions than for subjects in the two other conditions (Contrasts method, F = 13.327, p <.0005). Some main effects of academic level, and one interaction effect, were also revealed by such analyses. Finally, no significant gender effects were found in the present study.

3 Discussion and Conclusion

The performance outcomes obtained in this investigation suggest that social variables embedded (and neglected) in interactive learning situations may play an important role in performance variations, frequently observed in such situations. Indeed, consistent with our general hypothesis, we observed performance change whereas subjects did not communicate about the task.

Regarding Littleton & al.'s results, these findings suggest that the facilitative effects of co-working on children's paired performance may be due, *at least in part*, to social comparison, (undoubtedly more salient in co-working than in audience situations), which may have increased the subjects' desire to achieve a positive self-presentation in presence of a familiar coactor. As a consequence, subjects performed better when co-working than when working alone in presence of a peer-spectator. In line with this explanation, performance effects linked to slips-oversights in our own study suggest that more attention was allocated to the task by subjects in the positive comparison condition. In our view, the present findings come close to results such as those obtained by Robinson-Staveley and Cooper [9] in the facilitation paradigm, which demonstrated, in a computer based-learning situation with adults, that the presence of others differentially affects performance as a function of success expectancy (resulting in facilitation for positive expectancy and impairment for negative expectancy subjects).

More generally, given both the present findings and those presented by Robinson-Staveley and Cooper, it seems that future research conducted to illuminate the effects of interaction upon individual performance on problem solving tasks might dissociate independent variables related to both social presence and social comparison to those connected to verbal interaction itself.

References

1. Guerin, B. *Social facilitation*, Cambridge University Press, Cambridge and Paris, 1993.
2. Zajonc, R.B. Social facilitation, *Science*, 1965, **149,** 269-274.
3. Chambres, P. Social comparison and knowledge construction. *Learning and Instruction*, 1993, **3,** 23-38.
4. Monteil, J.M. & Huguet, P. The influence of social comparison situations on individual cognitive task performance: Experimental illustrations, *International Journal of Psychology*, 1993, **28,** 627-643.
5. Blaye, A., Light, P. & Rubtsov, V. Collaborative learning at the computer - How social processes 'interface' with human-computer interaction, *European Journal of Psychology of Education*, 1992, **7,** 257-267.
6. Blaye, A., Light, P., Joiner, R. & Sheldon, S. Collaboration as a facilitator of planning and problem solving on a computer-based task, *British Journal of Developmental Psychology*, 1991, **9,** 471-483.

7. Littleton, K., Light, P., Joiner, R., Messer, D. & Barnes, P. Pairing and gender effects on children's computer-based learning, *European Journal of Psychology of Education*, 1992, **7,** 311-324.
8. Monteil, J.M. & Huguet, P. The social context of human learning: Some prospects for the study of socio-cognitive regulations. *European Journal of Psychology of Education*, 1993, **8,** 131-150.
9. Robinson-Staveley, K. & Cooper, J. Mere presence, gender, and reaction to computers: Studying human-computer interaction in the social context, *Journal of Experimental Social Psychology*, 1990, **26,** 168-183.

Learning in co-acting groups: The role of social comparison and gender norms

P. Huguet & J.M. Monteil

Laboratoire de Psychologie Sociale de la Cognition, C.N.R.S., U.R.A. 1719, Université Blaise Pascal, 34 Avenue Carnot, 63006 Clermont-Ferrand, France

Abstract

Three experiments were conducted in which male and female children performed a cognitive-perceptual task in co-acting groups involving the presence of possibly inferior peer co-actors while subjects anticipated, or not, overt social comparison of task performance. The results suggest that task performance depends, at least in part, on the consistency of the social context of cognition with gender motivations or appropriate norms. They are discussed as illustrations of social regulations of cognition in relation with interactive learning processes.

1 Introduction

Many results in the area of gender differences in self-evaluation of performances and abilities (e.g., Daubman, Heatherington & Ahn [1]) support the idea of a greater concern by females for the problems of superiority in face-to-face interactions, consistent with the well-documented finding, from self-concept studies, that more males value difference and individuation whereas more females value connection and relationships (see Josephs, Markus, & Tafarodi, [2]).

According to Daubman et al., females, more than males, could be motivated by the desire for interpersonal harmony and by the necessity to protect other(s) from a negative social comparison, thereby protecting the other(s)' self-esteem and avoiding an interpersonally uncomfortable situation. Thus, in social situations in which personal achievements are discussed, female subjects "might be concerned not only with others' evaluations of them, but also others' evaluations of themselves and with the implications that social comparisons about such evaluations and achievements might have for the immediate relationships" (p. 190).

In this paper, we assume that, as in the case of self-evaluations, task performance itself is dependent on such motivations or gender norms when the task is performed in presence of possibly less fortunate other(s). We hypothesized that the social context may interact in some way with gender, with the emergence of a suboptimal task performance as the possible consequence of the incompatibility between: (i) different characteristics of this context, such as those enhancing public positive individuation versus anonymity, and (ii) different gender motivations or appropriate norms, such as individuation and dominance for males versus connection and relationships for females. Indeed, separate works (see Monteil, [3]); Monteil & Huguet, [4]) have demonstrated the negative influence of being submitted to inconsistent events for the self on cognitive task performances.

Thus, we predicted that subjects led to anticipate performing well on the task in the presence of possibly inferior others should perform better in a situation which is rather more consistent (i.e., public situation for males; private situation for females) than inconsistent (i.e., private situation for males; public situation for females) with gender motivations or appropriate norms.

2. Empirical investigations

Method

In the three studies, 64 children (32 males and 32 females (10 to 12 years old), from a summer camp, performed a cognitive-perceptual task in the presence of possibly inferior peer co-actors while they anticipated, or not, overt social comparisons of their task performance, through face-to-face interactions at the end of the session. Since it can be assumed that knowledge about gender is acquired very early in development (see Bauer, [5]), the influence of such a manipulation on task performance should differ for male and female children led to anticipate to performing well on the task, as suggested in our introduction.

In the first place, the subjects performed a bogus task in presence of their coactors. Appropriate feedback on this prior task then led them to anticipate performing well on the experimental task, without receiving information about the present others (Study 1), with receiving information inducing a clear superiority of the self regarding the present others (Study 2), and with receiving information inducing a clear superiority of their co-acting group (i.e., the self and the 3 co-actors) regarding other groups in the camp (Study 3).

The task consisted of studying a figure for a short time (90 seconds) and reproducing it from memory. The figure, a nonsense geometrical one, was taken from Rey-Osterrieth's complex figure reproduction test, which is not affected by gender. Task performance was measured in terms of both the number and the quality of reproduced units of the Rey-Osterrieth figure.

Results and discussion
In the three studies, the data were analyzed in a 2 (Sex, male vs female) x 2 (Comparison of Task Performance, anticipated vs not anticipated) analysis of variance (ANOVA).

Consistent with our expectations, the analysis performed on data of Study 1 revealed a significant gender by social comparison interaction effect, F $(1, 60)=16.43$, $p <.001$. As predicted, male subjects' task performance was better when subjects anticipated overt comparisons of their performance than when they did not F (1, 30)=8.75, p <.006, while a reverse effect occured for females' performance F (1, 30)=7.68, p <.001. In addition, male subjects' performance was clearly better than that of females in the social comparison condition F (1, 30)=21.79, p <.001. However, this effect was slightly reversed in the condition in which comparisons of task performance were not anticipated F (1, 30)=3.13, p <.087.

In accord with our hypothesis, these findings seemed then to indicate that the level of individual task performance might vary, at least partially, as a function of the degree of consistency or compatibility of the social context of cognition regarding gender motivations or appropriate norms. Obviously, it should be noted that data linked to gender schemas, or subjects' knowledge of sex-role stereotypes, for instance, are not available in our investigation. Thus, although performance outcomes were entirely consistent with our hypothesis, it seems difficult to interpret the present findings in a theoretically satisfying manner.

Different possible explanations of the provocative interaction effect found in Study 1 could have been tested in Study 2. However, taking into account the exploratory nature of Study 1, Study 2 was designed, instead, to test whether the present interaction effect is replicated when subjects perceive themselves as clearly superior to the present coactors. Surprisingly, results of Study 2, in which the self was more clearly and positively individuated from others, failed to replicate the phenomenon found in Study 1.

Indeed, in Study 2, both male and female subjects performed worse on the task in the public situation than in the private situation F (1, 60)=9.02, p <.003, suggesting that our general hypothesis has boundary conditions: When it is undoubted and very strong, positive public individuation could have a negative effect on performance for both males and females.

Finally, the results of Study 3 demonstrated the importance of group membership regarding the performance effects found in the two previous studies. Indeed, in this last experiment, both male and female subjects performed worse on the task in the private situation than in the group-score comparison situation F (1, 60)=15.06, p <.001. Thus, inducing a positive collective individuation (instead of a positive personal individuation), in which subjects become members of a group that stands out from the rest, then in which they can perceive themselves as very similar to some people and, in the same time, as very different of many others, might participate to enhance cognitive task performance in both males and females led to anticipate overt comparisons with less fortunate others.

3 Conclusion

In the present investigation, the processes mediating the observed performance effects remain unspecified. Nevertheless, these effects support Levine, Resnick, and Higgins's [6] recent "sociocognition orientation" which suggests treating cognition as a fundamental social activity (see also Monteil, [7,8]; Monteil & Huguet, [9]). Indeed, they demonstrate the necessity of taking into account both gender, one of the most basic categories in social life, and the social context of cognition to predict cognitive task performance. Interestingly, this set of experiments suggest that appropriate motivations or norms elaborated by individuals from their earliest years and throughout their lives might play a crucial role in determining human cognitive functioning in social contexts, in particular those involving social comparison episodes.

Of particular interest for the study of interactive learning are the ideas that (i) performance facilitation or inhibition in social interaction situations can be due, at least in part, to social comparison cues embedded in such situations (ii) the influence of such cues on task performance can depend on subjects' expectations about the co-workers' abilities on the task, gender norms, and social resources or social support available in the subjects' environment. In short, independent variables not related to social interaction *per se* could partially explain many results obtained in studies on interactive learning.

References

1. Daubman, K.A., Heatherington, L. & Ahn, A. Gender and the self-presentation of academic achievement, *Sex Roles*, 1992, **27,** 187-204.
2. Josephs, R.A., Markus, H.R. & Tafarodi, R.W. Gender and self-esteem, *Journal of Personality and Social Psychology*, 1992, **63,** 391-402.
3. Monteil, J.M. Social regulation and individual cognitive function: Effects of individuation on cognitive performances, *European Journal of Social Psychology*, 1991, **21,** 225-231.
4. Monteil, J.M., & Huguet, P. The influence of social comparison situations on individual cognitive task performance: Experimental illustrations, *International Journal of Psychology*, 1993, **28,** 627-643.
5. Bauer, P.J. Memory for gender-consistent and gender-inconsistent event sequences by twenty-five-month-old children, *Child Development*, 1993, **64,** 285-297.
6. Levine, J.M., Resnick, L.B. & Higgins, E.T. Social foundations of cognition, *Annual Review of Psychology*, 1993, **44,** 585-612.
7. Monteil, J.M. Toward a social psychology of cognitive functioning: Theoretical outline and empirical illustrations, Chapter 2, *Social representations and the social bases of knowledge*, eds M. Von Cranach, W. Doise & G. Mugny, pp 42-55, Hogrefe & Hubert, Lewiston, New-York & Bern, 1992.

8. Monteil, J.M. *Soi et le contexte: Constructions autobiographiques, insertions sociales et performances cognitives*, A. Colin, Paris, 1993.

9. Monteil, J.M. & Huguet, P. The social context of human learning: Some prospects for the study of socio-cognitive regulations, *European Journal of Psychology of Education*, 1993, **8**, 131-150.

Does immediate group feedback of student's performance improve their learning experience?

A. Irving[a] & A. Hunt[b]

[a] *Department of Psychology, University of Portsmouth, King Charles Street, Portsmouth PO1 2ER, UK*
[b] *School of Pharmacy and Biomedical Sciences, University of Portsmouth, Portsmouth, UK*

Introduction

Feedback is an essential ingredient for successful active learning (Anderson[1], Bilodean[2]) It is the mechanism by which students put their efforts into context and learn from their misunderstandings and lack of knowledge. Evidence from other studies (Lewis & Anderson[3]) suggest that the more immediate the feedback the more useful it is in terms of learning. However, it is this individual marking, writing of feedback and discussing of students work that takes a considerable amount of time and is often repetitive for the teacher, with long delays between submission and return of the work for the students. With increasing numbers of students, it is often this feedback element that gets reduced, thereby providing a poorer quality and less effective learning experience for the student.

In Pharmacy education various techniques have been developed to overcome some of these problems. For example, the Royal Pharmaceutical Society has made it's professional exams multiple choice to ensure speed and accuracy of assessment, but a single grade does little to tell students where they went wrong. The Pharmacy Consortium for Computer Aided Learning (PCCAL) has developed 8 packages for undergraduate teaching and other products are available for post-graduate and professional training education.(Bilham et al[4]). 75% of the UK Pharmacy Schools now use PCCAL software and first evaluation results (PCCAL[5]) indicate that students enjoy using Computer Aided Learning (CAL) and teaching staff feel it is useful and appropriate.

Although CAL overcomes the problems of teacher's time for assessment, and provides immediate feedback to individuals, its traditional one to one computer approach is not suitable for all subjects, it limits interaction and can prevent learning from the teacher and the group as a whole. Students are missing out on that human touch.

The University of Portsmouth School of Pharmacy ran its final year undergraduate Clinical Pharmacy practicals in a traditional way, with students working in pairs during the class, but producing individual reports for assessment. These were marked with general misunderstandings discussed in class at the beginning of the next practical session 3 weeks later, when the reports were returned. This approach involved the teacher in a considerable amount of repetitive assessment, and generated limited enthusiasm for the class discussion. Nor did it help prepare students for the multiple choice assessment they would meet in their professional Pharmacy exams. Hence the teacher of the practicals wanted a new method of teaching that would use Multiple Choice Questions (MCQ) and generate group discussion to help students learn more from their experience.

Group Decision Support Systems (GDSS) have been used for some time in industry to support groups making decisions (Gear & Read[6]). In essence GDSS provide a structured process by which information / opionions are collected from the group, analysed and fed back for the final decision.

This approach was adopted by Portsmouth, using a computer based GDSS system called 'Teamworker', which presented and collected students' answers to MCQ and then fed back the class's answers straight away for a group discussion led by the teacher. This group interactive approach was compared with the more traditional method of paper and pencil MCQ in terms of students' performance and perception of their learning experience.

Method

Design
A within subject design was used. Within their normal 3 practical groups, final year BSc Pharmacy students were randomly allocated to condition A (n = 30) : pencil and paper MCQ (Task 1) followed by Teamworker MCQ (Task 2) and condition B (n = 29): Task 2 followed by Task 1.

Equipment & Questionnaires
The Teamworker system comprises a set of individual handsets (each with a numeric keypad, a 2 line LCD display and radio transmitter) a radio receiver linked to a personal computer with the Teamworker software, which in turn is linked to a video projector and printer. See Diagram 1.

Two questionnaires were developed for this study using positive and negative statements (with 5 point Likert scale ranging from strongly agree to strongly disagree) together with several open questions to obtain some non structured opinions.

Diagram 1: The Teamworker System

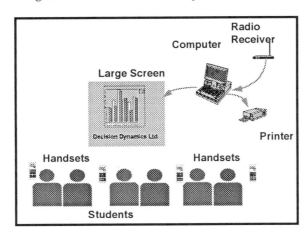

Procedure

To keep the practicals in a similar format of other Year III 'Clinical Pharmacy' practicals the students worked in pairs and were able to discuss their answers with each other, but each individual recorded his or her own choice of answer. This procedure enabled the marks attained in these practicals to be compared with the students' performance in other more traditional practicals.

Task 1: 20 MCQ were presented on paper and students were asked to record their answers on a sheet of paper and to hand this in at the end of the exercise. As is usual with this type of practical, this exercise was open book. Discussion of the results followed three weeks later, after the exercise had been marked. On completion of the MCQ, students were asked to anonymously complete a short attitudinal questionnaire on the use of MCQ. Questions used in this exercise were selected from a sample "Open Book Pre-Registration Exam Paper" issued by the Royal Pharmaceutical Society of Great Britain.

Task 2: 24 MCQ were projected in turn onto a large screen by the Teamworker system. As each question was presented the student selected the appropriate answer via their individual handset. When all students had selected an answer a histogram of the responses was projected onto the screen. The histogram indicated the groups performance but did not identify any individuals. Students' individual responses needed for assessment records were stored by the computer and printed off later.

Where there was disagreement among the students as to the correct answer, the groups' responses were discussed before the correct answer was identified. In the few cases where there was total agreement and the answer correct, no discussion was required. On completion of the MCQ, students were asked to anonymously complete a short attitudinal questionnaire on the use of Teamworker.

Questions used in this exercise were completed without the use of reference sources and were selected from a sample "Closed Book Pre-Registration Exam Paper" issued by the Royal Pharmaceutical Society of Great Britain and were therefore slightly easier than those used in task 1.

Results

Task 1
Students liked MCQ because of the large number of topics that could be covered in short periods of time (83%), and because they are a useful way to review knowledge (63%). However the aspects of MCQ that students didn't like was inability to justify one's choice of answer (60%) and the difficulty of choosing between very similar answers (50%).

In response to the open questions, (n = 58) 29% of students identified being guided by the choice of answers as the biggest advantage of MCQ, followed by 27% liking the shortness and speed of MCQ and 24% liking the large area of work that can be covered.

The major disadvantages were seen as being the difficulty of answering the questions (39%), no opportunity to explain choice of answer (22%) and the ambiguous and confusing nature of some of the questions (22%).

No students identified the lack of interactive group discussion as a problem or disadvantage.

Task 2
Nearly all the students enjoyed using the Teamworker system (96%) and most found the immediate feedback and group discussions very useful (82%, 93% respectively). The students also liked to be able to see how every one else in the class answered (82%) [information not usually made public], and 84% of the students felt that Teamworker allowed them to get more involved in the group discussions.

The two aspects of the system disliked by the students was the 'pressure to answer' the questions (17%) and having to wait for other students to answer (14%).

Other uses for the system suggested by the students (n=50%) included tutorials (24%) and course revision (20%)

Task 1 Vs Task 2
Following the completion of both tasks, students were asked which method of MCQ they preferred. 99 % (n = 58) preferred Teamworker.

The Teacher's Experience
MCQ type of assessment obviously involves the teacher in less marking than traditional practicals, but provides little opportunity for feedback on the 'why' or for general group discussion.

With the Teamworker system the practical set up time was increased slightly by the need to input the MCQ into the system. However students were more actively engaged in the discussions and with no marking of reports or the need to discuss the answers with individual students, the over all teacher time involved in the practical was significantly reduced. The teacher felt that Teamworker significantly enhanced the group interaction and the individual student learning experience.

Discussion

When used as an assessment tool with no immediate discussion of results, MCQs were not well received by students. Questions were felt to be hard to answer and the students disliked not being able to explain their answers. Combining multiple choice with an interactive computer system, whilst not statistically improving their academic performance, did appear to improve their learning experience; students indicating that they found the procedure enjoyable and welcoming the immediate feedback and discussion. The use of a GDSS would also appear to have potential as a revision / tutorial tool which would ensure the involvement of all members of the group.

The staff involved in the project identified two major advantages of using Teamworker. Firstly, it provided the opportunity to focus the discussion, as an immediate indication of group performance was available and areas of concern identified clearly. Where there was disagreement as to the correct answer, students could discuss their ideas of what was right and why before the correct answer was revealed and if needed an explanation could then be given. Within the group discussions, students usually arrived at the correct answer themselves with very little prompting from the teacher.   Secondly, the time spent on marking could be greatly reduced (a print out of results being immediately available, as opposed to an average of 9 hours to mark traditional 'pen and paper' practical reports for a group of 60 students). Although the time savings could be great, caution would have to be exercised in placing too much emphasis on the use of GDSS as a formal assessment tool given that although discussion takes place immediately after a choice has been made it is the initial choice which would determine the mark awarded rather than subsequent discussion and so the problems associated by students with MCQs would not have been totally addressed. The GDSS does however appear to offer an effective and acceptable method for tutorial / revision sessions for both staff and students alike.

Conclusions

The use of a GDSS such as Teamworker combines the advantages of multiple choice questions and computer assisted learning with group discussion. A large subject area can be reviewed quickly by a large number of students with everyone having to participate. Both students and members of staff have an opportunity to quickly and easily monitor both individual and group performance. In addition such a system offers excellent opportunity to stimulate and target group discussion on the key areas of concern as they are encountered rather than at a later date when the material may not be fresh in the minds of the students. Both these aspects, relying on the immediate feedback of the groups performance, appear to improve the students learning experience.

Whilst Teamworker may not be wholly appropriate for formal examination procedures it could prove an invaluable aid for general teaching, and revision / tutorial sessions. The fact that it is perceived as being fun must also be an added bonus.

References

1.   Anderson, J.R. *Cognitive Psychology and its Implications.* 3rd ed., Freeman, New York, 1990.
2.   Bilodean, I. M. Information feedback, *Principles of Skill Acquisition,* ed. E.A. Bilodean, Academic Press, New York.
3.   Lewis, M.W. Anderson, J.R. Discrimination of Operator Schemata in Problem Solving - Learning from Example, *Cognitive Psychology,* 1985,17,26-65.
4.   Bilham T, Christie P, Jenkins R, Moss S, Redfern P. Computer-Assisted Learning - A survey of access and acceptability, *Pharm J,* 1991, 24,**7,** R41.
5.   PCCAL Newsletter No5, School of Pharmacy and Pharmacology, University of Bath, March 1994.
6.   Gear, T. & Read, M.J. On-Line Group Support, *Omega,* 1993.

Task influences on spontaneous peer learning in the classroom

A.C. Kruger

Department of Educational Psychology and Special Education, Georgia State University, Atlanta, Georgia, USA

Abstract

A number of experimental interventions have confirmed the effectiveness of peer collaboration for the acquisition of concepts such as conservation. However, no study to date has described the process or effectiveness of peer learning as it takes place in classrooms. The present study documented episodes of spontaneous peer interaction during academic tasks in a progressive school. Results indicated that the type of task performed influenced the structure of the interaction. Open-ended or discovery tasks such as story-writing promoted more exchange of information and more argumentation than did skill tasks that had only one right answer. Skill tasks were related to more negative behaviors, such as refusals and rejections, and resulted in more time spent off task. The interactive behavior observed during engagement with discovery tasks is consistent with the interactive style related to cognitive growth in laboratory studies of peer interaction.

1 Introduction

During the last two decades educators have increasingly included peer learning alternatives in their traditional classrooms. This rapid and enthusiastic change toward the use of peers constitutes a "movement" in education (Damon

& Phelps[1]).   Broad acceptance of peer learning can be credited to the considerable body of experimental literature on the subject.   The effectiveness of peer collaboration in the acquisition of conservation (e.g., Doise & Mugny[2]), spatial coordination (e.g., Emler & Valiant[3]), legal thinking (Roy & Howe[6]), moral reasoning (e.g., Kruger[4]), and mathematics (Phelps & Damon[5]) is well-documented. However, these studies all relied on laboratory or school-based interventions that were structured and maintained by adults.   To date no one has described the process of peer learning as it spontaneously occurs in the classroom, often with minimal adult facilitation.

The purpose of the present study was to examine the structure of peer learning in a classroom designed to allow spontaneous interactions among children.   The research questions investigated were:
1) Will the organization of peer interaction in the classroom resemble the organization of peer interaction in the laboratory?
2) In laboratory studies, peer interaction that is effective for learning features social engagement and the criticism of ideas.   Will this happen in the classroom?
3) Will the type of task the children are working on affect the nature of their interaction?

Following Damon and Phelps[1], it was predicted that peers would be more actively engaged with each other's ideas when working on tasks requiring creativity or discovery.   It was further predicted that children would be less interactive when working together on tasks that require the practice of skills.

2 Method

Subjects.
Subjects were 16 (eight males, eight females) middle and upper-middle class children.   Thirteen of the children were European-American, one was Latin-American, one was Asian-American, and one was African-American.   Their mean age was 7.6 years.   The 16 subjects represent a subset of a

first/second grade classroom of 28 children taught by two full time teachers in a progressive private school.

Observational Procedure.
Children's classroom interactions were videotaped and audio taped as unobtrusively as possible. Thirteen episodes (mean length = 18 min) of spontaneous peer interaction were selected for taping. During these episodes the subjects worked with one or more partners on various academic tasks. No instruction on how to work with partners was provided, but teachers occasionally prompted children who were having difficulties.

Coding Procedure.
The <u>tasks</u> the subjects worked on were coded as either

> 1) <u>Discovery</u> tasks, such as story-writing and code-breaking, or
> 2) <u>Skill</u> tasks, such as measuring and arithmetic puzzles.

The characteristic that distinguishes these two types of task is the presence or absence of only one right answer. Open-ended tasks were coded as discovery tasks. Tasks with only one answer were coded as skill tasks.

The videotaped <u>episodes</u> were coded for the amount of time children spent in different types of social interaction. On a moment-to-moment basis, each subject was coded as being in one of the following 10 interactive states.

> 1) <u>Egalitarian</u> - subjects are working together, sharing equally in the task
> 2) <u>Asymmetrical</u> - one subject is focusing on the thoughts of the other as follows
>> a) <u>onlooking</u> - monitoring a partner's independent work
>> b) <u>giving help</u> - providing assistance to the partner
>> c) <u>requesting help</u> - asking for assistance from a partner

d) <u>refusing to help</u> - declining to give assistance
   when it is requested
e) <u>persuading</u> - making an argument to the
   partner in favor of an idea
f) <u>countering</u> - making an alternative argument
   to the persuading partner
g) <u>rejecting</u> - actively refusing to engage in
   discussion of an idea

3) <u>Independent</u> - the subject is focused only on his/her
own work and is not in a   social   interaction

4) <u>Off Task</u> - the subject is no longer attending to the
task at hand

3 Results

The amount of time (in seconds) spent in each of the 10
coded states was summarized for each subject. The mean
durations for each state during discovery task episodes
were compared to those during skill task episodes via a
series of t-tests. Subjects performing discovery tasks spent
the same amount of time in Egalitarian interactions as did
subjects performing skill tasks. The two groups also spent
similar amounts of time in Independent states. However, as
predicted, subjects performing discovery tasks spent
significantly more time in Asymmetrical states than did
those working on skills. In particular, discovery tasks
promoted more onlooking, giving help, requesting help,
persuasion, and countering than did skill tasks. Skill tasks,
by contrast, promoted significantly more Off Task behavior,
more refusal to help, and more rejection of persuasion than
did discovery tasks.   See Figures 1, 2, and 3.

4 Discussion

The type of task subjects worked on influenced the nature of
their peer interaction. Discovery tasks, compared to skill
tasks, promoted more lively discussion of ideas as measured
by the argumentation codes and more exchange of
information as measured by the helping codes.
Interestingly, skill task subjects were more likely to engage
in negative behaviors, such as refusing to help or rejecting
the partner's ideas. Furthermore, they were significantly

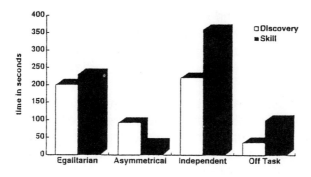

Figure 1: Task influences on social interaction

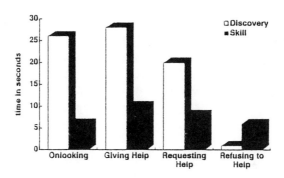

Figure 2: Task influences on helping

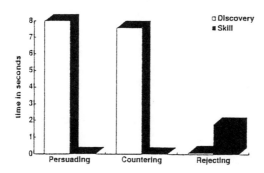

Figure 3: Task influences on argumentation

more likely to spend time off task. Thus, discovery tasks promoted a more engaging exchange between partners; this type of lively peer interaction has been shown to produce more cognitive benefits in the laboratory (e.g., Kruger[4]).

The present data are limited in that they are observational. No outcome measures were taken. However, this study is an important step toward identification of the circumstances and tasks necessary for effective peer learning in the classroom.

5 References

1. Damon, W., & Phelps, E. Critical distinctions among three approaches to peer education. *International Journal of Educational Research,* 1989, 1 3, 9-19.
2. Doise, W., & Mugny, G. Individual and collective conflicts of centrations in cognitive development. *European Journal of Psychology,* 1979, 9, 105-108.
3. Emler, N., & Valiant, G.L. Social interaction and cognitive conflict in the development of spatial coordination skills. *British Journal of Psychology,* 1982, 7 3, 295-303.
4. Kruger, A.C. The effect of peer and adult-child transactive discussions on moral reasoning. *Merrill-Palmer Quarterly,* 1992, 3 8, 191-211.
5. Phelps, E., & Damon, W. Problem solving with equals: Peer collaboration as a context for learning mathematics and spatial concepts. *Journal of Educational Psychology,* 1989, 8 1, 639-646
6. Roy, A. W., & Howe, C. Effects of cognitive conflict, socio-cognitive conflict and imitation on children's socio-legal thinking. *European Journal of Social Psychology,* 1990, 2 0, 241-252.

'Stimulating the students' - Self-activation in the context of a cooperative learning setting

R. Lamberigts

Department of Educational Sciences, University of Nijmegen, PO Box 9103, Nijmegen, The Netherlands

ABSTRACT

Recent psychological research into learning shows that the acquisition of knowledge and skills is not so much the result of a direct transmission of the formalized and abstract learning material, but more an effect of the mental activities of the learner. In this constructivist view instruction is defined as process-oriented. In order to be effective, process-oriented instruction should (1) be activative by stimulating and demonstrating processing content and strategy learning, and (2) take place in the context of a cooperative learning-setting, in which learning activities are visible and have an observable status.

To illustrate this, we have carried out a small - scale intervention study in the field. The implementation of activative instruction in the context of a cooperative learning setting is carefully controlled by on-line observations of the lessons in an experimental and control-group.

The implementation turns out to have a positive impact on academic achievement (reading comprehension and spelling) and partly on subject-specific motivation.

1. THEORETICAL FRAMEWORK

In traditional instructional design, instruction is mainly conceived of as the direct transmission of formalized knowledge and explicit skills to the students. In order to be effective, this direct teaching should decompose a complex learning task into atomic component-tasks, formulating and sequencing the objectives and assessing the extent to which these goals are met by the students (Rosenshine and Stevens, 1986). Rarely, however, students are stimulated to undertake learning activities. And, if so, neither the mental activities are specified, nor is demonstrated the way these activities should be initiated (Stevens, Slavin and Farnish, 1991). Recent psychological research into learning has shown that knowledge and skills cannot be transmitted directly but are the result of mental activity of the learner (Brown, 1987; Schuell, 1988). The quality of the learning outcomes students attain is largely dependent on the learning activities they employ.

1.1   Activative instruction as a tool for constructivism.

In traditional teaching (Rosenshine and Stevens, 1986) all the instructional-learning functions are performed by the teacher or, in other words are taken over by the teacher. So the five tasks, underlying the processing activities of the learner are performed by the teacher: the teacher prepares the learning of students, decomposes the complex learning task into pieces for them, regulates the learning by testing, questioning or judging the learning progress, povides feedback and tries to keep the students motivated and concentrated.

Also the regulation of learning (orientation; planning, testing, monitoring, etc.) is taken over by the teacher.

In learning by students, however, the central actvity in the classroom, the teacher is inclined to give the students their authentic learning functions back. So, he lets the students perform all these functions by themselves; he stimulates the students to relate, structure and analyse on the one side and he stimulates them to regulate their own learning.

Stimulating learners to employ the right thinking-, learning- and regulation activities is called process-oriented instruction (Klauer, 1987; Palincsar, Stevens and Gavelek, 1989; Collins, Brown and Newman, 1989) and can function as a tool for constructivism.

1.2   Activative instruction in a cooperative learning setting.

Learning as a constructive activity and teaching as activative instruction, stimulating and demonstrating constructive information-processing and self-regulation of learning, can pre-eminently be tuned to each other in an interpersonal (social) system of learning (Glaser, 1991). That interpersonal system is described in the literature as a cooperative learning setting (Slavin et al (eds) 1985; Sharan (ed), 1990).

Starting point of cooperative learning is the thesis of the social genesis of human development and human learning (Vygotsky, 1978; G-H. Mead, 1934). Conceptual development often involves internalizing cognitive activies, experienced in social settings.

Especially a group of cooperating peers can - from a cognitive contructivist perspective - serve several roles:

1)   A cooperative group-setting as a social context elevates thinking in the classroom to an observable status. As students participate in group-learning tasks, the details of various problem solving procedures, strategies of learning and reasoning and techniques for accomplishing goals become apparent. In traditional whole-class settings, instruction by the teacher as transmission of knowledge is visible, but the learning of students is rarely a visible and observable enterprise. Individual learning is mostly - and should be - a silent process in a crowded whole class setting. Hence shaping thinking activities through external influences is limited.

2)   A group of peers, guided by a scaffolding teacher, is a fruitful basis for creating learning situations in which students can function as apprentices, who observe how knowledge is used in expert-performance. A number of cognitive theorists have suggested that cooperative learning can be an important component in cognitive apprenticeship (Brown and Palincsar, 1989; Collins et

al. , 1989).

3)   In cooperative learning-groups, as research on cooperative learning has shown (Webb, 1982), students who give to and receive from fellow-students elaborate explanations of learning content, learn better than those who simply receive the correct answers from their peers. In cooperative situations students are encouraged to teach their fellow-students. By teaching they restructure the learning content and are motivated to explain the content, more than they are triggered to memorize.

Reviewing the role of a cooperative learning setting in an activative instruction, we may say that the setting can help their individual members to become teachers for themselves in a natural way by being a teacher for each other. The setting can also help their individual members to (re)construct knowledge collaboratively and to make individual learning strategies observable for each other.

2.   AIMS OF THE STUDY

We want to investigate the surplus-value of ACtivative instruction (AC) in a COOPerative setting (in COOP) as compared to DIrect teaching (DI) in a Whole CLass-setting (in WCL).

We have chosen an intervention-study,   because the implementation of activative instruction in a cooperative setting is generally not put into the practice of education but is an experimental enterprise. Nevertheless we have tried to implement the intervention in a careful way on a small scale within a class of lower level students in a secondary school. This implementation of activative instruction in a cooperative learning setting during regular education is processed gradually. In order to be effective the experimental teacher first was induced to execute direct teaching elements in an adequate way. That means that the teacher gives reviews, examples, orientations, etc. Second, the teacher was advised to stimulate the students to give reviews, examples, etc. by themselves after he/she has given an adequate demonstration how to prepare reviews etc. Finally - in the last phase of experimental period - the students were stimulated to give reviews, etc. to each other and to co-construct reviews in a peer-group. In this period individual students were given the opportunity to internalize the learning strategies and to regulate their own learning (self-regulation).

3.   METHOD

3.1   Subjects
Twenty seven students (age fourteen to sixteen years) in two classes of the lower level of a secundary school (MAVO-LHNO) participated in the study. The two classes were randomly assigned to an experimental (AC in COOP) and a control group (DI in WCL). The two teachers - nested in the experimental and control group - were experts in native language teaching and were both willing to participate in this field-experimental study.

3.2   Procedure

The procedure of the field experiment lasted seven weeks in the beginning of 1991, and was divided into a baseline period (three weeks) and an experimental period (four weeks). In the baseline period some preliminary tests were done and checks on the ongoing teaching activites were processed by on line observations.

3.3   Description of measures used

Included are a check on the implementation of the intervention, and measurements of dependent, independent and moderator (aptitude) variables.

3.3.1   Check on the implementation of the intervention.

On line time-sampling observation of the experimental and control teacher in the baseline and experimental period-during lessons was performed. Every twenty-second period the occurence of teaching events was coded in four basic categories: (1) the class structure (whole class vs. individual vs. small group) (2) the lesson fragment (presentation vs. guided learning vs. seat work) (3) formal instruction (direct teaching vs. activate instruction (4) instructional activities (giving explanations vs. questioning vs. giving feedback, etc.).

3.3.2   Measures of the dependent variables.

- The academic achievement was measured by a test on spelling and reading comprehension, which can be combined to an overall measure of reading achievement. This test was used as pre- and posttest. The test was an ad-hoc test, composed by the teachers out of the regular curriculum test items. Because the researchers found it important not to interrupt the progress of the curriculum during the intervention, it was decided to relinguish the claim of standardized tests. All (sub)measures turned out to be sufficiently reliable (Cronbach's Alpha .70 - .85)
- The motivational attitude toward the curriculum was measured by a 32-item questionnaire about the experienced pleasure, relevance/practical utility, difficulty/fear and devotion/interest with respect to the actual curriculum (pretest and posttest).
  The (sub)measures turned out to have an excellent reliability (.86 - .95).

3.3.3   Meaures of moderator variables.

- A test of General Learning Ability (GLA) was constructed on the basis of factor-analysis (principal component) of the grades on related subject-matter (foreign languages, biology, chemistry, geography, history and economy). The mean score of the factor scores of the first factor (which explained more than 50 % of the total variance) was a sufficiently reliable indication of the overall (general) achievement level of the students.
- The general motivational orientation (GMO) is derived from the existing AMS (Achievement Motivation Scale), constructed by Gjesme and Nygard (1970). The 30-item test yielded two factors: inclination to avoid failure (failure-orientation) and inclination to gain succes (succes-orientation). The two factors received more than sufficient reliability (Cronbach's Alpha .81 resp. .95).

3.3.4   Scheme of variables underlying the different measures.

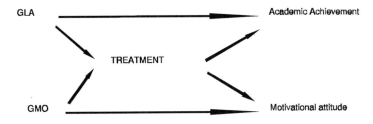

3.4   SUMMARY OF RESULTS

Implementation checks carried out during the intervention period (baseline period and experimental period) by means of on-line observations indicate that the assignments and guidelines of the research group were carefully implemented by both the experimental and the control teacher.

Formal instruction	E-teacher			C-teacher		
	bp	ep	p.	bp	ep	p.
Direct teaching	81.81	62.27	.01	92.97	90.33	.58
Activative instruction	18.12	37.37	.01	6.48	9.56	.45

Figure 1:   Percentages of time spend on formal instruction (direct teaching vs. activative instruction) by the E(xperimental) and C(ontrol) teacher, tested on the difference between baseline (bp) and experimental period (ep).

Analysis of covariance (MANOVA) on achievement scores reveals a significant treatment effect on the overall measure of academic achievement ($F = 4.52$; $p < .05$). This effect is substantial and not moderated by the General Learning (achievement) Ability (GLA) of the students.

Results on the motivational attitude toward the curriculum is more complex. Analysis of covariance (MANOVA) on the factor scores of the four subscales (pleasure; relevance; fear and devotion) indicates a great influence of the covariate, that is the existing motivational attitude before the intervention

Only with respect to the relevance of the curriculum, the experimental treatment condition has a positive effect (F.= 4.97; p<.04), moderated by the success-orientation (SO) of the students. So mainly success-oriented students are perceptive to the radiating practical- utility-power of AC in COOP.

LITERATURE

Brown, A.L. (1987). Metacognition, executive control, self-regulation and other more mysterious mechanisms. In F. Weinert and R. Kluwe (Eds.), *Metacognition, motivation and understanding*. Hillsdale: Erlbaum, 65-116.

Brown, A.L. & Palincsar, A.S. (1989). Guided, cooperative learning and individual knowledge acquisition. In L.B. Resnick (Ed.) *Knowing, learning and instruction*. Essays in honor of Robert Glaser (pp. 393 451). Hillsdale: Erlbaum.

Collins, A., Brown, J.S. & Newman, S.E. (1989). Cognitive apprenticeship: teaching the craft of reading, writing and mathematics. In L.B. Resnick (Ed.), *Knowing, learning and instruction*. Essays in honor of Robert Glaser (pp. 453-494).

Gjesme, T. & Nygard (1970). *Achievement -related motives.* Theorectial considerations and construction of measurement instrument. Unpublished manuscript, University of Oslo.

Glaser, R. (1991). The maturing of the relationship between the science of learning and cognition and educational practice. *Learning and Instruction, 1,* 129-144.

Klauer, K.J. (1987). *Paradigmatic teaching of inductive thinking.* Paper presented at second EARLI-conference. Tübingen. September 19-22.

Mead, G.-H. (1934). *Mind, self and society- form the standpoint of social behaviourist.* Chicago, Pyttel.

Palincsar, A.S., Stevens, D.D. & Gavelek, J.R. (1989) Collaborating with teachers in the interest of student collaboration. *International Journal of Educational Research, 13,* 41-53.

Rosenshine, B. & Stevens, R. (1986) Teaching functions. In : M.C. Wittrock (Ed.), *Handbook of research on teaching* (3rd. ed.) New York: Mc. Millan (pp. 376-391)

Sharan, S. (ed.) (1990). *Cooperative learning, theory and research.* New York: Praeger.

Shuell, T.J. (1988). The role of the student in learning from instruction. *Contemporary Educational Psychology, 13,* 276-295.

Slavin, R. et al. (eds.) (1985) *Learning to cooperate, cooperating to learn.* New York: Plenum.

Stevens, R.J., Slavin, R.E. & Farnish, A.M. (1991). The effects of cooperative learning and direct instruction in reading comprehension strategies on main idea identification *Journal of Educational Psychology, 83,* 8-16.

Vygotsky, L.S. (1978). *Mind in society*. Cambridge MA: Harvard University Press.

Webb, N. (1982). Student interaction and learning in small groups. *Review of educational research, 52,* 421-445.

Social comparison of expertise: Interactional patterns and dynamics of instruction

M.J. Liengme Bessire, M. Grossen, A. Iannaccone &
A.N. Perret-Clermont
*Séminaire de Psychologie, University of Neuchâtel, CH-2000
Neuchâtel, Switzerland*

Abstract
The aim of the present study is to examine the effects of social comparison on individual performance after an interaction session and the variation of the interactional dynamics depending upon the reciprocal perception children have of their level of expertise. The experiment is a pretest-interaction-posttest design with two experimental conditions manipulating the reciprocal perception an expert and a novice have of their level of expertise. Results show that the novices gain more individual benefits when they think they have the same level of expertise as the expert during the interaction session than when they believe themselves to have a lower level of expertise. Further results concerning the interactional dynamics of the interaction session show that there are more collaborative patterns when the children perceive themselves as equal. The presentation of the latter results will constitute the core of this paper.

I. Introduction
Research on the role of peer interaction in cognitive development has so far focused on the cognitive and social conditions enabling a child to benefit from a peer interaction session: a first approach has been to compare the child's performance before and after an interaction session (pretest-posttest comparison) (PERRET-CLERMONT, 1980; DOISE & MUGNY, 1984; PERRET-CLERMONT & NICOLET, 1988; GILLY, 1989); a second approach has been to analyse the interaction sessions in order to describe the interactional patterns which account for children's appropriation of knowledge (ROGOFF, 1990). Whereas the first approach has usually been adopted by post-Piagetian scholars trying to uphold Piaget's claim that peer interaction is an essential factor of development, the second approach has been used either by post-Piagetian or by post-Vygotskian researchers: the former with the aim of looking for interactional patterns, explaining improved performance between the pretest and the posttest, while the latter aimed at studying how the partners (generally an expert and a novice) could reach a joint attention and construct an intersubjectivity within the novice's zone of proximal development (TUDGE & ROGOFF, 1991 WERTSCH, 1991). Although their theoretical framework and their aims were not the same, these lines of research have both emphasized the role of two main processes: socio-cognitive conflict on the one hand and intersubjectivity on the other (GROSSEN, 1988). The point common to both these studies has been to focus on the socio-cognitive processes responsible for the appropriation of a new competence, but to some extent they have neglected the **relational setting** in which the socio-cognitive

processes are mobilized (LIGHT, 1986; PERRET-ŒRMONT, PERRET & BELL, 1991; SCHUBAUER, PERRET-CLERMONT & GROSSEN, 1992). With regard to this point, a few questions may be asked: which are the interactional conditions necessary for the construction of an intersubjectivity? In which conditions are the partners able to solve the socio-cognitive conflicts they experience? When the partners' competence is asymmetric, is the expert's point of view necessarily taken into consideration by the novice? With what consequences for the organization of their interactions? These questions refer to two classical problems within the field of social psychology: the first concerns the **perception of the source of influence** and the second **the role of social comparison processes** in the construction of self and other identity.

The general hypothesis of the present study is that in some social situations, the reciprocal perceptions of the partners might either facilitate or inhibit the taking into account of the other's point of view and hence differentially contribute to promoting the search for a cognitive solution to solve conflicts.

The aim of this study is to examine the links between **the individual benefit children** take from the interactional dynamics and **the partners' reciprocal perceptions** Our main hypothesis is that perceiving the partner as equal affects the way the children interact with the each other and take their partner's perspective into consideration. Perceiving the partner as equal should facilitate the construction of an intersubjectivity and hence the cognitive solving of the socio-cognitive conflicts which could occur during the interaction session.

We shall first present the experimental procedure. We will then recall the main results concerning the pretest-posttest comparison in order to present our new data concerning the interactional patterns observed in the two experimental conditions during the oral presentation of our paper.

II. Presentation of the study

1. Procedure

The task requires a mastery of right and left recognition and is inspired by a study done by Claude Dalzon in Aix-en-Provence (France) (DALZON, 1992). The procedure consists of a four-step experimental design, which is a variation of the classical pretest-posttest design (cf. figure 1).

Figure 1: Experimental design

PRETEST	
CONDITION 1 Attribution of **unequal** level of expertise	CONDITION 2 Atttribution of **equal** level of expertise
INTERACTION SESSION	
POSTTEST	

The first step is an individual pretest consisting of three series of subtests:

a) the first series concerns right and left recognition on oneself or on an object oriented in the same direction as the child (0^0 subtests);

b) the second series concerns right and left recognition when the object forms a 90^0 angle in relation to the child's body (90^0 subtests);

c) a third series concerns right and left recognition when the object forms a 180^0 angle in relation to the child's body (180^0 subtests)

The novices recognize their own right and left, but not that of an object oriented at 90^0 or 180^0 in relation to their own body, while the experts have a good mastery of the right and left on objects oriented at 90^0 or 180^0 although they do not have full mastery of it. After the pretest, dyads of experts and novices of the same sex are constituted.

The second step is an "attribution session" in which equal or unequal perception of expertise is manipulated. Children are called two by two, a novice and an expert, into a special room of the school. They are told that first there will be a training session to get familiar with the task. Each dyad is presented with a short path drawn on the floor. One child after the other has to guide a LOGO floor turtle from the beginning to the end of a path without straying from it. For the purpose of the experiment, only three programmed cards (FORWARD, TURN LEFT, TURN RIGHT) are proposed to the children. The situation is manipulated in such a way that in condition 1 (unequal attribution) only the expert is able to guide the turtle without straying from the path, while in condition 2, both the expert and the novice are led to perceive themselves as being equally capable.

The interaction session immediately follows the attribution session. Both children sit at one end of the path and give orders to the experimenter by means of cards (on which is written FORWARD, TURN LEFT, TURN RIGHT) that they put in a small basket. They have to guide the same turtle along a longer path made up of 14 turns:

7 form a 90^0 angle in relation to the child's body ("easy turns"); 6 form a 180^0 angle in relation to the child's body ("difficult turns") and a turn which forms no angle in relation to the child's body, this will not be taken into consideration for the analysis. Carrying out the task correctly therefore implies the mastery of right and left after a 90^0 or a 180^0 rotation in relation to the children's position.

The last step is an individual posttest undergone both by experts and novices which is the same as step 1.

2. Hypothesis
The main hypothesis is that the perception by the child of his/her own expertise has a differential impact on the relationship the children establish during the interaction. We expect the "equal attribution" condition to bring about more collaboration between the children and the "unequal attribution" to reinforce the expert's leadership, thus resulting in different types of interactions. The experimental conditions should also have a different impact on individual benefits in the posttest: we expect the children of the "equal attribution" condition to gain more expertise than the children of the "unequal attribution" condition.

3. Subjects
The population selected after the pretest resulted in 52 seven to eight year old children, 26 in each experimental condition. The novice and the expert of each dyad were of the same sex.

4. Results
We shall first present the analysis of the individual cognitive gains between the pretest and the posttest. We shall then examine some results regarding the analysis of the interaction session. The other results will be presented orally.

4.1. Comparison between the pretest and the posttest
The comparison between the pretest and the posttest has been carried out separately for each series of subtests. One of the indicators measuring the evolution between the two sessions is the frequency of regressions, stabilities and progressions in each experimental condition. The performance of the **novices** in the 90^0 subtests shows that the frequency of subjects progressing between the pretest and the posttest is significantly higher in the equal condition:

SUBTESTS 90^0				
	Regressions	Stabilities	Progressions	N
Condition 1 (unequal)	5 38%	3 23%	5 38%	13 100%
Condition 2 (equal)	1 8%	2 15%	10 77%	13 100%

Table 1: Subtests 90°: Frequency of regressions, stabilities and progressions between the pretest and the posttest in each experimental condition. (Jonkheere test: z = 01.85; p = 0.03)

As table 2 shows, the tendency is in the same dirrection for the 180^0 subtests, although the difference is not statistically significant:

SUBTESTS 180^0				
	Regressions	Stabilities	Progressions	N
Condition 1 (unequal)	4 31%	4 31%	5 38%	13 100%
Condition 2 (equal)	3 23%	2 15%	8 62%	13 100%

Table 2: Subtests 180°: Frequency of regressions, stabilities and progressions between the pretest and the posttest in each experimental condition. (Jonkheere test: z = 0.75; p = 0.32)

Table 3 presents the number of subjects progressing in neither the 90^0 nor 180^0 subtests, the number of those who progress in one of the two series and the frequency of those progressing in both series. Subjects are progressing more frequently in both series of subtests in the equal attribution condition than in the unequal one.

SUBTESTS 90^0 and 180^0				
	No progress	Progress in 90^0 or 180^0	Progress in 90^0 and180^0	N
Condition 1 (unequal)	4 31%	8 62%	1 7%	13 100%
Condition 2 (equal)	1 7%	6 46,5%	6 46,5%	13 100%

Table 3: Subtests 90° and 180°: Number of novices in each experimental condition. (no progress; progress in 90° or 180° subtests; progress in both subtests) (Jonkheere test: z = 01.85; p = 0.03)

Concerning the results of the experts, the table 4 shows no significant difference between the experimental conditions. However, if we look at the raw scores, we observe a difference, statistically significant, the experts of the equal attribution condition progressing more than those in the inequal attribution.

SUBTESTS 180^0				
	Regression	Stabilities	Progressions	N
Condition 1 (unequal)	4 31%	2 15%	7 54%	13 100%
Condition 2 (equal)	4 31%	-	9 69%	13 100%

Table 4: Subtests 180°: Frequency of regressions, stabilities and progressions between the pretest and the posttest in each condition. (Jonkheere test: z = 0.31; p = 0.37)

4. 2. Analysis of the interaction sessions

All the interaction sessions have been registered on videotapes and transcribed along seven dimensions. We shall focus here on two of them:
a) the decision: how do children reach a decision about the order to be given to the turtle? And who takes the decision ?
b) the actions: who puts the card in the basket ?
For each dimension, the level of conflict is taken into consideration.
The first step of our work has been to examine who makes the decision. We expect the proportion of joint decisions to be higher for the FORWARD orders than for the "easy" and the "difficult turns' " orders and the experts to make the decision more frequently in condition 1 than in condition 2. The next table shows how the decision is taken depending upon the type of orders and the experimental conditions:

	Condition	Novice	Joint	Expert	N	N condition 1 and 2
Forward	Condition 1 (unequal)	11 6%	128 66%	53 28%	192 100%	383 100%
	Condition 2 (equal)	23 12%	139 73%	29 15%	191 100%	
Easy turns	Condition 1	17 19%	22 25%	49 56%	88 100%	179 100%
	Condition 2	39 43%	16 18%	36 39%	91 100%	
Difficult turns	Condition 1	17 23%	18 24%	39 53%	74 100%	152 100%
	Condition 2	35 45%	16 20%	27 35%	78 100%	

Table 5: Who makes the decision depending on the type of orders and the experimental condition

A non-parametric analysis of variance calculated on these data indicates that there is a significant effect of the experimental conditions ($k=23.63$; $p<0.01$) but no significant effect of the type of order ($k=1.28$; $p=0.47$) and no significant interaction between these two variables ($k=2.97$; $p=0.17$). Whatever the type of order, experts always make more decisions in condition 1 (unequal attribution) than in condition 2 (equal attribution) and the reverse is true for the novices who more often make the decision in condition 2 (FORWARD: $z=3.32$; $p=.0004$/ "Easy" turns: $z=2.84$; $p=.002$) "Difficult" turns: $z=2.68$; $p=.003$).
We will present orally the second step of the analysis concerning specific behavioural patterns. The results show that the patterns of interaction observed for the "easy" and the "difficult turns" vary depending upon the experimental conditions, but only when it is the expert who decides which card to choose and not when it is the novice who leads the choice.

Conclusion
The results of this study show that the perception the expert and the novice have of their own expertise and of that of their partner has an effect on the benefit they draw from an interaction session. When the partners perceive themselves as being of equal expertise, the novice gains more competence between the pretest and the posttest. The analysis concerning the interaction session itself shows that the interactional patterns

vary depending upon the experimental conditions, with more collaborative patterns in the condition in which children perceive themselves as equal. Further analysis is now necessary to examine the links between individual performance and the type of interactional patterns observed during the interaction session.

Acknowledgement
This research has been carried out with the help of a grant of the Fonds National suisse pour la Recherche Scientifique (contrat n0 11-285190)

References
Perret-Clermont, A.-N. (1980). *Social interaction and cognitive development in children.* New York: Academic Press (original work published 1979).
Doise, W., & Mugny, G. (1984). *The social development of the intellect.* Oxford: Pergamon Press (original work published 1981).
Perret-Clermont, A. N. & Nicolet, M. (1988). *Intéragir et connaître.* Cousset (Fribourg CH): Delval.
Gilly, M. (1989). A propos de la théorie du conflit socio-cognitif et des mécanismes psycho-sociaux des constructions cognitives. In C. Bednarz & Garnier (Eds), *Construction des savoirs- Obstacles et Conflits.* Québec: Cirade, éd. Agence d'Arc)
Rogoff, B. (1990). *Apprenticeship in thinking. cognitive development in social context.* New York: Oxford University Press.
Tudge, J., Rogoff, B.(1991). Peer influences on cognitive development: piagetian and vygotskian perspectives. In: M. Bornstein & J. Bruner (Eds), *Interaction in Human Development.* Hillsdale, N.J: Erlbaum.
Wertsch, J.V. (1991). *Voices of the mind: a sociocultural approach to mediated action.* London: Harvester Wheatsheaf.
Grossen, M. (1988). *L'intersubjectivité en situation de test.* Cousset (Fribourg): Delval.
Light, P. (1986). Context, conservation and conversation. In M. Richards & P. Light (Eds.), *Children of Social Worlds. Development in a Social Context.* Cambridge: Polity Presss.
Perret-Clermont, A.-N. , Perret, J.-F. & Bell, N. (1991). The social construction of meaning and cognitive activity in elementary school children. In L. B. Resnick, J. M. Levine & S. D. Teasly (Eds), *Social Shared Cognition.* Washington, D. C: American Psychological Association.
Schubauer, M.L., Perret-Clermont, A.-N., & Grossen, M. (1992). The construction of adult child intersubjectivity in psychological research and in school. In M. Von Cranach, W. Doise & G. Mugny (Eds.), *Social representations and the social bases of knowledge* (Vol. 1). Bern and Lewiston: Swiss Psychological Society and Hogrefe & Huber Publishers.
Dalzon, C. (1992). Interaction entre pairs et construction de la notion droite-gauche chez des enfants. In *Bulletin de Psychologie,* XLV, 404, pp.21-27

The significance of group dynamics in peer tutoring in higher education

H. Soini & E.-L. Kronqvist
Department of Behavioral Sciences, University of Oulu, PO Box 222, FIN-90571 Oulu, Finland

The aim of this research was to examine the kind of peer tutoring which emphasizes the meaning of group dynamic factors for the learning of the student group, starting out from the assumption that such elements occupy a highly significant position in the evaluation of collective forms of teaching both as facilitating factors as well as barriers to learning. Pre-eminently interactive skills, individual responsibility, the function of leadership and the setting of targets for one's learning were underlined. The results showed that student -led tutoring is a useful method for increasing students' understanding of the significance of group dynamics in the learning process.

I Introduction

Tutoring can be used in a variety of ways to help students' learning process. There are numerous reports available on tutoring experiments (Jacobi[1]), and mention has been made of both the advantages of the model and the points at which it could be developed further. These tutoring models mostly emphasise instrumental or utilitarian considerations. The instrumental approach looks at tutoring mainly as a relatively narrow intermediary process aimed at ensuring that the students advance in their studies in accordance with the curriculum and achieve the aims laid down at each stage. Tutoring can also be viewed as a developmental matter, however, in which case the focus is on examining the students' activities in a broader perspective, paying attention to the hidden or subconscious factors in individuals and organizations that prevent learning. (Bramley[2], Baum [3], Wildman, et al.[4].)

Modern learning theory emphasizes the active participation of the individual in the learning event, self-regulation, the setting of one's own learning targets and the adoption of the role of subject in the process. It is easy to accept the importance of these factors but in practical teaching situations the teacher is frequently stopped in his or her tracks when the students will not set their own targets or they remain unaware of them. This is often seen as the student's problem, but the main point of this study is to point out the role of the teaching organisation so that it changes its own ways of working to correspond to the demands which it sets for its students. From the point of view of group behavior a good teacher will above all help students to learn for themselves and to accept more responsibilty for their own learning.

 Mostly   tutoring methods have been developed as a means of support for students with learning difficulties but relatively few studies have dealt with the possibility of using tutoring as a method of promoting the quality of students' work and especially of increasing their understanding of the signifigance of group dynamics in the learning process. Also the importance of tutor-training has been emphasized (Barron & Foot[5]). The starting point of this exercise was to develop a Peer-Tutoring-Model, in which an older student meets with first or second-year students to study with them or advise them in their studies. The purpose of the present study was also to examine the impact of peer-tutoring on learning, when the tutors have been instructed to take into account group dynamic factors. Especially interactive skills, individual responsibility, and the function of the leadership were emphasized.

II Method

30 students participated in two courses dealing with Higher Education and Social Psychology. The courses consisted of lectures, small group activities led by peer-tutors, and in social psychology also a large group exercise as a part of examining the course. Before and during the courses, peer tutors were trained for the tutoring with lectures by the authors, common sessions and conversations dealing with group dynamics and progress in each small group. It was especially emphasized, that peer-tutors are not leaders of the group in the traditional sense, but more   facilitators of communication. The main task of the peer-tutors was to conduct students in discussing their primary task and also to take into account group dynamic factors such as the function of leadership, the responsibility of individual members of the group, and adequate use of the resources of the group.

In the large group exercise the task of the students was to produce a common product, which points out as concretely as possible the factors which must be taken into account when the teaching methods in higher education are sought to be changed. Before the exercise the students were required to lay out posters produced by them in small groups in the lecture rooms. The posters dealt with the topics adequate for the common product in the large group exercise.

In the small group meetings a record was drawn up, the sessions of each group were videotaped, the progress of the action in groups was appraised in the tutors' sessions, and finally the students answered the semi structured questionnaire which concerned the way of action in the course. In addition, at the end of the social psychology course the students' action was appraised separately in the exercise of the large group. The activity of the tutors was appraised separately with a questionnaire and by interviewing them personally at the end of the course.

III Problems

1. The behavior in the groups and the changes that occured in it during the course.

2. The ideas of the students about the meaning of the group dynamic factors for the behavior of the student group, and the ability of the students to recognize these factors.

IV Results

1. The basic orientation models of the small group work.

During the courses one could observe two kinds of basic orientation towards the work in the behavior of the groups (Table 1). The orientation models did not appear separately, but some features of both could be noticed in different groups. Especially on a first course and on the other hand at the beginning of work the instrumental orientation was given emphasis. While appraising their own behavior the groups realized that they had rushed into the task too fast and spent too little time for planning the sensible way to proceed and appraising the meaningfulness of their own action.   Instrumental orientation seemed to be appropriate to the structure of the curriculum as developmental orientations presuppose more freedom and individuality in the arrangement of personal study programs.

Table 1. Basic orientation types in small group work.

DEVELOPMENTAL ORIENTATION   INSTRUMENTAL ORIENTATION

typical themes of discussion in the beginning of group work

What are the goals of the group?	What are the demands of the teacher?
How is this course engaged with other studies?	How could we divide the group task into different parts?
How to organize the work of group?	Election of chairman or secretary without discussion about his/her role.
Do we need the leader in the group?	

typical features of working in the beginning of group work

Slow progress.	Rapid progress.
Differences of opinion,conflicts.	Effective performance by some
Frustration because of slow	group members.
progress and vague idea of the task.	A lot of homework.
A lot of discussion.	

typical features of working during the performance phase and at the end of the group work

Expresion of individual responsibility.	Expression of frustration by passive group members.
Rational division of labor.	Absences.
Working together with	Working alone at home.
group members and tutors.	Motivation problems.
Lack of time.	

2. The appraising of the small group action

In appraising the action in small groups the students had paid attention mostly to their personal ways of working as group members. Instead it seemed difficult for them to recognize the meaning of organizational factors, such as leadership and the resources of the group, for the learning of the group. The most important things that the students learned from the small group activity were:

1. Listening to another student and respecting his/her thoughts in the group.
2. The difficulty of taking personal responsibility. Unwillingness to commit oneself or be responsible in a realistic way?
3. The difficulty of changing personal ways of working.
4. The importance of giving expression to one´s own ideas and hopes in group work.

Typically the students did not see the role of leadership as important to their working group. The leader was elected but "the group was still democratic" or "we did not need a leader in the group". The role of peer-tutors in group work was evaluated for facilitation. The students were understood that they should themselves do the work and not the tutor. The role and the personality of the tutor had an effect on the function of the group. A very active peer-tutor, who immediately revealed his opinions and took the leadership for himself in the group was experienced as confusing. Also a very passive and quiet peer -tutor had a negative and controlling impact on the group.

3. The large group proceedings

To demonstrate through experience the resistance, the meaning of individual responsibility and the function of leadership to the students, a large group exercise was carried out at the end of the course in social psychology.

At the beginning of the exercise the students were unable to change their earlier group compilations and working methods and their "escape" to small groups. Some students expressed strongly their disappointment to the teachers, who did not pay any attention to their posters even though they were required to be laid out. By degrees the students noticed that they must reorganize themselves so that a common result could be achieved. A representative from each small group came to the leading group, and when the problem of leadership was solved the students noticed that they must use posters made by all groups in order to achieve a common result. This observation was made only about 15 minutes before the end of the exercise.

After the large group exercise the students were asked once more the meaning of group dynamic factors in their own student work. The following factors were given emphasis in the opinions of the students:

1. The meaning of leadership for organizing the action of the group. Many students thought that only the large group exercise helped them to understand the meaning of leadership in perfoming the task in a group. In small groups the

leadership was examined from the point of view of power and status, in a large group from the point of view of performing the task.

2. The recognition of individual resistance to change. "It was a shock to notice all those modes of behaviour in one's own action that make the group work more difficult".

3. The problems of changing the action of organizations as well as the action of students themselves was brought forward very clearly in the exercise.

V Discussion

The results showed that student -led tutoring increased the understanding of the significance of group dynamics in the learning process. In general emphasizing the group dynamic factors changed the work of the student group. They became more conscious of their personal impact in the group. They realized the importance of listening and respecting others' opinions and ideas for the learning process. The crucial point in this research was the students attitudes towards the function of leadership in the group. It seemed to be difficult for students to evaluate the function of the leadership. In the small group work it was evaluated more from the point of view of status and power but not from the point of view of task performing. In the beginning of the course students typically neglected the meaning of the leader, but afterwards they regarded it as important to understand the meaning of leadership as a facilitating factor in group work. Consequently students should be guided to study group phenomena and recognize features of their own behaviour as members of a student group.

References:

1. Jacobi,M. Mentoring and undergraduate academic success. A Litterature review. *Review of educational research.*,61 (4), 505-532. 1991
2. Bramley, W. *Group tutoring. Concepts and case studies.* Kogan Page, London.1979.
3. Baum, H.S. Mentoring: Narcissistic fantasies and oedipal realities. *Human relations,* vol 45, No 3. 1992.
4. Wildman, T. & Magliaro, S., Niles R., Niles,J. Teacher monitoring: An analysis of roles, Activities and condition. *Journal of Teacher Education,* vol 43, no 3, 205 - 213. 1992.
5. Barron, A-M., Foot, H. Peer tutoring and tutor training. *Educational Research.* 1991,33,174-185.

Authors' Index